Archiv für Rechts- und Sozialphilosophie
Archives for Philosophy of Law and Social Philosophy
Archives de Philosophie du Droit et de Philosophie Sociale
Archivo de Filosofía Jurídica y Social

Herausgegeben von der Internationalen Vereinigung für Rechts- und Sozialphilosophie (IVR)
Redaktion: DR. ANNETTE BROCKMÖLLER, LL. M.

Beiheft 179

www.steiner-verlag.de/brand/Archiv-fuer-Rechts-und-Sozialphilosophie

EAST MEETS WEST: JUSTICE, LAW, AND POLITICS

The 13th Kobe Lecture and the 2nd IVR Japan International Conference, Chiba, September 2023

Edited by
Makoto Usami and Hidehiko Adachi

Franz Steiner Verlag

Cover illustration: Justitia, Landgericht Ulm
Source: shutterstock.com / Georg_89

Bibliographic information published by the German National Library:
The German National Library lists this publication in the Deutsche Nationalbibliografie; detailed bibliographic information is available at
dnb.d-nb.de.

Maybachstraße 8, 70469 Stuttgart
service@steiner-verlag.de
www.steiner-verlag.de
Layout and production by Franz Steiner Verlag
Typesetting: DTP + TEXT Eva Burri, Stuttgart
Print: Beltz Grafische Betriebe, Bad Langensalza
Printed on acid-free and age-resistant paper.
Printed in Germany.
ISBN 978-3-515-14052-2 (Print)
ISBN 978-3-515-14057-7 (E-Book)
DOI 10.25162/9783515140577

Preface

Among non-Western societies, Japan probably has the longest history of studies on Western legal philosophy. The introduction of European legal thoughts into the country dates back to the late 19th century. After World War II, an increasing number of Japanese legal thinkers have studied Western positivism, natural law, and various historical thoughts. Based on such a rich legacy, the Japanese section of the International Association for Philosophy of Law and Social Philosophy (IVR Japan) has held Kobe Lectures since 1990. More than ten worldly celebrated legal and political philosophers to date have delivered insightful and inspiring lectures.

In 2018, IVR Japan launched a series of international conferences to provide a new opportunity for the multinational exchange of scholarly opinions and observations. Kobe Lecture was repositioned as one of the conference's two plenary sessions. The second conference "East Meets West: Justice, Law, and Politics," which had been postponed due to the COVID-19 pandemic, eventually took place at Chiba University from the 16th to 18th of September 2023. A renowned political philosopher Daniel A. Bell was invited to deliver a Kobe Lecture, and Hirohide Takikawa gave the other plenary speech. 106 researchers and graduate students from 17 countries/regions participated in the three-day event. After the conference, full papers submitted for publication were carefully reviewed, and 16 papers were finally selected. The result is a set of highly unique articles included in the current issue, which cover a great variety of subjects, ranging from the history of legal thoughts to cutting-edge topics in legal and political philosophy.

Our special thanks are due to the host university's representative Takayuki Kawase and the Secretary General Michihiro Kaino. We are also grateful to all other members of the IVR Japan Executive Committee for their dedicated efforts to ensure the success of the conference. For the publication of this issue, we greatly appreciate Annette Brockmöller's seasoned editing management. Kobe Lectures have long been supported by the Kobe Fund, while also benefiting from the fund provided by the Kikawada Foundation in 2018.

Makoto Usami and Hidehiko Adachi

Contents

Part 3
Legal Theory

Part 4
The Role and Reality of Judges

Part 5
Law and Science

Introduction

MAKOTO USAMI / HIDEHIKO ADACHI

The idiom "East Meets West" has been widely used in cultural and commercial realms at both ends of the Eurasian Continent. Early examples of its usage include a 1978 book published by the Japanese fashion designer Issey Miyake and a 1995 Japanese Western film directed by Kihachi Okamoto. The idiom in these realms has appealed to Westerners' orientalistic curiosity about Asian traditions and heritages or reflected Easterners' admiration of Western contemporary cultures. Meanwhile, the 1990s witnessed a growing tension in a discourse on political values in the international community. Some political leaders in East and Southeast Asia, notably Lee Kuan Yu in Singapore and Mahathir Mohamad in Malaysia, condemned liberal democracy, individual freedom, and human rights as Western-centric ideas, invoking the notion of Asian values. Against this backdrop, in his book *East Meets West*, Daniel A. Bell offered a thought-provoking defense of Asian challenges to Western-style liberal democracy and human rights.[1]

A quarter century later, East and Southeast Asian societies are in remarkably different situations from those in the past. For instance, in the Democracy Index 2023 published by the Economist Group, Japan, South Korea, and Taiwan are all ranked as full democracies, while Italy and the United States are included among flawed democracies. In the Human Rights Index by the V-Dem Institute, Japan and Taiwan indicate very high scores. As for the economic growth of Asian countries and regions, a noticeable fact is that China's gross domestic product (GDP), adjusted for purchasing power parity (PPP), accounts for one-fifth of the world's GDP. Also, Singapore and Macao have much larger per capita GDP (PPP) than most Western nations.

Of course, the political and economic development of East and Southeast Asian societies does not mean that they are thoroughly westernized. Non-negligible differences exist between Asian countries and their Western counterparts in terms of law, politics, and culture. Thus "East Meets West" does make sense still today. In the present situation, however, this old cliché needs to be reinterpreted in a new perspective, which supposedly differs from traditional orientalism, admiration of the West, and alleged Asian values. The question is: how can we conceptualize, describe, and evaluate the contemporary and historical issues surrounding law and politics in Asian and

1 Daniel A. Bell, *East Meets West: Human Rights and Democracy in East Asia*, Princeton, NJ: Princeton University Press, 2000.

Western countries? This broad question is what contributors to the current special issue endeavor to answer or keep in mind.

This issue consists of seven parts, displaying a great variety of theoretical and empirical topics surrounding the law and politics of Eastern and Western societies. Two papers in the first part "Monarchy and Democracy" discuss political regimes from different angles. Bell presents a powerful but provocative defense of what he calls symbolic monarchy, in which a monarch is limited by the constitution to ceremonial powers without actual power. He begins with the fact that monarchies are among the most successful democracies, also achieving social peace and respect for diversity. Next, he stresses the significance of rituals, citing his personal experiences and events in Chinese history. After mentioning the dangerousness of absolute monarchy, Bell argues that symbolic monarchy can promote social reform, environmental sustainability, concern for foreigners, and political stability. Most importantly, "the monarch can be the symbol of a non-partisan, intergenerational national community that makes the people feel as one." He proceeds to note that contemporary populist leaders have appeared in societies with no monarchs. Finally, he argues that the institution of symbolic monarchy may be appropriate for China's political future, with references to contemporary Chinese scholars.[2]

Hirohide Takikawa scrutinizes two arguments for the legitimate authority of democracy, while examining whether each argument can apply to authoritarianism. The instrumentalist argument says that democracy, as well as some types of authoritarian regimes, can have legitimate authority because of their epistemic function. The proceduralist argument claims that only democracy has legitimate authority; however, democracy implies the outsider problem. To address this problem, he argues that democracy has the legitimate authority to establish a global rightful state. The paper concludes by noting that some forms of authoritarianism can have legitimate authority if they protect every citizen's equal right to freedom.

The second part "Historical Thoughts and Contemporary Realities" sheds a new light on three great figures in the history of legal thought, Francisco de Vitoria, Immanuel Kant, and Hans Kelsen, by linking them with contemporary views and realities. Carlos Isler Soto focuses on principles of the rule of law or legality, propounded by Lon L. Fuller. He argues that Vitoria pioneeringly defended at least four of Fuller's eight principles: generality, public promulgation, constancy, and no contradiction. When defending these principles, Vitoria posits that the legislator is primarily the political community as a whole and can be only secondarily a king, the parliament, or a king in the parliament. On the other hand, the thinker gave no suggestion as to institutional issues such as the separation of powers.

---

2 For his recent works on related topics, see Daniel A. Bell and Wang Pei, *Just Hierarchy: Why Social Hierarchies Matter in China and the Rest of the World*, Princeton, NJ: Princeton University Press, 2020.

Henry Vumjou critically examines Western Enlightenment hospitality, Kant's universal hospitality in particular, by closely looking at the plight of refugees crossing the Myanmar borders to India. India is not legally obliged to assist refugees from other countries because it has not been a signatory of the 1951 Refugee Convention or a party to international refugee protocols. Nonetheless, the Zo people inhabiting Mizoram in the country have continually offered humanitarian aid to the refugees from Myanmar. Vumjou describes aid activities of what he calls Zo hospitality and its underlying philanthropic principle *tlawmngaihna*. In conclusion, he finds Kant's hospitality inadequate and suggests that it should meet Zo hospitality.

Monika Zalewska explains why Kelsen's pure theory of law can apply to East Asian legal systems, with special attention to Japan. She notes that some elements of the pure theory, including the positivistic aim of legal science, can explain its universality, but only to some extent. Next, it is argued that other elements, such as coercion associated with empowerment, make the pure theory of law more successful than its positivistic rivals. Then, she maintains that the hierarchical structure of law *Stufenbau* makes this theory objective and universal, enabling it to apply to both East Asian legal cultures and Western continental legal traditions. Finally, she identifies two types of relationships in *Stufenbau*: vertical and horizontal.

The third part "Legal Theory" begins with a novel proposal of the aesthetics of law. Inspired by Gustav Radbruch's ideas, Kamil Zeidler, Paula Chmielowska, and Dawid Kostecki advance the aesthetics of law as the fifth branch of legal philosophy, distinct from the ontology, epistemology, logic, and ethics of law. In their account, this subarea challenges us to reconcile the need for order and justice with various interpretations of beauty in different societies. They identify five phenomena in which aesthetics matters: creating, binding, observing, applying, and interpreting. They also distinguish between an external approach, in which the researcher is outside of the object studied, and an internal approach, in which she belongs to it. Then, they aesthetically examine some allegorical drawings and signs from Western and Eastern cultures.

The subject of Motoki Miura's paper is the shift of emphasis in a debate over coercion in law: contrary to the long-standing treatment of coercion as a putative constituent of the concept of law, an increasing number of theorists have recently considered the nature of coerciveness of law as a matter of degree. He begins by explaining the secondary, auxiliary role assigned to coercion in law, which is assumed by H. L. A. Hart and Joseph Raz but challenged by Frederick Schauer and Kenneth Einar Himma. Next, Miura sketches the degree of coerciveness function, recently proposed by Lucas Miotto. Then, he discusses what a conception of law's coerciveness as a matter of degree would imply for jurisprudence.

Nobuaki Yamamoto explicates legal causation, more specifically factual causation in non-deterministic cases, like pollution and medical malpractice litigations. After briefly examining the necessary element of a sufficient set (NESS) test and the probability-rising theory, he describes the interventionist account of causation and its implications. The interventionist account states that a causation exists between X and Y if and only if it is possible to indirectly manipulate Y by directly manipulating X. Among interventionist models, Yamamoto focuses on the extended causal model (ECM) proposed by Joseph Halpern. He points out some limitations of the ECM, proposes the modified ECM (MECM), and concludes that the MECM applies to both deterministic and non-deterministic cases.

The fourth part "The Role and Reality of Judges" consists of two papers. Tomasz Widłak elaborates on the meaning of judicial virtue by proposing a theoretical model of virtue that accommodates the judicial role in a democratic jurisdiction. First, he examines why virtues can be regarded as helpful in considering the judicial role. Second, his discussion turns to the issue of relationships between judicial and overall virtues. Christine Swanton advances the target-centered virtue ethics, according to which the features that make traits of character virtues are determined by their targets or aims. Drawing on Swanton's works, Widłak proposes the target model of virtue, which accommodates the role-oriented view of judicial virtues.

Teresa Chirkowska-Smolak and Marek Smolak empirically study the psychological wellbeing of judges in the midst of Poland's constitutional crisis, revealing their work-related stress and burnout in the challenging political environment. They analyze responses from 475 judges with the Perceived Stress at Work Scale and the Oldenburg Burnout Inventory. The findings indicate that Polish judges experience moderate to high levels of perceived stress and burnout, which are significantly higher than those of other social professionals in the country and legal professionals in other European countries. This result underscores the need for systemic interventions in the judiciary, such as mental health support and workload management.

In the fifth part "Law and Science," Amelia Shooter focuses on Blackstone's ratio, which reads "it is better that ten guilty persons escape, than that one innocent party suffer." This principle can be eroded by the legal professionals who prioritize rational legal decisions over the evaluation of substantive scientific concerns, as observed in a body of U. S. case law. Shooter posits that such a situation is due to legal professionals' greater familiarity with legal reasoning rather than scientific knowledge. To address the situation, she proposes that law schools harness their position to provide contextual scientific education for their students. This proposal will, so argues she, support science-led decisions and reduce the risk of miscarriages of justice, striving to uphold Blackstone's ratio.

Tomasz Pietrzykowski investigates traditional and alternative medicine, which raises a challenge for the public and legal policy-making. A plethora of healing practices rooted in pre-scientific traditions remain prevalent worldwide, although they are not supported by credible empirical evidence or consistent with basic scientific knowledge. Pietrzykowski shows that two extreme regulatory models – laissez-faire and prohibitionist – are indefensible on account of their practical deficiencies and flawed philosophical underpinnings. As an alternative, he offers a middle-way model of respect for the patient's genuine autonomy, based on informed consent. Last, he notes the need for the development of legal measures to make patients' decisions accurately and sufficiently informed.

Three papers in the sixth part "Cosmopolitanism vs. Culture?" deal with cultural diversity and human mobility in the contemporary world. Kosuke Kiyama begins with what he calls the cultural diversity respect requirement, which advocates some kind of respect for different cultural systems when human rights are envisaged. Next, he turns to the argument that the international human rights regime benefits all cultural proponents and thus can be supported despite cultural diversity. He objects to this argument by complaining that benefit does not entail support and that the argument provides no room for new international mechanisms protecting the rights of members of a cultural group. He advocates an alternative approach that bases international human rights norms on universally shared interests, offering a more nuanced framework of respect for cultural differences.

To address the question of how cosmopolitanism can be universally accepted in the culturally diverse world, Kento Miyata strives to provide an intercultural ground for the permissibility and rationality of cosmopolitan hope. He examines the overlapping consensus approach proposed by Charles Taylor and the constructivist approach by Rainer Forst, reaching the evaluation that the latter is more suitable than the former. However, Miyata notes that the constructivist argument must be supplemented by the unity requirement, which demands theoretical reason and practical reason functioning with no contradiction. Finally, he explains how the unity requirement can foster cosmopolitan order and contribute to the constitution of practical identity, rendering cosmopolitan hope permissible and rational.

Yuichiro Mori overhauls Daniel Sharp's relational egalitarian argument against immigration restrictions. While affluent states' immigration restrictions on disadvantaged immigrants are morally objectionable because they are an exercise of unequal power, so the argument goes, similar restrictions on those coming from affluent states are not. Mori challenges Sharp's restrictive view on who can make a complaint about immigration restrictions by invoking relational equality. After describing the view, he objects that it should lead to the condemnation of restrictions to immigrants from affluent states. Then, he replies to three possible criticisms of his objection: criticisms based on democracy, structural injustice, and the danger of territorial domination.

The final part "Law and Sexuality" focuses on a group of LGBTQ-related legal issues across cultures: the decriminalization of homosexual conduct and the legalization of same-sex marriage. Ming Yuan Chin addresses a conflict between personal autonomy – a fundamental human right that underpins freedom – and the good defined by the state in the context of legalizing same-sex marriage in Taiwan. Drawing on John Stuart Mill's harm principle and Raz's autonomy-based principle, he explores the evolution of personal autonomy, advocates value pluralism, and examines a tension between the harm principle and Razian perfectionism. Also, he criticizes Raz's dismissal of the right to autonomy and discusses an interplay between autonomy and constitutional theories.

Kuan-Ting Chen objects to John Rawls's concept of public reason by arguing that it might not inherently guarantee stability, which is highly valued by Rawls himself. Putting the idea of public reason into the context of the same-sex marriage debate in Taiwan, he argues that this idea excludes religious and comprehensive doctrines, pushing citizens to offer external or weaker internal reasons. In the early 2010s, the public reason idea was expected to have positive impacts on the legalization of same-sex marriage. However, the conservative backlash in the 2018 public vote called its effectiveness into doubt. Chen investigates the relationship between this idea and different conservative actors' motivations in order to uncover the causes of the idea's failure to ensure stability.

Seow Hon Tan closely looks at the history of criminalization and decriminalization of consensual male homosexual conduct in Singapore. Such conduct, whether private or public, had been kept punishable by a Penal Code provision, which was inherited from colonial times and retained even in the 2007 review. In 2023, the provision was eventually repealed alongside the introduction of a constitutional provision to safeguard the laws and policies related to heterosexual marriage. Tan explicates this shift in the government's stance as to the regulation of homosexual conduct, identifying the social forces and legal thoughts that underlie the shift.

Many papers included in the current issue analyze various cutting-edge jurisprudential or politico-philosophical topics, while some unpack realities in the contemporary law and politics of East and Southeast Asia, Europe, or the United States. By doing so, they all cast a new light on the cliché "East Meets West." Hopefully, this issue opens a new chapter of international academic dialogue and collaboration between Asian and Western researchers in the fields of philosophy of law and political philosophy.

References

Bell, Daniel A. (2000). *East Meets West: Human Rights and Democracy in East Asia*. Princeton, NJ: Princeton University Press.

Bell, Daniel A. and Wang Pei (2020). *Just Hierarchy: Why Social Hierarchies Matter in China and the Rest of the World*. Princeton, NJ: Princeton University Press.

Makoto Usami
Graduate School of Global Environmental Studies, Kyoto University; Institute for Ethics in Artificial Intelligence, Technical University of Munich
usami.makoto.2r@kyoto-u.ac.jp

Hidehiko Adachi
Faculty of Law, Kanazawa University
hadachi@staff.kanazawa-u.ac.jp

Part 1
Monarchy and Democracy

In Defense of Symbolic Monarchy
The Case of China

DANIEL A. BELL

Abstract: This essay opens by critically evaluating the case against monarchy. Then the author distinguishes between three types of monarchical systems and argues that symbolic monarchy is most appropriate for the modern world. He concludes with an argument for restoring (symbolic) monarchy in China.

Keywords: symbolic monarchy, China, constitutionalism, rituals, Confucianism

Why am I writing this essay?[1] I'd like to say it's a change of mind driven by somewhat surprising social scientific evidence. It's true that I had a bias against monarchy. Like other "progressive" thinkers of my age, I thought that monarchy was an archaic relic from the past. It seems irrational to empower people just because they happen to be born into families with "good" bloodlines. Why should states be ruled by hereditary monarchs rather than by politicians selected on the grounds they can effectively implement policies that benefit the people? Surely people want to choose their own rulers?

Yet it turns out that monarchies – political systems headed by single rulers selected largely if not exclusively on the basis of family background[2] – are among the world's most successful countries in the modern world. As Tom Ginsburg shows, 22 % of the countries today are monarchies, and they tend to do well on global indices of success, whatever they measure: eight of the world's top fifteen democracies are constitutional monarchies and many of the richest countries in the world are monarchies, including the constitutional monarchies of Europe and Japan and the absolute monarchies in

1 I am grateful to the International Association for Philosophy of Law and Social Philosophy for the invitation to deliver the 2023 Kobe Lecture and to Princeton University's "Transitions to Democracy" workshop for the opportunity to present an earlier version of this draft, along with students and scholars for helpful questions and comments. I'd particularly like to thank Hidehiko Adachi, Tom Ginsburg, James Hankins, Tatsuo Inoue, Dongxian Jiang, Alexandre Lefebvre, Yuichiro Mori, Yuri Pines, Justin Tiwald, Makoto Usami, Adrian Vermuele, Wang Pei and Lynn White III for helpful comments on an earlier version of this paper. I should note that some scholars kindly provided critical comments even though they forcefully disagreed with the main argument.

2 There are other types of monarchies – monarchs can be selected by other mechanisms such as merit, elections, or lot – but hereditary monarchy is the most common form (including in China) and it is also the form most likely to generate feelings of being part of an intergenerational community.

the Middle East.[3] In 2013, I co-published (with Mo Yingchuan) a "Harmony Index" that ranks countries according to level of harmony, meaning social peace and respect for diversity, and somehow failed to notice that five out of the world's eight most harmonious countries, including the top two (Norway and Sweden), are monarchies.[4] At the very least, it seems difficult to argue against the proposition that monarchies are compatible with forms of government that deliver the goods people care about in the modern world. But I've settled on an even stronger claim: a particular form of monarchy – symbolic monarchy – has advantages that should cause political reformers to consider adopting this form of government even in countries that have abolished monarchies in the past.

A Personal Story

I confess, however, that my change of mind was not solely driven by the empirical evidence. When I was about ten years old, my mother – a francophone from Quebec – married Anthony Meech, a sweet and highly intelligent man who never changed his British citizenship even though he had lived in Canada for nearly three decades. I dearly loved my step-father who provided much-needed stability in the midst of family turmoil. I confess, however, to mocking his habit of watching the Queen's Christmas message delivered every year on television. I could not understand why my step-father so reverently listened to a hereditary monarch deliver almost the same set of platitudes year after year. Eventually, I came to sympathize with his charming habit – and I delivered an emotional ode to monarchy at his funeral in 2008 – though I still couldn't understand his habit from an intellectual point of view: Why do we need such empty rituals presided over by hereditary rulers in the modern political world?

As often happens, it takes personal experience to change one's mind. I served as dean at Shandong University's School of Political Science and Public Administration from 2017 to 2022 and the last two years of my deanship consisted almost entirely of symbolic rituals.[5] I had been hired (at least partly) to internationalize the faculty but internationalization was dead in the water due to Covid and I had hardly any work of substance. I hosted dinners for visitors and participated in welcoming and graduation ceremonies. I learned to talk like a typical Chinese bureaucrat – flat affect and stick to three points, regardless of the substance of what's communicated – but it was mainly

3 Tom Ginsburg, "East Asian Monarchy in Comparative Perspective," in *The Long East Asia*, ed. Wang Zhengxu (Singapore: Springer, 2023), p. 199.
4 Daniel A. Bell and Mo Yingchuan, "Harmony in the World 2013: The Ideal and the Reality," Social Indicators Inde, Sept. 2013, 118(2), pp. 797–818.
5 The next three paragraphs draw on my book *The Dean of Shandong: Confessions of a Minor Bureaucrat at a Chinese University* (Princeton: Princeton University Press, 2023), pp. 153–156.

"propaganda" (宣传) for our faculty, such as short speeches to parents of first-year students before the start of the academic year to assure them we'd take good care of their (adult) children.

I felt somewhat useless but turned to history to help make sense of symbolic rituals and came to appreciate the value of my work. The case for symbolic rituals may be clearer at the highest level of government. The remarkable longevity and constitutional stability of the Republic of Venice, as Edward Muir has explained, was achieved "through a pious, intensely conservative adherence to ritual and legend, a habit that rendered the political order both mystical and sanctified."[6] Consider what happens when leaders stop performing rituals. There's one famous example in the history of China: Emperor Wanli, who reigned from 1572 to 1620. As documented in Ray Huang's excellent book *1587: A Year of Significance, The Ming Dynasty in Decline*, the most important tasks for the Chinese sovereign were personnel management and ceremonial procedure. The highly intelligent and sensitive Wanli, however, slowly became disenchanted when he could not get his way on key decisions, such as selecting a successor. In the last two decades of his rule, he basically went on strike, withdrawing from public life and refusing to play the emperor's role in government, leading to widespread alienation that contributed to the end of the Ming dynasty. In retrospect, the problem was not so much that he withdrew from the substantial task of personnel management, since much of that work could be done by meritocratically-selected public officials in the bureaucracy. The main problem was his failure to oversee the symbolic work of ritualistic proceedings that could not be replaced by anyone else.[7] It's perhaps understandable why the emperor, who "lost much of his personal identity and had little private life" might want to rebel.[8] Rituals were extremely taxing, if not completely exhausting. But such rituals were invested with (belief in a) cosmic spirit that kept the Empire going, as noted by the First Grand Secretary at the time:

> In providing the best leadership to an empire such as ours, there was no substitute for ritualistic proceedings. The emperor did not have a formidable army at his command; he did not even have a very large land base. He remained the Son of Heaven only because everyone believed he was. This belief required the ritualistic exercises involving the sovereign and his chief ministers to be enacted with vigor and regularity, completely in a public spirit, and accompanied by aesthetic and moral overtones. Pageantry or not, the many rounds of kowtowing reaffirmed imperial supremacy; yet merely the fact the emperor attended the ceremonies indicated that he was subjecting himself to the cosmic order and moral

6 Edward Muir, *Civic Ritual in Renaissance Venice* (Princeton: Princeton University Press, 1981), p. 186.

7 Some rites could be delegated to kinsmen and ministers but many of the most important ones had to be performed by the emperor himself.

8 Ray Huang, *1587: A Year of Significance, The Ming Dynasty in Decline* (Yale University Press, 1981), pp. 3, 76.

> law. It was precisely because the messages taken from the basic classical sources were dull and trite that one must be prepared to listen to them again and again. The heat and cold and the pre-dawn hour only tested the human will. This idea of discipline and endurance had been emphasized by Censor Keng. Even in the emperor's farming ritual obviously a degree of make-believe was involved; but make believe is not necessarily unreal. One must realize how powerful an instrument of government it was when all participants shared a belief in it.[9]

So when Emperor Wanli neglected his symbolic duties, he shattered the "magical" edifice that underpinned the whole system. To use contemporary language, the emperor's participation in ritual proceedings made others believe the political system was legitimate and the system could not survive for long without this belief.

I also came to appreciate the work of my step-father's favorite monarch, Queen Elizabeth II: It's both extremely difficult and extremely important to serve as a symbolic ruler. As Queen Mary put it to Elizabeth before she was formally anointed in the (semi-fictitious) show *The Crown*, "To do nothing is the hardest job of all. And it will take every ounce of energy that you have, to be impartial is not natural, not human." I'm aware that the stakes are not so high for a minor bureaucrat with symbolic responsibilities, but I sought direct inspiration from the Queen when participating in ritualistic ceremonies. Doing nothing is hard work! Consider distributing certificates to graduating students. We – the leaders – had to stand straight for three hours without a bathroom break and hand out certificates to hundreds of students. We wore colorful (and highly uncomfortable) outfits that drew on a mixture of Western and Chinese traditions, with different colors corresponding to the different hierarchies in the administration (deans wore red and black, and I confess that I envied the university president and university party secretary, who wore yellow robes, similar to the emperor's standard costume). We couldn't show our preferences. I tried not to show my enthusiasm when I met my own students and tried not to respond to smiling faces. I had to say "congratulations" (祝贺) to each student and sound equally enthusiastic every time. But I also knew the work was important to keep the university going and make the students feel part of the university.

In short, I came to realize that we need leaders to carry out symbolic rituals that provide a sense of continuity, stability, and a sense of community to those who partake of the rituals. Far from mocking those who preside over such rituals, we should respect if not revere them: it's extremely hard work and they need to be fully devoted to the common cause rather than pursue their own interests and act on their own political preferences. Of course, I've been asked to contribute an academic essay and I do not mean to imply that my own experience should persuade anybody else. So let me now

9 Ray Huang's summary of the First Secretary view in Ibid, pp. 46–47.

turn to the academic case for symbolic monarchy in the modern world. I will first discuss the case against monarchy and show it rests on a dubious premise. Then I will distinguish between three kinds of monarchical systems and argue that symbolic monarchy is most appropriate for the modern world. I will end with a tentative argument for restoring symbolic monarchy in China.

What's Wrong with Monarchy?

Tom Ginsburg, professor of law at the University of Chicago, is one of the few academics in the United States who is willing to openly put forward a case for monarchy in the modern world. It's worth asking why the argument is so controversial. Ginsburg blames the Marxist tradition: "communism is almost always fatal to monarchy; ideas matter and there are no more distant ideas in political theory than Marxism and monarchy."[10] The revolution in Russia did abolish monarchy in the form of Tsarist rule. And subsequent revolutions in China, North Korea, Cuba, Vietnam, and Laos did not implement monarchical forms of rule, at least on the surface. But is actually-existing communism really "fatal" to monarchy? Cambodia, ruled by a political party formed under communist ideology, restored the monarchy in 1993.[11] It can be argued that rulers such as Stalin and Mao were similar to monarchs, with the exception that they did not inherit their rule or pass it on their children. The Kim family dynasty in "communist" North Korea exhibits most of the characteristics of an absolute monarchy. In today's Russia, President Putin explicitly draws on symbols that echo Russia's Tsarist past, and in China President Xi draws on the legacy of imperial ritual performance to resume "the positioning in the polity once presumed to be held by emperors."[12] Monarchy may not have been officially restored in "communist" countries, but it's pretty close in reality.

At the level of ideas, there is a clear incompatibility between Marxist theory and monarchy. The state's function, according to Marx, is mainly to provide legitimacy and legal force to property relations that benefit the ruling class. Since the monarchy is part of the state, its main function is to benefit the ruling class. Marx himself didn't spend much time attacking the monarchy – his main target was capitalism – but post-capitalist societies are supposed to be governed first by the "dictatorship of the proletariat"

10 Ginsburg, "East Asian Monarchy in Comparative Perspective," p. 224.

11 Even more surprising, the political rulers in Cambodia recently adopted a form of "rule by political primogeniture" with monarchical roots, with the posts of prime minister and key ministers being passed on to the eldest sons (https://www.scmp.com/week-asia/politics/article/3230641/cambodias-hun-manet-likely-lead-cabinet-princelings-move-stability-over-democracy; accessed Aug. 18, 2025).

12 Vivienne Shue, "Regimes of Resonance: Cosmos, Empire, and Changing Technologies of CCP Rule," *Modern China*, January 11, 2022, p. 26 (https://journals.sagepub.com/doi/full/10.1177/00977004211068055; accessed Aug. 18, 2025).

and then, in higher communism with material abundance, the state will have withered away because there will no longer be any classes and people will be free to develop their creative talents rather than work for a living. There is no need for monarchy in communist society.

The case against monarchy, however, is much older than Marxism in both theory and history. In the seventeenth century, John Locke argued against the divine right of kings to rule and for the view that legitimate governments must have the consent of the people. A century later, American revolutionaries overthrew monarchical rule from the British Crown and established the United States founded on the principles of liberal democracy. In the Francophone world, Jean-Jacques Rousseau, Baron de Montesquieu, and other Enlightenment thinkers argued against the traditional authority of the absolute monarch and for the view that legitimate power derives from the people,[13] and French revolutionaries went on replace monarchical rule with a form of government founded on the rights of man and citizen.

At the heart of these revolutions against monarchy – of which Marxism can be viewed as a sub-branch – is the belief that moral progress means overthrowing social hierarchies and moving towards a future where people are treated as moral equals. Monarchy is the mother (or father) of all social hierarchies so naturally it's the first target of revolutionaries who fight for moral progress. The mainstream Enlightenment narrative of modernity developed centuries ago continues to influence progressive thinkers in the West and the rest of the world. Here's a (somewhat crude) sketch of this narrative. Traditional hierarchies expressed and institutionalized unjust values such as racism, sexism, and aristocratic privilege (with monarchy at the apex of aristocratic privilege). These traditional hierarchies can and should be replaced by relations of social equality and individual freedom that set the moral standard for future progress. There remains a large gap between the ideal and the reality, but hardly anybody in "right thinking" progressive circles openly argues for a return to the bad old days of rule by powerful men and women from aristocratic and royal families. There may be a prudential case to maintain some social hierarchies if it's difficult or costly to change the system, but in principle they ought to be abolished and it's just a matter of time till we get rid of them.

These questions are deep and complex but it's not difficult to find flaws in this narrative of moral progress.[14] For one thing, we need to ask: Is it possible to completely do away with social hierarchies? Efficiency is a clear benefit of hierarchy and it's impossible to connect large numbers of people in an efficient way without a hierar-

13 In the case of Rousseau, however, he defended the institution of the monarchy for large states such as Poland, but argued it should not be a hereditary post (https://www.files.ethz.ch/isn/125482/5016_Rousseau_Considerations_on_the_Government_of_Poland.pdf; accessed Aug. 18, 2025).

14 The next two paragraphs draw on Daniel A. Bell and Wang Pei, *Just Hierarchy: Why Social Hierarchies Matter in China and the Rest of the World* (Princeton: Princeton University Press, 2020), Introduction.

chically structured social organization. As Peter Turchin explains, "The only way that large human groups can arrive at a common course of action is by [hierarchically] structuring interpersonal connections … Societies that were larger and better organized outcompeted smaller and more shambolic ones … It's a pipe dream to imagine a large-scale society (e.g. a million or more – a small nation by today's standards!) in a nonhierarchical, horizontal way. Hierarchy (in a neutral sense) is the only way to organize large-scale societies."[15] History bears out this thesis: efforts to consciously build large-scale organizations of societies without hierarchies have failed miserably. Edmund Burke famously criticized the French revolutionaries for seeking to equalize relations of common and obedience in the military and predicted such efforts would lead to the rise of an even more autocratic strongman. In China's Cultural Revolution, the effort to stamp social hierarchies led to mass violence and populist tyranny. In the United States, populist backlashes against elites empower strongmen such as Donald Trump with scant regard and respect for traditional constraints on political power. So the effort to combat all forms of hierarchy will not only fail; it may lead to something even worse from a moral point of view. The right question to ask is not how abolish hierarchies *tout court*, but rather how to stamp out (or minimize the influence of) unjust hierarchies that benefit only the power-holders and how to promote morally legitimate social hierarchies that benefit those on the bottom of hierarchies. Some social hierarchies can be beneficial to those with less power: think of teacher-student or parent-child relations. In principle, teachers and parents are supposed to exercise their power for the benefit of students and children. In reality, things can go wrong, but only the most dogmatic cynic would deny that social hierarchies sometimes benefit those with less power. In the case of monarchy, it's a (moral) problem if the system only benefits the hereditary rulers, but we need to ask if it is possible to identify and promote forms of monarchical rule that benefit the people who are ruled by monarchs.

Three Models of Monarchy

Absolute monarchy – a political system that gives the monarch unlimited power – is the oldest and most common form of monarchical rule. It is also the worst form of monarchy and fortunately, on its way out. Today, there are only five absolute monarchies (including Vatican City) and they are relatively small states (Saudi Arabia, with a population of 36 million people, is the largest). Why did absolute monarchies come to have such a bad name? The problem is not that absolute monarchs exercised totalitarian rule that controlled every aspect of their subjects' lives: whatever their aspirations,

15 Peter Turchin, "The Evolution of Hierarchy," December 20, 2014, https://peterturchin.com/the-evolution-of-hierarchy/; accessed Aug. 18, 2025.

monarchs lacked the ability and the technology to do so. The problem is rather that absolute monarchs can and did interfere with subjects' lives in arbitrary and cruel ways and were themselves not subject to any constraints: In a word, they often acted like tyrants. To get away with their nasty deeds, absolute monarchs often claimed to have some sort of divine legitimacy: they were the direct heirs of God, reincarnation of spirits, or appointed as representatives of "Heaven." Hence, they could do more or less do what they wanted because they were not subject to the whims of earthly endorsement. Today, few people believe such myths and it's hard to believe an effort to revive them could succeed without North-Korean style control of outside information. That said, it's abstractly conceivable that an all-wise and benevolent Aristotelian monarch or Confucian sage-king will rescue the world from suffering and misery. But even if there is one, the successors are not likely to be equally up to par (Mencius, the most idealist of the Confucians, said the sage-kings come only once every five hundred years). And even if the sage monarch is talented and virtuous and his or her successors are equally sage-like, the system would not work well without talented and virtuous public officials at lower levels of government who are willing and able to effectively implement the monarch's decisions and to report the country's problems without fear or favor, which makes the system even more unlikely in reality.

In the Chinese tradition, scholars thought of endless schemes to limit the absolute monarch's power. The "Legalist" thinker Han Feizi argued that monarchs should put in place a system of harsh laws and punishments that control the people and then withdraw from politics on the grounds that rulers accumulate more mystique and power by rarely intervening in worldly affairs: the not-so-implicit result is that the monarch would be neutralized and the system could operate even with mediocre rulers.[16] In imperial China, meritocratically selected public officials often acted as a de facto check on the emperor's power and court historians recorded the words and deeds of emperors in the hope that emperors would worry about negative evaluations by posterity. Emperors were educated in Confucian norms so that they could be made to rule in a more humane way. The multi-volume Tang dynasty text on *The Essentials of Governance* was used to educate emperors in the art of good government in subsequent dynasties.[17] A more direct check came in the form of Confucian "censors" who criticized what they considered to be mistaken policies (though they were rarely so foolhardy as to attack the emperor himself). More radical proposals were circulated *samizdat*: the recently unearthed "Zhouxun" (Instructions of the Zhou) from the Western Han argued for the meritocratic selection of heirs rather than succession based solely on primogen-

---

16 Yuri Pines, "Submerged by Absolute Power: The Ruler's Predicament in the *Han Feizi*," in *Dao Companion to the Philosophy of Han Fei*, ed. Paul Goldin (New York: Springer, 2013), pp. 67–86.
17 For an English translation, see Wu Jing, *The Essentials of Governance* (Cambridge: Cambridge University Press, 2021).

iture or the nobility of the maternal lineage.[18] The Confucian scholar Huang Zongxi suggested that emperors be subject to monthly, semi-public questioning by scholar-officials.[19] But none of these proposals succeeded in eliminating arbitrary rule and even the least bad emperors in Chinese history sometimes caused the people to suffer in ways shocking to contemporary sensibilities.[20] If the moral purpose of politics is to benefit the people, it seems like a reckless gamble to pin hopes on absolute monarchy.

More surprisingly, absolute monarchy can be bad for the monarch. On the face of it, it seems desirable to have as much power as possible without any constraints. But power corrupts the soul, and absolute power corrupts the soul absolutely.[21] In book 9 of The *Republic*, Plato criticized tyrants enslaved by their passions and concluded that the tyrant's life is desperate, paranoid, and miserable. No wonder some absolute monarchs sought to exit from the system. In Denmark, Christian VII was crowned king in 1766 and publicly announced he would live out his inner wildness rather than rule the kingdom: "He embarked on a regime of debauched violence that, in its sheer relentlessness, seemed almost a calculated attempt to persuade the administration at the court of the fatal flaws in their belief in absolute monarchy as the best form of govern-

---

18 Andrej Fech, ed. and translator, *Mad Rulers and Worthy Sons: A Translation and Analysis of the Newly Excavated* Zhouxun (St. Petersburg, FL: Three Pines Press, 2023). One disadvantage of such proposals without clear lines of succession is that they often lead to infighting among potential heirs fighting for political power (in the Roman case, the imperial office was not strictly hereditary but also involved questions of merit and consent, which led to periods of good government but the system eventually broke down into the more common dynastic form of succession; see Allen Guelzo and James Hankins, *The Golden Thread: A History of the Western Tradition* (New York: Encounter, 2025), ch. 4). In the case of symbolic monarchy, however, an incompetent ruler is not so dangerous because the ruler does not have real power (so clear lines of hereditary succession to, say, the eldest child, is not so problematic) and if there are some meritocratic or consensual mechanisms meant to influence the succession, the result is not likely to lead to vicious infighting because the post of symbolic monarch is more of a burden than a benefit (for the office holder) and will more likely to appeal to those with other regarding personalities rather than power-hungry would-be-tyrants (see note 50).

19 Huang Zongxi, *Waiting for the Dawn: A Plan for the Prince*, trans. Wm. Theodore de Bary (New York: Columbia University Press, 1993), p. 83.

20 That said, it's probably true that every single political system prior to the twentieth century caused some people to suffer in ways that would be shocking to contemporary sensibilities (think of the suffering caused by extreme forms of exploitation of women that were almost universal until recently).

21 There may be some counter-examples to the principle that absolute power corrupts absolutely, such as the third century BCE Emperor Ashoka, who changed from a ruthless conqueror of territory to a defender of Buddhist-inspired non-violence once he assumed near absolute power over an area larger than the Indian subcontinent (see Patrick Olivelle, *Ashoka: Portrait of a Philosopher-King* (New Haven: Yale University Press, 2024) and the Roman Emperor Augustus (63 BCE – 15 CE) who was transformed from a populist warlord to a visionary statesman once he became a powerful monarch (see James Hankins, "Augustus and the Salvation of Rome," *First Things*, Nov. 7, 2023, https://www.firstthings.com/web-exclusives/2023/11/augustus-and-the-salvation-of-rome; accessed Aug. 18, 2025). Again, however, the system will not be stable without a guarantee that successors are equally up to par and without lower-level officials who are unusually talented and virtuous.

ment for Denmark."[22] To remedy the system, the physician and royal adviser Johann Friedrich Struensee ruled the country and implemented political reforms designed to curb the power of the monarchy, such as abolition of the Royal Court's aristocracy and the introduction of complete freedom of the press, thus paving the way for the constitution of 1849 that formally abolished absolute monarchy in favor of a system where the monarch only has formal power.

The newer and far more popular form of monarchy is constitutional monarchy, meaning that the monarch's powers are limited by a constitution and informal norms that substantially limit his or her power compared to absolute forms of monarchy. Today there are 43 constitutional monarchies and they help to minimize the abuses of absolute monarchy. Still, the term "constitutional monarchy" covers too many regime types and we need more nuance for normative evaluation. The constitutional monarch can still wield plenty of political power, depending on the content of the written constitution and informal constitutional norms. If a relatively powerful monarch is benevolent and revered by the people, the system can produce good outcomes: In 1973, for example, King Rama IX in Thailand offered shelter and protection in his palace to students who demanded that the military resign and let them draft a new, democratic constitution, which saved the students and led to the resignation of the military government.[23] In 1992, the King intervened again to help de-escalate violence and pave the way for an eventual return to democracy. Recent developments in Thailand, however, expose the downside of a system which invests much executive power in the hands of the monarch: after his son King Rama X took power, "He took back the holdings of the Crown Property Bureau into his personal control and management, preserving his status near the very richest of monarchs in the world … He took over direct command of the military units guarding Bangkok, essentially ensuring that no coup could be organized without him. And he spent much of the COVID-19 pandemic in Germany with a large harem."[24] Meanwhile, one of the world's strictest lèse-majesté laws punishes insults to the monarchy with imprisonment of three to fifteen years, thus helping to shield the Thai monarchy from criticism. In short, constitutional monarchy *per se* is not sufficient to minimize the risk that monarchs abuse their power: the (formal or informal) constitution must ensure that monarchs are limited to ceremonial or symbolic powers, without any actual power or direct political influence (except in highly unusual situations). Let's label this form of monarchy – a sub-species of constitutional monarchy – "symbolic monarchy."

---

22 Robert Ferguson, *Scandinavians: In Search of the Soul of the North* (London: Head of Zeus Ltd., 2016), p. 141.

23 Eugénie Mérieau, "Establishing the King as the Source of the Constitution: Shifting 'Bricolaged' Narratives of Buddhist Kingship from Siam to Thailand," in *Buddhism and Comparative Constitutional Law,* eds. Tom Ginsburg and Benjamin Schonthal (Cambridge: Cambridge University Press, 2023), p. 191.

24 Ginsburg, *East Asian Monarchy in Comparative Perspective,* p. 222.

Symbolic monarchy, as an idea, has a long history. In the Chinese tradition, the Warring States Confucian thinker Xunzi argued that powerful ministers should do most of the policy decision-making and selection of personnel, with monarchs sticking largely to symbolic rituals and ceremonies. But such plans for "symbolic monarchy" rarely constrained the "Son of Heaven" in imperial Chinese history who could and often did intervene at will. In the Kingdom of England, the Glorious Revolution of 1688 helped to institutionalize constitutional monarchy but monarchs continued to exercise a degree of personal and political power until the nineteenth century. In his influential work *The English Constitution* (1867), the British writer (and editor-in-chief of *The Economist*) Walter Bagehot argued that monarchs should stick largely to ceremonial duties and informal political powers such as the rights to encourage, to warn, and to be consulted, which more or less became the reality in the British system. Today, symbolic monarchs in the United Kingdom and Japan (the world's two largest monarchies) exercise little or no actual power or direct political influence: the monarch reigns but does not rule.[25] In short, symbolic monarchy has more or less successfully curbed the tendency of monarchs to abuse their power.

But it's not just a matter of boxing in monarchs. The argument that it's possible and desirable to limit their power won't convince skeptics of monarchical rule that the system has advantages compared to, say, democracies without symbolic monarchs such as the United States and France. So what is the positive case for symbolic monarchy? One empirically informed study by Mauro F. Guillen shows that contemporary monarchies protect property rights to a greater extent compared to republics, which translates into higher GDP per capita, because they control internal conflict by virtue of being a symbol of unity, reduce the negative effects of executive tenure through dynastic continuity, and offset the discretion of the executive branch by providing an additional veto point, and that the latter two effects are particularly strong in the case of democratic constitutional monarchies where the monarch reigns but does not rule.[26] In the United Kingdom, the economic case for monarchy is especially compelling: In 2017, according to Brand Finance, the royals contributed 1.77 billion pounds to the UK economy through a combination of the Crown Estate's revenues and indirect benefits for tourism, trade, media and the arts, far outweighing the estimated 345 million pounds annual cost of the monarchy.[27] "Monarcho-socialists" put forward another economic argument for symbolic monarchy: peasants and workers can ally with progressive

---

25 https://www.ucl.ac.uk/constitution-unit/explainers/what-role-monarchy#:~:text=The%20King%20reigns%2C%20but%20he,to%20follow%20the%20government's%20advice; accessed Aug. 18, 2025. In Japan, the monarch had largely symbolic powers prior to the Meiji restoration, so it was more a matter of restoring that form of emperorship after World War II.

26 Mauro F. Guillen, "Symbolic Unity, Dynastic Continuity, and Countervailing Power: Monarchies, Republics, and the Economy," *Social Forces*, 97(2), Dec. 2018, pp. 607–648.

27 https://www.aljazeera.com/economy/2023/5/2/how-much-does-the-british-royal-family-cost-its-complicated; accessed Aug. 18, 2025. Needless to say, such figures are context dependent – no doubt the cost

monarchies for the purpose of radical social reform.[28] As theologian and monarchist John Ritzema points out, "One of the great things about having a hereditary system is that you can't buy it,"[29] which provides a bulwark against the destructive power of international capital. That said, there is scant historical evidence to suggest that monarchs in the modern world have contributed to redistributive outcomes that favor the less well-off and it seems overly optimistic to expect that they will often sacrifice the interests of "natural" allies in the aristocracy in cases of conflict.

Perhaps a stronger progressive argument for monarchy is that it can help with the cause of environmental sustainability (one of King Charles III's favorite causes).[30] In electoral democracies, nobody represents the interests of future generations and their interests are likely to be sacrificed in cases of conflict with the current generation of voters. But a hereditary head of state, as Jiang Qing explains, "is answerable not only to the present generation but also to ancestors and generations to come. He can provide a check on the political power that destroys the environment for the worldly interests of a given group of people. He can use state power to give advice, question, encourage, and warn people in the various important areas of national life and suggest to the political authorities that they cannot use ecological destruction to … harm the interests of future generations."[31] Along those same lines, the symbolic monarch can represent the interests of foreigners who do not otherwise have a voice in a democratic political system that only gives political rights to voters. Perhaps it's not a coincidence that four countries with symbolic monarchs (Luxembourg, Norway, Sweden, and Denmark) lead the world in terms of foreign aid given per capita.[32]

Yet another argument in favor of symbolic monarchy is that it contributes to political stability. Dong Fangkui argues that "drastic implementation of the republic political system [as opposed to symbolic monarchy] will inevitably bring political chaos and economic or financial hardships … in the 27 years between 1952 and 1979, [most mil-

---

of the British monarchy outweighed the economic benefits when tourism to the dried up in the first two years of Covid – and newer and smaller monarchies may not be so successful at international marketing.

28 John Last, "A King for the People," *Noema*, May 2, 2023 (https://www.noemamag.com/a-king-for-the-people/; accessed Aug. 18, 2025).

29 Quoted in Ibid. See also Robert McNair Wilson, *Monarchy or Money Power* (Dublin: Omnia Veritas Ltd., 2015).

30 See Charles HRH, The Prince of Wales, *Harmony: A New Way of Looking at the World* (N.Y.: Harper Collins, 2010). Similarly, Prince Frederik of Denmark was a strong advocate of environmental sustainability and embraced the fight against climate change (https://www.nytimes.com/2024/01/02/world/europe/denmark-prince-frederik-royal-family.html; accessed Aug. 18, 2025). It is likely that two monarchs will be less public in their commitments qua King given they that are expected to refrain from explicitly taking sides in public debates, but they may continue to exercise moral power behind the scenes.

31 Jiang Qing, *A Confucian Constitutional Order: How China's Ancient Past Can Shape Its Political Future*, trans. Edmund Ryden, eds. Daniel A. Bell and Fan Ruiping (Princeton: Princeton University Press, 2013), pp. 92–93.

32 https://www.insidermonkey.com/blog/10-countries-that-give-the-most-foreign-aid-per-capita-1184118/10/; accessed Aug. 18, 2025.

itary coups] took place in countries with the republic political system, bringing social instability and disorder."[33] Conversely, countries with symbolic monarchs experienced more political stability. In the Arab Spring, for example, all the monarchies avoided major turmoil but the republics were shattered to pieces. In the case of Japan, "General MacArthur's decision to preserve the [symbolic] emperor induced conservatives to cooperate with the Occupation authorities and allowed the successful reconstruction of Japan."[34] Without the emperor, right-wing outrage and wealthy landlords could have sabotaged massive land reform and the transition to democracy. Still, these arguments provide strong reasons for maintaining symbolic monarchy where it already exists, but they won't be so persuasive in political contexts that do not have monarchies.

The strongest case for symbolic monarchy is psychological: people have a need to identify with a broader community and a symbolic monarch can satisfy it.[35] In the modern state, the monarch can be the symbol of a non-partisan, intergenerational national community that makes the people feel as one (perhaps, say, national victory in the World Cup can generate similar feelings, but they are more fleeting). It's not necessarily an elitist point that divides people into a tiny minority of Platonic guardians guided by reason and morality versus the ignorant and emotional masses. Nor do we need to endorse a Confucian-style division between Confucian *junzi* (exemplary persons) fit to rule versus *xiao ren* (petty people) who pursue narrow self-interest and lack compassion for others. And we do not need to agree with Walter Bagehot's defense of symbolic monarchy on the grounds that it is designed to impress and secure the loyalty of the narrow-minded and unintelligent lower orders, thus leaving the actual policy-making to the minority of people with substantial political capacities. Rather, the division between emotion and reason is mainly within people, not between them. Even highly-educated people (such as my step-father) often have a need to identify with a unified, intergenerational community and a symbolic monarch can satisfy that

33 Dong Fangkui, "The Constitutional Monarchy and Modernization: Kang Youwei's Perspective of "Keeping the Emperor and the Royal System in China," *Canadian Social Science*, Vol. 10, No. 2, 2014, p. 7.

34 Ginsburg, "East Asian Monarchy in Comparative Perspective," p. 218.

35 In principle, people can be emotionally attached to an abstract entity such as an intergenerational political community without particular people who represent the nation. In practice, however, the phenomenon is too rare, weak, and fragile to serve as a foundation for a political culture. For purposes of getting people more or less wholeheartedly on board – especially from an emotional point of view – we need concrete entities (or people) to stand in for the nation. There have been proposals to replace the monarchy with machines, but not surprisingly none has yet to be realized. As early as the 18th century, Sophie de Grouchy suggested that the king and his entourage be replaced by automata as a cost-saving measure (Sandrine Berges and Eric Schliesser, "Against power," https://aeon.co/essays/the-radical-political-writings-of-sophie-de-grouchy; accessed Aug. 18, 2025). That said, it is possible that technology develops to the point that imaginary avatars or anime characters are so life-like that people can become attached to a non-human entity that serves as symbolic monarch, similar to the avatars that serve as symbols of some Japanese cities (but I find it hard to imagine that anything non-human can generate the sorts of emotions generated by, for example, the picture of Queen Elizabeth II mourning the death of her husband in forced solitude due to Covid constraints at the time).

need. Perhaps a handful of saints and sages can transcend this human need, but for the rest of us, it's quite natural. How many people would turn down an invitation for lunch with, say, King Charles III at Buckingham Palace? And not feel a bit of magic?

Again, the point is not to argue that monarchs should have political power: symbolic and political powers must be separated. We tend to think of the separation of powers as the separation of legislative, executive, and judicial powers.[36] But it is equally, if not more important, to separate the two most important powers of the head of state: The power to make political decisions for the good of the people and the symbolic, ritualistic power to represent the state in official ceremonies.[37] In the United States and China, the two powers are merged in one person: The president. In the United Kingdom and Japan, they are separated. The monarch has symbolic, ritualistic power, and the elected prime minister has the power to decide on policy (with the support of his or her party and the majority in the legislature).

Other things being equal, the separation of symbolic and political powers is a good idea. The symbolic monarch can spend his or her time on rituals. Success does not depend too much on talent. In the United Kingdom, the King's task is mainly to appear contented,[38] read speeches written by others and greet visiting heads of state. He may not be the most brilliant person in the room, but it doesn't matter. Nor could he abuse her power, even if he wanted to. He is not supposed to interfere in policy-making. And since the symbolic monarch represents the state, including past and future generations, he can exert a pull on people's emotions. Citizens can project their love of country onto him, while being more rational in evaluating the decisions of the elected prime minister.[39] Meanwhile, the top political decision-maker can spend his or her

---

36 The next three paragraphs draw on my book *The Dean of Shandong*, pp. 151–153.

37 That's not to say symbolic monarchs should *never* intervene in politics: As symbols of national unity, they can (and perhaps should) occasionally intervene to protect the interests of otherwise vulnerable minority groups. For example, Sultan Ibrahim Ismail, the ruler of Johor who was installed as Malaysia's ceremonial king in January 2024 (the country rotates the crown every five years among nine hereditary state sultans), excoriated a Malay Muslim laundromat owner who announced he would not serve people of other faiths, saying "this is not a Taliban state" and the owner quickly fell into line (Kishore Mahbubani, "Anwar Ibrahim's Quiet Triumph," *Project Syndicate,* November 2, 2023).

38 I say "appear" to be contented because the task of presiding over endless rituals can be mind-dulling and physically exhausting and can lead to unhappiness (as we see from members of royal families in Japan and the United Kingdom who experience depression or decide the flee the system). From a legal point of view, monarchs in Japan and members of the Imperial family are deprived of the right of vote and of rights to free speech and the freedom of association granted to ordinary citizens. I feel sorry for royals who feel trapped in a gilded cage, but I also have great admiration for royals who stick with the system even at great personal cost and do what they are supposed to do in the interests of the community.

39 Conversely, some people can project negative emotions on the monarch – for example, they can despise King Charles – while being more rational when it comes to evaluating the real power holder. In countries without symbolic monarchy, some people will project an unreasonable form of hatred onto the real power holder, which can undermine the legitimacy of the whole political system.

time thinking about appropriate policies benefiting the country and not waste time cutting ribbons and officiating at national ceremonies.

Conversely, it's much easier for things to go wrong in political systems that merge symbolic and political powers at the highest level of government. In the United States and China, the president of the country is both the channel for people's emotions and the most important political decision-maker. So citizens are more likely to support bad decisions by the political leader since he or she also represents the state as a whole. There is no other channel for people's emotions at the top and citizens are less likely to critically evaluate the decisions of the leader. Even worse, the leader in a merged political system can create a cult of personality that's dangerous for the long-term good of the country. As Tom Ginsburg notes, "With the presence of a monarch, there is no way a populist can claim to be the one true leader representing the people," which helps to explain why populists such as Recep Tayyip Erdogan, Hugo Chavez, Saddam Hussein and Muammar Gaddafi emerge in countries without symbolic monarchs. George Orwell made a similar point: "In England the real power belongs to unprepossessing men in bowler hats: the creature who rides in a gilded coach behind soldiers in breastplates is really a waxwork ... It is at any rate possible that while this division of function exists a Hitler or Stalin cannot come to power."[40] In the United States, many citizens project their patriotic love of country on President Donald Trump, regardless of how incompetent or morally debased he may be. In China, President Xi abolished term limits for President and the media celebrates his thought. It's hard to be optimistic about the long-term good of any country with personality cults at the top, even if we like the policies of rulers in merged systems. If citizens project their emotions on the political ruler, will the political system appear to be less legitimate once the ruler "reports to Karl Marx," as they used to say in China?

Restoring (or Reinventing) Monarchical Rule in China

If we agree that it's important to separate political power and symbolic power, there is a strong case for institutionalizing symbolic monarchy even in republican countries without any form of monarchy. But political culture sets constraints on what's feasible and the argument is a non-starter in, say, the United States, a country strongly influenced by anti-monarchical principles from its earliest days and with an ancient constitution that's almost impossible to amend or in post-colonial contexts where the monarchy is strongly associated with racist impulses and imperial legacies. In China, it's a different (hi)story. The country was ruled by monarchs since the beginning of known history and its relatively short history of non-monarchical rule dates from 1912, when

40 Quoted in Last, "A King for the People."

absolute monarchy was abolished. In the twentieth century, the main tradition was anti-traditionalism, but history has made a raging comeback in the twenty-first century, with even the highest levels of government seeking legitimacy in China's imperial history and the continuity of China's great cultural traditions, including Confucianism that helped to legitimize imperial China's political system.[41] So why not consider restoring the monarchy in a symbolic form fit for the modern world?[42] It may not happen soon, but what about a few decades from now?

Kang Youwei was China's most influential political reformer at the turn of the twentieth century. He was also a die-hard monarchist until the end of his days in 1927, sixteen years after the collapse of the imperial system. In the late Qing, Kang advocated for a form of constitutional monarchy similar to that in rapidly modernizing Meiji Japan. His ideas inspired the Hundred Days Reform designed to modernize China's political system in 1898, but Empress Dowager Cixi and her conservative supporters staged a coup that ended the reforms and Kang was forced to flee to Japan. Following the collapse of absolute monarchy in 1911 and the establishment of a Republic under Sun Yat-sen in 1912, Kang argued for restoration of the monarch but with powers clearly circumscribed by the constitution and republican branches of government. Without a monarch who could serve as a unifying symbol for the nation, he worried that China would descend into chaos with military factions competing for power, which is more or less what happened until the victory of the CCP in 1949.

Kang's political views were largely discredited in the eyes of his contemporaries when he participated in the abortive restoration of the Qing ruler in 1917.[43] Today, however, "New Confucians occasionally suggest that the Republican Revolution of

---

41 See my book *China's New Confucianism: Politics and Everyday Life in a Changing Society* (Princeton: Princeton University Press, 2008).

42 China's long experience with an absolute form of monarchy is central to its political culture and may limit the appeal of symbolic monarchy (even China's limited experience with a more symbolic form of monarchy – the Zhou royal family in the Spring and Autumn period – is usually remembered as an unfortunate loss of prestige and influence). But countries such as the United Kingdom evolved from a long experience with absolute monarchy to symbolic monarchy so it shows it can be done (though China's challenge is greater given the formal break with monarchy *tout court*).

43 The ideal of monarchy suffered an earlier shock in late 1915 and early 1916 in the form of the short-lived, highly unpopular and ultimately disastrous effort by Yuan Shikai to restore a strong form of constitutional monarchy with himself as a powerful monarch (Yuan was advised by the American legal scholar Frank Goodnow who tried to turn China into a country that fit his paternalistic and racist worldview: see Jedidiah Kroncke, "An Early Tragedy of Comparative Constitutionalism: Frank Goodnow and the Chinese Republic," 21 Pac. Rim L & Pol'y J. 533 (2012). Available at: https://digitalcommons.law.uw.edu/wilj/vol21/iss3/6; accessed Aug. 18, 2025). For some strange reason, *The Economist* has compared my efforts to those of Frank Goodnow and I was similarly criticized by a commentator at Princeton University on an earlier version of this paper (see https://www.economist.com/china/2012/10/27/embarrassed-meritocrats; accessed Aug. 18, 2025). But I am a social critic, not an adviser to the throne, and my political theorizing aims to articulate and make systematic ideals grounded in Chinese history and culture that could be politically realistic and morally defensible in the contemporary era, not to impose a political ideal from outside against a reluctant population.

1911 was a mistake, because China was already headed toward a constitutional monarchy more suited to its 'national character.'"[44] China, the argument goes, would have been better off – more stable, with less violence and a smoother path to modernization – if it had adopted a symbolic monarchy in 1912 rather than abolishing the whole monarchical system. So it should not be surprising that Kang's ideas have made something of a comeback in Chinese intellectual circles. Zhang Yongle, professor at Peking University's law school (the leading law school in China), has written a strong defense of Kang Youwei's idea of "Without commonality there cannot be 'diversity in harmony'" (不能共则不能和). The Confucian idea of "diversity in harmony" is desirable, but it cannot be achieved without a sense of commonality that underpins the political community. More concretely, Kang interpreted commonality to mean a strong state with the capacity to provide railways, telegraphs, banks and other infrastructure for modernizing the country as well as a monarch who could serve as a unifying symbol for the political community.[45] Zhang argues in favor of Kang's idea of commonality but does not endorse the proposal for a constitutional monarchy.[46] Dong Fangkui, professor at the College of History and Culture at the Central China Normal University in Wuhan, openly defends Kang's ideal of constitutional monarchy. Dong argues that establishing a constitutional monarchy was the most suitable choice for China in Kang's time and he argues for the ideal in other political contexts as well. Dong concludes that "the Constitutional Monarchy should be acknowledged and promoted."[47] He doesn't add "in China," but the implication is clear.

The contemporary Confucian scholar Jiang Qing is more explicit. He openly advocates the restoration of monarchy in China in the form of what he calls "虚君", which literally means empty or imaginary ruler but it's similar to the British model of symbolic monarchy.[48] Jiang explicitly appeals to Kang for inspiration and spells out the implications for contemporary (or future) China in great institutional detail. Controversially, Jiang also proposes *who* should be the symbolic monarch in China. He argues

44 Yao Yang, *China and the West: A Pragmatic Confucian's View* (Singapore: Palgrave Macmillan, 2023), p. 27.

45 In *Datongshu* (The Book of Great Unity), published posthumously, Kang argued that (symbolic) constitutional monarchy should be viewed as an intermediary stage before the final state of human development when the barriers of race, religion, class, sex, and the family are eliminated and replaced by an egalitarian, communal society under a universal government. But the final stage was so distant from the political reality in Kang's day (and remains so in our day) that one must wonder if it was meant to be taken seriously (I'm reminded of Allan Bloom's argument in the introduction to his translation of Plato's *Republic* that Plato put forward a utopian idea of communism, including abolishing the family for the ruling class, that was so far-fetched it was meant to discredit the idea).

46 Zhang Yongle, "不能共则不能和": 晚期康有为的国家建构论与政体论" ["Without commonality there cannot be 'diversity in harmony'": Kang Youwei's Later Theory of State Construction and the Political System,"] 思想战线, Vol. 42 (6), 2016, pp. 55–63.

47 Dong, "The Constitutional Monarchy and Modernization," p. 8.

48 With the exception that Jiang grants more political power to the monarch, such as the power to appoint political personnel.

that a symbolic monarch in today's China can be legitimate in the eyes of the people if the monarchy has a noble and ancient lineage, if the lineage is political in nature, if it can be shown that the lineage is direct and unbroken, if the lineage is so unique as to exclude competition from other lineages, and if the citizens universally respect and accept the person with noble political lineage. Jiang shows that descendants of past emperors cannot meet those conditions. He then goes through each condition and argues that only one person qualifies as the symbolic monarch in today's China: "the direct heir of Confucius."[49]

We can argue about who should occupy the post of symbolic monarch – Kang himself wavered between supporting Confucius's descendant as symbolic monarch and restoring the Qing emperor – but the larger point is that the institution of symbolic monarchy may be appropriate for China's political future.[50] Symbolic monarchy is

---

49 Jiang, *A Confucian Constitutional Order*, ch. 3. One common objection to Jiang's proposal is that Confucian's heir would not be viewed as legitimate by minority groups in Tibet and Xinjiang. In Confucius's home town (Qufu), however, Muslim minorities take pride in their Confucian heritage and do not experience a conflict between commitments to Islam and to Confucianism (see Kong Xinfeng and Daniel Bell, "曲阜：儒家文化之城" [Qufu: The City of Confucian Culture], in Daniel A. Bell and Avner de Shalit, eds. 城市的精神II [The Spirit of Cities II], (重庆： 重庆出版社, 2017), pp. 53–85). Note that Kongzi's direct descendant Kong Decheng lived in Taiwan until his death in 2008 and a symbolic monarch who descends from the Kong family may also help to buttress cultural unity between mainland China and Taiwan. East Asian countries with a Confucian heritage such as South Korea may balk at the idea that a member of the Kong family should serve as an important symbol of Chinese cultural unity, but on the other hand it is not inconceivable that East Asian countries at some point in the future join a commonwealth under the Kong-led monarchy similar to the British commonwealth and that the Kong monarch helps to secure peaceful ties and a values-based connection between China and other East Asian countries with a Confucian cultural heritage.

50 In Chinese history, the "father-to-son" succession orders with a tendency towards primogeniture mitigated the tendency to vicious infighting and helped to facilitate relatively smooth transfers of power compared to the vague succession rules of nomad-led dynasties such as the Mongol Yuan dynasty (the Qing was relatively stable because Chinese-inspired succession practices triumphed over tribal customs of brother-inheritance and election that often led to vicious infighting). See Andrej Kokkonen, Jorgen Moller, and Anders Sundell, *The Politics of Succession* (Oxford: Oxford University Press, 2022), ch. 9. Given the history of murderous infighting in Chinese history about who will assume the post of monarch when the lines of transmission were not clear, it may seem optimistic to assume that the debate about who will occupy the post of monarch can be settled without bloodshed. But the post of symbolic monarch, to repeat, is not so desirable because the monarch does not exercise substantial power: if anything, the job is a burden that requires an other-regarding and self-sacrificing personality and the challenge may be to persuade someone to accept the post (as opposed to the expectation that people will fight for the post). In view of these considerations, the next in line in a hereditary system of symbolic monarchy would ideally have the right of refusal, and the system would include a procedure to select someone who is more likely to accept the post. If it's a descendant of Kongzi (Confucius), the issue may be settled by a convocation of Kong family descendants who choose a leader, similar to the way the College of Cardinals selects a pope (the Kong family tree is perhaps the world's longest recorded family history). Another possible scenario is that the current Chinese leader tires of political decision-making and assumes a formal post as symbolic monarch (this scenario would also reduce the risk that political enemies seek revenge after retirement from politics because he would still be the symbolic leader of the country rather than a relatively vulnerable former leader with no formal power). In any case, it's worth noting that Chinese history offers some flexibility in terms of who should occupy the post of symbolic monarch – unlike Japan, the new dynasties did not restore old lines – and new, as yet unforeseen possibilities may arise.

compatible not just with Western-style democracy, but also with Chinese-style political meritocracy that aims to select and promote public officials with superior ability and virtue who do the actual decision-making:[51] elected politicians and/or meritocratically selected public officials can do the ruling and the symbolic monarch can do the reigning. Still, the restoration of monarchy in China might seem far-fetched. Perhaps the main practical obstacle is that it seems difficult to recover the sense of awe and mystique that underpins monarchical systems. But monarchies have been successfully restored in other countries. King Charles I was executed in 1649 but the English restored the monarchy eleven years later. When Norway became independent from Sweden in 1905, the people voted overwhelmingly to reject republicanism in favor of monarchy and they recruited a monarch from Denmark (Norway's former colonial master) and few question the legitimacy of the Norwegian royal family today. The Spanish monarchy was reestablished in the form of a constitutional monarchy in 1978 after more than four decades of rule by the populist (fascist) General Francisco Franco. Buganda – a Bantu Kingdom within Uganda – abolished the monarchy in 1966 (when Uganda was declared a republic) but it was restored as a ceremonial kingdom in 1993 following decades of horrific violence. Cambodia abolished the monarchy in 1970 but it was restored as a ceremonial monarchy in 1993. In short, a wide range of political systems have reestablished relatively weak forms of constitutional monarchy in a peaceful way.

But how to restore the magic, one might ask? After all, if symbolic monarchy lacks an aura of awe and majesty, the institution is less likely to serve its function of satisfying people's need to feel part of an intergenerational community. Without these feelings, the best we can hope for is something like Singapore's elected presidency, a recently invented institution that allows citizens to select a largely ceremonial state leader from a small group of establishment candidates: the President is respected but not revered.[52] For more, we can turn to the insights of Xunzi, perhaps the greatest political theorist in China's history. Writing at a time of constant warfare (third century BCE), Xunzi deliberately avoids utopian assumptions about human nature and society. In fact, he begins with the pessimistic assumption that "human nature tends to badness" (ch. 23). If people follow their bodily natures and indulge their natural inclinations, aggressiveness and exploitation are sure to develop, resulting in cruel tyranny and poverty (ch. 19). Fortunately, that's not the end of the story. People can "become good by

---

51 For a systematic defense of the ideal of "democratic political meritocracy" for the Chinese context, see my book *The China Model: Political Meritocracy and the Limits of Democracy* (Princeton: Princeton University Press, 2015).

52 The same is true of Presidents in countries such as India, Germany and Israel that perform largely symbolic duties. Such presidents are supposed to be non-partisan and to represent the interests of the political community as a whole, but they are respected rather than revered. A hereditary monarchy, with the monarch viewed as part of an intergenerational family that has represented and will continue to represent the national community, is far more likely to generate emotions of reverence and magic that can satisfy the human to feel part of an intergenerational community.

conscious exertion" (ch. 23). They can learn to contain their natural desires and enjoy the benefits of peaceful and cooperative social existence.

The key to transformation is ritual propriety (ch. 23). By learning and participating in rituals, people can learn to contain their desires, there will be a fit between people's actual desires and the goods available in society, and social peace and material well-being will result (ch. 19). Rituals provide bonds on based solely on kinship that allow people to partake of the benefits of social existence. Hence, Xunzi advocates the extensive use of ritual by the monarch to create bonds with people both at home and abroad, though (as mentioned above) he argues that much of the actual ruling should be left to the prime minister and ministers. For rituals to work their magic, they must engage with the emotions:[53] hence, they should be accompanied by stirring music and be viewed by participants as grounded in a revered tradition that people feel honored to partake of, though the details can be changed in accordance with particular circumstances.[54] Such views are not so archaic: the term for ritual (礼) still sounds positive in contemporary Chinese[55] and the term is often paired with music (礼乐) similar to ancient times precisely because it is assumed that rituals work on the emotions. Note, however, that music-infused rituals should only be performed on special occasions: if they are performed on a regular basis, the magic tends to wear off (a wedding ceremony accompanied by the wedding march is less likely to move the participants if it's frequently performed). More generally, we can borrow the Daoist/Legalist insight that rulers accumulate some mystique by remaining somewhat hidden, which helps to stir people's hearts when they do make their appearances. So now we have a clear mechanism for restoring the magic of monarchy in China: it may take some time, but if the political system can reinvigorate ancient rituals, accompanied by beautiful music, that guide the actions of the symbolic monarch in his or her interaction with people at home and abroad, and if the rituals are only performed on very special occasions, the symbolic head of state may come to embody the "sacred, historical, lofty, and eternal mysterious power of attraction and transcendent power in his [or her] person" and people's need for a "heartfelt sense of belonging" can be satisfied.[56]

---

53 Cross-cultural evidence supports Xunzi's argument that rituals serve to generate a sense of community, bonding, and mutual caring between people: see Dimitris Xygalatas, *Ritual: How Seemingly Senseless Acts Make Life Worth Living* (Boston: Little, Brown Sparks, 2022).

54 For a more systematic articulation and defense of Xunzi's view on ritual, see my essay, "Hierarchical Rituals for Egalitarian Societies," in *Ritual and the Moral Life: Reclaiming the Tradition*, eds. David Solomon, Ping-Cheung Lo, and Fan Ruiping, eds. (Dordrecht: Springer, 2012), pp. 173–194.

55 In the West, the Catholic religion emphasizes rituals combined with music but the strong hostility to "empty ritual" owes much to the Protestant hostility to Catholicism.

56 Jiang, *A Confucian Constitutional Order*, p. 90.

Bibliography

Bell, Daniel A. *The Dean of Shandong: Confessions of a Minor Bureaucrat at a Chinese University*. Princeton: Princeton University Press, 2023.

Bell, Daniel A. and Wang Pei. *Just Hierarchy: Why Social Hierarchies Matter in China and the Rest of the World*. Princeton: Princeton University Press, 2020.

Bell, Daniel A. *The China Model: Political Meritocracy and the Limits of Democracy*. Princeton: Princeton University Press, 2015.

Bell, Daniel A. and Mo Yingchuan, "Harmony in the World 2013: The Ideal and the Reality," *Social Indicators Index*, Sept. 2013, 118(2), pp. 797–818.

Bell, Daniel A. "Hierarchical Rituals for Egalitarian Societies," in *Ritual and the Moral Life: Reclaiming the Tradition*, eds. David Solomon, Ping-Cheung Lo, and Fan Ruiping, eds. Dordrecht: Springer, 2012.

Bell, Daniel A. *China's New Confucianism: Politics and Everyday Life in a Changing Society*. Princeton: Princeton University Press, 2008.

Berges, Sandrine and Eric Schliesser, "Against power," (https://aeon.co/essays/the-radical-political-writings-of-sophie-de-grouchy; accessed October 5, 2025).

Charles HRH The Prince of Wales. *Harmony: A New Way of Looking at the World*. N. Y.: Harper Collins, 2010.

Dong, Fangkui. "The Constitutional Monarchy and Modernization: Kang Youwei's Perspective of 'Keeping the Emperor and the Royal System in China'," *Canadian Social Science*, Vol. 10, No. 2, 2014.

Fech, Andrej, ed. and translator. *Mad Rulers and Worthy Sons: A Translation and Analysis of the Newly Excavated Zhouxun*. St. Petersburg, FL: Three Pines Press, 2023.

Ferguson, Robert. *Scandinavians: In Search of the Soul of the North*. London: Head of Zeus Ltd., 2016.

Ginsburg, Tom., "East Asian Monarchy in Comparative Perspective," in *The Long East Asia*, ed. Wang Zhengxu. Singapore: Springer, 2023.

Guelzo, Allen and James Hankins. *The Golden Thread: A History of the Western Tradition*, Vol. 1. New York: Encounter, 2025.

Guillen, Mauro. F. "Symbolic Unity, Dynastic Continuity, and Countervailing Power: Monarchies, Republics, and the Economy," *Social Forces*, 97(2), Dec. 2018.

Hankins, James. "Augustus and the Salvation of Rome," *First Things*, Nov. 7, 2023. https://www.firsthings.com/web-exclusives/2023/11/augustus-and-the-salvation-of-rome (accessed October 5, 2025).

Huang, Ray. 1587: *A Year of Significance, The Ming Dynasty in Decline*. New Haven: Yale University Press, 1981.

Huang, Zongxi. *Waiting for the Dawn: A Plan for the Prince*, trans. Wm. Theodore de Bary. New York: Columbia University Press, 1993.

Jiang, Qing. *A Confucian Constitutional Order: How China's Ancient Past Can Shape Its Political Future*, trans. Edmund Ryden, eds. Daniel A. Bell and Fan Ruiping. Princeton: Princeton University Press, 2013.

Kokkonen, Andrej, Jorgen Moller, and Anders Sundell. *The Politics of Succession*. Oxford: Oxford University Press, 2022.

Kong, Xinfeng and Daniel Bell, "曲阜：儒家文化之城" ["Qufu: The City of Confucian Culture"], in Daniel A. Bell and Avner de Shalit, eds. 城市的精神*II* [*The Spirit of Cities II*]. 重庆：重庆出版社, 2017.

Kroncke, Jedidiah. "An Early Tragedy of Comparative Constitutionalism: Frank Goodnow and the Chinese Republic," 21 Pac. Rim L & Pol'y J. 533 (2012). Available at: https://digitalcommons.law.uw.edu/wilj/vol21/iss3/6 (accessed October 5, 2025).

Last, John. "A King for the People," *Noema*, May 2, 2023 (https://www.noemamag.com/a-king-for-the-people/; accessed October 5, 2025).

Mérieau, Eugénie. "Establishing the King as the Source of the Constitution: Shifting 'Bricolaged' Narratives of Buddhist Kingship from Siam to Thailand," in *Buddhism and Comparative Constitutional Law*, eds. Tom Ginsburg and Benjamin Schonthal. Cambridge: Cambridge University Press, 2023.

Muir, Edward. *Civic Ritual in Renaissance Venice*. Princeton: Princeton University Press, 1981.

Olivelle, Patrick. Ashoka: *Portrait of a Philosopher-King*. New Haven: Yale University Press, 2024.

Pines, Yuri. "Submerged by Absolute Power: The Ruler's Predicament in the Han Feizi," in *Dao Companion to the Philosophy of Han Fei*, ed. Paul Goldin. New York: Springer, 2013.

Rousseau, Jean Jaques. *Considerations on the Government of Poland and on its Proposed Reformation*. April 1772 (https://www.files.ethz.ch/isn/125482/5016_Rousseau_Considerations_on_the_Government_of_Poland.pdf; accessed October 5, 2025).

Shue, Vivienne. "Regimes of Resonance: Cosmos, Empire, and Changing Technologies of CCP Rule," *Modern China*, January 11, 2022 (https://journals.sagepub.com/doi/full/10.1177/00977004211068055; accessed October 5, 2025).

Turchin, Peter. "The Evolution of Hierarchy," December 20, 2014 (https://peterturchin.com/the-evolution-of-hierarchy/; accessed October 5, 2025).

Wilson, Robert McNair. *Monarchy or Money Power*. Dublin: Omnia Veritas Ltd., 2015.

Wu, Jing. *The Essentials of Governance*. Cambridge: Cambridge University Press, 2021.

Xygalatas, Dimitris. *Ritual: How Seemingly Senseless Acts Make Life Worth Living*. Boston: Little, Brown Sparks, 2022.

Yao, Yang. *China and the West: A Pragmatic Confucian's View*. Singapore: Palgrave Macmillan, 2023.

Zhang, Yongle, "不能共则不能和"：晚期康有为的国家建构论与政体论" ["Without Commonality There Cannot Be 'Diversity in Harmony': Kang Youwei's Later Theory of State Construction and the Political System,"] 思想战线， Vol. 42 (6), 2016.

Daniel A. Bell
Faculty of Law, University of Hong Kong
dabell@hku.hk

Legitimate Authority in Democracy and Authoritarianism

HIROHIDE TAKIKAWA

Abstract: This paper examines the conditions under which political authority can be regarded as legitimate, with a focus on evaluating democracy and authoritarianism. I analyze two main arguments for democratic authority: instrumentalism and proceduralism. The instrumentalist argument suggests that democracy, as well as some forms of authoritarian regimes, can have legitimate authority due to their epistemic value. By contrast, the proceduralist argument maintains that only democracy has legitimate authority, though it faces the outsider problem. To address this problem, I propose the global approach, according to which democracy has legitimate authority as a means of establishing a global rightful state. Finally, I argue that some forms of authoritarianism can have legitimate authority only insofar as they protect everyone's equal right to freedom.

Keywords: authority, legitimacy, democracy, authoritarianism, instrumentalism, proceduralism, the outsider problem

1 Introduction: Democracy and Authoritarianism

Thirty years ago, in his *The End of History and the Last Man*, Francis Fukuyama declared that humanity had reached the end of history. That is, liberal democracy is the end point of mankind's ideological evolution and the final form of human government.[1] Today, his diagnosis is being challenged. Some argue that democracy is in "recession"[2] or "backsliding"[3]. Many observers see that while the number of authoritarian regimes in power had been decreasing since the end of the Cold War, it has recently been in turn on the rise[4]. Democracy may not be the final form of human government.

Reflecting a current landscape in international real politics, there has been a vigorous debate between democracy and authoritarianism in terms of effective governance. Some argue that authoritarian regimes can address urgent issues more quickly and comprehensively. Others argue that democratic regimes will do better even in a rapidly

1 Fukuyama (1992)
2 Diamond (2015)
3 Bermeo (2016)
4 Frantz (2018), 40

changing world. My aim is not to get involved in the debate. Rather, I aim to compare the two regimes in terms of legitimate authority.

The topic of democratic authority has been widely discussed in philosophical scholarship. The core question of democratic authority is whether a democratic government has legitimate authority over the governed, and if so why. A traditional answer to this question is the consent theory: a democratic government has legitimate authority because the governed have given consent to it. Because the consent theory is now seen as having many intractable flaws, a variety of alternative arguments have been proposed.

In this paper, I will examine the question of authoritarian authority by drawing on the arguments for democratic authority. I will do so by focusing on legitimate authority not from within but from without. In other words, I will approach it by examining so-called global issues. For example, climate change demands that we act to mitigate its anticipated effects and adapt to its inevitable consequences. We are urged to change many aspects of our lives by regulating greenhouse gas emissions, improving energy efficiency, subsidizing renewable energy, developing early warning systems, planting heat-resistant crops, and so on. Governments must not act in isolation, but in a globally coordinated way to meet the targets.

The actions and inactions of any government have a significant impact not only on its citizens, but also on those who live outside its territory. It is important to ask whether the decisions of the government have legitimate authority over those who do not have the right to vote in the jurisdiction. Policies adopted in a developed country affect people in other countries, especially poor people living in underdeveloped countries. Some argue that global poverty is central to the problem of climate change.[5] Climate change is expected to have negative impacts such as floods, droughts, typhoons, heat waves and infections in tropical areas where many poor people live. As we consider how to address climate change, we should ensure that our climate change laws and policies emphasize the reduction of global poverty.

However, the global poor generally lack effective means to influence and control the policies of developed countries. Although the global poor suffer from more impacts of climate change policies, they usually have less, and often no, power to challenge these policies. More generally, many of those affected by such policies have no official representation in environmental politics. For example, citizens of Tuvalu do not have the right to vote in the presidential elections of the United States or in the National People's Congress of the People's Republic of China.

This argument holds true for future generations. They will likely face greater impacts of climate change than our generation, but they must simply accept our decisions because they have no representatives in our democratic decision-making process. De-

5 Moellendorf (2014)

mocracy structurally ignores, or at most very indirectly reflects, the interests of future generations.

We are faced with the question of legitimate authority. When we make some decisions about politically important issues, the effects of those decisions sometimes spill over and affect people outside the demos. My question is: Can we claim legitimate authority over "outsiders"? If we can, why? This is often called the boundary problem, but I will call it the outsider problem. It is one of the most fundamental questions facing theories of legitimate authority, and yet, as Simmons puts it, it is a question "rarely raised by democratic theorists".[6]

In this paper, I first examine the concept of legitimate authority and then present two arguments for democratic authority: the instrumentalist argument and the proceduralist argument in Section 2. In Section 3, I argue that the epistemic argument for democratic authority, which is part of the instrumentalist argument, shows that some forms of authoritarianism are no worse than democracy. In Section 4, I argue that the procedural argument seems to show that democracy is better than authoritarianism because democracy embodies the intrinsic value of equality through its process, but it is not because democracy, like authoritarianism, has the outsider problem. Democracy lacks legitimate authority over domestic and global outsiders. To solve the outsider problem and acquire legitimate authority, I argue, both democracy and authoritarianism must meet certain conditions.

2 Legitimate Authority

2.1 The Paradoxes of Authority

First, I briefly examine the notion of authority. Any inquiry into questions of authority should start with the paradoxes of authority. The paradoxes of authority derive from the alleged incompatibility of authority with other important values. Joseph Raz mentions two paradoxes: reason and autonomy.[7]

The first value conflict is between authority and reason. When we plan and carry out an action, reason requires that we weigh the pros and cons and act accordingly. It is irrational to obey an authority that tells us to do something that seems to be wrong. Obeying authority contradicts our conception of ourselves as rational agents.

The second value conflict is between authority and autonomy. On the one hand, autonomy urges us to decide for ourselves what to do. On the other hand, authority

6 Simmons (2016), 73
7 Raz (2009), 3

requires us to surrender our own judgment and follow official directives. Obeying authority is incompatible with our conception of ourselves as autonomous agents.

I can add a third value conflict: that between authority and equality. The basic capacities of human beings are roughly equal. There is indeed some inequality among them, but it is not so great as to justify an authoritarian relationship. The concept of authority, however, assumes that there is a substantial inequality among them, and therefore inferiors should obey the directives of superiors. Obedience to authority contradicts our conception of ourselves as equals.

These value conflicts around authority are called "paradoxes" because authority plays an important role in our lives, but it also compromises other important values. Because authority has these three seemingly contradictory characteristics, authority is said to be paradoxical.

The paradoxes of authority must be resolved because we value morally ideal human relationships. Our fundamental assumption is that our rationality, autonomy, and equality carry moral importance in our human relationships, and therefore we must treat people, including ourselves, as rational, free, and equal agents. Nevertheless, an authoritative relationship appears to defy this assumption. If we deviate from morally ideal relationships, we must justify the deviation on some acceptable grounds. It is morally impermissible to treat people as irrational, unfree, and/or inferior without some acceptable reason. If we successfully justify the allegedly unacceptable human relationships, we can claim that they are in fact legitimate. The idea of legitimacy is a moral justification of seemingly unacceptable human relationships. Conversely, if we did not value morally ideal human relationships among rational, free, and equal agents, authority would never be paradoxical.

2.2 The Superiority Condition

To resolve the paradoxes of authority, what conditions must authority satisfy? I argue that authority must meet at least two conditions: the superiority condition and the preexisting condition. One of the most influential solutions to the paradoxes of authority is given by Raz. The main idea is as follows:

> [T]he normal way to establish that a person has authority over another person involves showing that the alleged subject is likely better to comply with reasons which apply to him (other than the alleged authoritative directives) if he accepts the directives of the alleged authority as authoritatively binding and tries to follow them, rather than by trying to follow the reasons which apply to him directly.[8]

---

8 Raz (1986), 53

This is what Raz calls "the normal justification thesis". Let me illustrate it with the example of the doctor's authority. A doctor has the authority to treat her patient because the patient is more likely to cure his illness by following her instructions than by devising his own remedies, while a teacher has the authority to educate her student because her instructions are more likely to promote his intellectual development than his own style of learning. Simply put, authority is justified if it improves the conformity to reason of its subject, who in this example is to be cured. We have good reason to follow authority as an effective means of achieving our own ends.

The core of the normal justification thesis is the rationalization of authority. The phenomenon of authority seems irrational because obedience to authority seems to be incompatible with our rational agency, as the paradox of authority shows. The normal justification thesis makes authority and rationality compatible by claiming that authority is justifiable only if it enhances rational behavior. A person has legitimate authority not because he decides to do whatever he wants, but because he shows us the right thing to do. We can call this an intellectualist understanding as opposed to a voluntarist understanding of authority.

The normal justification thesis is an indirect justification for obedience to authority. To understand what "indirect" means in this context, it is helpful to examine the contrast between direct and indirect consequentialism. To evaluate an action, consequentialism focuses on its consequences: i. e., those actions that make outcomes better are right, whereas those actions that make them worse are wrong. The more good consequences an action produces, the better the action. Thus, the good consequences produced by an action serve as the evaluative standard for consequentialism. To understand the contrast between direct and indirect consequentialism, it is important to note the distinction between the evaluative standard and the decision-making rules. On the one hand, direct consequentialism uses the imperative "make the consequences better" not only as an evaluative standard, but also as a decision-making rule. It requires an agent to follow the "make the consequences better" rule when deciding what to do. On the other hand, indirect consequentialism uses the "make the consequences better" imperative as an evaluative standard, but not as a decision-making rule. If an agent only considers consequences, she may make decisions that do not produce good consequences. Indirect consequentialism recommends that the agent use other rules to achieve her goal. For example, to minimize the anxiety of speaking in front of a large audience, it would be more useful for the speaker not to worry about his delivery than to repeat to himself, "Don't be nervous". Often an indirect route is a beneficial shortcut.

The normal justification thesis appeals to "indirectness" in this sense. Obedience to authority looks irrational to achieve one's goal because it might seem better to decide for oneself. The normal justification thesis claims that authority can be justified if obedience to authority is an indirect but better way to comply with one's reason than is one's self-determination. Simply put, authority is justifiable as an indirect but better way to achieve the goal.

I regard the normal justification thesis as a necessary condition for authority to be justified. The basic idea is to compare following authority with making decisions on one's own and to show that the former is superior to the latter for reaching one's goal. Therefore, I call it "the superiority condition" of authority.

2.3 The Preexisting Condition

Raz argues that the normal justification thesis is related to another thesis about authority, which he calls the dependence thesis. The main idea is as follows:

> [A]ll authoritative directives should be based on reasons which already independently apply to the subjects of the directives and are relevant to their action in the circumstances covered by the directive.[9]

The dependence thesis essentially requires that authoritative directives rely on "dependent reasons"[10]. These descriptions would not make the dependence thesis clear; in fact, it is quite elusive. But to see the point of the dependence thesis, it would be better to illustrate it in terms of theoretical authority. Experts have theoretical authority. Ordinary people have a reason to believe experts' advice because the experts tend to have better access to relevant credible information. It is important to note that such information is not special, as ordinary people would refer to this information when trying to form their own opinions. Experts depend on information that already exists independently of the question at hand before they tell ordinary people to believe it. In many cases, it is useful for ordinary people to follow the experts' advice because it saves them the cost of collecting and examining relevant information. In this sense, people generally have good reasons to follow theoretical authority, and the same is true of practical authority. It follows that authority in general is justifiable if it relies on dependent reasons.

Even with this explanation, the dependence thesis may be difficult to understand. It may be helpful to examine what the thesis denies rather than what it prescribes. When an authority issues a directive, the reasons the subject should consider change. For example, when a father tells his daughter to study, she considers whether to follow the directive. She considers the merits and demerits of studying (better grade versus boredom) as well as the merits and demerits of not studying (enjoying SNS versus worse grade). Additionally, she considers how her father will feel and react when she follows

9 Ibid., 47
10 Ibid., 41

or does not follow his instruction. She considers both the content of his directive to study and his possible reactions to her obeying or disobeying it.

The dependence thesis requires that authority should be based on the former rather than the latter. Authority must not refer to what the subject expects the authority to do in response to obeying or disobeying its directive, because these considerations arise only after the directive has been issued.

To illustrate this point, consider that a student follows his teacher's instruction because he expects to be punished if he does not comply with it. Regardless of whether his teacher's command is right or wrong, he may believe that it is wise to comply with it because of the negative consequences of disobeying it. According to the dependence thesis, these considerations do not justify authority because they arise only after a directive is issued. If this were allowed, any authority could create new reasons for people to obey its directives. This implies that any authoritative directives could be justified. The dependence thesis claims that authority should be based only on reasons that exist before a directive is issued. Because the dependence thesis is a necessary condition for authority, I will call it "the preexisting condition" of authority.

2.4 What Is a Preexisting Duty?

David Enoch presents a conception of authority that seems to be similar to the preexisting condition.[11] He claims that there are two cases in which the paradoxes of authority are resolved and therefore obedience to authority is justified.

The first case is when there is a preexisting duty to do as the authority requires.[12] In this case, obedience to authority is morally justified because there was a preexisting duty to obey authority before the directive was issued. The claim that there is a duty to obey authority because there is a preexisting duty to obey authority seems to be either tautological or prone to the problem of infinite regress. Enoch suggests that there is a preexisting duty to obey authority when consent makes a difference.[13]

The second case is when there are quasi-protected reasons to obey authority, such as when there is a rationale for not deliberating about some reasons.[14] For instance, when the subject lacks a sufficient ability to evaluate reasons there is a rationale not to deliberate about those reasons, and therefore obedience to authority is justified. Enoch claims that the paradoxes of authority are resolved in these two ways.

It is important to note that I have suggested that the preexisting condition for authority is different from a preexisting duty to obey authority. The preexisting condi-

11 Enoch (2014)
12 Ibid., 314
13 Ibid., 329
14 Ibid., 321

tion stipulates that authority is morally justified only if we have a preexisting duty, but that duty cannot simply be a duty to obey authority. What I have emphasized is that the duty must exist *independently of* one's relationship with authority. Otherwise, the paradoxes of authority remain unresolved. If we want to resolve the question of how to justify the unequal relations of authority, we cannot appeal to a preexisting duty to follow authority without begging the question.

According to the preexisting condition for authority, it is crucial important to identify what kinds of preexisting duties we have. It is safe to say that we have several kinds of natural duties, such as the duty not to harm or lie to others, the duty to keep promises, and the duty to help those in need. I cannot discuss them in detail in this paper, but in section 4 I will refer to the natural duty to respect other people as free, equal agents.

2.5 Two Arguments for Democratic Authority: Instrumentalist and Proceduralist

So far, I have discussed the two conditions of authority in general. The next question I attempt to answer concerns democratic authority. Do democratic decisions have legitimate authority, and if so, why? Is democratic authority consistent with the ideal of rational, free, and equal agents?

Democracy as a collective decision-making process can be justified in two ways: intrinsically or instrumentally.[15] The former argues for democracy because it is intrinsically valuable, and the latter argues for it because it is instrumentally better.

First, democracy is justified because it embodies an important value through the democratic decision-making process. This intrinsic argument of democracy refers to intrinsic values that are realized within the process itself. A variety of approaches have suggested that intrinsic values are inherent in the democratic process, including self-governance as equality among citizens, collective political autonomy, fairness as anonymous procedure, and public recognition of citizenship. These values are intrinsic in the sense that they are embodied in the democratic decision-making processes despite the value of their outcomes.

Second, democracy is justified because the democratic process is a useful instrument to produce better outcomes. Democracy is valuable because it tends to causally bring about better outcomes. The instrumental argument of democracy refers to values produced by but not existing within the democratic process. Those values include a correct solution to political issues, the construction of a peaceful society, the cultivation of civic virtue through political participation, and the reduction of non-domination.

---

15 List and Goodin (2001); Christiano (2008); Christiano and Bajaj (2022)

The difference between the intrinsic and instrumental arguments concerns whether the focus is on the value of the *process* or on one of its *products*. The former explains democracy with no reference to the outcomes of the democratic process. The latter includes the criteria for evaluating the outcomes independently of the value of the process itself. In John Rawls' terminology,[16] the former is based on pure procedural justice in the sense that it does not contain substantive evaluative standards of outcomes. Decisions cannot be right without referring to its procedure. The latter relies on imperfect procedural justice in the sense that it is likely to reach correct answers, but it will not always do so. Whereas perfect procedural justice has an independent criterion against which outcomes are evaluated to be right or not and it always produces the right outcome, imperfect procedural justice sometimes fails to produce the right outcome. A typical case of imperfect procedural justice is criminal procedure. It usually succeeds in finding guilty those who are guilty and not guilty those who are innocent, but it sometimes fails in both ways. Democracy as an illustration of imperfect procedural justice is similar to the criminal procedure in this way.

3 The Epistemic Argument for Legitimate Authority

As discussed in section 2, authority is justified if the subject is more likely to comply with reasons that apply to him/her by following the authoritative directives rather than by deciding based on reasons that apply to him/herself directly. Authority is justified as an indirect strategy to achieve the subject's goal, or as a better instrument to reach the goal. In this sense, the superiority condition for legitimate authority is consonant with the instrumental argument for democratic authority. Both seem to suggest that authority is justified if it improves compliance with reason for the subject.

The question is: how does democratic authority help the subject be more likely to comply with reason? One promising way is to focus on the epistemic value embedded in democratic decision-making procedures. An epistemic argument for democracy has recently attracted a growing number of supporters. Proponents of epistemic democracy argue that the aim of democracy is to track the truth in politics. Democracy is better than other types of decision-making processes because it is more likely to provide a correct answer to social issues. In other words, democratic decision-making process can provide better answers in terms of correctness for problem solving and predicting the future.

16 Rawls (1999), 75

3.1 The Condorcet Jury Theorem and the Diversity Trumps Ability Theorem

The epistemic value of democracy is usually explained by the Condorcet Jury Theorem, the Miracle of Aggregation Theorem, and the Diversity Trumps Ability Theorem.[17] These theorems show that democratic decision-making process is more likely to produce right outcomes than other decision-making methods.

The Condorcet Jury Theorem suggested by Condorcet has two main claims. First, when the average voter in a group is more likely to be correct than not, the majority vote is more likely to be correct than individual voters acting separately. Second, the more such voters there are, the more correct the outcome of the majority will be.[18] The plausibility of the Condorcet Jury Theorem is easy to understand intuitively. Suppose each voter is more likely to reach a correct answer than is random choice, say at a probability of 0.6. The majority vote of a group of three voters can reach it with the probability of 0.648[19]. The group is wiser than its individual members. The Condorcet Jury Theorem is dependent on the law of large numbers: the larger, the wiser.[20]

The Condorcet Jury Theorem is valid only if at least two conditions are met: competence and independence.[21] First, the competence condition requires that voters are better than random, meaning that they must make correct choices with a probability greater than 50 %. Some scholars are pessimistic regarding the competence of ordinary voters and cite votes on socially important topics, such as the Brexit vote and the election of Donald Trump, as examples of their ignorance. These worries are increased when spatially and/or temporally large problems are at stake. For instance, there is reason to be concerned about ordinary people's knowledge about the causes and effects of climate change and the appropriate policies for mitigation and adaptation.

---

17 See List and Goodin (2001); Landemore (2013). An important exception is Estlund's argument (Estlund 2008). He argues that democracy has epistemic value because it is more likely to recognize right laws and policies than are other decision-making procedures. He calls this position "epistemic proceduralism". Although his epistemic proceduralism appeals to the epistemic value of democracy, Estlund claims only that democracy tends to be better than random decision-making. He admits that it does not necessarily lead to correct results. Estlund rejects "correctness theory", which claims that correct results give its procedure political legitimacy. Therefore, he does not use the Condorcet Jury Theorem to defend the epistemic value of democracy, and he describes several problems the theorem would face. Estlund defends epistemic proceduralism by appealing to "the qualified acceptability requirement". Simply put, this requirement for political legitimacy states that political authority is legitimate if it is acceptable to all qualified (or reasonable) points of view. He rejects epistocracy because it would not be acceptable to all qualified persons. His fundamental tenet is that the qualified acceptability requirement is the primary criterion for political legitimacy. He then claims that, because democracy has epistemic value, it meets the qualified acceptability requirement for political legitimacy.

18 Goodin and Spiekermann (2018), 5

19 The probability that all three voters are correct is $0.6 \times 0.6 \times 0.6 = 0.216$. The probability that exactly two voters are correct and one voter is incorrect is $0.6 \times 0.6 \times 0.4 \times 3 = 0.432$. Therefore, the probability that the majority of the three voters is correct is $0.216 + 0.432 = 0.648$.

20 Landemore (2013), 166

21 Goodin and Spiekermann (2018), chap. 2

However, the ignorance of voters does not necessarily raise such serious problems for the Condorcet Jury Theorem. The competence condition does not require every voter to be better than random at judging social issues; i. e., only the average voter needs to be better than random. Therefore, when the mean voter in a group is more than 50 % likely to vote for the correct answer to political questions, the theorem still holds. Moreover, the competence condition does not require voters to be knowledgeable about the questions. All it requires is that they make better than random decisions. The lack of information among voters is not necessarily detrimental to the epistemic value of democratic decision-making processes.

Second, the independence condition requires that voters are independent of each other. When voters are not independent, such as when they follow the same charismatic leader's opinion or when only one dominant media outlet is allowed to broadcast, there is effectively a single voter in the society, because the voters are sufficiently similar. It follows that collective decisions made by dependent voters are no better than any individual decision.

However, the independence condition does not prohibit voters from referring to the same source of information. The ultimate goal of the Condorcet Jury Theorem is to show that democratic decision-making process has epistemic value: a better understanding about what it is going on in the world. Therefore, voters are allowed to share objective statistical data in order to understand the world correctly. The independence condition only prohibits voters from blindly following an authoritative opinion without examining its background data.

In addition to the Condorcet Jury Theorem, the Diversity Trumps Ability Theorem is often used as another justification for the epistemic value inherent in the democratic decision-making process.[22] The main idea of the theorem is that a group of diverse people is more likely to give the correct answer than a group of wise people who think alike.[23] For example, suppose that a firm is planning to employ people to solve a difficult problem. 1,000 applicants get scores ranging from 60 to 80. Should the firm hire (X) the person who gets the highest score, (Y) 20 people who get the next highest score, or (Z) 20 people randomly selected from all the applicants? The Condorcet Jury Theorem shows that (Y) is better than (X). The Diversity Trumps Ability Theorem suggests that (Z) is better than (Y) under some conditions.[24] The theorem holds true only if (1) the problem is so difficult that no single person can always find the right answer, (2) all the applicants are capable, (3) the selected people are diverse, and (4) the group of applicants and the selected people are large.[25]

22 Anderson (2006); Landemore (2013)
23 Landemore (2013), 105
24 Hong and Page (2004), 16385
25 Page (2007), 159–162

Among the conditions, the most important one is the diversity condition, which requires that the selected people are diverse in terms of perspectives (ways of representing situations and problems), interpretations (ways of categorizing or partitioning perspectives), heuristics (ways of generating solutions to problems), and predictive models (ways of inferring cause and effect).[26] In other words, it requires cognitive diversity among the problem solvers. The main point of the Diversity Trumps Ability Theorem is that when a group of people has cognitive diversity, the collective decision of the group is more likely to get the right answer than the smartest individual.

Both the Condorcet Jury Theorem and the Diversity Trumps Ability Theorem argue for democracy based on epistemic value through different routes. By way of majority vote or diverse perspectives, democratic decision-making process is better than other processes because it is more likely to reach the best solution.

3.2 The Epistemic Argument for Democratic Authority

By combining the two theorems with the superiority condition, we can provide an epistemic argument for democratic authority. Suppose that we have reason to deal properly with social problems. To solve the problems properly, we must find the best solution to them and implement it. The epistemic theorems show that a democratic decision-making process is more likely to produce the best solution than any individual judgment. Combining this insight with the superiority condition, it follows that democratic authority is justified because it improves our conformity with reason. The logical structure of this argument can be analyzed as follows:

EA1. We have a preexisting reason to solve social problems and find the best solution to them. [the preexisting condition]

EA2. Democratic decisions are wiser than our own personal decisions. [the epistemic superiority]

EA3. We are more likely to comply with the reason by accepting democratic decisions than by acting on personal decisions. ∵EA2

EA4. EAuthority is legitimate if it improves our conformity with reason. [the superiority condition]

EA5. Therefore, democratic decisions have legitimate authority.

Therefore, we have good reason to comply with democratic decisions, even if our personal opinions differ on what the best solution is. We should not adhere to our own judgment but rather defer to the collective decisions derived from the democratic decision-making process because those decisions are more likely to be accurate than our

26 Ibid., 7–9

own judgment. When people disagree on which policies to use for addressing social issues like climate change, like whether to prioritize mitigation policies or adaptation policies, they should follow democratic decisions. Even if we think that the collective decisions are wrong, we should follow them because democratic decisions are more likely to track the truth than are our own opinions. The "truth" here can be assessed in terms of efficiency (which policy is more efficient overall), human rights (which policy protects human rights more fully), ecological value (which policy preserves nature more holistically), and so on. We should obey democratic decisions not because it is fair to do so, but because they are correct.

The epistemic argument for democratic authority might be regarded as flawed in at least two ways. Let me discuss these objections in turn. The first objection pertains to coordination problems. As for the first defect, Raz rejects what he calls the "recognitional conception" of practical authority, which regards practical authority as a special kind of theoretical authority.[27] The recognitional conception holds that authoritative directives for the subject to do something are a reason to believe that the subject has a reason to act as told, but not necessarily a reason for action. Raz objects to the recognitional conception because it fails to explain the role of authority in the solution of coordination problems, which are problems for which a solution, whatever it may be, must be determined. A paradigmatic coordination problem is the choice between driving on the right side or driving on the left side of the road. According to Raz, practical authority can coordinate the behaviors of people by declaring which rule should be followed. Authority plays a decisive role in such coordination problems, but not because it is epistemically superior. If it were, it would give the subject a reason to believe, even though there is no objectively preferable rule in such coordination situations. Rather, authority accomplishes its task because its directives are taken as a reason for the subject's actions. It seems to follow that the epistemic argument of practical authority misses the point concerning coordination problems.

However, in ordinary political situations we do not face *pure* coordination problems in which everyone prefers some solution to no solution, with no preference for any particular solution, as in the case of driving on the left or the right. Instead, most coordination problems are "partial conflict coordination problems" in which everyone prefers some solution to no solution, but individuals differ in the solutions they prefer.[28] These kinds of coordination problems are known as "the battle of the sexes" in game theory. For example, although everyone agrees that there should be some restrictions on greenhouse gas emissions, they may disagree about the kinds of legal restrictions that should be enacted. When we face partial conflict coordination problems, we must judge which solution will be better than others. The epistemic argument for democrat-

27 Raz (1986), 28–31
28 Waldron (1999), 103

ic authority claims that the democratic decision-making process plays an important role in determining the solution because it is epistemically superior, and then it can identify which solution is better. Therefore, it is safe to say that the epistemic argument for democratic authority holds true with the typical kinds of coordination problems.

The second objection to the epistemic argument for democratic authority concerns experts. As shown above, democratic authority is justified only when democracy is more likely to give the right answer than individual voters are. It follows that experts who are knowledgeable and scientifically intelligent may not have a duty to obey democratic decisions. Suppose we have a duty to address climate change. According to the epistemic justification for democratic authority, experts on climate change have a duty *not* to obey democratically decided policies on climate change because complying with such decisions is less likely to fulfill their duty than is acting on their own judgment. In other words, democratic decisions may have no authority over experts because of their epistemic inferiority. This seems to be a serious flaw in the epistemic argument for democratic authority.

However, experts usually specialize in a particular area and have knowledge limited to that specific area. No one knows everything. For example, climate scientists are experts in the field of climate, but not on climate policy. Climate policy researchers may be experts in either energy, transportation, forestry, water resources, agriculture, disaster management, or public health, but not all of them. Each expert plays his or her own role in the "division of epistemic labor" to fulfill our duty.[29] In this scenario, when a democratic decision-making process deals with a large package of public policies based on a wide range of scientific knowledge, experts probably have a duty to follow the democratic decision.

3.3 Epistemic Value in Authoritarianism

From the argument above, it seems to follow that democracy is superior to authoritarianism because a democratic decision-making process allows a larger number of more diverse voters to participate in the process than an authoritarian one. This seems to imply that democracy is more likely to be legitimate than authoritarianism because it is more likely to satisfy the superiority condition for legitimate authority.

However, the epistemic argument for democratic authority does not necessarily demonstrate that democracy is better than authoritarianism in terms of epistemic value. As seen above, democracy is distinguished from authoritarianism by the presence of free and fair elections.[30] Political leaders are selected through free and fair elections

29 Goodin and Spiekermann (2018), chap. 8

30 An election is free when most adults can vote. An election is fair when multiple parties can participate and compete on a relatively even playing field (Franz 2018, 12). The conditions for free and fair elections may involve many other factors (V-Demo Codebook 2003).

in democracy but not in authoritarianism. If the epistemic argument for democratic authority is valid, then democracy is better than authoritarianism in terms of selecting political leaders. However, two questions must be considered.

The first question concerns the quality of political leaders. Are governors in democracies better than those in authoritarian regimes? Are democratic representatives wiser than authoritarian leaders? Extensive empirical research is needed to answer these questions definitively. Here I will simply assume that there is no patently obvious superiority of political leaders in democracy over those in authoritarianism in terms of epistemic capacities.

The second issue concerns the subject of majority rule in a democracy, specifically what is decided by the majority of ordinary voters. As discussed above, democracy, in contrast to authoritarianism, is characterized by free and fair elections. Therefore, in a democracy, political leaders are supposed to be chosen through these elections. In other words, contemporary democracy is assumed, either explicitly or implicitly, to be an indirect or representative democracy. Laws and policies are created by elected representatives rather than by the general public. This means that in modern democracy, ordinary citizens do not have a direct right to vote on every law and policy. Rather, modern democracy includes an aristocratic element, with a much smaller and less diverse group of representatives than the general population.

On the other hand, there are several forms of authoritarian regimes.[31] I will discuss three of them: personalist, military, and dominant-party authoritarianism[32]. In personalist authoritarianism, a single individual holds the ultimate decision-making power over most major laws and policies. He is often supported by political elites, but he can exercise discretionary prerogatives independently of his followers. According to the epistemic arguments, the dictator has no legitimate authority because he does not satisfy the superiority condition. When the dictator makes policy decisions, he often issues directives that are detrimental to the welfare of his subjects and then fails to improve their conformity with their preexisting reason. Democracy is much better than dictatorship, especially in ordinary situations.

In military authoritarianism, most political leaders are middle-aged or older male military officers. Although military authoritarianism includes a larger and more diverse group of rulers than personalist authoritarianism, the military elite is both limited in number and diversity. According to the Condorcet Jury Theorem and the Diversity Trumps Ability Theorem, when the group of decision makers is small and monotonous, their decisions tend not to be correct. This may explain why military authoritarianism is on the decline while electoral authoritarianism is on the rise mark-

31 Franz (2018), chap. 5

32 Other than these three forms, Franz suggests monarchic dictatorship by ruling family in the typology of authoritarian regimes, but this form is not distinct from personalist or military authoritarianism in terms of epistemic value.

edly. Therefore, military authoritarianism lacks legitimate authority because it does not improve the subject's compliance with its reason.

However, it is possible that dominant-party authoritarianism has better epistemic capacities. Although the dominant party, by definition, is never exposed to free and fair elections, it does have some level of internal diversity. In fact, the structure of dominant-party authoritarianism is very similar to the structure of democracy.[33] As for the diversity condition, a congress in dominant-party authoritarianism is composed of less diverse members than that in democracies, but a dominant party often has internal factions. As for the capacity condition, political elites in dominant-party authoritarianism are not worse than representative in democracies in terms of political epistemic capacity due to a competitive promotion system. Dominant-party authoritarianism may therefore be on a par with democracy in terms of epistemic value. As long as democracy has legitimate authority due to its epistemic capacities, so does dominant-party authoritarianism.

4 The Proceduralist Argument for Legitimate Authority

4.1 The Proceduralist Argument for Democratic Authority

Now I turn to another approach to legitimate authority. According to the superiority condition of authority, authority is justified if the alleged subject is more likely to fulfill his duty by accepting the directives of the alleged authority than by trying to follow his own directives. According to the preexisting condition of authority, such a duty must exist before authority can operate. From these two conditions, it follows that democratic authority is justified if we have a preexisting duty that can be fulfilled in the very process of democratic decision-making. A promising candidate for such a duty is the duty to treat people as equals. In nondemocratic decision-making processes, some people have a greater influence on outcomes than others. In some forms of authoritarian regimes, the dictator alone has wide discretion over major policies, or only military elites have political power, but ordinary people have no way of influencing policy outcomes. Democracy ensures political equality in the sense that everyone is granted an equal say in the decision-making process. The supposedly fundamental principle of democracy is one person, one vote: that is, no one has more votes than anyone else. Because we have a preexisting duty to treat people as equals and because we are more likely to fulfill our duty by accepting democratic decisions than by acting on personal decisions, democratic decisions have legitimate authority. A logical structure of the argument is analyzed as the following:

33 Ibid., 75

PA1. We have a preexisting reason to treat people as equals. [the preexisting condition]
PA2. We are more likely to conform to the preexisting reason by following democratic decision-making procedures than by our own personal activities.
PA3. Authority is legitimate if it improves our conformity with reason. [the superiority condition]
PA4. Therefore, democratic decisions have legitimate authority.

This argument can be called the proceduralist argument for democratic authority. It focuses on the process itself, not on the products produced by the process. The proceduralist argument for democratic authority claims that democratic authority is justified not because the democratic decision-making process is a better instrument for finding the right answers, but rather because the process itself has intrinsic value. It embodies an important value in the very process that is based on the democratic principle of one person, one vote.

The proceduralist argument for democratic authority takes several forms. Intrinsic values embodied in the democratic process include equality among citizens and collective autonomy or self-determination of the people. In democratic decision-making processes, all members are granted equal opportunities to participate in collective decision-making. Thereby, they enjoy an equal opportunity to influence collective decision-making.[34] Also, through the granting of these equal opportunities, all are publicly recognized as equal members.[35] This is not the place to go into these details, but the bottom line is that we are more likely to fulfill our duty to treat people, including ourselves, as free, equal, and rational agents in democratic decision-making processes.

The proceduralist argument is a more attractive way to defend democracy than the epistemic argument. First, the proceduralist argument never fails to defend democracy as long as the intrinsic value of the democratic process is sound. The intrinsic value is embodied in democratic procedures whenever the procedures are implemented, because it is inherent in democratic decision-making processes themselves. This becomes clear when contrasted with instrumental value. If a process produces good results, it has instrumental value, but if it fails, it loses instrumental value. The attainment of intrinsic value is necessary, though the attainment of instrumental value is accidental. This point becomes clear when we compare the logical structure of the epistemic argument (EA1-EA5) with that of the proceduralist argument (PA1-PA4). The latter lacks a presupposition equivalent to EA2. PA does not depend on such an empirical presupposition and is therefore immune to empirical refutation.

34 Viehoff (2014); Kolodny (2023)
35 Christiano (2008)

Second, the proceduralist argument always defends democracy over authoritarianism because democracy, by definition, holds free and fair elections that embody the political equality of all members. The proceduralist argument, if successful, shows that authoritarianism does not acquire legitimate authority through its procedural value. On the other hand, the epistemic argument may end up defending authoritarianism rather than democracy when authoritarian leaders are wiser than democratic politicians. In fact, the epistemic argument is often used to refute democracy and then to argue for epistocracy, in which more knowledgeable people have more votes than ordinary people. For example, John Stuart Mill proposes a plural voting system, in which people have had a certain career in office or who have graduated from a prestigious university have multiple votes.[36]

Let us suppose that PA1 is true: we have a preexisting reason to treat people as equals. It is morally wrong to treat some other people as second-class citizens. It is morally wrong not to give some other people unequal opportunities to influence political outcomes. It seems to follow that the proceduralist argument succeeds in showing that democratic decisions have legitimate authority and that democracy is better than authoritarianism in terms of legitimacy.

4.2 The Outsider Problem

But the proceduralist argument for democratic authority has several flaws. Its most serious flaw becomes apparent when we consider "outsiders". Every democratic process has its insiders and outsiders. Democratic insiders are the "demos", or those who are allowed to participate in democratic decision-making processes. Democratic outsiders are those who do not have the right to participate in, and are therefore excluded from, the decision-making process. Obvious examples of democratic outsiders include minors, foreigners (both resident and non-resident), and prisoners. Democratic outsiders are not treated as equals because they are not given the same right to vote as ordinary citizens. Democratic outsiders are second-class citizens, if not slaves. The proceduralist argument shows that democracy lacks legitimate authority at least over democratic outsiders. I will call it "the outsider problem".

The outsider problem implies a serious conclusion. Because the democratic decision-making process lacks legitimate authority over outsiders, outsiders have no duty to obey democratic decisions. Minors, foreigners, and prisoners have no duty to follow the laws and policies that are established through democratic decision-making procedures. If the government attempts to force them to obey its policies, it does so through brute coercion. Although democratic outsiders may have prudent reasons to obey

36 Mill (1998), 336

democratic directives, such as avoiding sanctions, they have no moral obligation to do so. To be sure, it sounds odd to say that prisoners do not have a moral duty to obey the law just because they have violated it by committing heinous crimes and thereby lost their right to vote in elections. By *reductio ad absurdum*, the proceduralist argument for democratic authority is false.

The outsider problem arises not only in democracy, but also in authoritarianism. Every authoritarianism also has its own insiders and outsiders. Authoritarian outsiders are those who are excluded from the authoritarian decision-making process. According to the definition of authoritarianism, ordinary citizens do not enjoy free and fair elections and are therefore excluded from substantial decision-making processes. Authoritarian outsiders are placed in the same position as democratic outsiders. This suggests that democracy appears as "authoritarianism" to democratic outsiders in the sense that they are not allowed to participate in free and fair elections. Both democratic and authoritarian outsiders are procedural outsiders. They are treated unequally against their reason. From the proceduralist argument for legitimate authority, it seems to follow that both democracy and authoritarianism lack legitimate authority over their procedural outsiders.

4.3 The Inclusive Approach

The proceduralist argument for democratic authority can take the inclusive approach to address the outsider problem. The inclusive approach requires that democracy include those excluded from decision-making processes and then reduce the number of procedural outsiders as much as possible, ideally to zero. Indeed, some advocates call for granting voting rights to prisoners, resident aliens, and teenagers. When a democratic political society fully implements the inclusive approach and grants them full political rights, it can acquire legitimate authority over all its members, according to the proceduralist argument.

The inclusive approach does not show that democracy is better than authoritarianism in terms of legitimate authority. Rather, it shows that all democratic regimes today have some authority deficits because they grant full participation rights only to some selected people. As long as they include prisoners, aliens, and minors who do not have the right to vote, they are to some extent similar to authoritarian regimes.

More importantly, even when the inclusive approach is fully implemented, the outsider problem remains. To illuminate the remaining problem, it would be helpful to distinguish two types of procedural outsiders: domestic and global. Domestic outsiders are those who live within a state's jurisdiction but lack its participatory rights. They include prisoners, foreign residents, and minors. Global outsiders are foreigners living under the jurisdiction of other states. Democracy can take the inclusive approach to domestic outsiders to solve the outsider problem. But it would be almost unimaginable to take the inclusive approach to global outsiders. Would it be possible for all people on earth to have the right to vote not in their own state, but in all jurisdictions? It implies that democracy lacks legitimate authority if it does not extend the franchise to global outsiders.

This global outsider problem is clear in the case of climate change. Public policies in an industrialized country to control the emissions of greenhouse gases will have far-reaching effects on various types of people, including global outsiders as well as future generations. Because these outsiders will be affected by such policies, they may wish to have an equal say in the decision-making process. But today they are not allowed to participate in the process. Do such policies have political authority over global outsiders if they are democratically decided? No, according to the proceduralist argument for democratic authority, because global outsiders are not treated as equals in the decision-making process. It is inevitably true that global outsiders are subject to such policies; that is, they must accept the bad and good effects of their implementation. The point is that such policies lack legitimate authority over global outsiders even when democratic regimes take the inclusive approach to domestic outsiders.

The paradoxes of authority remain unresolved. Global outsiders are unavoidably subject to those policies they have no opportunity to influence. This fact undermines the moral ideal of equality among free rational agents. Given our commitment to building human relationships based on the moral ideal, we cannot maintain the proceduralist argument for democratic authority.

Some might object that there is no authority relationship between a state and its global outsiders. A state's policies affect not only those people who live within its territory but also those who do not, i. e., global outsiders. However, they have authority only over domestic insiders, but not over global outsiders. Global outsiders have no obligation to obey the authoritative directives of the state. If the state introduces a new policy of lifting the strict regulations on greenhouse gas emissions, it will affect global outsiders badly, but it does not impose any obligation on them. This means that the paradoxes of authority never arise between the state and its global outsiders because there is no authority relationship between them.

However, it is not conceptually necessary that the exercise of legitimate authority generates an obligation to obey.[37] An example from international institutions would be illustrative. The United Nations Security Council exercises authority when giving member states the liberty to use non-armed and armed measures.[38] It does not obligate member states to take such measures; rather, it only permits them to do so. Moreover, it does not impose any obligation on the international enemy. It only generates the liability of being a target of international action. That is, the international enemy loses

37 Applbaum (2010), 222
38 Christiano (2012)

the claims against the member states not to take such measures. Legitimate authority has power to change legal relations from duty to liberty, from immunity to liability, and the like.

Another example from domestic relations would be helpful to see the point. If a government exercises legitimate authority and permits a factory to discharge polluted water into a river, the residents living along the river will be adversely affected by the government's authoritative decision. But the residents have no obligation to obey it. In modern administrative states, ordinary people are indirectly affected by authoritative directives. The government exercises authority in regulating corporations and then the corporations affect the general public. The relationship between the government and the public is indirect, but the paradoxes of authority remain. Authority may seem to conflict with the reason, autonomy, and equality of ordinary people. Therefore, authority needs justification, which is the starting point of this paper. The same is true for global outsiders; they are indirectly subject to the authority of all the states from which they are politically excluded.

4.4 The Global Approach

Some might object that democratic government has no legitimate authority over foreigners. According to Raz, foreigners may feel that they have reason to obey the laws of their host country for prudential reasons, but they have no general obligation to obey the law, or in other words, democratic government has no authority over foreigners.[39] As is clear here, Raz makes a distinction between the reason to obey the law and the authority of the government. Even if some people do not recognize the authority of the government, they may have various reasons to obey the law; they may want to avoid legal sanction, try to preserve their reputation, or intend not to damage social stability. It follows that both democratic and non-democratic government lack legitimate authority over foreigners.

Another objection could be added. Suppose that the democratic decision-making process has authority even over those who do not have the right to vote. This would mean that everyone has a moral obligation to obey *all* directives issued through the democratic decision-making process, However, this leads to an absurd conclusion that people have a moral obligation to obey orders from a gang of burglars who make decisions by majority rule. Therefore, we must reject the assumption that the democratic decision-making process creates authority over outsiders.

Against these objections, I argue that a government has *pro tanto* authority over outsiders under certain conditions. My argument consists of three steps. First, I assume

---

39 Raz (1986), 101

that we have a universal duty to establish a global rightful state, following Kant.[40] This duty is often referred to as a natural duty of justice in the modern literature.[41] The basic idea is that our fundamental moral duty is to exit from the state of nature, where no one enjoys their right to freedom, and to enter a global rightful state, where everyone enjoys their equal right to freedom.

Second, to fulfill this duty, it is an effective way to divide the globe into territories and assign a group of people, called "citizens", to each territory. This idea is developed and coined by Robert Goodin as "the assigned responsibility model".[42] To illustrate the model, let us use the example of caring for hospital patients. Suppose that a hospital has 5 doctors and 100 patients. What is the best way to care for these patients? It is not efficient for all five doctors to spend one-hundredth of their time on each patient. This inefficiency results from the fact that we care less when we share. A better way is for each doctor to care for his or her assigned patients (e.g., 20 patients each). The doctors can fulfill their responsibility to care for all patients by focusing on their own patients. Similarly, we can fulfill our duty to establish a global rightful state (basically) by focusing on our own assigned territory.[43] The government in each territory is responsible for issuing directives to construct a global rightful state in its own territory. A global order consisting of multiple states is an effective way to fulfill our duty to build a global rightful state. The overall picture is one of a global division of labor in fulfilling our fundamental duty.

It is important to note that the epistemic argument for democratic authority can solve the outsider problem. The democratic decision-making process can have authority over those who cannot vote because it still has epistemic value to produce better outcomes. According to the epistemic argument, the larger and more diverse the group of voters, the more accurate the outcome. The demos would be wiser if they included the outsiders in their democratic decision-making process, but the democratic government is still wiser than any individual, including the outsiders. Therefore, even outsiders have a reason to follow the decisions of the democratic process in which they have no franchise. Thus, democracy can have legitimate authority over global outsiders. We have reason to accept the judgments of other democratic governments because, by virtue of their democratic character, they tend to be more correct than our own judgments.

We have another reason to accept the policies of other democratic governments if we are treated equally as free, rational agents by the global order. The global decision-making process can embody important values if it treats all earthlings as equal, free, rational agents and assigns each government a fair share of responsibility for es-

40 Kant (1797)
41 Rawls (1999), 293
42 Goodin (1988)
43 I have argued a more refined version of the assigned model elsewhere (Takikawa 2020).

tablishing a rightful state within its own territory. If these conditions are met, a foreign government can have legitimate authority over us according to the proceduralist argument for legitimate authority even though we have no right to vote in its jurisdiction. It is similar to the fact that other local governments have legitimate authority over us even though we do not have the right to vote in their elections. A fair global division of labor achieves intrinsic values through the global process.

The global approach is entirely consistent with the preexisting condition for authority, which holds that authority is justified if it is based on a preexisting duty for the alleged subject. Democratic government has authority over all of us, including global outsiders, because we have a preexisting duty to construct a global rightful state. We have a moral duty to comply with the directives of democratic government, even if we have no right to participate in its decision-making process. This is because it is an indirect but better way to achieve the goal.

This is a deduction from the idea of a global rightful state to the *pro tanto* legitimate authority of each government. Let me describe the same theme from the opposite direction: induction. Most people believe that laws and policies that are established through a democratic decision-making process are binding, even on global outsiders. This is not because they are backed by legal sanctions, but because they have legitimate authority. This intuition cannot be explained and justified without the basic assumption that we have a universal duty to construct a global rightful state, and that each government plays its own role in the global division of labor.

The global approach shows that our democratic government has legitimate authority over domestic and global outsiders when its laws and policies do not contradict the ideal of a global rightful state. It also implies that foreign governments have legitimate authority over us despite our lack of voting rights. It is important to note that this implication applies not only to democratic governments, but also to authoritarian governments. We, as foreigners, do not have the right to vote in other democratic and authoritarian states, but foreign governments can have legitimate authority over us if they can be seen as actors in the project of establishing a global rightful state. Democracy may be better than authoritarianism at achieving a global rightful state due to the intrinsic and instrumental values of democratic decision-making procedures. But whether democratic or authoritarian, the conditions for legitimate authority are the same.

Conclusion

Authority must be legitimate because it seems to be incompatible with rationality, freedom, and equality. To resolve the paradox of authority, authority must satisfy at least two conditions: the superiority condition and the preexisting condition. Two arguments have been proposed to defend democratic authority: instrumentalism and proceduralism. The epistemic argument claims that democracy can have legitimate authority due to its epistemic value; however, some forms of authoritarianism can also have legitimate authority. The proceduralist argument, by contrast, maintains that only democracy has legitimate authority. However, democracy faces the outsider problem, as does authoritarianism. I have examined two approaches to the outsider problem: the inclusion approach and the global approach. I defend the global approach, which asserts that democracy has legitimate authority as a means of establishing a global rightful state. Similarly, some forms of authoritarianism can have legitimate authority only insofar as they protect everyone's equal right to freedom.

Bibliography

Applbaum, Arthur Isak (2010). Legitimacy without the Duty to Obey. *Philosophy & Public Affairs*, 38(3), 215–239.

Anderson, Elizabeth (2006). The Epistemology of Democracy. *Episteme*, 3(1–2), 8–22.

Bermeo, Nancy (2016). On Democratic Backsliding. *Journal of Democracy*, 27(1), 5–19.

Christiano, Thomas (2008). *The Constitution of Equality: Democratic Authority and Its Limits*. Oxford: Oxford University Press.

Christiano, Tom (2012). Authority. *The Stanford Encyclopedia of Philosophy*. https://plato.stanford.edu/archives/sum2020/entries/authority/, accessed 30 August 2025.

Christiano, Tom, and Sameer Bajaj (2022). Democracy. *The Stanford Encyclopedia of Philosophy*. https://plato.stanford.edu/archives/spr2022/entries/democracy/, accessed 30 August 2025.

Coppedge, Michael, John Gerring, Carl Henrik Knutsen, Staffan I. Lindberg, Jan Teorell, David Altman, Michael Bernhard, Agnes Cornell, M. Steven Fish, Lisa Gastaldi, Haakon Gjerløw, Adam Glynn, Sandra Grahn, Allen Hicken, Katrin Kinzelbach, Kyle L. Marquardt, Kelly McMann, Valeriya Mechkova, Anja Neundorf, Pamela Paxton, Daniel Pemstein, Oskar Rydén, Johannesvon Römer, Brigitte Seim, Rachel Sigman, Svend Erik Skaaning, Jeffrey Staton, Aksel Sundström, Eitan Tzelgov, Luca Uberti, Yiting Wang, Tore Wig, and Daniel Ziblatt (2023). "V-Dem Codebook v13" Varieties of Democracy (V-Dem) Project.

Diamond, Larry (2015). Facing Up to the Democratic Recession. *Journal of Democracy* 26(1): 141–155.

Enoch, David (2014). Authority and Reason-Giving. *Philosophy and Phenomenological Research*, 89(2), 296–332.

Estlund, David M. (2008). *Democratic Authority: A Philosophical Framework*. Princeton; Oxford: Princeton University Press.

Franz, Erica (2018). *Authoritarianism: What Everyone Needs to Know*. New York: Oxford University Press.

Fukuyama, Francis (1992). *The End of History and the Last Man*. New York: Free Press.

Goodin, Robert E. (1988). What is So Special about Our Fellow Countrymen? *Ethics*, 98(4), 663–686.

Goodin, Robert E., and Kai Spiekermann (2018). *An Epistemic Theory of Democracy*. Oxford: Oxford University Press.

Hong, Lu, and Page, Scott. E. (2004). Groups of Diverse Problem Solvers Can Outperform Groups of High-Ability Problem Solvers. *Proceedings of the National Academy of Sciences*, 101(46), 16385–16389.

Kant, Immanuel (1797). *Die Metaphysik der Sitten*. Ak. VI, 203–493.
Kolodny, Niko (2023). The Pecking Order: Social Hierarchy as a Philosophical Problem. Cambridge, MA: Harvard University Press.
Landemore, Hélène (2013). *Democratic Reason: Politics, Collective Intelligence, and the Rule of the Many*. Princeton; Oxford: Princeton University Press.
List, Christian, and Robert E. Goodin (2001). Epistemic Democracy: Generalizing the Condorcet Jury Theorem. *Journal of Political Philosophy*, 9(3), 277–306.
Mill, John Stuart (1998 [1861]). Considerations on Representative Government. In: John Gray (Ed.): *On Liberty and Other Essay*. Oxford: Oxford University Press.
Moellendorf, Darrel (2014). *The Moral Challenge of Dangerous Climate Change: Values, Poverty, and Policy*. New York: Cambridge University Press.
Page, Scott E. (2007). *The Difference: How the Power of Diversity Creates Better Groups, Firms, Schools, and Societies*. Princeton, NJ: Princeton University Press.
Rawls, John (1999). *A Theory of Justice*, Revised Edition. Cambridge, MA: Belknap Press of Harvard University Press.
Raz, Joseph (1986). *The Morality of Freedom*. Oxford: Clarendon Press.
Raz, Joseph (2009 [1979]). *The Authority of Law: Essays on Law and Morality* (2nd ed.). Oxford: Oxford University Press.
Simmons, A. John (2016). *Boundaries of Authority*. New York: Oxford University Press.
Takikawa, Hirohide (2020). Drawing National Boundaries for Global Governance. In: Hirohide Takikawa (Ed.): *The Rule of Law and Democracy*. Stuttgart: Franz Steiner Verlag.
Viehoff, Daniel (2014). Democratic Equality and Political Authority. *Philosophy & Public Affairs*, 42(4): 337–375.
Waldron, Jeremy (1999). *Law and Disagreement*. Oxford: Clarendon Press.

Hirohide Takikawa
Graduate Schools for Law and Politics, The University of Tokyo
tkkw@j.u-tokyo.ac.jp

This research was funded by Grants-in-Aid for Scientific Research (C) 21K01108 and 24K04490 from Japan Society for the Promotion of Science (JSPS).

Part 2
Historical Thoughts and Contemporary Realities

Francisco de Vitoria and the Rule of Law*

CARLOS ISLER SOTO

Abstract: Lon Fuller held that there was an internal morality of law, which he called the "Rule of Law", consisting of a set of requirements that every legal system has to comply with in order to be effective, for instance, that laws ought to be prospective, general, stable, among others.

I argue in this paper that Francisco de Vitoria had already defended at least four of the eight requirements identified by Lon Fuller as elements of the Rule of Law, and that he defended them as implications of a more profound idea of the Rule of Law, namely, that the political community and not parliament, king or prince is the true legislator. However, there is in his theory no defense of an institutional aspect of the Rule of Law, such as the separation of powers or checks and balances among them.

Keywords: Francisco de Vitoria – Rule of Law – Lon Fuller – Thomas Aquinas – Internal Morality of Law – Promulgation of Laws

1 Introduction

The English phrase "Rule of Law" has many senses, and its exact meaning depends always on the context. In its most basic form, it conveys the idea that standing rules, and not men, should govern, and in this form is found in the work of many political philosophers since at least Plato[1] and Aristotle[2]. In constitutional contexts, it normally conveys the idea of checks and balances defended by Montesquieu and *The Federalist Papers*.

More recently, in legal philosophy the phrase has been associated with the name of Lon Fuller. In his book *The Morality of Law* (1964), he defended the idea that the whole rationale of law consists in subjecting human action to the rule of impersonal rules, and that this implies that every legal system has to comply with a set of require-

---

* This conference presentation was supported by the Vicerrectoría de Investigación y Doctorados of the Universidad San Sebastián, Chile – Fondo USS-FIN-23-CNGI-14.

1 Consider, especially, the passage of the VIIth Letter (a letter whose Platonic authorship, is, however, debated) of 334c, where Plato advises his readers never to submit the city to a man, but only to the laws.

2 See, this famous passage of the *Politics*, where Aristotle states that the government of laws differs from that of men in that the rule of laws is like the rule of intelligence, calling it also a rule by God, while the rule of men adds an animal element, namely the passions: 1287a28–32: 'ὁ μὲν οὖν τὸν νόμον κελεύων ἄρχειν δοκεῖ κελεύειν ἄρχειν τὸν θεὸν καὶ τὸν νοῦν μόνους, ὁ δ' ἄνθρωπον κελεύων προστίθησι καὶ θηρίον· ἥ τε γὰρ ἐπιθυμία τοιοῦτον, καὶ ὁ θυμὸς ἄρχοντας διαστρέφει καὶ τοὺς ἀρίστους ἄνδρας. διόπερ ἄνευ ὀρέξεως νοῦς ὁ νόμος ἐστίν'.

ments to attain that end. This set of requirements, which can never be completely fulfilled, are: a) that laws ought to be general, b) promulgated, c) prospective, not retroactive, d) clear, e) not contradictory among themselves, f) not impossible to fulfill, f) stable through time, g) and there ought to be congruence between the law and its enforcement by public officials.

He called this whole set of requirements the "internal morality of law", which had to be distinguished from the external morality of law, namely, the ends that law purports to attain. Even if this internal morality is purely procedural, Fuller was convinced that it sets limits to which external ends can be attained by law.

In the Postscript to the second edition of the book, he called this whole set of requirements "the Rule of Law"[3], and since that time in legal philosophy, what is called the "Rule of Law" is normally the set of requirements that constitute the internal morality of law according to Fuller. We have, then, a meaning in English where the phrase does not necessarily convey the idea of checks and balances or separation of powers, which the related phrases *Rechtsstaat, État de droit, Stato di Diritto* or *Estado de derecho* convey in German, French, Italian or Spanish, respectively[4]. Of course, we also find in the English-speaking world philosophers who use a thicker conception of the Rule of Law than that of Fuller, namely, one that approaches the one used in constitutional contexts in that English-speaking world and the concept expressed by the corresponding phrases *Rechtsstaat, État de Droit, Estado de Derecho* or *Stato di Diritto* in other languages: for instance, John Finnis, after reviewing Fuller's account of the Rule of Law, says that "the Rule of Law involves certain qualities of process which can be systematically secured only by the institution of judicial authority and its exercise by persons professionally equipped and motivated to act according to law. Obviously, much more could be said about this institutional aspect of the Rule of Law – of what historical experience has shown to be further desiderata, such as the independence of the judiciary, the openness of court proceedings, the power of the courts to review the proceedings and actions not only of other courts but of most other classes of official, and the accessibility of the courts to all, including the poor."[5]

Now, returning to the "thinner" Fullerian sense of "Rule of Law", in the same postscript to the second edition of *The Morality of Law,* Fuller recognizes that most of the requirements identified by him had already been identified by Aquinas[6].

---

3 See Fuller (1969), 209–210.

4 So, for instance, we may see that Roberto Bin, in his work on the *Stato di diritto,* says that this Italian expression comes from the German phrase *Rechtsstaat,* and does not mention the English equivalent "Rule of Law": "L'espressione Stato di diritto nasce in Germania all'inizio del XIX secolo: è infatti la traduzione letterale del termine tedesco *Rechtsstaat*": Bin (2010), pos. 275.

5 Finnis (1980), 271.

6 This fact had been pointed out by Ovid C. Lewis (see Lewis 1968, 565), and Fuller endorses this claim in the postscript, though it qualifies it by saying that "It may be stretching things a bit to say that Aquinas recognized the principle of congruity between official action and declared rule": Fuller (1969), 242, n. 52.

Aquinas indeed recognized most of the elements of this Rule of Law, although his treatment of the subject is brief and can be found dispersed among his reflections on law. Let us recall that this "Rule of Law" does not imply the notion of division of powers, a notion that Aquinas did not explicitly defend even though it may be said to be adumbrated in his defense, following Aristotle, of the mixed form of political regime as the best one.

We find a more explicit treatment of the subject in one of his followers, the Spanish Dominican Francisco de Vitoria (1483–1546), who is otherwise famous as one of the founders of the idea of International Law[7] and for his defense of the idea of the existence of natural rights[8]. Quentin Skinner has also found in Vitoria's thought, and in that of other Spanish Scholastics as well, antecedents of modern constitutionalist ideas, like that of the consent of the people as the source of the legitimacy of government[9], and even that of social contract[10].

However, little attention has been paid to the fact that, as was mentioned before, there are already traces in Vitoria of the Fullerian account of the Rule of Law.

Now, it is important to explain what we will find in Vitoria's treatment of the Rule of Law and what not: we do not find in his work a theory of the Rule of Law, namely, a full-fledged exposition of it as a subject worth studying in itself, with all the implications of its requirements. We find, instead, in his work, doctrines that correspond to some of the requirements of the Fullerian Rule of Law, but dispersed among discussions about other topics, especially, about the nature of human law.

Secondly, we do not find in him any trace of the institutional side of Rule of Law as explained by Finnis and as expressed by the phrase "Rule of Law" in constitutional contexts.

Thirdly, as will be seen, we find in him very well expressed the idea conveyed by the Platonic and Aristotelian doctrines of Rule of Law, namely, that laws and not men ought to rule. Indeed, the requirements of the Fullerian Rule of Law that he defends are defended as implications of this deeper idea.

---

7 Other candidates to that title are, as it is widely known, Hugo Grotius and Alberico Gentili. On Vitoria as the possible founder of international law, see especially Hernández (1995).
8 On the issue of human rights in Vitoria, see Araujo (2012) and Isler (2022).
9 See, Skinner (1978).
10 See Skinner (1978), 155–161.

2 Requirements of the Rule of Law defended by Vitoria

So, regarding human law, Vitoria says that, before it is promulgated, it has no force whatsoever[11]. And the reason is quite congenial to the idea of Rule of Law, namely, that the legislator is a public person, and to legislate is to speak, and, therefore, a public person has to speak in a public manner[12], and this public way of uttering the law is the promulgation. This obligation to speak in a public manner applies to every official, so that even judges have to promulgate, i. d., utter in a public way, their judgments, before they can have any legal effect[13].

Furthermore, this promulgation has to be a "solemn promulgation", namely, it has to be such, that everyone may have the possibility of knowing the content of the new law[14].

Vitoria also mentions in his commentary on Aquinas's *Treatise of Law*, although briefly, the requirement that laws ought to be general[15], referring, without further commenting it, to the text of Aquinas he is expounding[16]. In another work, his *relectio* on the power of the Pope and of the Council, he says that "the legislator makes laws in general terms and about future things"[17].

Similarly, laws ought to be stable. He thinks that the legislator ought to change a statute only in the case mentioned by Aquinas. Therefore, he says, expounding Aquinas's doctrine, that "in order for the law to be changed, it does not suffice that something better occurs, since custom fosters much compliance with the law"[18], and that "human laws ought not to be so fixed as divine laws are. If a statute contains a manifest iniquity, it has to be changed"[19]. But, what happens if the legislator changes the law when the change is not justified? For example, if he wrongly abrogates a good law that

11 "De lege humana positiva sit PRIMA PROPOSITIO: *Quod non obligat sine promulgatione, nec habet vim aut effectum*": De Lege Commentarium in Primam Secundae QQ. 90–108 (henceforth, *De Legibus*), quaestio 90, articulus quartus, lectio 122, p. 102 (page 102 of the edition of Barrientos García and Langella).

12 "legislator est persona publica; ergo non habet vim condendi legem nisi promulget et in publico": ibid.

13 "Item quia iudex postquam fecit sententiam potest revocare illam, si nondum promulgaverat. Ergo signum est quod antea non tenebat. Et simile de lege": ibid.

14 "SECUNDA PROPOSITIO: *Ad hoc quod lex humana obliget, non sufficit promulgatio privata apud aliquos, nec etiam ipsos scientes; oportet quod sit solemnis promulgatio*": ibid.

15 "Respondet [Aquinas] quia lex respicit in bonum commune, debent dari in communi et durare in republica": *De Legibus*, q. 96, a. 1, lectio 124., page 134.

16 When Vitoria simply refers to a text by Aquinas which he is commenting, that means that he endorses the doctrine there expounded and that he considers that doctrine and the justification given by Aquinas to be so clear, that no further comment is needed.

17 "legislator fert leges in universali et de futuris": *de Potestate Papae et Concilii relectio*, 468.

18 "*ad hoc quod lex mutetur non sufficit quod occurrat aliquod melius, quia multum iuvat consuetudo ad servandum legem*": *De Legibus*, q. 97, a. 2, lectio 127, page 158.

19 "*leges humanae non possunt esse ita fixae sicut leges divinae. Si lex contineat manifestam iniquitatem, debet mutari*": ibid.

was widely respected. If this situation arises, then the positive law is indeed abrogated, even if the legislator may sin abrogating it without just cause[20].

And here we point to a key aspect of Vitoria's (and Aquinas's) doctrine of the Rule of Law: some of its requirements are of a moral nature, and it may be the case that transgression to them be impossible to punish at the institutional level[21].

Consider, then, his answer to the question, key for a doctrine of the Rule of Law, of whether the legislator is bound by his own laws. His answer follows Aquinas's: he is bound by his own laws regarding their *vis directiva*, not regarding their *vis coactiva*[22]. What does that mean?

To say that the legislator is bound by the directive force of his own laws, means that he has a moral duty to comply with them. But, if he does not follow the directive force of his laws, namely, if he unjustifiably does not apply them in a given case, then he cannot be coerced (the coactive force) to it by another. He has a non-enforceable moral obligation to follow his own laws. Of course, he may always amend them, since he is the legislator, but, if not amended, he ought to apply them in all cases except those of extreme necessity.

That may sound a little bit disappointing and even farcical to the modern reader. Does this not sound like the doctrine of the divine rights of kings, accountable only to God? But before discarding it so easily, let us understand the rationale behind this idea, which is not so alien to our modern ideas. Most, if not all, contemporary legal systems have an institution, normally a court, that tests whether the legislator's statutes are congruent with the Constitution and exercises the corresponding power of judicial review of legislation. In contemporary legal systems, therefore, it seems that there is no legislator bound only by moral rules, but that there are also institutional checks for its activity. But if one asks oneself, what happens if the constitutional or supreme court does not follow the Constitution it pretends to apply, and simply disregards it when applying it in an exercise of judicial activism[23], then one has sincerely to answer that

20 "*amplius non est* [a law] *nec habet vim legis, si scilicet legislator abrogavit, quantumque sine causa*": ibid, p. 160. Similarly, "respublica cum rege posset abrogare quamcumque legem": ibid.

21 This is not necessarily incompatible with Fuller's conception of the Rule of Law: remember that he calls it also the "internal *morality* of law".

22 "Respondet Doctor [Aquinas] quod legislator non obligatur vi coactiva, nec posset puniri a superiori propter transgressionem. Ratio est quia nullus potest proprie cogi a seipso. Sed tamen quantum ad vim directivam obligantur omnes, etiam legislatores, hoc est quod peccant transgrediendo leges": *De Legibus* q. 96, a. 5, lectio 126, p. 152. Similarly, he says that in monarchical regimes, kings are as bound by their laws as aristocrats or the people in aristocratic or popular regimes: "in aristocratico principatu senatus consulta obligant ipsos senatores, auctores senatorum consulti; et in populari regimine plebiscita obligant ipsum populum. Ergo similiter leges regiae obligant ipsum regem. Et licet sit voluntarium regi facere legem, tamen non est in voluntate sua se obligari vel non obligari": *De Potestate Civili*, 21, p. 62.

23 On the dangers of judicial activism, possible indeed only where there is judicial review of legislation, see Bork (2003), for the American case, García and Verdugo (2013) and Silva Irrarázaval (2023) for the Chilean case, and Rüthers (2016) for the German one.

there is no institutional solution for this problem. The whole system of judicial review of legislation rests on the idea that judges will apply the Constitution and not their personal political ideas. However we call this duty, whether as a moral or a legal duty, one has to recognize that it is not enforceable. Constitutional judges are, as a matter of fact, bound by the Constitution only according to its *vis directiva*, not by its *vis coactiva*. The idea behind Aquinas's and Vitoria's thought is, then, that whatever the distribution of powers in a legal system, there will be always at least one institution that will be bound by the Constitution or the laws only according to their directive force and not according to their coactive force[24], and this idea seems to be valid even for contemporary legal systems.

We can then understand now Vitoria's doctrine regarding the necessity of applying the law consistently (another of Fuller's desiderata). Vitoria says that "the officials of the king ought to judge according to the written laws"[25]. This has to be well understood, according to written laws implies judging not only according to the tenor of the law, but also according to its spirit[26].

But what about the king himself? First of all, he says that, if the king acts as a judge, then he ought always to judge according to the written laws. But, applying them outside a court, he may dispense some subject if there is reasonable cause[27].

3 The Rule of the Community as the foundation of the Rule of Law

Now, according to Vitoria, the duty to follow his laws by the legislator is of moral nature. What is the source of this duty? Here we come to a key aspect of Vitoria's thought, one that is not explicitly expounded by Aquinas, namely, that the legislator's power to legislate is delegated and belongs first and foremost to the political community of

---

24 As was previously stated, one could find some anticipation of the idea of the institutional side of the Rule of Law in Aristotle's, Cicero's and Aquinas's preference for the mixed form of government, namely, one that combines aspects of the three pure forms: monarchy, aristocracy and rule by the people. Vitoria too defends this mixed form as the best form: "Verum est autem quod *tutissimus principatus et administratio videtur esse mixtus ex tribus*, qualis videtur esse Hispaniorum": *De Potestate Civili*, 11, p. 42.

25 De Justitia, 2–2 qq. 57–66 (henceforth, *De Justitia*), q. 60, a. 5.

26 The necessity of appealing to the intention of the law is manifest in situations of necessity: "*Si emergat casus necessitatis ubi servando legem manifeste constat esse contra intentionem legis, non debet impleri ad verbum, sed ad intentionem*": *De Legibus* q. 96 a. 6, lectio 126, p. 154. Notice how he speaks of the intention "of the law", not of the legislator, conveying the idea that obedience to rules is obedience to an impersonal authority with its own (artificial) volition.

27 "Respondeo quod nullo modo potest judicare contra leges, quamvis in illis possit dispensare. Et sic non est simile. Nam judicium nihil aliud est quam diffinitio et declaratio iuris. Et hoc non potest esse nisi secundum leges scriptas, quia non judicat rex ad dispensandum in jure, sed ad faciendum conformiter ad leges. Et ideo peccaret faciendo contra leges, quia convenientes ad judicium, hoc solum petunt, ut diffiniatur ius secundum leges scriptas. Sed dispensare potest in legibus extra judicium ex rationabili causa, ut caveat ab injustitia, ut omnia sint aequalia …": *De Justitia* q. 60, a. 5.

which it is an organ. Or, better, that the true legislator is the political community and, only secondarily, the "nominal legislator", be it king, parliament, king in parliament, or whatever. He says that the nominal legislator has the duty to obey the laws because it is the organ of the true legislator. He is not merely above every single part of the community, but it is also a part of it[28].

This idea of the political community as the true legislator explains also why he can accept that, in some cases, good statutes given by tyrants may be valid: they are converted into valid statutes by the consent of the political community, which prefers to be ruled by these statutes instead of having no statutes on a certain matter at all. They are valid statutes because, in fact, they are commanded by the true legislator: the political community[29]. Notice, moreover, how this idea is also an expression of the more basic idea of the necessity of rules to be stable: if all the rules given by a tyrant were invalid, then chaos and disorder would follow. A legal system has to be stable over time.

Consider, on the other hand, how this is the key idea behind Aristotle's and Plato's conception of the Rule of Law. They defended the idea that rules, not men, should govern. One can only make this intelligible if one supposes that the true legislator is not parliament or the prince, or whatever, but the political community itself. In his *Relectio* on political power, Vitoria repeatedly says that political power pertains firstly to the community itself and this original political power is prior to and the source of any political power any political organ may have: so, for instance, the republic, or the majority of its people, has the power to create a king[30]. He even says that the republic never alienates its political power (*potestas*) to the king, but only its authority (*auctoritas*)[31]. Political power belongs first and in itself to the republic, and secondarily and as delegated powers to the magistrates[32]. In brief, "the [material] cause, in which this kind of power is, indeed by natural and divine right, is the republic itself, to which pertains by itself to govern and manage itself, and to direct all of its powers to the common good"[33]. Vitoria is quite clear that this political power belongs to the political commu-

---

28 "quantumcumque princeps est supra totam rempublicam, est tamen pars reipublicae": *De Legibus* q. 96, a. 5, lectio 126, p. 152.

29 "Certe videtur quod *leges quae sunt convenientes reipublicae, etsi ferantur a tyranno, quod obligent,* non quidem quia a tyranno procedunt, sed quia ex consensu reipublicae, cum utilius et sanctius sit quod serventur illae leges latae a tyranno quam quod nullae serventur": *De Potestate Civili* 23, p. 64.

30 "*Sicut maior pars reipublicae regem constituere potest*": *De Potestate Civili*, 14, p. 44.

31 "Respublica enim in regem non potestatem, sed propriam auctoritatem transfert": *De Potestate Civili*, 8, p. 34.

32 "Quamquam autem haec potestas et auctoritas sit primo et per se in ipsa republica, eadem autem auctoritas est in principibus et magistratibus, quibus respublica vices suas et munimenta commisit": *De Potestate Civili* 7, p. 26. See also, *De potestate Ecclesiae prior*, 320: "Tota potestas principum saecularium est a communitate et republica".

33 "*Causa vero [materialis], in qua huiusmodi potestas residet, iure quidem naturali et divino, est ipsa respublica,* cui per se competit seipsam gubernare et administrare, et omnes suas potestates in commune bonum dirigere": *De Potestate Civili*, 7, p. 24.

nity by natural and not positive law. Political power, says Vitoria, is the power to create positive rules and, therefore, it cannot proceed from a positive rule. Consequently, it can only proceed from natural law[34].

4 Conclusion

We have seen, then, that in Francisco de Vitoria's thought we find a defense of some of the requirements of Fuller's Rule of Law, and that he defended these requirements as an expression of a deeper idea of Rule of Law, namely, that laws and not men should govern, an idea as old, at least, as Plato and Aristotle, and also that Vitoria considers that this deeper idea implies the doctrine that the political community, and not its organs, is the true legislator. We find, however, in him, no full-fledged theory of the Rule of Law such as one that we can find in modern and contemporary philosophers.

There is no explicit defense in Vitoria of the institutional aspect of the Rule of Law, namely, the idea of checks and balances, but we can say that this idea is adumbrated by his defense of the traditional doctrine of the mixed regime as the best political regime.

Bibliography

Araujo S.J., Robert (2012): "Our Debt to de Vitoria: A Catholic Foundation of Human Rights". In: Ave Maria Law Review 10: 313–329.

Aristotle (1988): Aristotelis Politica, (ed. W.D. Ross). Oxford: Oxford University Press.

Bin, Roberto (2010): Lo Stato di diritto. Bologna: Il Mulino, Kindle Edition.

Bork, Robert (2003): Coercing Virtue: The Worldwide Rule of Judges. Washington D.C.: AEI Press, Kindle Edition.

Finnis, John (1980): Natural Law and Natural Rights. Oxford: Clarendon Press.

Fuller, Lon L. (1969): The Morality of Law. New Haven and London: Yale University Press.

García, José Francisco and Verdugo, Sergio (2013): Activismo judicial en Chile. ¿Hacia el gobierno de los jueces? Santiago: Ediciones Libertad y Desarrollo.

Hernández O.P., Ramón (1995): Francisco de Vitoria. Vida y pensamiento internacionalista. Madrid: Biblioteca de Autores Cristianos.

Isler Soto, Carlos (2022). "Alcance de la defensa de los derechos humanos en Francisco de Vitoria". In: Cauriensia vol XVII: 195–211. doi: https://doi.org/10.17398/2340-4256.17.195

Lewis, Ovid C. (1968): "The High Court: Final … But Fallible". In: Case Western Reserve Law Review, 19, 3, 528–643.

Rüthers, Bernd (2016): Die heimliche Revolution. Vom Rechtsstaat zum Richterstaat. 2nd. ed. Tübingen: Mohr Siebeck.

---

34 "Item ius omne positivum est a republica: ergo oportet quod ipsa respublica et potestas condendi ius sit ante ius positivum. Et per consequens sequitur quod talis potestas sit in republica iure divino et naturali": *De Potestate Civili* 7, p. 26.

Silva Irrarázaval, Luis Alejandro (2023): Entre la Justicia y la Ley. Un ensayo sobre la judicialización de la política. 2nd. ed. Santiago: Ediciones Libertad y Desarrollo.
Skinner, Quentin (1978): The foundations of modern political thought, vol 2. New York: Cambridge University Press, Kindle edition.
Vitoria, Francisco de (1934): *De Justitia*, ed. Vicente Beltrán de Heredia, O. P., first volume, 2–2, qq. 57–60. Madrid: Publicaciones de la Asociación Francisco de Vitoria.
– (1960a): *De potestaete Ecclesiae prior*, in Francisco de Vitoria, *Obras de Francisco de Vitoria*, ed. Teófilo Urdanoz O. P. Madrid: Biblioteca de Autores Cristianos, 242–327.
– (1960b): *De Potestate Papae et Concilii relectio*, in Francisco de Vitoria, *Obras de Francisco de Vitoria*, ed. Teófilo Urdanoz O. P. Madrid: Biblioteca de Autores Cristianos, 430–490.
– (2008): *Relectio de Potestate Civili*, ed. Jesús Cordero Pando. Madrid: Consejo Superior de Investigaciones Científicas.
– (2010): *De Legibus*, ed. José Barrientos García and Simona Langella. Salamanca: Ediciones Universidad de Salamanca.

Prof. Carlos Isler Soto
Facultad de Derecho y Ciencias Sociales, Universidad San Sebastián
carlos.isler@uss.cl

Where Kant's Hospitality Meets "Zo Hospitality"?*

HENRY VUMJOU

Abstract: This paper juxtaposes the Western hospitality propounded by Immanuel Kant to one of the East's hospitality, what this paper refers to as 'Zo hospitality', against the backdrop of the refugee crisis caused by the recent political upheaval in Myanmar. It explicates the lesser-known Zo concept of hospitality to unveil its unique role in addressing the plight of refugees crossing the Myanmar border to India. Since India is neither a signatory of the United Nations 1951 Refugee Convention nor a party to international refugee protocols, it is not obligated to take in any refugees. However, the Zo People, a trans-border community of the Indo-Burmese border continue to provide aid, relief and shelter to the conflict victims from Myanmar who seek refuge in the Indian state of Mizoram. The paper calls this phenomenon "Zo hospitality". Unlike Kant's hospitality, Zo hospitality is undergirded by the age-old philanthropic principle called *tlawmngaihna. Tlawmngaihna* is a cultural, moral, and, to an extent, a political phenomenon. But most of all, it is a practical philanthropic phenomenon. It is *tlawmngaihna* that propels Zo People to go beyond the call of duty and extend humanitarian aid to refugees from Myanmar despite the Indian state legal announcement to prevent the influx of refugees. On the other hand, Kant distinctively states that hospitality is a category of law, not philanthropy. The paper, through a close reading of *Perpetual Peace* and the *Metaphysics of Morals,* also extrapolates Kant's hospitality which is constitutive of the Cosmopolitan Law. As Benhabib (2003) rightly observes, Kantian hospitality is inadequate to address issues such as refugees, migrants and asylum seekers because its guarantee lies with the state i. e. the state can deny entry to any refugee. Considering a comprehensive approach to the refugee crisis worldwide, this paper holds that Kant's hospitality alone is inadequate to address the increasing complexity of refugee crises worldover. The plight of refugees can be better addressed in a world where Kant's hospitality *meets* Zo hospitality, as has been the case with Myanmar refugees.

Keywords: Hospitality, Kant, Zo, *Tlawmngaihna,* Refugees

* Acknowledgement: I thank my colleague Swetha and dearest Toinu for the helpful suggestions, and the participants of the IVR Japan 2023 Conference for the insightful comments.

1 Introduction

The 2021 political upheaval in Myanmar displaced over 1.3 million citizens who rebelled against the tyranny of the military junta to neighbouring countries. So far, an estimated 50,000 Myanmar Chin refugees are recorded to have crossed over to the Indian state of Mizoram, where they are provided temporary relief by the Zo People.[1] India is not a signatory to the 1951 Refugee Convention or its 1967 Protocol and does not have a national refugee protection framework.[2] So, as a sovereign nation-state, it is not obligated to take in any refugees. When handling refugees, the Indian state can easily maintain an ambiguous position since it has no formal refugee policy. It is evident that the Bharatiya Janata Party (BJP) led National Democratic Alliance (NDA) government at the centre is not in favour of receiving coup refugees from Myanmar. This is evident from the fact that the security forces guarding the state borders of India bordering Myanmar have been instructed "to prevent the influx and deport those who have come in since the coup".[3] The Zo[4] People in contradistinction to the central Indian government's adamant refugee policy welcomed and accepted the coup refugees escaping the tyranny of the junta in the North East Indian state of Mizoram. They provide them rehabilitation – food, rations, blankets, mosquito nets and clothes – from local sources under the aegis of the Young Mizo Association (YMA)[5] and Mizo Student Associations without the aid of the central Indian government.[6] This is an uncanny affair; one that this paper terms as "Zo hospitality".

This paper attempts to explicate the principle constituting Zo People's hospitality in providing relief measures towards the coup refugees from Myanmar, even at the ex-

1 Fishbein, Emily (2023): "In India's Mizoram, ethnic ties drive response to Chin conflict." In: Frontier Myanmar. https://www.frontiermyanmar.net/en/in-indias-mizoram-ethnic-ties-drive-response-to-chin-conflict/ (Accessed 11 July 2023).

2 "UNHCR Global Appeal 2011 (update) – India." https://www.unhcr.org/in/media/unhcr-global-appeal-2011-update-india (Accessed 28 September 2023)

3 Kaushik, Krishn (2021): "Disagreement over coup refugees from Myanmar: Mizoram wants to help but Centre says stop, deport." The Indian Express. https://indianexpress.com/article/north-east-india/mizoram/myanmar-refugees-mizoram-mnf-bjp-7236424/ (Accessed 06 June 2023).

4 The Zo People are an ethnic group that inhabits the present day North East India, Bangladesh and Myanmar. They are known by various names, such as Chin, Kuki, and Mizo/Zomi. These various ethnic groups constitute Zo People, and they are ethnic minorities in these three countries. cf Vumson (1987): *Zo History: With an Introduction to Zo Culture, Economy, Religion, and Their Status as an Ethnic Minority in India, Burma, and Bangladesh*. Aizawl: Published by the author.

5 The YMA is one of the largest philanthropic organisations of the Zo People worldwide with its headquarters in Aizawl, Mizoram. It was constituted initially as the Young Lushai Association in 1935. https://centralyma.org/about-us/ (Accessed 28 September 23).

6 Hazarika, Sanjoy (2023): "'Now this is home for us': Chin refugees from Myanmar find a welcoming sanctuary in Mizoram." Scroll.in. https://scroll.in/article/1045343/now-this-is-home-for-us-chin-refugees-from-myanmar-find-a-welcoming-sanctuary-in-mizoram (Accessed 01.08.2023).

pense of going against a state policy. The Zo society is regulated by the principle called *tlawmngaihna*. *Tlawmngaihna* is a philanthropic principle inculcated and upheld well within Zo People. The paper argues that the *tlawmngaihna* ethic serves as the law for Zo People's hospitality, in general, and in this particular case, towards the Myanmar coup refugees. To bring out the concept of Zo hospitality more clearly, the paper juxtaposes it with the Western understanding of hospitality propounded by Immanuel Kant. In *Perpetual Peace* and *Metaphysics of Morals*, Kant limits the cosmopolitan law to hospitality. Hospitality entails the act of not treating a stranger or foreigner with hostility. Kant's hospitality is categorically 'non-philanthropic', it is a matter of law. The discourse adopted in this paper shows that Zo's hospitality and Kant's hospitality do not have to be mutually exclusive. Kant's hospitality only tells the host *what not to do* towards strangers or refugees, such as not turning a stranger away if it will lead to the stranger's death which is not clear a law to operate with in today's refugee crisis. Zo hospitality, through *tlawmngaihna* ethic, compels human beings to show love and compassion to persons in dire need, especially someone seeking refuge. Zo hospitality can complement Kant's hospitality, the combination of the two offers a better-suited option to address the evolving refugee crisis globally.

2 Kant's "Non-Philanthropic" Hospitality

What do we do when foreigners or citizens of a different country enter our territory? Here, we are referring to Myanmar citizens crossing the international border over to India and becoming refugees in the Indian state of Mizoram. With the country mired in war, they are compelled to leave Myanmar one way or the other; staying back would render their lives in danger as the country's military resorts to bombing its civilian settlement areas amidst the civil war. They have no choice but to escape the country because staying put would mean they will meet the same fate as those who are killed by the bombings. Fleeing the country implies that they crossed international boundaries and landed in another country's territory without a legal permit. Kant's answer, in *Perpetual Peace*, to any person or people who enters another's territory or state is to treat them with hospitality.

By hospitality, Kant means

> The right of a stranger not to be treated with hostility when he arrives on someone else's territory. He can indeed be turned away, if this can be done without causing his death, but he must not be treated with hostility so long as he behaves in a peaceable manner in the place he happens to be in. The stranger cannot claim the right of a guest to be entertained, for this would require a special friendly agreement whereby he might become a member of the native household for a certain time. He may only claim a right of resort, for all men are

> entitled to present themselves in the society of others by virtue of their right to communal possession of the earth's surface.[7]

Kant places the concept of hospitality in the relationship between the host and the stranger. The host can be the state or an individual within a state. The stranger can be a foreigner, a migrant, a refugee, an asylum seeker or an individual outside of the state who seeks interaction with the host or the state. Kant's hospitality entails that the stranger is not treated in a hostile manner upon their arrival in the host's territory. He cautions, however, that the rule is not guaranteed for a stranger to be necessarily welcomed into another's territory. The host can turn away a stranger. This turning away, however, is conditioned upon the stranger's life not being threatened or harmed or led to its destruction (*Untergang*) in doing so.[8] Hospitality does not mean the stranger's ability to claim the right of a guest to the host or the state. There is no necessary obligation upon the host to entertain the stranger. However, the state cannot treat the foreigner as an enemy.[9] Hospitality, then, is the right to present oneself in the society of others by initiating contact or communication. It is the right to temporary sojourn in others' territory but not a right to permanent settlement. A contract is required to be able to settle on another's land permanently, Kant insists.

Kant possibly does not picture 'refugees' as the foremost issue to be addressed by hospitality. What he pictured was 'foreign arrivals' not necessarily the 'refugee' we have in contemporary parlance. Broadly, there can be two distinct cases of arrivals, namely accidental arrival and intentional arrival. The first is a case for arrival due to undue circumstances, and the second is arrival with intent, meaning one willfully chooses to go to that state's territory. In today's understanding, accidental arrival can be an individual arriving in a foreign territory due to a shipwreck or a plane crash, where an individual outside of the state has to seek refuge in another's territory because their life is at stake. According to Kant's condition of *Untergang*, it is clear that such a foreign individual cannot be turned away or denied entry by the host state because it will destroy their life. In case of accidental arrivals, such as shipwrecks or plane crashes, an entry cannot be denied because the intention is not to arrive in that territory per se, but individuals end up by accident. Kant does not specify the possible kind of foreign arrivals, thereby leaving room for interpretation when it comes to arrivals. Apart from accidental arrivals, intentional arrivals can be of varying kinds. One is the intentional arrival of individuals on a foreign territory with the purpose of establishing trade, commerce,

---

7 Kant, Immanuel (1991): Towards Perpetual Peace, 8:358. In: Kant: Political Writings, (Ed) Hans Reiss, (Trans) H. B. Nisbet, Second ed, Cambridge: Cambridge University Press.

8 *Untergang* means the opposite of 'the good life' or 'human flourishing', cf. Knowles, Adam (2017): "Hospitality's Downfall: Kant, Cosmopolitanism, and Refugees". In: The Journal of Speculative Philosophy, vol. 31, no. 3, 347–357.

9 Kant, Immanuel (1991): Metaphysics of Morals, 6: 352. In: Kant: Political Writings.

tourism, etc, by fulfilling legal formalities. In these cases of intentional arrivals, there is room for a clear-cut implementation of Kant's *Untergang* condition. The state can deny any individual outside the state who wishes to establish contact. Another is the intentional arrival of individuals into a foreign territory as refugees, asylum seekers, or people who seek refuge because they are forced to flee one territory. Refugees, for instance, share a stark contrasting background compared to individuals who come to another's territory to establish trade, commerce, tourism, etc. As for refugees, their lives are under threat, while for traders, it is not necessarily the case.

In the context of coup refugees, they are forced to flee to India and other neighbouring countries because their life is under threat in Myanmar. They are foreigners moving into another state's territory. It is the case of foreign arrivals but not primarily with the intent to communicate and establish commercial relations. Kant does not differentiate between the two possible kinds of arrivals on a host's territory. In both cases, Kant's hospitality states that a state should not treat a stranger with hostility. It does not state anything further. Moreover, the condition of *Untergang* applies to both cases of intentional arrivals. This means that, just as a foreigner who seeks to establish trading with another state can be turned away, refugees can equally be turned away. In the case of Myanmar coup refugees, they do not enter through the legal process. Then the question arises: Are all persons who seek arrival in another state's territory of the same background? They are not. Persons who seek entry into another's territory for commercial relations come with means. The condition of *Untergang* can be easily applied to them, and they can easily be denied entry. The case of Myanmar coup refugees presents us with a case of illegal entry yet they cannot be turned away because turning them away would lead to the destruction of their lives.

Benhabib ties Kant's hospitality to the claim of temporary sojourn, not permanent residency. It can be refused on certain conditions. However, if refusal harms or leads to the destruction (*Untergang*) of the stranger, then refusal ceases to be an option. So, in cases of victims of religious wars, piracy, or shipwrecks, it is clear that claims of temporary residency cannot be refused.[10] However, Kant's hospitality is wanting when it comes to refugees – it offers no clear-cut mechanism to address refugee issues. It is unclear whether Kant's hospitality involves acts of supererogation among peoples and nations, requires going beyond the call of moral duty, or entails a particular sort of moral claim about respecting the right of humanity in the person of the other.[11] There needs to be more clarity in the details of Kant's hospitality. It is unclear whether the rights of refugees are rights in the sense of reciprocal moral obligation grounded upon our mutual humanity. It is also unclear whether they are legally enforceable rights that an individual can claim in such a way that the denial of it leads to punitive measures.

---

10 Benhabib, Seyla (2004): The Rights of Others: Aliens, Residents, and Citizens. Cambridge University Press, 27f.

11 Benhabib (2004), 28.

Kant's hospitality to be able to address the rights of refugees requires the backing of a sovereign authority wielding a supreme law to enforce it legally. However, such a sovereign has to be a sovereign of the world state. Establishing a world state sovereign contradicts Kant's republican commitment.[12] Kant's hospitality remains a law that can only be arbitrarily granted to strangers and foreigners by a state sovereign.[13] It is inadequate to address the issues at the borders of the state, especially the refugees. Kant's hospitality fails to take into account the moral obligation of the state to provide refuge to those in need.

3 *Tlawmngaihna:* Zo Law of Hospitality

There is no word-for-word translation of 'hospitality' in any of the Zo languages. But this does not imply that the sense of hospitality is absent in Zo culture. Today, one often comes across vloggers who visit and interact with Zo People in Mizoram, lauding their 'hospitable' nature. Brown presents hospitality as "the cordial and generous reception of guests that is receptive and open-minded to their particular ways of living".[14] In a broader understanding, hospitality is one's conduct towards a stranger. Even to Kant, hospitality is a host's conduct towards their guest(s)/stranger.[15] Going by this understanding, the practice of hospitality is very much alive amongst the Zo People. Warmly receiving a *'mikhual'* to one's household or village, can be explained as '*mikhual laka thatna*' or 'good conduct towards a stranger', is an age-old tradition for Zo People. *Mikhual* is any person not native to the place or village, so the term applies to strangers. Lorrain and Savidge, presented *mi-khual* as "a stranger, one belonging to another village."[16] In literal terms, *mi* is a person, and *khual* implies a foreign land. Hence, *mikhual* is a person from other lands – a stranger, a foreigner. The usage of the term refers to the time a Zo person's worldview was confined to their village republics. So, any person outside of a particular village, a non-local is a *mikhual*. In today's parlance, a *mikhual* can be a refugee, an alien, an asylum seeker, an outsider, a visitor and even a tourist. It may extend to any person outside of Mizoram, considering modern state or provincial boundaries are at play now. The Zo Duhlian[17] language has a particular word for "refugee" called *raltlan*. The Duhlian word *raltlan* literally translates as

---

12 Kant, Perpetual Peace, 8: 367, 352.

13 Benhabib (2004), 29

14 Brown, G. W. (2006): "Kantian Cosmopolitan Law And The Idea Of A Cosmopolitan Constitution." In: History of Political Thought, 27(4), 662.

15 Kant (1991), Perpetual Peace, 8:357.

16 Lorrain, J. H., & Savidge, F. W. (1898): A Grammar and Dictionary of the Lushai Language. Assam: The Assam Secretariat Printing Office, 143.

17 The language spoken today by the Mizo people is called Duhlian language. Mizos are the predominant Zo People inhabiting the North East Indian state of Mizoram. Cf. Vumson "Zo History".

an "escapee of war", *ral* – war, *tlan* – runaway, escapee. Undergirding the good conduct towards a *mikhual* or *raltlan* is the concept of *tlawmngaihna*.

Tlawmngaihna is a concept rooted particularly to the Mizo people and to the Zo People in general. *Tlawm* means less, *ngaihna* is philia or love, so *tlawmngaihna* literally translates as 'love of the less'. It is akin to concepts such as the Surinamese *Ala Kondre*, African *Ubuntu* and the Finnish word *Sisu*. *Ala Kondre* is an inclusivist concept that refers to "all countries, all denominations, all colours" in Suriname. *Sisu* refers to a cultural attitude among the Finns to never give up – a sense of tenacity.[18] It can also refer to values like bravery, hardiness, resilience etc. *Ubuntu* has numerous connotations, such as humanity, humanness, virtue, politeness, kindness, greatness of the soul, etc.[19] All these concepts are similar in that they are culturally rooted to a particular people. However, their meanings and references are not all quite the same.

Tlawmngaihna, however, is difficult to define accurately, at least to audiences outside of the Zo cosmos.[20] To say this, however, is not to render the concept as elusive or meaningless. It is difficult to define precisely as there is no equivalent word for it in the English language. Also, *tlawmngaihna* can connote a lot of meanings. Ask any Zo person to explain *tlawmngaihna*, the explanation will vary from person to person. *Tlawmngaihna* is not a rule or law like Kant's law of hospitality. It is not a written rule. Mostly, what is described are day to day manifestations of *tlawmngaihna*. *Tlawmngaihna* embodies the Mizo code of ethics and Dharma, a guiding principle that prioritises the welfare and interests of others over personal gain or self-interest.[21] It is a profound moral force, compelling individuals to demonstrate self-sacrifice and actively serve others.[22]

---

18 Brueggeman, M.A. (2008): "An Outsider's View of Beginning Literacy in Finland: Assumptions, Lessons Learned, and Sisu." In: Literacy Research and Instruction, 47(1), 4.

19 Gade, C.B.N. (2011): "The Historical Development of the Written Discourses on Ubuntu." In: South African Journal of Philosophy, 30(3), 307f.

20 Lorrain, J.H. (1975): Dictionary of the Lushai Language (1940). Royal Asiatic Society of Bengal, 513, presents *tlawmngaihna* as connoting various meanings:

1. to be self-sacrificing, unselfish, self-denying, persevering, stoical, stouthearted, plucky, brave, firm, independent (refusing help); to be loth to lose one's good reputation, prestige etc; to be too proud or self- respecting to give in etc.
2. to persevere, to endure patiently, to make light of personal injuries, to dislike making a fuss over anything.
3. to put one's own inclinations on one side and do a thing which one would rather not do, with the object either of keeping up one's prestige etc, or of helping or pleasing another, etc.
4. to do whatever the occasion demands, no matter how distasteful or inconvenient it may be to oneself or to one's inclinations.
5. to refuse to give in, give way, or be conquered.

21 Joshi, Nandini (2015): "What Indians can learn from the Mizo spirit of Tlawmngaihna during natural disasters." In: NewsGram. https://www.newsgram.com/general/2015/03/16/what-indians-can-learn-from-the-mizo-spirit-of-tlawmngaihna-during-natural-disasters, (Accessed 01 August 2023).

22 Sharma, Tithiya (2011): "The code of a warrior." In: Hindustan Times. https://www.hindustantimes.com/columns/the-code-of-a-warrior/story-c9v7KjUEstagNXgJlViZzH.html, (Accessed 12 August 2023).

In the book *Pi Pute Nun*, Challiana presents *tlawmngaihna* thus:

> It [*tlawmngaihna*] is a marvellous concept, and it has wide connotations. Diligence, bravery, endurance, selflessness, benevolence, kindness, selflessness, it includes all. The very name for it is adorable. It is one of the most adored [values], taught the most by parents to their children. Since Mizoram widely uses it, *tlawmngaihna* naturally adorns Mizo land the most. On the bad days and the good, a *tlawmngai* person's action lends adoration and comfort.[23] (translation is mine)

Challiana emphasises that *tlawmngaihna* is a multifaceted concept, encompassing a wide array of virtues within its embrace – diligence, bravery, endurance, selflessness, benevolence, and kindness, to name a few. The actions of an individual guided by *tlawmngaihna* exude admiration and offer solace. They serve as a source of adoration and comfort during challenging and favourable times, alike. For Challiana, the term *tlawmngaihna* is, by itself, adorable. It is this adoration for *tlawmngaihna* that urges Zo People to carry out deeds of *tlawmngaihna*. All these references draw from the manifestations of the usages of *tlawmngaihna* in everyday affairs.

The essence of *tlawmngaihna* runs deep within the tapestry of Zo society, manifesting itself through various altruistic practices, notably in the handling of death, grave-digging, and the care for the sick and departed.[24] While it may not transcribe into a direct equivalent in other cultures, this ethos of selfless care and community support remains a cornerstone of Zo societal values. A palpable representation of *tlawmngaihna* in contemporary times is witnessed in the solemn ritual of *mithi thlan laih* or the act of digging a grave for the deceased.[25] Upon the occurrence of death amongst the Zo People, the youth of the community voluntarily engage in the solemn task of preparing the final resting place for the departed soul. Importantly, this is not an obligation borne out of coercion or monetary reward; instead, it is a deeply ingrained sense of duty and compassion stemming from the ethos of *tlawmngaihna*. When inquired about their motivation, the resounding response echoes the concept of *tlawmngaihna* – the principle of selflessly caring for others, irrespective of familiarity or personal gain. This practice transcends mere burial preparations; it embodies the Zo People's historical inclination towards caretaking. In the past, this act of caring for the sick or deceased was a communal competition to be the best caregiver, showcasing the extent to which *tlawmngaihna* permeates their societal fabric. Central to Zo hospitality too is this ethos of *tlawmngaihna*, where displaying care and compassion towards strangers or those in

23 Challiana, P (1972): Pipu Nun. Aizawl: The Trio Book House, 8.

24 Cf. *"Mi zawn, Bo Zawn, Khawhar in riah, mithi in tlaivar, thlan laih, khawhar in len"*, Ralte, L (2023): "Mizo Tlawmngaihna: Then and Now." In K. C. Baral (Ed.), Cultural Forms and Practices in Northeast India. Springer Nature Singapore, 201–4.

25 Challiana (1972), 10.

need comes naturally. The act of offering assistance to a sick stranger or handling the burial of a deceased person is an expression of this inherent sense of Zo hospitality. It is a way of extending care to those in vulnerable situations without expecting any form of remuneration or recognition.

Tlawmngaihna is a lot about self-denial, too.[26] It is when a man is hurt, but he will insist that he is not. He will decline aid, saying that he can bear it. As Challiana points out, for somebody who does not understand *tlawmngaihna*, it can easily be mistaken for *lying*. If it is a long walk and tiresome, the idea is to keep on walking, resisting the aid of others, never openly confessing that one is tired. However, another *tlawmgai* person would acknowledge the pain or tiredness and insist on relieving the other person. There is a sense of reciprocity with the practice of *tlawmngaihna*, and this is how it continues to this day.[27]

Within the Zo community, *tlawmngaihna* is a term everybody understands but nobody can quite define. The point is that there is not one perfect definition for *tlawmngaihna*. This is, at least, to say that there is no single definition to understand the term. The particular definition changes with time and place; *changes* does not imply that the ethic of *tlawmngaihna* is arbitrary. It rather points to the fact that *tlawmngaihna* pervades all forms of Zo life and is relatable or applicable to a Zo person in all walks of life. The understanding may vary from person to person, young and old and to an extent from one locale to another. This is because when people speak about or attempt to describe *Tlawmngaihna*, it is usually the manifestation of it that they talked about.

Tlawmngaihna is tied to a Zo person in every form of life. In the past, it found its usages and roots in the Zo religion called *Sahkhua*. Some scholars are of the view that *tlawmngaihna* is the religious ethic of *Sahkhua* that continued to be retained in some kind or form.[28] The *Sahkhua* of old withered with the coming of Christianity. However, *tlawmngaihna* finds its way into Zo-Christian culture. British missionaries and administrators historically viewed *Tlawmngaihna* differently, with missionaries initially dismissing it due to its association with non-Christian practices. Eventually, the Church embraced it, recognising its alignment with Christian principles, contributing to the Mizo cultural renaissance. Today, Zo People themselves see *tlawmngaihna* as a constitutive part of Zo identity.

Tlawmngaihna does not fit the conventional definition of a law or rule. It stands distinct from Kant's law of hospitality. *Tlawmngaihna* is not explicitly codified but exists implicitly. It is intangible, present yet elusive – a principle that defies clear definition. Rather than a written rule, *tlawmngaihna* operates more as a predisposition – a readiness or willingness to extend help to others. It encompasses a spectrum of actions that reflect a love for humanity and a philanthropic ethic inherent in the Zo People.

---

26 Challiana (1972), 8.
27 Challiana (1972), 13.
28 Ralte (2023), 199.

Despite varying interpretations based on circumstances, at its core, tlawmngaihna embodies a philanthropic law – a commitment to care for others. This philanthropic ethic embedded within the Zo cultural fabric serves as the impetus driving their hospitality towards coup refugees in Mizoram. Even in the absence of a specific refugee law within the Indian state, it is this inherent principle of *tlawmngaihna* that compels the Zo People to extend their hospitality and aid to refugees, reflecting their unwavering commitment to humanitarian values.

Human societies are guided by their own moral codes, and their structures evolve from the ground of the belief system that is held. Zo People have for so long been regulated by the way of life called *Tlawmngaihna*.[29] Over the years, it has become the natural orientation of the Zo People to aid the needy who come to them or whom they come across. This orientation has been inculcated in each person growing up within the Zo community. This orientation is guided by the Zo ethic – *tlawmngaihna*. This brings us to the *raltlan* people from Myanmar – the coup refugees. So far, the Zo people have been rehabilitating and providing humanitarian aid to the coup refugees from Myanmar who crossed the border towards the Indian state of Mizoram. It is none other than the spirit of *tlawmngaihna* that propels the Zo People to extend humanitarian aid to the refugees from Myanmar. A *tlawmngai* person would always be ready to receive a *mikhual,* or would show *tlawmngaihna* to them. Likewise, for a society that thrives on *tlawmngaihna,* it is an inbound duty as a community to come together to aid the less fortunate. The Zo People's hospitality towards the coup refugees is propelled by their strong sense of *tlawmngaihna* towards the others who are much more in a dire situation than them.

4 Active Hospitality Towards Refugees

'Refugees' constitute a distinct case of entry into another's territory unlike shipwreck victims or traders. When it comes to refugees, Kant's hospitality is limited. Kant's hospitality only insists on what not to do with refugees. The distinction between Kant's hospitality and the Zo hospitality, guided by *tlawmngaihna,* is quite apparent, especially concerning refugees. Kant's hospitality primarily outlines what should not be done to strangers, refugees, asylum seekers, or migrants. It emphasises refraining from hostility, violence, or treating them as enemies and even prohibits turning away a stranger if it leads to their harm or destruction. Essentially, it is a prohibitive guideline, a negative law.

29 Pillai, S.K. (1999): "Winds of change in the bamboo hills: Learning from a Mizo way of life." In: India International Centre Quarterly, 26 (2), 128.

However, the Zo law of hospitality takes a more proactive and practical approach, particularly concerning refugees. Rooted in *tlawmngaihna,* it goes beyond mere abstention from negative actions. It inherently advocates for the rehabilitation and compassionate treatment of strangers, refugees, or asylum seekers. Unlike Kant's approach, Zo hospitality does not merely instruct what not to do. Instead, it directs the hosts to display good conduct and care toward refugees actively. This encompasses providing food, shelter, and support, reflecting a more comprehensive and affirmative approach to accommodating those seeking refuge.

Zo hospitality, rooted in the ethos of *tlawmngaihna,* transcends mere abstention from hostility toward strangers. It embodies a profound obligation incumbent upon the host. When a stranger seeks refuge within the host's territory, *tlawmngaihna* dictates not just the avoidance of hostility but demands a genuine commitment to treat them with kindness and care. This principle places the responsibility squarely within the host's control. While the stranger rightfully expects not to face hostility, the pivotal question arises: What role does the host undertake? The host's duty extends beyond mere avoidance of hostility. It requires an active display of hospitality towards the stranger. The essence of the host's role lies in practising *tlawmngaihna* toward the stranger. Being hospitable translates to embodying *tlawmngaihna* by extending genuine care, compassion, and kindness to the stranger seeking refuge. Hospitality signifies an active demonstration of this inherent ethical principle in Zo People's treatment and conduct towards a foreigner.

Tlawmngaihna, in the old Zo society, found its nurturing ground within an institution known as *Zawlbuk. Zawlbuk* served as an all-male dormitory where boys learned essential life skills and cultural values, including *tlawmngaihna,* as they transitioned into adulthood. This institution played a pivotal role in sustaining and imparting the principles of *tlawmngaihna,* as every Zo individual was required to be a part of it. Through *Zawlbuk, tlawmngaihna* was instilled in the younger generation, ensuring its continuity. In contemporary times, the YMA has taken up this responsibility, serving as a modern equivalent to impart Zo cultural values, including *tlawmngaihna.* This transition signifies that *tlawmngaihna* is not inherently ingrained in individuals but rather a learned principle. The fact that it can be taught and transmitted through these institutions suggests its applicability beyond Zo culture – to anyone willing to practise it worldwide.

The collective upbringing and guidance within the YMA have unified the Zo People, fostering a shared commitment to upholding *tlawmngaihna.* This cohesive upbringing is reflected in their collective stance against the central Indian government's policy regarding the rehabilitation of coup refugees. The Zo People collectively took a stand against the central government policy of not receiving coup refugees.[30] The unanimous opposition towards the central Indian government's plan of 'not rehabilitating the coup refugees' from the entirety of Mizoram illustrates their steadfast adherence to the principles ingrained in them through the YMA.[31] The unity and shared values cultivated within the YMA have enabled the Zo People to support and rehabilitate coup refugees independently, relying on their collective contributions without relying on aid from the central government. This ability to provide assistance and refuge to those in need is a testament to the strength of their shared cultural values and their unwavering commitment to *tlawmngaihna*.

5 Conclusion

There have been reported instances where the Zo People of Mizoram may not have consistently extended the same level of *tlawmngaihna* to other ethnic communities like the Chakmas or Brus. These instances, while noteworthy, do not diminish the overarching projection of *tlawmngaihna* as a cornerstone of Zo hospitality. It is worth noting that Zo hospitality, much like Kant's requires the foreigner to remain non-hostile. Reflecting on the past, there were periods, notably in the 1990s and early 2000s, where the Zo People exhibited hostility towards ethnic Chin refugees because there was hostility on their part.[32] However, this disposition has undergone transformation and evolution over time. Presently, there is a significant shift in their approach, displaying *tlawmngaihna* towards these refugees. Despite facing limitations in resources, the Zo People strive to rehabilitate coup refugees to the best of their abilities. This evolution underscores the dynamic nature of *tlawmngaihna* as an evolving ethic. It emphasises a continuous process of growth and change, indicating that the attitude towards extending hospitality is not fixed or stagnant. The current benevolent treatment of coup refugees stands as a testament to this evolution, showcasing the potential for extending similar

30 Chief Minister of Mizoram, Pu Zoramthanga, refutes the central Indian government directive, saying, "This (MHA advisory) is not acceptable to Mizoram. I understand that there are certain foreign policy issues where India needs to proceed cautiously. However, we cannot ignore this humanitarian crisis" Gupta, Nishtha (2021): "Mizoram CM writes to PM Modi, wants asylum for Myanmar refugees." In: India Today. https://www.indiatoday.in/india/story/mizoram-cm-writes-to-modi-wants-asylum-for-myanmar-refugees-1781647-2021-03-20 (Accessed 09 August 2023).

31 "We cannot ignore the conditions of our brother Chin refugees who suffered a lot and are taking refuge in Mizoram. We will give all our efforts for them, for their safety and livelihoods," said Professor Malsawmliana, assistant secretary of the central office of the YMA. This sentiment was shared by Ricky Lalbiakmawia, spokesperson of the MZP, "[Chin people] are running from death, so it is not good to look the other way," he said. "Even though the Indian government is against what we are doing, we are doing it … It is our duty as Christians, and as humanitarians, and as brothers and sisters." Fishbein, (2023).

32 Fishbein, 2023.

hospitality to any other refugees in the future, underscoring the adaptability and evolving nature of *tlawmngaihna* as a guiding principle of hospitality among the Zo People.

The existence of refugee laws are undoubtedly crucial, but their mere presence is not sufficient to ensure the well-being and proper care of refugees. Addressing the global refugee crisis necessitates an active demonstration of hospitality and compassion. *Tlawmngaihna*, although lamented for its decline in some instances, has experienced a resurgence, especially in the context of taking care of refugees.[33] This resurgence highlights the relevance and adaptability of *tlawmngaihna* in responding to contemporary challenges, particularly in providing aid and refuge to those displaced by conflict or crisis. While legal frameworks are essential, the active application of hospitality and the humanitarian ethos embedded in *tlawmngaihna* play a crucial role in addressing the multifaceted concerns of refugees. It is not merely about having laws in place but actively practising and demonstrating care, compassion, and a sense of responsibility towards those seeking refuge. Kant's hospitality, with its emphasis on avoiding hostility towards strangers, sets a foundational standard for how individuals and societies should treat refugees. On the other hand, Zo hospitality provides a deeper, more intrinsic ethic rooted in care, compassion, and active support for the less fortunate, creating a more comprehensive and humane approach. The plight of refugees can be better addressed when Kant's hospitality *meets* Zo's hospitality.

Bibliography

Benhabib, Seyla (2004): The Rights of Others: Aliens, Residents, and Citizens. Cambridge University Press.

Brown, Garrett Wallace (2006): "Kantian Cosmopolitan Law And The Idea Of A Cosmopolitan Constitution." In: *History of Political Thought* 27 (4): 661-84.

Brueggeman, M.A. (2008): An Outsider's View of Beginning Literacy in Finland: Assumptions, Lessons Learned, and Sisu. In: *Literacy Research and Instruction*, 47(1), 1-8.

Challiana, P. (1972): *Pipu Nun*. The Trio Book House.

Fishbein, Emily (2023): "In India's Mizoram, ethnic ties drive response to Chin conflict." In: Frontier Myanmar. https://www.frontiermyanmar.net/en/in-indias-mizoram-ethnic-ties-drive-response-to-chin-conflict/ Accessed 11 July 2023.

Gade, C.B.N. (2011): The Historical Development of the Written Discourses on Ubuntu. In: *South African Journal of Philosophy*, 30 (3), 303–329.

Gupta, Nishtha (2021): "Mizoram CM writes to PM Modi, wants asylum for Myanmar refugees." In: India Today. https://www.indiatoday.in/india/story/mizoram-cm-writes-to-modi-wants-asylum-for-myanmar-refugees-1781647-2021-03-20. Accessed 09 August 2023.

Hazarika, Sanjoy (2023): "'Now this is home for us': Chin refugees from Myanmar find a welcoming sanctuary in Mizoram." In: Scroll.in. https://scroll.in/article/1045343/now-this-is-ho

33 Saitawka (1932): "Tlawmngaihna (Newspaper Archive)." In: Mizo Leh Vai Chanchin, 12 f.

me-for-us-chin-refugees-from-myanmar-find-a-welcoming-sanctuary-in-mizoram. Accessed 01 August 2023.

Joshi, Nandini (2015): "What Indians can learn from the Mizo spirit of Tlawmngaihna during natural disasters." In: NewsGram. https://www.newsgram.com/general/2015/03/16/what-indians-can-learn-from-the-mizo-spirit-of-tlawmngaihna-during-natural-disasters. Accessed 01 August 2023.

Kaushik, Krishn (2021): "Disagreement over coup refugees from Myanmar: Mizoram wants to help but Centre says stop, deport." In: The Indian Express. https://indianexpress.com/article/north-east-india/mizoram/myanmar-refugees-mizoram-mnf-bjp-7236424/. Accessed 06 June 2023.

Knowles, Adam (2017): "Hospitality's Downfall: Kant, Cosmopolitanism, and Refugees." In: *The Journal of Speculative Philosophy* 31 (3): 347-357.

Lalchhanhima (2015): Mizote Leh Tlawmngaihna. In: *Mizo Literary Journal, USA*, 2(1), 74-84.

Lorrain, J. H. (1975): *Dictionary of the Lushai Language* (1940). Royal Asiatic Society of Bengal.

Lorrain, J. H., & Savidge, F. W. (1898): *A Grammar and Dictionary of the Lushai Language - Primary Source Edition*. The Assam Secretariat Printing Office.

Pillai, S. K. (1999): "Winds of change in the bamboo hills: Learning from a Mizo way of life." In: *India International Centre Quarterly, 26*(2), 125-137.

Ralte, L. (2023): Mizo Tlawmngaihna: Then and Now. In K. C. Baral (Ed.), *Cultural Forms and Practices in Northeast India* (pp. 199-213). Springer Nature Singapore.

Saitawka (1932): Tlawmngaihna [Newspaper Archive]. In *Mizo Leh Vai Chanchin* (pp. 12-14).

Sharma, Tithiya (2011): "The code of a warrior." In: Hindustan Times. https://www.hindustantimes.com/columns/the-code-of-a-warrior/story-c9v7KjUEstagNXgJlViZzH.html. Accessed 12 August 2023.

UNHCR India (2011): "UNHCR Global Appeal 2011 (update) – India." UNHCR India website. https://www.unhcr.org/in/media/unhcr-global-appeal-2011-update-india. Accessed 12 August 2023.

Vumson (1987): *Zo history: With an introduction to Zo culture, economy, religion and their status as an ethnic minority in India, Burma, and Bangladesh*. Aizawl: Published by the Author.

YMA, Central (n. d): "Young Mizo Association." Central YMA. https://centralyma.org/about-us/. Accessed 09 August 2023.

Henry Vumjou
HSS, IIT-Bombay
henryvumjou.iitb@gmail.com

The Universality of Hans Kelsen's Pure Theory of Law*

MONIKA ZALEWSKA

Abstract: This chapter attempts to critically examine the universality of Hans Kelsen's pure theory of law. The argument posits that the universality of Kelsen's theory is grounded in the nature of all positivistic theories of law, which aspire to objectivity. Additionally, this study contends that Kelsen's theory incorporates unique elements, contributing to the success of the pure theory of law. Specifically, the analysis centers on the empowerment and hierarchical structure of law, as encapsulated in the Stufenbau metaphor. The clarification of these elements gains further depth when viewed through the lens of conceptual metaphors and scientific models.

The paper adopts a focused approach, delving into the examination of the applicability of Kelsen's theory within the legal cultures of Eastern Asia and continental Western legal traditions. By scrutinizing these specific contexts, this study seeks to provide nuanced insights into the universality and adaptability of Kelsen's theoretical framework in diverse cultural and legal landscapes.

Keywords: Hans Kelsen, Pure Theory of Law, Japanese legal system, Stufenbau, legal positivism

Introduction

In the legal world, Hans Kelsen's Pure Theory of Law is like a meeting point where East and West come together. Despite the pronounced differences characterizing these distinct legal cultures, there exists a notable consensus in treating Kelsen's theory as a central reference point. The question of why Hans Kelsen's Pure Theory of Law holds significance across diverse legal cultures often elicits two primary explanations. Firstly, it aligns with the objectives of legal positivism, a perspective that examines the fundamental concept of law and purports to be objective and universally applicable across various legal systems. Secondly, in contrast to common law traditions, Kelsen's theory demonstrates a notable compatibility with civil law systems. Therefore, Kelsen's the-

* This research has been financed by National Science Centre (Poland) within the framework of research project: 2021/41/B/HS5/01174.

ory should apply to any civil law system, including those outside Europe. However, attributing its widespread acceptance solely to its alignment with legal positivism and compatibility with civil law systems proves to be an incomplete rationale. This explanation falls short of addressing the essential inquiry: why, amidst various positivistic theories applicable to civil law systems, has Kelsen's theory consistently emerged as one of the most successful?

Through this analysis, I endeavour to underscore the distinctive features that characterize Kelsen's Pure Theory of Law and explore how its conceptualization of legal elements contributes to its broader resonance in comparison to other positivistic frameworks. In this context, I will focus on a hierarchical structure of law (Stufenbau); I will also demonstrate how Kelsen's understanding of coercion and sanction might have contributed to the extended universality of his theory distinguishing it from other positivistic perspectives. It is worth adding here that I understand 'universality' as a matter of degree rather than 'either-or' quality.

In the context of universality, a particularly interesting case is the legal culture of Eastern Asia, which, at first glance, is associated with Confucian tradition and its emphasis on tradition and social structure outside the legal scope. This is a counter-example of what the pure theory of law has to offer. Yet, Kelsen's thought continues to attract attention in that context. Examining the cultural richness of social systems in Japan, China, and Korea within the limits of a single chapter and thoroughly analyzing them through the lens of Hans Kelsen's Pure Theory of Law proves to be an impossible task. Consequently, the scope of this study will be delimited to focus specifically on Japan. Japan, while influenced by Chinese legal perspectives, has cultivated its unique approach to law, which should enrich the analysis.[1]

Given the universal claims of the Pure Theory of Law, this analysis will be limited to those elements consistent with its conceptual framework. The objective is to illustrate that the Pure Theory of Law can offer insights into specific aspects of Japan's legal culture. It is not imperative to comprehensively expound upon the entire legal landscape of any given country through the scope of pure theory of law. This theory inherently possesses limitations, and a discerning acknowledgement of its inability to encompass the entirety of legal phenomena is essential to apply this theory properly.

My analysis contains three steps. First, the standard features of positivistic theories of law will be analysed. Among these are well-known features, such as the positivist commitment of legal science to constructing a theoretical framework that secures the objectivity of its inquiry. This part will conclude that although these elements provide some explanation of why the pure theory of law is, to a grand extent, universal, they do not provide a full explanation. In the second part, I will argue that there are also elements unique to the pure theory of law, which make it more successful than other

1 Haley (1995), 3.

positivistic doctrines of that time. In this part, I will introduce the first such element, the underlying mechanism of imposing coercion associated with empowerment.

The following parts will analyse the main element that makes the pure theory of law unique and universal simultaneously: the hierarchical structure of law, known in German as Stufenbau, which can be translated into 'stairway'. The third part will delve into an examination of the metaphorical construct of 'Stufenbau,' designed to conceptualize a hierarchical structure of law. Commencing with an exploration of its linguistic metaphorical underpinnings, this section will subsequently examine its cognitive dimension as developed by Lakoff and Johnson. The fourth section will examine the concept of 'Stufenbau' from a different perspective, which is the perspective of the philosophy of science. I will argue that the stairway metaphor serves as a model for two distinct forms of relations within the legal hierarchy: vertical relations of empowerment and horizontal relations defined by normative content.

1 The universality of the positivistic doctrine of law

Unsurprisingly, Hans Kelsen's doctrine has the strongest impact on civil law legal systems, especially in Central Europe. This region was influenced by the Austrian-Hungarian Empire, where Kelsen made his first steps as a lawyer and legal theorist. His theory is positivistic in nature, and particularly in his earlier writings, reflects the structure of the Austrian legal system – especially in the field of public law.[2]

The majority of legal concepts employed by Kelsen were not singular to his own contributions; rather, he drew influence from German legal positivists who had been engaged with this doctrinal framework several decades prior to Kelsen's work. Influenced by legal positivism, Kelsen endeavoured to conscientiously fulfil its overarching agenda, which aimed at formulating a scientifically grounded theory of law. Scientific theory requires several conditions to be satisfied; among others, it must be objective. Objectivity is supposed to ensure the universality of the theory.

Hence, the category of objectivity is crucial for legal positivism. Marmor notes that such objectivity means that criteria allow lawyers to determine the law on certain issue coherently.[3] Spaak compellingly argues that such understood objectivity concerns only the level of the sources of law as the process of interpreting and applying the law inherently incorporates a moral dimension.[4] Spaak defines legal positivism in this context as

2 Kelsen (2019).
3 Marmor (2001), 139.
4 Spaak (2004), 267.

> a general and descriptive theory about law […] and not a theory telling the judge how to decide on complex cases or when civil obedience is justified […]. Legal positivism thus conceived could perhaps be described as a meta-theory, a theory about theories of law because it aims to lay down requirements that any adequate theory of law must meet.[5]

Spaak observation is by the scope of the pure theory of law, which is also focused on the problem of the sources of law. Hence, I will follow this understanding of objectivity in this Chapter.

One of the ways of proving that the positivistic program was successful was the consequence of the universality of such a theory. If the positivistic theory is universal and accepted by as many legal cultures as possible, then the positivistic program could be declared a success. Undeniably, Hans Kelsen's Pure Theory of Law turned out to be very successful, which brings us to the question of what is so distinct about Kelsen's pure theory of law that this theory became so successful, and no any other positivistic theory of that time.[6]

Even though Kelsen is widely regarded as the most prominent representative of legal positivism in his time, his theory significantly differs from earlier attempts to conceptualize law in a similar manner. Kelsen was younger compared to famous legal positivists such as Georg Jellinek or Hans-Magnus Bergbom, and he became a fierce critic of his older colleagues. Namely, he disagreed with perceiving law as a social fact, the fundamental thesis for legal positivistic doctrine. Instead, he claimed that law can be only reduced to Ought since it contains norms; reduction of law to fact falls under the naturalistic fallacy. Furthermore, Kelsen introduced and, in some cases, refined already existing concepts to establish distinctive elements within his theoretical framework. These include the Is-Ought separation, basic norm, hierarchical structure of law (Stufenbau), and the concept of imputation, each contributing to the unique character of Kelsen's legal theory.

In Kelsen's view, the objectivity of legal science is ensured by its theoretical character – that is, by abstracting from the content of law and focusing solely on its form. Kelsen was convinced that the form of law is objective and unchangeable. If certain conditions are fulfilled, the normative system acquires the attribute of law. In contrast, the content of law is supposed to be subjective, which means the content of legal provisions can change at any time. The content of law depends on politics – or, as Kelsen preferred to put it, on the ideology prevailing in a particular place at a specific time. In a democracy, the content of the law is constantly negotiated and reformulated due

5 Ibid., 256–57.

6 I abstract here from Herbert H. L. A. Hart theory, probably even more successful than Kelsen's theory, which is constructed specifically for common law system and deal with different problem than PTL. For these reasons these theories are not necessary in competition, they can be both influential at the same time and place, tackling with different problems of jurisprudence.

to democratic processes. Given the inherently subjective nature of ethical inquiries – with each individual possessing a distinct moral compass – Kelsen argues that the form of law should maintain neutrality towards values. He posits that the negotiation of values is more appropriately situated within the content of the law itself.[7]

Interestingly, such a positivistic account is advantageous when describing the Japanese legal system since Japan can be characterised by a lack of unified moral standards for political and social control. This particular characteristic, the lack of such shared moral foundations, acts as a restriction for the emergence of some universal natural law doctrine within the Japanese legal framework. This distinguishes Japan from other Eastern legal orders, which put more emphasis on Confucianism, which contains strongly defined standards of conduct that are external to the law. While Confucianism has maintained a historical presence in Japan, it has often been perceived as an external influence among a variety of available social principles.[8]

According to Haley, this leads to an interesting question: what is the source of legitimacy in Japan, if not some universal moral rules? He argues that this function is performed by consensus.[9] This, in turn, is compatible with Kelsen's vision of law as an order to ensure peaceful co-existence. Even though Kelsen perceived law in the narrow sense, eliminating external normative rules, his vision of a well-functioning society bears resemblance. He rejects the vision of a well-functioning society based on some universal ideal of justice. As he argues: 'The longing for peace means, as a rule, a renunciation of the original ideal of justice.'[10] In formulating his democratic theory, he contends that a peaceful and respectful coexistence within a well-functioning society can be achieved through consensus-building; particularly within the democratic framework that advocates for tolerance and pluralism.[11]

In Japan, however, the consensus is supposed to be reached mainly through means external to the law. Legal control has much less significance compared to Occidental countries. Much more significant are informal, extra-legal rules. At this point, the similarity is diminished; however, what matters the most is that the main idea underlying the legitimacy of law is similar and involves consensus/peaceful coexistence. From this perspective, it appears that the Japanese conceptualization of law may align even more closely with Kelsen's vision than its Western counterpart. In Japan, executing the law without consensus is considerably more difficult than in Europe. This implies that the deliberative process holds greater significance in Japan compared to Europe. In Japan, the collaboration between parties is essential, while in Europe, the argumentative

---

7 Kelsen (1945), 391.
8 Haley (1995), 194.
9 Ibid., 195.
10 Kelsen (1945), 441.
11 Kelsen (2010), 1575–90.

model of politics is common.[12] As a result, it can be concluded that the Japanese idea of law, as not representing moral commands but legitimising social order and the order based on consensus, is, in this aspect, Kelsenian in nature.[13]

Summing up, the methodological assumption of objectivity predestines the legal theory to be universal, even when comparing disparate cultures such as Western Europe and Eastern Asia, exemplified by Japan. Later, by discussing universality, I use this contrast as my scope. The contrast between such distinct cultures and the fact that the pure theory of law can embrace the richness of each of them should also emphasise my thesis that the degree of Kelsen's theory is high. In the following sections, I will argue why Kelsen's amendments to positivistic doctrine caused the pure theory of law to be the most universal. I will start with the problem of empowerment and coercion, then move to the concept of the hierarchical structure of law, Stufenbau, and its metaphorical aspect. The final section will discuss the metaphor of Stufenbau from the angle of the philosophy of science and theory of models and argue about its universal and unique character it.

2 Purpose of the norm: legitimacy and coercion

The concept of consensus is, in this context, linked to another fundamental legal element, coercion, within the positivist framework. This distinction sets positivistic theories apart from the Japanese notion of law, where law functions as a tool to legitimize norms rather than a mechanism of coercion.[14] As Haley argues:

> In this sense, institutional or structural patterns become cultural phenomena by definition. Thus, Japan's dependency on consensus can be argued to have acquired from habit and expectation a particular and self-reinforcing legitimacy. In this context, formal law-making and law-enforcing processes – whether legislative, bureaucratic or judicial – function in considerable measure as consensus-building processes rather than avenues for command and coercion.[15]

This quote indicates the significance of consensus in law-making processes and introduces a consequence of such an approach, which is less emphasis on commanding and coercion. At first glance, this could serve as a counter-argument to the thesis of compatibility of the pure theory of law with the Japanese understanding of this phenomenon. After all, positivistic theories of law signify coercion as one of the most crucial

12 Haley (1995), 198.
13 Ibid., 197.
14 Ibid., 199.
15 Ibid, 198.

aspects of the law. However, when looked closely, it can be seen that Kelsen rejected command as a primary norm. For him, such a norm is superfluous because what counts in law is the norm which contains *empowerment*.

In traditional legal positivism, the normative structure was conceptualized as comprising two distinct types of norms. The primary norm encompassed an obligation, exemplified by statements like 'you shall not steal.' Complementing this, the secondary norm included the consequences in the form of coercion for violating the primary norm, for instance, 'if A has stolen a car, then A should be punished.'

Kelsen reversed this order, arguing that the norm, which refers to consequences, is the primary norm, while the norm, which relates to obligation, is secondary.[16] This allowed Kelsen to demonstrate a distinctive feature of the law: the initiation of consequences occurs through a process of empowerment, defined by Kelsen as follows: 'The normative function of empowering means: conferring on an individual the power to posit and apply norms.'[17] Many normative systems foresee the consequences of breaking the obligation. However, only the law does that in an institutionalised manner in the form of empowerment. As a result, the primary norm took the form in which empowerment is on the first plan, rather than coercion:

If A stole a car, then the organ *ought* to be empowered to do Y (e.g. impose a sanction)

As Kelsen notes: 'Since the law regulates its creation and application, the normative function of empowering plays a fundamental law in law. Only individuals on whom the legal order confers this power can create or apply legal norms.'[18] This quote indicates the central place for the empowerment category in his theory since the second edition of 'Pure Theory of Law.'[19] There is no law without empowerment; on the other hand, the question of whether a law without coercion is possible is left by Kelsen rather open. Kelsen does not often use the phrase 'coercion' or sanction. He prefers to use these categories in concrete examples or just write about 'consequences,' Such an approach indicates that some kind of consequence is essential for law. However, it is not determined that this consequence must occur in the form of coercion. In the light of efficacy, which conditions validity, it can be assumed that Kelsen meant coercion and force in particular; however, it seems that Kelsen leaves some margin of interpretation here. This margin allows Kelsen's theory to be more universal than theories that operate more straightforwardly in this case.

Hence, in the legal cultures that put more emphasis on consensus, Kelsen's pure theory of law can be interpreted as follows: the law is not about commanding; the law is

16 Kelsen (1979), 56–58.
17 Ibid., 102.
18 Ibid.
19 The importance of empowerment category is compellingly argued by: Paulson (1988).

about empowering an organ to issue another norm when specific conditions are met. This reasoning takes the emphasis away from sanctions and towards empowerment. This shift in focus from sanctions to empowerment could find resonance in legal cultures such as Japan, where coercion within the legal system assumes a secondary role.

However, in Kelsen's case, even when considering the interpretation favouring empowerment, coercion is essential, but rather concerning the efficacy of the legal system, which, in turn, conditions validity. On the other hand, if efficacy is ensured by authority and social control in Japan, coercion loses its significance. It seems that such interpretation is still possible in the framework of the pure theory of law. In this framework, validity would have to be somewhat bound with legitimacy rather than efficacy. Valid law would legitimise norms obtained by the consensus. These norms are efficacious not because of the valid legal system but because of the existing consensus. Therefore, the law reflects the consensus that such a specific norm exists in society at a certain time.

Such an understanding of validity deviates from the standard interpretation of the pure theory of law. However, the advantage of such a reading is that the tension between efficacy and validity ceases to exist. Instead, the relations between Is and Ought are redefined. On one hand, there is no such sharp division between Is and Ought. Since the law reflects the factual consensus, this relation is relatively harmonious. Conversely, this does not mean separating these two domains is wakened. In the framework described here, the domain of Ought can be easily distinguished from the Is domain. Such interpretation in Japanese spirit stays in sharp contrast to the interpretation known from continental Europe, where the tendency exists to read Kelsen in a manner that strongly emphasises coercion.[20] Overall, the richness and sophistication of Kelsen's thought allow us to interpret his theory in a way that, depending on the type of legal culture, will put more emphasis on one element and less on others. What matters here is that Kelsen included all the relevant 'ingredients,' leaving the question regarding its importance to the interpreter of the text, depending on the legal culture.

3 The universality of the metaphor of Stufenbau?

The conception of Stufenbau is one of the most crucial components of Hans Kelsen's pure theory of law. However, this translation does not express the richness of the metaphor used. In the law domain Stufenbau is associated with the metaphor of a 'stairway' or 'pyramid.' This metaphor reveals Kelsen's vision regarding the legal system's structure. This system is supposed to be hierarchical, in which one 'step' is necessary

20 See: Kletzer (2018).

to make another step.[21] Both Western and Eastern cultures can easily adopt this metaphor due to its notion of hierarchy. In both legal cultures, the law, especially in the public law domain, is envisioned as a hierarchy in which each legal norm has its place.

This metaphor is also strong due to its cognitive dimension. Stufenbau can be analysed more profoundly as a conceptual metaphor described by Lakoff and Johnson.[22] This framework claims that some metaphors reveal profound thinking patterns when translating more abstract concepts into less abstract ones. For instance, the 'argument' in Western cultures is understood in terms of 'war,' which is reflected in such phrases as: 'I have defeated my opponent,' 'I have won this argument,' 'his argument was stronger than mine,' and so on.[23] Hence, the linguistic expression of some abstract concepts is secondary to understanding these concepts and reflects this understanding on a cognitive level. In such case, the 'Stairway' refers to the group of metaphors called 'orientational,' referring to how humankind perceives the body in its surrounding reality. They are associated with space, hence 'up' is more important in some aspect than 'down.'[24] By extrapolating it into pure theory of law, Kelsen and earlier Merkl, using the stairway metaphor, referred to a primordial understanding of law as a hierarchical structure with strict order. This can be seen in phrases such as: at the top of the legal hierarchy is constitution', 'the lower norm must conform to the higher norm,' and 'the individual norm is at the bottom of legal hierarchy'; such understanding of the law is typical for civil law culture, which was primarily described by Kelsen.

The importance of 'up' that is expressed by a 'higher' norm metaphor is reflected in Kelsen's emphasis that the validity of a lower norm is contingent upon the empowerment inherent in the higher norm. This emphasis is accompanied by the conviction that a lower norm must not contradict the higher norm and resonates with both cultural circles. However, the reasons why this notion is fundamental might be slightly different. While in Western countries, this requirement is associated with the rule of law, which in the end is supposed to guarantee freedom and liberties to people, Eastern cultures might resonate with this requirement of Stufenbau because of the vision of law acquired from China, where two traditions shaped its perception: namely Confucianism and legalism.[25] Confucianism, which emphasizes the hierarchical structure of society[26], might cause the idea of Stufenbau to resonate powerfully since law reflects or at least should reflect the social structure.

Japan is no exception here. Primarily, the concept of law has been derived from China and its bureaucratic tradition, which emphasizes the narrow idea of law, limiting it

21 Kelsen (1967), 221–29.
22 Lakoff and Johnson (2003).
23 Ibid., 4.
24 Ibid., 14–17.
25 Gao and Walayat (2021), 237.
26 Chang et al. (2017), 352.

to administrative aspects and law-making processes and penal functions, leaving aside most of the norms which govern the aspects of private life.[27] As Haley notes: 'Conceptually, law meant the regulatory commands of those who ruled. There was no concept of law as a means of private autonomous ordering.'[28] Such a vision of law is compatible with the scope of the pure theory of law, which focuses on similar aspects of law, leaving aside the civil law problematics and contract law in particular, where the Stufenbau structure might not fit, at first glance at least.

It seems that the idea of Stufenbau in Western culture also resonates strongly. Yet, it is attached to the liberal paradigm, which stems from (among others) Immanuel Kant's and John Locke's assumption regarding freedom as the fundamental governing society. Kant believed that 'every rational being had an innate right to freedom and a duty to enter a civil condition managed by a social contract to realise and preserve freedom.'[29] Locke assumed that human beings are naturally free and equal. In the social contract framework, they can transfer some of their rights to the government, which has a duty to protect their freedom, life and property.[30] The notion of freedom underpins the emergence of the rule of law, positing that all individuals, including those in positions of authority, are subject to legal constraints. This social contract materializes in the form of a constitution, positioned at the top of the legal hierarchy, encompassing freedoms and liberties applicable to all. Freedoms and liberties are ensured by the rule that the lower norms are valid only if they are not contradictory to constitutional provisions. Consequently, the Stufenbau establishes a formal rule of law, safeguarding the efficacy of the Constitution and upholding all the rights and liberties enshrined within it.

As mentioned before, this metaphor and its strong inclination to a top-down structure raises problems for legal systems which are decentralised, for instance, the legal system of the European Union, international law or even much more decentralised common law, compared to civil law. The concept of 'Stufenbau,' while instrumental in defining a particular type of legal system, seemingly constrains the universality of the pure theory of law in other instances. However, when looking closely at this concept, it might turn out that there is no contradiction between decentralised, multicentric legal systems and the idea of Stufenbau. Stufenbau reflects more aspects of law than can be decoded by the conceptual metaphor. To demonstrate that, another philosophical tool must be introduced, that is a scientific model.

27 Haley (1995), 194.
28 Ibid., 198.
29 Rauscher (2022).
30 Tuckness and Stanton (2024).

4 Stufenbau as a model of the structure of law

Despite the overarching universality of legal positivism and particularly Hans Kelsen's pure theory of law, there are specific domains where they exhibit lesser compatibility, such as in multicentric legal systems or common law. German legal positivism, tailored for civil law systems, encounters challenges in aligning with common law structures. The common law system places greater emphasis on judicial activity, and that falls beyond the scope of German positivistic doctrines, as previously noted. This does not imply an inherent incompatibility of Kelsen's theory with the common law; rather, it suggests a less seamless fit compared to its natural alignment with legal systems characteristic for continental Europe. Despite Kelsen's intent to adapt his theory to the common law, particularly evident in the General Theory of Law and State, his efforts met with limited success. In the United States, Kelsen is more prominently recognized for his contributions to international law and political theory rather than his direct influence on the common law system.

Moreover, Kelsen's theory appears to be incompatible with decentralized or multicentric legal systems like EU law. Decentralised or multicentric legal systems do not fall under the metaphor of the pyramid commonly associated with the interpretation of Stufenbau. Law perceived as a pyramid (the other translation of Stufenbau) does not necessarily fit decentralised law models, especially multicentric legal systems, such as the law of the European Union. It is argued that European Union law is instead characterized by equal centres, and for this reason, its structure should fit the metaphor of the network.[31] The same should apply to international law. However, Kelsen built his theory of international law and applied the category of *Stufenbau* to it in a compelling way.[32] To understand how Stufenbau could fit into such decentralised or even multicentric legal orders, it is necessary to comprehend the idea behind the metaphor of Stufenbau.

The key insight regarding Stufenbau is to recognize that it extends beyond mere hierarchy. Kelsen recognized that similar hierarchical arrangements are present in other normative frameworks, such as morality. A distinctive feature that sets law apart from morality lies in the nature of the relationships between specific norms within their respective hierarchies. In morality, these connections are substantive, relying on the content of the norm. For example, from the overarching norm 'you shall love your neighbor,' one can derive the lower norms specifying actions like helping or refraining from harming the neighbor. In contrast, legal structures exhibit a different pattern, where connections between norms have a formal character.[33]

---

31 Golecki and Wojciechowski (2009), 174. See also: Zirk-Sadowski (2009).
32 I have elaborated on this problem in: Zalewska (2022), 23–38.
33 Kelsen (1967), 195.

Therefore, there is more to the metaphor of Stufenbau than what is associated with conceptual metaphor in its orientational form, which is that 'up' is superior to 'down.' Merkl, the author of this metaphor, consciously used it not to highlight some form of hierarchy in law but to illustrate the specific and distinct structure of law, which reminds one of the steps in the stairway.[34] In other words, Merkl, followed by Kelsen, created a model of law represented by the Stufenbau.[35] In this model the linkage between norms is established through the empowerment embedded in the higher norm, authorizing the organ to issue the lower norm. This forms a structure reminiscent of distinct steps on a stairway. The norm-empowerment relationship represents the horizontal dimension of such a step, whereas the empowerment-norm signifies the vertical aspect of a step in the stairway. The Stufenbau serving as the model of law significantly contributes to considerations about the universality of the pure theory of law; to demonstrate that, the concept of the model needs to be clarified.

Models are representations of some phenomenon; that is, 'they stand for something else (namely the system they are used to investigate).'[36] As a representation, its objective is not to precisely mirror the phenomenon but rather to underscore essential elements of the phenomena at hand. A model as a representation of some phenomena means that deviations from the model are conceivable, and their presence does not necessarily render the model false.[37] Whether the model is successful or not can be stated by assessing whether the model is veridical. This implies that the model doesn't necessarily have to be entirely accurate; it suffices for the model to be 'true enough.'[38]

Such characteristics of models stem from the nature of science. "Science is not, cannot be, and ought not to be, a mirror of nature. Rather, science embodies an understanding of nature. Since understanding is not mirroring, failures of mirroring are not necessarily failures of understanding.'[39] In this quote, Elgin cogently articulates the role of models in science. Instead of mirroring nature, they facilitate *understanding* of it. While her reference pertains to empirical sciences, the principle is even more applicable to social sciences, where understanding takes priority to a greater extent than in empirical sciences, which predominantly rely on explicative methods.[40]

Understanding does not require accuracy, which is characteristic of empirical science. Understanding occurs in pure theory of law, for instance, when Kelsen distinguishes between an external manifestation of human conduct, which is perceived by

---

34 See: Merkl (2010), 1311–61.

35 The notion that Stufenbau is a model was primarily used by Potacs (2022), 61–70. I have elaborated this notion in: Zalewska (2022), 23–38.

36 Barberousse and Ludwig (2008), 56.

37 Frigg and Hartmann (2006), 56–57.

38 Teller (2008), 237–38,

39 Elgin (2009), 77.

40 The distinction between explanation and understanding was introduced by can be found in Weber (1949). Its elaboration, which could be relevant to Kelsen can be found in e. g. in: von Wright (1971).

senses and the meaning of it, for example, 'People assemble in a large room, make speeches, some raise hands, others do not – this is external happening. Its meaning is that a statute is being passed, that law is created.'[41] Kelsen suggests that particular interpretations attribute legal status to certain physical events. When examining the Pure Theory of Law from this perspective, its principal components revolve around the process by which legal professionals understand certain events as having legal significance. This process of understanding entails elements such as the Is-Ought separation, the basic norm, and so forth.[42]

The fact that models are associated with the mode of understanding and that they need to be 'true enough' offers a resolution to the argument that certain legal systems do not conform to the concept of Stufenbau. Models are one of the most essential tools which enable us to understand the phenomena in question. Some of them can even be considered fiction in the Vaihingerian sense; that is, even though they disagree with reality or are self-contradictory, they are useful in the sense that they add to the knowledge by enabling one to understand the phenomena in question.[43] This implies that presenting a counterexample to the model does not inherently disprove the model; instead, it offers an intriguing case study when the model encounters limitations, fostering a deeper understanding. While this may seem applicable to Stufenbau and multicentric legal systems, I will contend in the subsequent paragraph that, contrary to initial impressions, the model of Stufenbau is compatible with most multicentric legal systems.

The crux of the matter lies in grasping that the Stufenbau model diverges from the conventional model of legal hierarchy. Traditional models of legal structure focus only on the hierarchical aspect of law. Even though this feature is essential, it cannot distinguish law from other normative systems, most of which are hierarchical. The model of Stufenbau has added value. Not only does it represent the hierarchy of law, but it also represents the unique feature of the law, which is formal links between norms in the form of empowerment. The metaphor of the stairway depicts the structure unique for law where the content of the norm does not constitute the link between higher and lower norms; instead, the process has two stages. Primarily, the higher norm encompasses the authorization to promulgate the lower norm. Subsequently, the empowered organ issues the lower norm. These can be envisioned as a horizontal and vertical part of the step in the stairway.

41 Kelsen (1967), 2.

42 I have elaborated on this in the book, *The Dynamic Approach to Hans Kelsen's General Theory of Norms*, Hart Publishing, 2024.

43 For the problem of epistemological fictionalism by Vaihinger, its rejection and is rehabilitation in nineties see: Fine (1993): 1–18. The problematic of models understood in terms of fictions see: Barberousse and Ludwig (2008).

Such structure is much more universal than the vision of law as a pyramid. As noted before, the model of law depicted in the shape of the pyramid can be helpful in some domestic legal systems; however, such a model does not apply to decentralised or multicentric legal systems. In such cases, the network model better reflects the relation between specific 'centres', be it the states, bodies of international organisations, or some other actors such as NGOs.

On the other hand, the model encapsulated by the metaphor of Stufenbau does not serve as an alternative to the network or pyramid models; rather, it reveals distinct aspects of law in comparison to the pyramid or network models. Namely, the pyramid and network model represent relations between the norms in the legal system regarding their superiority or inferiority. The Stufenbau model brings more information because it is focused on the nature of the links between two norms, introducing the representation in the form of steps of the stairway, which presents a new dimension: the dimension of empowerment. Since empowerment is associated with both higher and lower norm, it adds a new dimension to the structure of law. The pyramid or network model operates on one dimension, the dimension of the norms, and envisions only vertical relations between norms. Hence, the Stufenbau model exhibits a high degree of universality as it is applicable to both pyramid and network structures.

The constraints of this model become apparent in Eastern Asian systems, particularly within the Japanese social structure. The Japanese system is founded not only on formal legal norms but also on informal rules that do not adhere to the concept of empowerment. While Kelsen's theory may align with the narrow concept of law in Japan, it falls short in elucidating the intricate complexity and richness of its normative system, which governs the society.

Concluding remarks

In this study, I investigated the proposition asserting the universality of the pure theory of law. I operated under the assumption that universality is a matter of degree rather than a binary either-or quality. Consequently, the central inquiry of this chapter revolves around determining the extent to which the pure theory of law can be considered universal and identifying any unique factors that contribute to its higher universality compared to other positivistic theories of a similar nature.

The conclusion is that the pure theory of law has a high degree of universality. Aside from the factors which predestine any positivistic theory to be universal, there is less emphasis on coercion, and the category of Stufenbau's universality is extended. However, this category resonates in both kinds of legal order, Western and Eastern, for different reasons. In Western legal systems, the hierarchical structure of law is linked to the idea of the formal rule of law. However, in Eastern legal systems, particularly in Japan, this categorization is more narrowly tied to law-making processes and bureaucracy. This limited association places constraints on the claim of universality for the pure theory of law, as the theory only elucidates a fraction of the broader system of social control prevalent in Japan.

Bibliography

Barberousse, Anouk and Ludwig, Pascal (2008): "Models as Fictions". In: Suárez, Mauricio: Fictions in Science: Philosophical Essays on Modeling and Idealization. Routledge.

Chang, Young-Hee, Junzhi Wu, Jack, and Weatherall, Mark (2017): "Popular Value Perceptions and Institutional Preference for Democracy in 'Confucian' East Asia". In: Asian Perspective 41, no. 3.

Elgin, Catherine (2009): "Exemplification, Idealization, and Scientific Understanding". In: Suárez, Mauricio (Ed.): Fictions in Science: Philosophical Essays on Modeling and Idealization. Routledge.

Fine, Arthur (1993): "Fictionalism". In: Midwest Studies in Philosophy 18, no. 1.

Frigg, Roman and Hartmann, Stephan (2006): "Models in Science". In: Stanford Encyclopedia of Philosophy Archive, 27 February.

Gao, Sophia and Walayat, Aaron J. (2021): "The Compatibility of Confucianism and Law". In: Pace Law Review 41, no. 1, 12 January, https://doi.org/10.58948/2331-3528.2028.

Golecki, Mariusz J. and Wojciechowski, Bartosz (2009): "The Application of Law within a Multicentric Legal System". In: ed. Marek Zirk-Sadowski / Golecki, Mariusz J. / Wojciechowski, Bartosz (Eds.): Multicentrism as an Emerging Paradigm in Legal Theory. Dia-Logos, Bd. 11. Frankfurt am Main: Peter Lang.

Haley, John Owen (1995): *Authority without Power: Law and the Japanese Paradox*, 1. issued as an Oxford Univ. Press paperback, Studies on Law and Social Control. New York, NY: Oxford Univ. Press.

Kelsen, Hans (1945): *General Theory of Law and State*, transl. Anders Wedberg. Cambridge: Harward University Press.

Kelsen, Hans (1967): *Pure Theory of Law*. The Lawbook Exchange, Ltd.

Kelsen, Hans (1979): *General Theory of Norms*. Oxford: Clarendon Press.

Kelsen, Hans (2010): 'Staatform Und Weltasnchauung'. In: Klecatsky, Hans / Marcic, Rene / Schambeck, Robert (Eds.): *Die Wiener Rechtstheoretische Schule*. vol. 2. Franz Steiner Verlag.

Kelsen, Hans (2019): *Allgemeine Staatslehre*. Ed. Matthias Jestaedt, Studienausgabe der Originalausgabe 1925. Tübingen: Mohr Siebeck.

Kletzer, Christoph (2018): *The Idea of a Pure Theory of Law: An Interpretation and Defence*. Oxford, UK; Portland, Oregon: Hart Publishing.

Lakoff, George and Johnson Mark (2003): *Metaphors We Live By*, 2nd edition. Chicago: University Of Chicago Press.

Marmor, Andrei (2001): *Positive Law and Objective Values*. Oxford [England]; New York: Clarendon Press.

Merkl, Adolf Julius (2010): "Prolegomena Einer Theorie Des Rechtlichen Stufenbaues". In: Klecatsky, Hans / Marcic, Rene / Schambeck Robert (Eds.): Die Wiener Rechtstheoretische Schule: Schriften von Hans Kelsen, Adolf Merkl Alfred Verdross. Franz Steiner Verlag.

Paulson, Stanley L. (1988): "An Empowerment Theory of Legal Norms". In: Ratio Juris 1, no. 1.

Potacs, Michael (2022): "Tree Diagram or Pyramid of Norms?". In: ed. Nicoletta Bersier, Christoph Bezemek, and Frederick Schauer (Eds.): Common Law – Civil Law: The Great Divide? Law and Philosophy Library. Cham: Springer International Publishing.

Rauscher, Frederick (2022): 'Kant's Social and Political Philosophy'. In: *The Stanford Encyclopedia of Philosophy*. Ed. Zalta, Edward N. and Nodelman, Uri. Fall. Metaphysics Research Lab, Stanford University. https://plato.stanford.edu/archives/fall2022/entries/kant-social-political/, accessed 10.01.2024.

Spaak, Torben (2004): "Legal Positivism and the Objectivity of Law". In: Analisi e Diritto.

Teller, Paul (2008): "Fictions, Fictionalization, and Truth in Science". In: Suárez, Mauricio: Fictions in Science: Philosophical Essays on Modeling and Idealization. Routledge.

Tuckness, Alex and Stanton, Tim (2024): "Locke's Political Philosophy". In: Zalta, Edward N. and Nodelman, Uri (Eds.): The Stanford Encyclopedia of Philosophy. Spring. Metaphysics Research Lab, Stanford University. https://plato.stanford.edu/archives/spr2024/entries/locke-political/ accessed 10.01.2024.

Weber, Max (1949): Methodology of Social Sciences. Transl. Shils, Edward and Heary, Finch. New Brunswick, NJ: Transaction Publishers.

Wright, Georg Henrik von (1971): Explanation and Understanding. Cornell University Press.

Zalewska, Monika (2022): "Network, or Stufenbau?". In: ed. Clemens Jabloner, Thomas Olechowski, and Klaus Zeleny (Eds.): Der Stufenbau Des Rechts Auf Dem Prüfstand. MANZ'sche Verlags- und Universitätsbuchhandlung GmbH. https://doi.org/10.5771/9783214250089-23.

Zalewska, Monika (2024): The Dynamic Approach to Hans Kelsen's General Theory of Norms. Hart Publishing, 2024.

Zirk-Sadowski, Marek (2009): "Soft-Kelsenism Versus Multicentrism". In: Golecki, Mariusz / Wojciechowski, Bartosz and Zirk-Sadowski, Marek (Eds.): Multicentrism as a Leading Paradigm in Legal Theory. Vol. 11. Dia-Logos, Peter Lang.

Monika Zalewska
Faculty of Law and Administration, University of Lodz
mzalewska@wpia.uni.lodz.pl

Part 3
Legal Theory

How Much Beauty in Law? How Much Law in Beauty? Aesthetics of Law as a Fifth Branch of the Philosophy of Law

KAMIL ZEIDLER / PAULA CHMIELOWSKA / DAWID KOSTECKI

Abstract: Following Gustav Radbruch's idea presented in a short chapter – titled "Ästhetik des Rechts" – in his famous book "Rechtsphilosophie" (1932) the authors would like to introduce the general concept of the aesthetics of law as a fifth branch of the philosophy of law.

The paper is devoted to the presentation of results in searching for the fifth branch of the philosophy of law, which – apart from the ontology of law, epistemology of law, logic, and legal ethics – completes its research areas analogically to general philosophy.

It turns out that the aesthetic aspects of the law may have practical significance in all five of its phenomena, that is: creating, binding, observing, applying, and interpreting. Moreover, the aesthetics of law also influences legal awareness and attitudes towards the law.

The whole argument is organised in such a way that: 1) external and 2) internal approaches to the aesthetics of law are distinguished and 3) the issue of law as a tool of aestheticisation, will be presented. All this is supported by examples taken from the world of culture and art, where the authors could present so many different allegorical manifestations of Justice, Law, and Politics – both in Eastern and Western art.

Keywords: aesthetics of law, philosophy of law, legal culture, west & east, law & literature

"Law can use art, and art can use law."
G. Radbruch

1 Introductory remarks

The idea of aesthetics of law can raise several doubts and even lead to the conclusion that this is an irrelevant point of view of the main trends in the theory and philosophy of law. That this endeavour probably is not worthy of greater attention for a researcher in the field.

Undoubtedly, the issue of legal aesthetics does not appear directly in the legal theoretical and philosophical literature, or at least those problems, that are important from an aesthetic point of view, are not always perceived from this perspective, much less examined in detail. However, it is worth emphasizing that after the deeper investigation of the literature, especially English, the considerations in the field of legal aesthetics are extensive, interesting, and inspiring, and the very concept of legal aesthetics is already well-established there.

Nevertheless, the authors will try to demonstrate that aesthetics is not a marginal issue, but its scope of influence in jurisprudence is broader than it may be noticed at first. Moreover, it will be tried to show that this broad issue, which includes aesthetic reflection on the law is not only extraordinarily interesting, but – what's more – it may turn out to be an important field also in a practical dimension.

Classic postulates towards law, understood as *lex* (law) come down to it being: *certa* (sure), *scripta* (written), *stricta* (exact), and *praevia* (anterior), and are appropriately connected with the traditional branches of philosophy such as: ontology, epistemology, logic and ethics. Reminding only, ontology is a theory of being, often also called metaphysics; epistemology, gnoseology, is the theory of knowledge; logic is the study of language and research activities, reasoning, defining, and classifying; ethics is science about morality.

In the field of jurisprudence, the interplay of beauty and law raises intriguing questions about the aesthetic dimensions of legal systems and whether they shouldn't be connected with the fifth postulate – *pulchra* (beautiful). Is the beauty we seek in law inherent in the system itself, or is it an appreciation of the elegant application of legal principles? The study of legal aesthetics prompts us to consider not only the structure and coherence of legal frameworks but also the ethical and moral foundations that define their beauty. This gives us a fifth branch of philosophy – aesthetics, which is the general theory of beauty.[1]

The aesthetics of law challenge us to reconcile the need for order and justice with various interpretations of what is aesthetic in the eyes of different cultures and societies. The dilemma between "beauty in law" and "the beauty of law" invites scholars and practitioners to engage in thoughtful dialogue about the subjective nature of legal aesthetics.

The cultural context of beauty in law introduces a rich range of perspectives, emphasizing the need for a global conversation about the universality of legal aesthetics. Also, law educators play a key role in shaping the next generation of lawyers by influencing their understanding of the beauty so deeply inherent in the practice of law. Ultimately, the study of beauty in law, or the beauty of law, encourages us to reflect on the profound connection between aesthetics, justice, and the continuous refinement of legal principles in our ever-changing world.

1 J. Zajadło, "Estetyka – zapomniany piąty człon filozofii prawa", Ruch Prawniczy, Ekonomiczny i Socjologiczny 2016, no. 4, p. 18.

It is important to be aware of the research methods used here – on the one hand, one should use the entire methodological toolkit of the legal sciences, on the other hand, it is necessary to use methods developed in the field of aesthetics, understood as a general philosophical reflection on beauty (the phenomenon of beauty). Additionally, when reaching for specific fields of artistic creation, such as literature, theatre, film, and fine arts, it is necessary to take into account the achievements of these fields. The most important thing – often in the field of law and even more often in the field of aesthetics, and, more broadly, in other areas of philosophy – is the evaluation of it and what comes out of it.

2 An outline of the concept

Although the word "aesthetics" comes from Greek, it has very little to do with the current understanding of the term. Traditionally, the term denotes a general philosophical consideration of beauty and all phenomena that are connected with it. However, in contemporary usage aesthetics is not only considered as a philosophy of beauty, but rather as a philosophy of art. Aesthetics relates to two spaces and one object – on one hand, to the process of creation (which affects in the emergence of a work), on other hand, to its perception and the aesthetic experience produced by an encounter with it. What is more, meta-aesthetics must also be considered, as all those attempts that seek to grasp the entirety of aesthetics within a specific theory.

Both in the work of Plato and Aristotle, we find reflections on art and reflections on beauty, yet they did not make a connection between these two. It was Alexander Baumgarten who linked reflections on art with reflections on beauty, at the same time distinguishing aesthetics as a general theory of beauty.[2] In Kant's writings aesthetics was understood rather differently. In his *Critique of Pure Reason* Kant linked it with sensory cognition, for later in his *Critique of Judgment*, referred it to the category of the beautiful. Initially, Kantian aesthetics was no more than an epistemology of phenomena, when in time came to be called phenomenology, while the term "aesthetics" took another meaning as an object experienced by someone may be a source of pleasure or unpleasantness or of offence. In the work of Georg W. F. Hegel, who, *inter alia*, conducted lectures in the philosophy of fine arts, aesthetics was narrowed down to beauty

2 See: N. Davey, "Baumgarten, Alexander G(ottlieb)" (in:) A Companion to Aesthetics, eds S. Davies, K. M. Higgins, R. Hopkins, R. Stecker, D. E. Cooper, 2nd ed., Blackwell Publishing, Malden- Oxford 2009, p. 162–163; see also: L. P. Wessell, "Alexander Baumgarten's Contribution to the Development of Aesthetics", Journal of Aesthetics and Art Criticism 1972, vol. 30, pp. 333–342; N. Davey, "Baumgarten's Aesthetics: A post Gadamerian Reflection", British Journal of Aesthetics 1989, vol. 2, pp. 101–115.

in art, the meaning of the term that is widely used nowadays. Lemcke and Mutermilch saw aesthetics in broader terms, as a "science of looking at the world".[3]

Within the philosophy of law, we have to refer to Gustav Radbruch's idea, inspired by his artistic interests, who wrote about the aesthetics of law: "Law can use art, and art can use law. Like all other cultural products, the law needs a sensual medium that allows it to be articulated: language, gesture, toga, insignia, symbolism, and impressive architecture. Therefore, sensual means of expressing law, like other means of this type, are subject to aesthetic evaluation".[4] He wrote that searching for a poetics in law was an unfortunate idea since law is one of the most ossified (cultural) institutions, while art is distinguished by an exceptional plasticity, capable of keeping up with the changing spirit of the times. Still, law and art remain in a state of enmity, that is quite natural to both of them.[5] Radbruch's attitude to the aesthetics of law resulted partly from his neo-Kantian philosophical principles, e. g. he considered law as a phenomenon of the culture world that is suspended between the world of ideal and the world of nature, but also partly from his biography as he was a lawyer showing a great deal of interest in art, creating many works in the theory of culture, art history and literary studies.[6]

When outlining the subject of the aesthetics of law there must be distinguished five research fields: 1) that of general problems of the aesthetics of law (which includes attempts to construct some baseline definition of the aesthetics of law but also attempts to elucidate its basic concepts);[7] 2) that of problems relating to aesthetic values and evaluation as a specific intellectual activity; 3) that of the comparison of activities in the researched field of aesthetics concerning the work of jurists (including all the five phenomena of law, which are: creation, validity, observance, application, and interpretation); 4) that of law as an object of aesthetics that applies to the shape and form of law, but also to its content, and last but not least 5) that of cultural products of varying kinds, e. g. works of fine arts and literary works referring to the law, its symbols, and

3 See: K. Zeidler, Aesthetics of Law, Gdańsk–Warsaw 2020.

4 G. Radbruch, Rechtsphilosophie, Verlag von Quelle & Meyer in Leipzig 1932 after: Gustav Radbruch Rechtsphilosophie. Studienausgabe, Herausgegeben von Ralf Dreirer und Stanley L. Paulson, 2., überarbeitete Auflage, C. F. Müller Verlag Heiderlberg.

5 Ibidem.

6 Radbruch personally valued the caricatures and satirical images of courtrooms and lawyers by Honoré Daumier (ill.1, 3, 54); see more: G. Radbruch, "Honoré Daumier: Gens de Justice" (in:) *idem*, Gesamtausgabe, vol. 5, ed. A. Kaufmann, Literatur-und kunsthistorische Schriften, ed. H. Kleiner, C. F. Muller Verlag, Heidelberg 1997, pp. 234–244; G. Radbruch, "Karikaturen der Justiz. Lithographien von Honoré Daumier' (in:) *idem*, Gesamtausgabe, vol. 5, pp. 245–289; see also: M. Tola, "The art of Law: Legal Drama in Artworks", Daily Art Magazine 2020.10.20.

7 This is important because: "Lack of precise definition is a great snag in every dispute, in every interpretation, leading ideas astray, and confusing and obscuring even the most transparent issue"; M. Mutermilch, Idea w sztuce, M. Arct, Warszawa 1902, p. 8.

phenomena.[8] However, it is necessary to adopt the broadest sense of the concept of law. Not only to include a certain formalized normative system, but also processes of legislation, that is its creation, application, and process of interpretation, together with research and teaching (that creates legal doctrine).

Radbruch wrote that the separation of law from art may be attributed to the fact that the aesthetics value of the law took on a separate autonomous manifestation, independent of any participation of art in its pure form. It is necessary to mention is that aesthetics in itself is not a law. It is something external to it, something extra-legal, however, it has undoubtedly its place within the law, just as the law does within aesthetics.

3 External and internal frame

When researching a system, including a normative system, the research process is also influenced by the researcher's relationship to the subject under study. He may study a system to which he is external because he is not an element of the system being studied does not recognise its principles or is indifferent to them. The subject of research may also be a system to which the researcher somehow belongs, is an element of it or is to some extent subordinated to it – either in the formal or actual sense, or both. Both approaches indicated above have their advantages and disadvantages. The first allows – as a rule – for greater objectivity, but is most often marked by a lack of empirical reflection on the subject of research because the researcher is outside the system. The second one – on the contrary – allows getting to know the subject being examined from the inside, but this may result in taking an even extremely subjective position towards the subject being examined.

In its external frame, the aesthetics of law is concerned with manifestations of the law, legal motifs, symbols, signs, and inspirations, which are noticeable in the fine arts through centuries. The nine daughters of Zeus and Mnemosyne[9], guardian deities of the fine arts and learning have gained another, tenth sister, Cinematographia, who might not be the last yet unknown sister, and maybe one of them would be related to legal studies. Probably, if considered deeply, the law could be of interest to each of the

---

8 See: K. Zeidler, Aesthetics of Law, Gdańsk- Warsaw 2020.

9 Erato (the beloved one, the muse of love poetry, presented carrying a small lyre), Euterpe (the joyous one, the muse of lyrics poetry, shown carrying an *aulos*), Clio (proclaiming fame, the muse of history, shown carrying a roll of papyrus), Calliope (fair of face, the muse of epic and heroic poetry, shown holding a stylus and a small tablet to write on), Melpomene (singing, the muse of tragedy, shown carrying a tragic mask), Thalia (the delectable one, the muse of comedy, shown with a comic mask and with a shepherd's staff and a wreath of ivy), Terpsichore (who loves dance, the muse of dance, shown carrying a lyre and a plectrum), Urania (the heavenly one, the muse of astronomy and geometry, shown holding compasses and a ball), Polyhymnia (the muse of sacred choral poetry, without any attribute, but always shown deep in thought).

Muses. We do, however already have a goddess – *Iustitia* (Lady Justice) who is holding scales to represent the impartiality of the court's decisions and a sword as a symbol of the power of justice. She is like a muse herself being depicted by artists across centuries. Because the concept of Justice is embodied in the shape of a woman, it is always a mixture of physiology and language, together with a mixture of how Lady Justice as an institution intends to present herself but also how viewers can actually interpret her.[10]

Zajadło notes that "in the history of literature, sculpture, painting, architecture, film, and theatre, it is possible to find countless examples of works in which the source of artistic inspiration has been what we can broadly understand as issues of law and lawyers".[11] A view of the law as "material for art" may be both external – when it relates to a non-lawyer looking at law and its performance from the sidelines, not being directly influenced by the law – or internal – when it refers to a participant in given legal events. However, in the broadest sense, everyone, without any exception, is an addressee of law.

Radbruch considered that law may be a material for art and as such enters within the scope of aesthetic valuation.[12] Yet, what is important is that in the external frame, the object of evaluation is not so much the law itself, but the work of the artist itself. Even though we might be tempted not only to judge the aesthetics of the creator that shaped his work but also on what constitutes the object of his work.[13] Thus, it is worth recalling that although the object of sensory inspection and aesthetic experience is the work of art, via art's agency and mediation that object may also be law itself. Radbruch himself is an excellent example. His achievements, also outside the scope of law, in the field of the history of art, literature, and philosophy of culture, are impressive. He wrote about many artists, among whom were: Michelangelo, Shakespeare, Tolstoi, and Goethe. Poetry, music, and the dance of death in art were only some of the topics he wrote about. His work is even more impressive since he was able to discover in the world of art dozens of examples of its varied links with law.[14] Fortunately, still today such general humanist interest can be found among authors.[15]

The object of the aesthetics of law in an internal frame is law itself. That means that the strictly juristic activity may be seen and examined as a creative activity as such.

---

10 V. Hayaert, Lady Justice, An Anatomy of Allegory, Edinburgh University Press 2023, p. 2.

11 J. Zajadło, "Estetyka – zapomniany piąty człon filozofii prawa", Ruch Prawniczy, Ekonomiczny i Socjologiczny 2016, no.4, p. 25.

12 G. Radbruch, Rechtsphilosophie, Verlag von Quelle & Meyer in Leipzig 1932 after: Gustav Radbruch Rechtsphilosophie. Studienausgabe, Herausgegeben von Ralf Dreirer und Stanley L. Paulson, 2., überarbeitete Auflage, C. F. Müller Verlag Heiderlberg.

13 J. Zajadło, "Estetyka – zapomniany piąty człon filozofii prawa", Ruch Prawniczy, Ekonomiczny i Socjologiczny 2016, no.4, p. 25.

14 G. Radbruch, Gesamtausgabe, vol. 4, ed. A. Kaufmann, Kulturphilosophische und Kulturhistorische Schriften, ed. G. Spendel, C. F. Muller Verlag, Heidelberg 2002; G. Radbruch, Gesamtausgabe, vol. 5.

15 See: S. Waltoś, Na tropach doktora Fausta i inne szkice, WSiP, Warszawa 2004.

Fig. 1 Biagio di Antonio Tucci, An Allegory of Justice, c. 1470–1475, Uffizi Gallery, Florence, photo K. Zeidler

If we start a discussion about the categories of aesthetics, it's worth starting with the Tatarkiewicz's *A History of Six Concepts* [Dzieje sześciu pojęć]. He distinguishes six fundamental categories of aesthetics: 1) art, 2) beauty, 3) form, 4) creativity 5) reproducibility and 6) aesthetics experiences.[16] Hence, we should ask six related questions to those categories in the aspects of aesthetics of law.

16 W. Tatarkiewicz, Dzieje sześciu pojęć: sztuka, piękno, forma, twórczość, odtwórczość, przeżycia estetyczne, PWN, Warszawa 1988, p. 393.

First, ask the question: can the law be seen as art? Recalling the words of Ulpian: *nam, ut eleganter Celsus definit, ius es tars boni et aequi* (as Celsus elegantly puts it, the law is the art of the good and the equitable). It might seem like a definition of law as such, but it also means something more, it renders the spirit of the law, its ultimate purpose both the legislator and for the judge and probably also for every addressee of a legal norm. The word "art", understood as a conscious act of human activity, has within it an impulse towards perfection, an ideal, that as we all know well, is impossible to attain.[17] The formulation of law as art can be already be found in literature from antiquity. Goodrich and Hayaert describe the encounter with legal books as: "The threshold of the text, the first encounter is with the image of the collection, of the tablets, tables or library of law, and then and more specifically with the boards and clasps of the individual volume. The frontispiece of the law book will classically have heavy letters, often in gothic typeface, coloured ink and an emblematic image, a frontispiece that forms the facies or face of the work".[18] It already sounds like an invitation to read an art piece, not just a technical document.

Second, beauty, or the question: can the law as such be beautiful? In subjective terms, one may like the law more than another. However, does this liking correspond to the aesthetic value that is beauty? Such evaluation can be made based on many factors and refer to many functions of law. We can consider the fact that the law is beautifully written, in good language, edited precisely, following all formal requirements, balanced, symmetrical, etc. On a macro level, the question relates to whether law as an idea of or a system of law, can be beautiful. Plato said: "The maintenance of measure and proportion is always beauty".

Third is form, or, the question: should law fulfil defined formal conditions, and if so, are any of those demands of an aesthetic character? Formal regulations do give a defined shape to reality. They put the world in order, and organise political, economic and social life. There is a poetic definition of law, which conveys the essence of the function of law in the aspect of the form: the law is a victory of order over chaos. It is worth citing Mutermilch here: "The most splendid idea that is not fixed in an appropriate form does not achieve anything great: only the ideal harmony of the external beautiful form (although in the sense that a given moment prescribes for beauty), with a rich internal content, creates a masterpiece".[19]

Fourth, creativity, or in the case of law are we dealing with creativity? If a demand for creativity is a novelty in action or work, then the creation of law itself is a kind of

17 Mutermilch remarks that: "We buried dreams of 'absolute beauty' long ago, and even the 'ideal' beauty of Greek sculpture is now so distant from us that we can admire it coolly"; M. Mutermilch, Idea w sztuce, M.Arct, Warszawa 1902, p.27.

18 M. Fumaroli, L'ecole du silence, Paris: Flammarion 1998; after: Genealogies of Legal Vision ed. P. Goodrich, V. Hayaert, Routledge, London–New York 2015, p.3.

19 M. Mutermilch, Idea w sztuce, M.Arct, Warszawa 1902, p.29.

creativity, as a result of which emerges a *sui generis* piece of work. In terms of the application of the law, or during its interpretation, we may, indeed, refer to a particular creative act, and it might possess creative character just as the interpretation of a literary work does. The result of both creating and interpreting is never fixed in advance. It is usually seen as a process of either finding the best solutions or searching for the truth within the framework of regulations contained in other legislative acts. Hence, they are in essence, creative acts of human will.

Fifth, reproducibility, or in the case of law do we have to do with reproducibility? The answer to this question always has to be yes. Zajadło put it accurately: "one can imagine discussions of the legislator which consider it as a collegiate (institutional) artist creating a work, and of judges who, depending on their legal-philosophical position, become in the process of applying and interpreting the law either faithful and barely creative copyist, or feeble forgers destroying the original, or finally, autonomous artists building their own work on top of the original".[20]

Finally, sixth, aesthetic experience, which leads us to the question: can the law be a source of aesthetic experience? The reception of the law, attitudes towards the law and in some concrete cases, specific court proceedings can certainly supply such experience. The reflections towards the idea that court procedure is a kind of performance is surely to agree. Many 'properties' have there purely aesthetic function. Stanisław Mikke is surely right in the way he understands the court in a literal sense: "The court is not a theatre. There – in the courtroom – there is no curtain, no smell of greasepaint. It is not a 'game of appearances' performed by people dressed in robes."[21] All that is true, however, do not those same procedures lead us to a mythologisation of the court's authority and power, give sanction to customs, not prescribe the participants in the court proceedings specific 'roles' and finally, compel lawyers to don costumes? Goodrich starts his book with a short story: "A judge springs out of his car on the way to court in downtown Chicago and takes photographs of an inflatable rat. A while later he inserts these photographs into a decision involving another insufflated rodent used in a union protest."[22] If only more of them did this!

Thus, if we finally refer to all six fundamental categories of aesthetics mentioned by Tatarkiewicz, and if we discuss e. g. the formal side of a legislative act, which is the final work of a complex legislative process, we can notice several of the mentioned above features of aesthetics in law.

---

20 J. Zajadło, "Estetyka – zapomniany piąty człon filozofii prawa", Ruch Prawniczy, Ekonomiczny i Socjologiczny 2016, no.4, p. 24.

21 S. Mikke, "Zachowaj ład, ('Bezmiar sprawiedliwości')," Edukacja Prawnicza 2007, no.6 (90), p. 46.

22 P. Goodrich, Judicial uses of images, Vision in decision, Oxford University Press 2023, p. 1.

Fig. 2 Honoré Daumier, The legislative Stomach, 1834, Metropolitan Museum of Art, New York

4 Law as a tool of aestheticisation

A third formulation of the aesthetics of law is law in functional terms. It becomes so, when law becomes a tool of aestheticisation of everyday life, and above all, an instrument of both negative and positive intervention in the process. Most often it concerns normative-legal regulations referring to art, but also such situations, in which legal norms mark out a place for what is aesthetic. We can at least distinguish dozen different fields where law is used as such a tool, only mentioned here briefly, as describing and giving examples could take the form of the entire new article.

First, one can find laws that aim to protect the language, where legislators usually refer to the aesthetic values of language, as a part of national identity worth defending in times of globalisation. This defence (e. g. as in Poland) can consist of: 1) care for the correct use of the language, at the same time enhancing the linguistic competences of its users, 2) resistance to the vulgarization of it (anti-aestheticisation), 3) broadening the knowledge of it and its role in culture, 4) spreading awareness about regional variants and dialects, 5) promoting the language in the world, 6) supporting teaching system at home and abroad.

Second is the cultural heritage law, which is today recognised as a complex branch of law.[23] It can be a separate legal act concerning protection and preservation of monuments together with implementing acts on e. g. conservation and archaeological work. It aims for all agencies of public administration (but not only them as private entities also play significant roles) undertaking any role in activities concerning the protection of monuments to regulate e. g. 1) legal, organisational and financial conditions to fulfil its role, 2) to prevent threats that could damage a monument and subsequently its value, 3) to thwart any future improper use and destruction of it, 4) to prevent illegal removal, theft or disappearance, 5) to monitor the state of maintenance and allocation of a monument, 6) to respect the other tasks mentioned in other legal acts concerning environmental matters or spatial planning

Third, city planning or in legal language spatial planning and management. It is based on the concept of 'spatial order' that is supposed to create a harmonious whole within orderly relations of socio-economic, environmental, cultural, compositional aesthetic factors and requirements.

Fig. 3 No spitting in wastebins – subject to a fine, Hong Kong, photo K. Zeidler

23 K. Zeidler, M. Wegrzak, Cultural heritage law as a complex branch of law, Gdańskie Studia Prawnicze, 2(50)/2021, p. 11–27.

Fourth, is architecture, that is regulated in vast acts. Worth mentioning is that it goes beyond the scope of architect himself, but regulates such matters as security of life and property, health, environment, accessibility of buildings for handicapped, all with the respect and consideration of artistic and historical values, the aesthetics of the architectural form and the unique character of the real estate.

Fifth, intellectual property law. One that in the era of AI and newest technologies is changing so fast. Its subject matter is every manifestation of creative activity taking any form, irrespective of value, purpose and means of expression. However, this law is pointed towards protection of creator and their rights.

Sixth, concerning the field of media and advertising. In a very distinctive manner it links law, ethics and aesthetics. The first two designate the framework for permitted activity, when the third is mainly regulated by the trends and specialist.

Seventh, the law of art, or being more precise, extensive legal acts regulating the variety of aspects of art. Starting with the widest, yet the base of legal rights, we should mention freedom of artistic expression and all the laws setting limits to this artistic freedom (the so-called restrictions). One can give many examples of interference of the law in the world of art, even those that lead to disputes in court.

Fig. 4 Women Only – Information about behaviour order, Tokyo, photo P. Chmielowska

5 Concluding remarks

To sum up the above considerations, the first stage of further research should be to organise the topics covered by the aesthetics of law. In this general outline, one can even encounter views that the aesthetics of law rises to the rank of an autopoietic, i.e. self-regulating, self-organising and self-creating system or idea.[24] To a large extent, lawyers have a great responsibility to ensure that beauty, harmony, and symmetry prevail, and not to let the ugliness triumph[25].

We should mention Chaim Perelman who once wrote an article "The Rhetorical Point of View in Ethics: A Program"[26], in which he suggests that contemporary research should focus on links between rhetoric and ethics, calling his suggestions a programme. This meets a demand formulated as well by Radbruch over 100 ago. He wrote that it was necessary to demand a systemic aesthetics of law, one that had not yet developed into a coherent whole.[27] It might appear bold to some to seek for connections between law and music, law and art and literature. Even more so, to call law an art! However, in the practical dimension, the most important, although not the only, dimension of research in the field of legal aesthetics is turning to the problem of shaping the legal awareness of society through means other than the text of a normative act.

This allows us to see how practically significant – although perhaps very imprecise and highly intuitive – the results could be. The aesthetics of law concerns the important issue of the impact of cognitive and emotional factors on the shape of law, as well as its prestige. Therefore, in the field of the aesthetics of law, it is the external view – that is, not so much that of lawyers themselves, but of people who shape their image of justice, law and lawyers through specific works – that will come to the fore.

Bibliography

Davey N., "Baumgarten, Alexander G(ottlieb)" (in:) A Companion to Aesthetics, eds S. Davies, K. M. Higgins, R. Hopkins, R. Stecker, D. E. Cooper, 2nd ed., Blackwell Publishing, Malden-Oxford 2009, p 162–163.

Fumaroli M., L'ecole du silence, Paris: Flammarion 1998; after: Genealogies of Legal Vision ed. P. Goodrich, V. Hayaert, Routledge, London–New York 2015.

Goodrich P., Judicial uses of images, Vision in decision, Oxford University Press 2023.

Hayaert V., Lady Justice, An Anatomy of Allegory, Edinburgh University Press 2023.

---

24 R. Kevelson (ed.), Law and Aesthetics, "New Studies in Aesthetics", vol. 11, New York 1992.

25 D. Kostecki, How much beauty in law? How much law in beauty? A Review of Kamil Zeidler's Aesthetics of Law, Archiwum Filozofii Prawa i Filozofii Społecznej 2022, vol. 3, p. 118.

26 Ch. Perelman, "The Rhetorical Point of View in Ethics: A Program", Communication 1981, vol. 6, pp. 315–320.

27 G. Radbruch, Rechtsphilosophie, Verlag von Quelle & Meyer in Leipzig 1932 after: Gustav Radbruch Rechtsphilosophie. Studienausgabe, Herausgegeben von Ralf Dreirer und Stanley L. Paulson, 2., überabeitete Auflage, C. F. Müller Verlag Heidelberg.

Kevelson R. (ed.), Law and Aesthetics, "New Studies in Aesthetics", vol. 11, New York 1992.
Kostecki D., How much beauty in law? How much law in beauty? A Review of Kamil Zeidler's Aesthetics of Law, Archiwum Filozofii Prawa i Filozofii Społecznej 2022, vol. 3.
Mikke S., "Zachowaj ład, ('Bezmiar sprawiedliwości')," Edukacja Prawnicza 2007, no.6 (90).
Mutermilch M., Idea w sztuce, M. Arct, Warszawa 1902, p. 8.
Perelman Ch., "The Rhetorical Point of View in Ethics: A Program", Communication 1981, vol. 6.
Radbruch G., "Honoré Daumier: Gens de Justice" (in:) *idem*, Gesamtausgabe, vol. 5, ed. A. Kaufmann, Literatur- und kunsthistorische Schriften, ed. H. Kleiner, C. F. Müller Verlag, Heidelberg 1997.
Radbruch G., "Karikaturen der Justiz. Lithographien von Honoré Daumier' (in:) *idem*, Gesamtausgabe, vol. 5, pp. 245–289; see also: M. Tola, "The art of Law: Legal Drama in Artworks", Daily Art Magazine 2020.10.20.
Radbruch G., Gesamtausgabe, vol. 4, ed. A. Kaufmann, Kulturphilosophische und Kulturhistorische Schriften, ed. G. Spendel, C. F. Müller Verlag, Heidelberg 2002; G. Radbruch, Gesamtausgabe, vol. 5.
Radbruch G., Rechtsphilosophie, Verlag von Quelle & Meyer in Leipzig 1932 after: Gustav Radbruch Rechtsphilosophie. Studienausgabe, Herausgegeben von Ralf Dreirer und Stanley L. Paulson, 2., überabeitete Auflage, C. F. Müller Verlag, Heidelberg.
Tatarkiewicz W., Dzieje sześciu pojęć: sztuka, piękno, forma, twórczość, odtwórczość, przeżycia estetyczne, PWN, Warszawa 1988.
Waltoś S., Na tropach doktora Fausta i inne szkice, WSiP, Warszawa 2004.
Wessell L. P., "Alexander Baumgarten's Contribution to the Development of Aesthetics", Journal of Aesthetics and Art Criticism 1972, vol. 30, pp. 333–342.
N. Davey, "Baumgarten's Aesthetics: A post Gadamerian Reflection", British Journal of Aesthetics 1989, vol. 2.
Zajadło J., "Estetyka – zapomniany piąty człon filozofii prawa", Ruch Prawniczy, Ekonomiczny i Socjologiczny 2016, no. 4.
Zeidler K., Aesthetics of Law, Gdańsk–Warsaw 2020.
Zeidler K., Wegrzak M., Cultural heritage law as a complex branch of law, Gdańskie Studia Prawnicze, 2(50)/2021.

Kamil Zeidler
Department of Theory and Philosophy of the State and Law, Faculty of Law and Administration, University of Gdansk
kamil.zeidler@ug.edu.pl

Paula Chmielowska
Department of Theory and Philosophy of the State and Law, Faculty of Law and Administration, University of Gdansk
paula.chmielowska@ug.edu.pl

Dawid Kostecki
Department of Theory, Philosophy and History of Law, College of Law Kozminski University
dkostecki@kozminski.edu.pl

Is It a Matter of Degree?*
On Recent Views on Law and Coercion

MOTOKI MIURA

Abstract: Our intuition tells us that questions of law often come down to ones of coercion, and vice versa. So, can the law itself be reduced to coercion? This long-debated problem has attracted as many answers as its participants. Even if we limit the scope to the last century, coercion has been subjected to many descriptions in relation to law, such as putative sources of the obligatory nature of laws or an institutional feature required by natural necessity but conceptually unnecessary, to name just two. Unlike these prior works, recent discussions on coercion in relation to the concept of law have seemed to focus on the law's *degree* of coerciveness. The present paper examines this approach to the coercive nature of law through its relationship with existing approaches.

Keywords: coercion, concept of law, natural necessity, society of angels, non-coercive regulatory methods, experimental jurisprudence

The concepts of law and coercion sit comfortably together in a single sentence. We discuss whether the law should authorise the use of coercive measures against certain kinds of behaviour, not just in university classrooms, but also on social media. Despite this apparent cogence, it is hardly obvious if law itself is coercion. Thus, legal philosophers have long discussed how coercion fares as a component of the concept of law. Does coercion serve the concept of law well? Is it a good candidate at all? These questions cut through different schools of legal philosophy, from legal positivism to natural law.[1] Therefore, it merits philosophical attention to ask if coercion is a necessary part of law.

Quite contrary to the philosophical concerns noted above, the place of coercion in law has become even more shaky in recent years, given developments in alternative regulatory technologies. Law can induce desired behaviours by changing the environ-

* This work was supported by JSPS KAKENHI grant number 22KJ2662. This paper was first presented at IVR Japan, at Chiba University, on 17 September 2023. I would like to thank the participants for their comments and questions, particularly one by Bertram Lomfeld, which motivated me to add two footnotes (15 and 42).

1 I leave it open to the reader to decide with which school it fits best.

ment surrounding ordinary citizens.[2] If one were to write a catalogue of regulatory methods, the section for non-coercive options would be more diverse than what it would have been in the past, from the physical barriers surrounding prisons to the makeup of online communications. There are even less intrusive means, such as nudging, that would add a few pages to the catalogue.[3]

The relationship between law and coercion has been the subject of heated philosophical discussions; however, it seems there has been a shift in these conversations' emphasis. Contrary to the long-standing treatment of coercion as a (putative) constituent of the concept of 'law', and thus sometimes asking 'Is coercion a necessary part of the concept of law?', an increasing number of papers are now dedicated to the nature of coerciveness of the law *as a matter of degree*. Of course, the *degree* of coerciveness can come in multiple modalities, such as: '*How* oppressive is it?' (descriptive), or 'Should it be *that* coercive?' (normative). Notwithstanding this possibility, or rather, all the more, given the variety of *degrees*, this paper asks the question broadly and examines what impact this shift of focus – if there is, indeed, a shift – could have on discussions of *law and coercion* in particular, or even the philosophy of law in general.

This paper consists of three parts. The first section summarises the place of coercion in relation to the concept of law. The second section describes recent challenges that treat the relationship between law and coercion as a matter of degree. The final section concludes with several suggestions.

1 A Summary of Coercion through Law

It seems only right to reserve the first section of this paper for a summary, to ensure that readers know what this paper aims to address, for law and coercion[4] meet at almost every corner of jurisprudence. The questions of law can often come down to

2 See Lessig (1998, p. 663). From walls to consumer products like computers and cars, the environment we take for granted shapes what we can do in it.

3 Thaler and Sunstein (2021).

4 The concept of coercion is a weighty theme in itself, so it is not reasonable to hope to provide a full account here. One way would be to equate coercion with threats, that is, the communication of psychological pressure. As Anderson (2010) points out, this kind understanding of coercion presupposes a '"success" term' (4) framework, as it all comes down to whether the threat successfully induces a desired course of action from the threatened party. Should one try to apply this explanation faithfully to a given legal system, it will suffer agent-relativity, given that, whether or not the law is seen as coercive hinges on the attitude of the citizen subject to the legal mandate. For instance, those who obey speed limits wholeheartedly, as well as those wealthy enough to regard speeding tickets as top-up for high-speed driving, would probably reject the coercive nature of speeding laws. The success term approach is useful for other purposes (as will be shown in Section 2.1), but not as a general or essential feature of law. For a working hypothesis, it suffices for now to say that law tracks compliance by initially setting (and often openly declaring) sanctions while simultaneously establishing safeguards through administrative and judicial enforcements. (For the compliance-tracking account of coercion, see Yaffe (2003).)

ones of coercion, whether civil or criminal. People are often so desperate that they resort to legal resolution, expecting to accomplish the *right* thing with, if necessary, an authorised use of force, so much so that one might think this is the point of legal resolution in the end. Conversely, coercion can become a matter of law: threats,[5] let alone the use of brute force, invite legal consequences. Though they are important in themselves, there is another question of law and coercion that digs into the root of these phenomena: Does the nature of law come down to coercion in the end? This section summarises how coercion has been treated in jurisprudence, especially regarding the concept of law.

Does the nature of law come down to coercion in the end? The situation used to be (or still is) rather desperate for those who argue in the affirmative. Especially after H. L. A. Hart's strenuous overhaul of John Austin and Jeremy Bentham's command theory of law, as well as Hans Kelsen's pure theory of law, coercion has assumed a rather minor role in explaining the essence of law. As Hart's canonical work claims, threatening citizens cannot possibly exhaust the role of law.[6] Laws help us to complete transactions safely, coordinate behaviours in groups and make collective decisions. As a concept, the point or the means of law precedes the need to coerce people, let alone their obedience. It twists the entire picture of the legal world if we only consider the last resort law can possibly deploy.[7]

The above was only true until Frederick Schauer's *Force of Law* (2015) was published. It pointed out that the secondary, auxiliary role assigned to coercion in law comes from the essentialist methodology of legal positivists, like Joseph Raz (and Hart to a certain extent). Schauer's book and his preceding works[8] had revitalised the debate over the law and coercion.[9] According to Schauer, Hart and those who adopt his framework have long assumed that the law should be understood from the perspective of 'puzzled' people, that is, of those who are 'willing to do what is required, if only [they] can be told what it is'.[10] Raz pushed this point further by arguing that law can be said to exist even in a society made up of agents devoid of intention to act against what the law says – that is, a society with a sanction-less legal system, or 'the society of angels'.

---

5 The 'threat' here refers to a broader mode of activities merely for the sake of introduction. It would be controversial to include blackmail under the category of threat. Nozick regarded blackmail as unproductive exchange because it can be coercive and will even undermine the (morally) expected baseline ((1974), 84–87; (1997), 29f & 344n.33). Rothbard, unconvinced by this argument, criticised the idea of productive exchange and suggested that we should take it as a business transaction (1998), 245–253.

6 Hart (2012).

7 Oberdiek (1976) and MacCormick ((1982), 232–246) are also aligned with Hart's views.

8 Schauer (2010) in particular.

9 Along with Bezemek and Ladavac (2016), several issues of *Jurisprudence* and *Ratio Juris* were dedicated to *The Force of Law*.

10 Hart (2012), 40.

Consider the following. It is gravely misleading to say the above-mentioned works were produced *solely* to answer the question 'Is law fully coercive?' Coercion can appear only marginal in relation to the key arguments in the abovementioned theories. For Hart, for instance, the putative connection between law and coercion was just one of the three underlying themes of *The Concept of Law*. Furthermore, the relevance of coercion often constitutes a presupposition of relevant arguments. They may even be corollaries of basics insights lying behind. Raz's iconic thought experiment as discussed in 1.3, for example, in a way harkens back to a much bigger picture of practical reasoning.

Having said that, let us take a look at those canonical works one by one. One can identify several focus points regarding the point of coercion in law: the putative source of the law's obligatory nature, natural necessity, and its conceptual (un)necessary nature.

1.1 The Putative Source of the Law's Obligatory Nature

Hart provides insight into the first two: the obligatory nature of law and natural necessity of coercion. He opens *The Concept of Law* with three persistent questions:

> How does law differ from and how is it related to orders backed by threats? How does legal obligation differ from, and how is it related to, moral obligation? What are rules and to what extent is law an affair of rules?[11]

The role of coercion in law is a theme that permeates *The Concept of Law*, as it appears Hart was anxious to distinguish law from mere coercion as much as from concepts of morality.[12] Hart hastened to add that a definition of the word 'law' cannot deliver full justice to these vexed questions. A contrast with Austin is of help here. Austin sought to define (positive) law as a triad of command, duty and sanction.[13] In this view, the idea of law directly incorporates the evil it brings in the event of disobedience to legal duty. By contrast, Hart's description of law yields a much more social nature: the union of primary and secondary rules.[14] Hart also mentions the context in which people

---

11 Hart (2012), 13 [emphasis added].

12 As Hart writes at the end of Ch. 1, the purpose of the book is to provide 'a better understanding of the resemblances and differences between law, coercion, and morality, as types of social phenomena' (ibid., 17.)

13 'Each of the three terms signifies the same notion; but each denotes a different part of that notion, and connotes the residue' (Austin (1995), 25).

14 Clearly, Hart was aware that he was trying to replace Austin's idea of the unlimited sovereign with secondary rules (rules of recognition, rules of change, and rules of adjudication) (2012), 110). As for the possibility of Hart mirroring Austin's theory, see Miura (2018). Perhaps he was speaking metaphorically when

speak of (legal) obligations from an internal point of view,[15] but he clearly did not regard coercion as central when describing the obligatory nature of law.[16] In this respect, Hart disagreed with the idea that coercion does a good job explaining the obligatory nature of law.

1.2 Natural Necessity

There is more to Hart's concept of law than the preceding part. He offers a second explanation of coercion in law, claiming that law is necessary in a practical way. To illustrate this, one needs to read beyond jurisprudentially popular chapters in *The Concept of Law* (Chapters I–VII). In Chapter IX, Hart tackles one of the central themes mentioned above, the distinction between law and morality.

After carefully trying to separate his view from a moralised, or teleological, account of the law, Hart draws readers' attention to basic natural conditions of law and tries to provide an empirical explanation for the intuitive association between law and morality.[17]

> We can say, given the setting of natural facts and aims, which make sanctions both possible and necessary in a municipal system, that this is a natural necessity; and some such phrase is needed also to convey the status of the minimum forms of protection for persons, property, and promises which are similarly indispensable features of municipal law.[18]

Within this case for natural necessity of coercive measures, Hart describes people's attitudes towards law:

> 'Sanctions' are therefore required not as the normal motive for obedience, but as a *guarantee* that those who would voluntarily obey shall not be sacrificed to those who would not. To obey, without this, would be to risk going to the wall. Given this standing danger, what reason demands is *voluntary* co-operation in a *coercive* system.[19]

---

he installed the rule of recognition to 'substitute for' the idea of the unlimited sovereign. Indeed, there are other things that we can find in Hart but not in Austin.

15 Hart (2012), 82–91.

16 Certainly, all rules do not exist to impose duties. Some rules specify conditions under which certain acts, even those of a private person, may be legally binding or effective ('power-conferring rules', Hart (2012), 27–41).

17 Hart's list includes: (1) Human vulnerability, (2) approximate equality, (3) limited altruism, (4) limited resources and (5) limited understanding and strength of will (2012), 194–198.

18 Ibid., 199.

19 Ibid., 198.

Two conditions should follow this explanation. First, as Hart admits, the natural necessity of coercion does not entail the conceptual necessity of law itself; it is rather practical.[20] It is practically necessary, yet 'ancillary', to borrow Hart's terminology.[21] This is why natural necessity should be treated separately from the putative source of the law's obligatory nature. One could say coercion is a motivational force, rather than one that reflects the conceptual structure of law. The second condition concerns civil law. What Hart says seems to fit well with crime and punishment, but it is rather a contortion to say all civil remedies are sanctions. Still, as MacCormick says, 'processes of the coercive enforcement of judiciary awarded remedies are an addendum, an additional security',[22] in case some people disregard the court's decisions.

1.3 Conceptual Necessity

Following the argument in Section 1.1, Hart's focus of discussion moves to the status of coercion in relation to the concept of law. To put it differently, the question 'is coercion a necessary part of the concept of law?' becomes more prominent, and the answers provided are more diverse than a simple yes or no. Let us consider the two sides of the argument.

It is not too farfetched to say Raz followed and further developed Hart's framework, pushing forward Hart's argument in one key respect. Though he recognised coercion as among the most 'general and important features', along with normativity and institutionality,[23] coercion will have to remain subsidiary regarding the role of law in practical reasoning. In Raz's view, law plays an important role in practical reasoning and provides special reason to its agents. Much like a parent's instruction to a child to take caution and avoid strangers when playing outside, the reasons for law's authority are not only rooted in the first order reasons to act upon, but also protected and exclusive reasons.[24] In this view, the role of coercion is merely auxiliary.[25] That is, the mere fact that certain legal directives are backed by sanctions and, ultimately, by the use of force, does not create a protected, exclusionary reason to act as law demands. Rather, sanctions and the use of force (usually but not necessarily) will tip the balance when people are tempted to act otherwise.

---

20 Hart (2012), 194; MacCormick (1982), 244. For a more detailed account of natural necessity, as distinct from conceptual or empirical connection between law and coercion, see Rapetti (2025).
21 Hart (2012), 39.
22 MacCormick (1982), 240.
23 Raz (1980), 3.
24 Raz (2009b), 17 f.
25 Raz (1990), 161 f.

To explain this point, Raz tells the story of an angelic society.[26, 27] Imagine a society made up of agents with a peculiar rationality. 'They differ from us only in having universal and deep-rooted respect towards their legal institutions and lacking all desire to disobey their rulings.'[28] They rely on a legislative assembly and an executive body to run their system. Raz claims even this society, 'the society of angels', would have a legal system, and he raises three points concerning it.[29] One is that, even among these 'angels', there would be factual disagreements that could necessitate official judgements. Another is that the standing law in this society would still leave some room for interpretation. Note that the angels happily comply with the legal directives, once they are clear and fixed. This does not mean they could dispense with choosing authorised adjudicators. Furthermore, the agents in this society could *inadvertently* cause damage to their friends, thereby leaving room to be held liable for their negligence. We do not know if Raz's angels might accidentally drop and ruin a vase belonging to a friend or accidentally bump into a cyclist while driving, but let us suppose so for the sake of argument. Criminal sanctions would be unnecessary, given the characteristics of the society's members, but civil remedies would still have a role to play quite distinct from deterrence through sanctions. Raz claims we can still bestow the notion of 'law' on the normative system in this society. This certainly hypothetical setting aims to provide clarification of our concept of law, and the mastery of a concept means, for Raz, grasping its essential properties.[30] As he put it, 'It is humanly impossible, but logically possible'.[31]

Raz's society of angels faces two challenges. Consider Himma's argument on the ordinary conception of law. He aims to defend what he calls a 'coercion thesis' by saying,

> [I]t is a conceptually necessary condition for the existence of a legal system that it backs some mandatory legal norms prohibiting breaches of the peace with the threat of detriment that rationally competent subjects have a practical reason to avoid.[32]

This looks very similar to what we have seen in the section on the natural necessity of law, for without the 'the threat of detriment' that assures mutual forbearance between competent agents, it would be impossible for law to keep the peace. However, there is one key step in which Himma deviates from Hart (and possibly Raz). Himma understands the concept of law as an 'artifact'. That is, it is dependent on intentional

26 Ibid., 157–160.
27 The term 'angels' may cause readers some trouble, especially because of its religious connotation. In that case, one might replace this term with 'agents with peculiar rationality' or 'people who are inclined to obey what the authorities say'. Doing so will suffice for understanding Raz's intent in this context.
28 Raz (1990), 159.
29 Ibid., 159 f.
30 Raz (2009a), 21 f.
31 Raz (1990), 158.
32 Himma (2020), 1.

creation for its very existence and supposed to serve specific purposes[33]. He further understands that our linguistic choices shape the concept of the law, and he contends the criteria of law are found in the canons of ordinary usage, that is, dictionaries.[34]

Based on this conception of law, Himma notes that a society of angels would not have laws.[35] His critical examination can be boiled down to a single point: to whom does the law belong? In this respect, Hart, Raz and Himma hold different presuppositions. On one hand, Himma explicitly appeals to the ordinary conception of the law shared by many people, mostly non-legal professionals (and possibly including the ordinary intuition of law-informed people, too, only to the extent that these are privately held views). Hart makes a striking contrast in this respect. Here, he explains the minimum conditions necessary and sufficient for the existence of a legal system:

> In an extreme case the internal point of view with its characteristic normative use of legal language ('This is a valid rule') might be confined to the official world. In this more complex system, only officials might accept and use the system's criteria of legal validity. The society in which this was so might be deplorably sheeplike; the sheep might end in the slaughter-house. But there is little reason for thinking that it could not exist or for denying it the title of a legal system.[36]

Raz aligns himself with Hart when he claims sanctions and the use of force are merely supplementary.[37] If so, then Himma's criticism merely exposes that they share nothing to begin with.[38] Still, we should note that the issue here concerns the status of coercion in relation to the concept of law. On one end is Raz, who gives it an auxiliary role from officials' point of view, and on the other is Himma, who views the law from an ordinary person's point of view.

It may not be practical to find a single story along the line of the debates presented this far. Still, it suffices to say that coercion has been (1) a candidate for the source of legal obligation, but (2) natural necessity and (3) the angelic society have pushed it to a relatively marginal place as a safeguard of the normativity of law, thus inviting criticism. However, this may not conclude how coercion is treated in philosophical investigations of law.

33 Ibid., 74 f.
34 Ibid., 23–47.
35 Ibid., 255–262.
36 Hart (2012), 117.
37 Furthermore, Raz certainly did not think conceptual questions could be reduced to a matter of linguistic usage: 'Those who offer explanations of the concept of law usually do mean, as Hart did, to explain the nature of a familiar social institution. It would have been possible for a language to contain a word which refers to this social institution and to nothing else. It may be mere accident that we do not have such a word, though there are good historical-intellectual explanations why 'law' has the meaning it has. But things being as they are the meaning of the expression 'the law' is not (identical with) the concept of law which Hart, and other philosophers of law, sought to explain.' ((2009a), 20)
38 See Woodbury-Smith (2020) for further scrutiny of angelic society.

2 The law's coerciveness as a matter of degree

The previous section explored how coercion has been treated in the philosophy of law, especially in relation to the concept of 'law' itself. However, a different tide has arisen in recent years. Questions concerning law and coercion used to expect a binary answer, yes or no (with variations, of course), but more recent works have examined law's coerciveness as a matter of degree as in: 'how coercive is it?'

The matter becomes clearer after taking a methodological detour. We examined Raz's angelic society in the preceding section, along with its critics. There is another criticism that cuts into the methodological nature of the angelic society argument. Schauer claims that legal philosophy has overlooked an important and stimulating aspect of jurisprudential enquiry by focusing on the 'puzzled' (Hart)[39] and 'angels' (Raz). He tries to draw our attention to the theoretical presuppositions of Hart-Raz positivism. In his attack on command theory, Hart suggested that the law is as much important for people who wish to play by the rules as for those who wish to ignore the law. This is where Schauer finds a vacuum:

> [W]e are putting ourselves in the place of someone who thinks that she ought to Φ on the basis of the full array of law-independent reasons, who then discover that the law requires not-Φ, and who then *because of the law*, proceeds to do not-Φ, proceeds to do it without regard to the possibility of punishment or any other form of legal coercion.[40]

One must exercise some caution here: Schauer aims not to convince us that virtually no one follows the law because it is the law; rather, he advises us to pause and reconsider the (Hart–)Razian quest for the essential property of law, as the quest for its essential property is merely a means for understanding this as a 'concept'. There are central cases, family resemblance and cluster concepts.[41] Once we refute our obsession

---

39 Hart (2012), 40.
40 Schauer (2015), 51f.
41 Ibid., 37–41. There is one philosopher who deserves attention in this context: Max Black. He points out that, for many concepts from the arts to law, the criteria can be 'very numerous, admit of variation in the degree to which they are met, and no simple conjunctive or disjunctive combination of them is both necessary and sufficient' (1954), 28. As suggested, methodological arguments ground Schauer's *The Force of Law*, and it sheds new light on one particular Japanese legal philosopher, Shimpei Kato (加藤新平: 1912–1999), who made a similar methodological claim with explicit reference to Black (the same paper referred to in Schauer (2015), 190, n.54.) Kato suggested that the concept of law is much more like a 'range' that accommodates variation than a definite class with some necessary and sufficient conditions. Such an open, flexible conceptual framework is particularly required to get an overview of research subjects (Kato (1976), 296f). In this spirit, Kato goes on to admit that the law generally is compulsory (ibid., 363–424). A legal system as a whole usually contains rules (Hart's primary rules) as its basis, not individual rules, and they are institutionally backed by coercion. 'That law entails coercion, one can only claim in such a broader meaning, not in the strict sense that examines every single legal norm for its coerciveness' (ibid., 377). Much of Kato's claim regarding the coercive nature of law echoes Schauer on the salience of coercion in law. This reminds us how

with the essential properties of law, coercion as a *salient* feature looms large. According to Schauer, this is worthwhile. Jurisprudential enquiry should be concerned with the practical study of effective rule. Law's arsenal is full, not only of coercion but also architectural (indirect) regulations, taxes, effects on reputation and so on. This is a radically different understanding of the coercive nature of law compared to Raz's angelic society, as the point of this criticism is not to refute essentialism but to highlight the usefulness of a non-essential approach to the concept of law. As Lamond points out,[42] Schauer's battlefront is not in the concept of law, but in improving its efficacy. Schauer readily admits this and leaves for further empirical study whether the law's coercive nature is good and if it is good at regulating human behaviour at all.[43]

If these views paved the way for a more flexible approach to the coerciveness of law, we now know of an account that allows for varying *degrees* of coerciveness. The frontrunner in this school of thought is Lucas Miotto.[44] He proposes a straightforward criterion for measuring the coerciveness of a given legal system. As noted earlier,[45] equating the coerciveness of law with a simple threat diminishes its explanatory power, as doing so means that everything hinges on the recipient of the threat and whether they really feel threatened. Thus, legal philosophers usually refer to coercive institutional features, like sanctions and use of force, when they talk about the coerciveness of law. Miotto takes advantage of this complexity and asks, 'How much does the law threaten people?' This is a useful question for both legal and political philosophers.

Concerning the 'degree of coerciveness' function Miotto proposes:

> Here is a rough way to determine the degree of coerciveness of a typical legal system. Take (A) the total number of actions a given typical legal system attempts to induce its population to perform or abstain from performing via systemic pressure; (B) the percentage of population on which legal pressure is operative and (C) the percentage of actions the

far philosophy can be timeless. For the sake of fairness, we must note the difference between them, too. Despite their anti-essentialist attitudes, when it comes to the purpose, Kato's work opts more for academic explanations, while Schauer's has a more practical goal of institutional design (Schauer (2015), 167). Still, this motivates us to re-examine what we have locally in our globalised world.

42 '[T]he underlying objection to contemporary jurisprudential methodology is not really to its (supposed) essentialism, but rather to its focus on the self-presentation of the law.' 'It is not coercion, but efficacy, that is the poor relation in contemporary legal philosophy' (Lamond (2018), 359).

43 Schauer (2018), 387 f.

44 Perhaps, Gkouvas's 'metric question' (2023) can be another example of a 'degree' shift, though from a different perspective. Given the complexity of the discussion over the necessity of coercion, Gkouvas suggests that we take a different approach to the 'necessity': within a given theory of law, how (much) is state coercion legally unavoidable? To emphasise the point he makes, the farther away reality is from legal actuality (i. e., the facts of lawmaking), the more difficult it is to avoid coercion. Unlike Miotto's cross-disciplinary project, Gkouvas's enterprise concerns the metaphysics of law.

45 See Note 4.

> system successfully induces citizens on which legal pressure is operative to perform or abstain from performing. We could then rely on a function – call it 'Dc function'–that takes (A), (B), and (C) into account.[46]

The viability of the Dc function aside, what is the point of measuring the coerciveness of a given legal system? It is supposed to serve as the basis of cross-disciplinary empirical enquiry.[47] In Miotto's analysis, this should aid in the moral evaluation of legal systems and the justification of their regulatory measures.[48]

Again, this is a very different sort of enterprise compared to the positions presented earlier. The questions we observed in Section 1 supposed more or less simple binary answers, while Miotto's understanding accommodates virtually any society, from Hart's human one to Raz's angelic one, and allows variations.

Lastly, we must admit that we have not yet confirmed if there is such a tendency towards the 'coercion of law as a matter of degree'. It may even be the case that the majority of jurisprudential thinkers align with Raz or other essentialist accounts of law, while recognising the value of empirical study. However, it could still be said that we now have more varying explanations when it comes to the coerciveness of law.

3 What will this shift in focus mean?

We have not yet confirmed if there is such a thing as a shift for *degree* questions, nor is such confirmation necessary. Let us put it in a bracket and play as if it were. What does the law's coerciveness as a matter of degree mean to jurisprudence? What are the shortcomings, if there are any?

One possibility is a departure from conceptual questions. Coercion as a *salient* feature of law (Schauer) requires no further explanation concerning why or how it is necessary, as the rest can be outsourced to empirical analysis. Will Schauer's *The Force of Law* (2015) be declared the winner in this respect? Has economics become a 'standard tool in law, reaching even a subject as philosophical as jurisprudence'?[49] Perhaps a departure from conceptual questions simply means a departure from the armchair to a questionnaire, if we reflect on Miotto's challenge in experimental jurisprudence.[50]

---

46 Miotto (2021b), 249.

47 Ibid., 249 f.

48 Assessing the coerciveness of legal systems in the strict sense of coercion is helpful for 'more precise evaluative judgements about the moral status of legal systems and provide a tailor-made justification for legal systems' use of coercion, a justification that may not extend to other types of actions that resemble coercion in some respects' (Miotto (2021a), 84).

49 Rasmusen (2017), 1188.

50 Miotto et al. (2023).

Another upshot of asking a *degree* question is a bridge between the law's coercive status with normative questions, and we have seen this motivates Miotto and Schauer in a much broader sense. There are normative questions about law: legal paternalism and political legitimacy of coercive legal measures. This may call our attention to other dubious effects, such as manipulation, nudging and persuasion, which resemble coercion. In the end, it may even help guide our choice of regulatory modes.

However, these possibilities will not render coercion a banal choice. The possibility of the *degree* question goes hand in hand with whose degree is at stake. We need to know whose coercion we are talking about before we can measure its degree. Indeed, as Schauer pointed out, the law's arsenal is full of wonder. In some cases, we can dispense with coercion, and there is no need to mention Lessig's architecture and Libertarian-Paternalistic nudging because we already know of these techniques through daily examples like guardrails and road signs. However, it is quite another question if non-coercive regulatory options obliterate law as we understand it. In the age of more automation through massive computational and network technology, it is worth asking if technology will replace law or extend it with one caveat to keep in mind. Prophecy is not the job of jurisprudence; bridging between reality and concepts is.

Bibliography

*Works with [J] at the end were published in Japanese.

Austin, John. (1995): The Province of Jurisprudence Determined (Originally published in 1832). Cambridge: Cambridge University Press.

Anderson, Scott A. (2010): "The Enforcement Approach to Coercion". In: Journal of Ethics and Social Philosophy 5 (1), 1–32.

Barnett, Randy E. (2014): The Structure of Liberty: Justice and the Rule of Law (2nd ed.). Oxford: Oxford University Press.

Black, Max. (1954): Problems of Analysis: Philosophical Essays. Ithaca, NY: Cornell University.

Gkouvas, Triantafyllos. (2023): The Place of Coercion in Law. Cambridge: Cambridge University Press.

Hart, Herbert Lionel Adolphus. (2012): The Concept of Law (3rd ed.). Oxford: Oxford University Press.

Himma, Kenneth Einar. (2020): Coercion and the Nature of Law. Oxford: Oxford University Press.

Kato, Shimpei. (1976): Introduction to Jurisprudence (法哲学概論). Tokyo: Yuhikaku. [J]

Lamond, Grant. (2018): "Everything in its Right Place". In: Jurisprudence 9 (2), 353–360. doi: 10.1080/20403313.2017.1333258.

Lessig, Lawrence. (1998): "The New Chicago School". In: Journal of Legal Studies 27 (2), 661–691. doi: 10.1086/468039.

MacCormick, Neil. (1982): Legal Right and Social Democracy: Essays in Legal and Political Philosophy. City: Clarendon Press.

Minobe, Tatsukichi. (1935): Collected Works of Minobe Tatsukichi Vol. 2: The Essence of Law (美濃部達吉論文集: 法の本質). Tokyo: Nihon-Hyoron-Sha. [J]

Miotto, Lucas. (2021a): "Law and Coercion: Some Clarification". In: Ratio Juris 34 (1), 74–87. doi: 10.1111/raju.12302.
Miotto, Lucas. (2021b): "What Makes Law Coercive when it is Coercive?" In: Archiv für Rechts- und Sozialphilosophie 107 (2), 235–250. doi: 10.25162/arsp-2021–0013.
Miotto, Lucas., Guilherme da Franca Couto Fernandes de Almeida, and Noel Struchiner. (2023): "Law, Coercion and Folk Intuitions". In: Oxford Journal of Legal Studies 43 (1), 97–123. doi: 10.1093/ojls/gqac014.
Miura, Motoki. (2018): "Re-examining Austin's Command Theory" https://hdl.handle.net/10086/29572 accessed 30.09.2024.
Nozick, Robert. (1974): Anarchy, State, and Utopia. City: Blackwell Publishing.
Nozick, Robert. (1997): Socratic Puzzles. Cambridge, MA: Harvard University Press.
Oberdiek, Hans. (1976): "The Role of Sanctions and Coercion in Understanding Law and Legal Systems". In: American Journal of Jurisprudence 21 (1), 71–94. doi: 10.1093/ajj/21.1.71.
Rapetti, Publo A. (2025). "Towards a Neo-Hartian Account of the 'Natural' Relation Between Law and Coercion: Distinct, Rational, Necessary, Quasi-Constitutivist." In: Stefano Bertea and Jorge Silva Sampaio (eds.). Metaethical Issues in Contemporary Legal Philosophy: A Constitutivist Approach. London: Routledge, 218-242.
Rasmusen, Eric. (2017): "Law, Coercion, and Expression: A Review Essay on Frederick Schauer's *The Force of Law* and Richard McAdams's *The Expressive Powers of Law*". In: Journal of Economic Literature 55 (3), 1098–1121. doi: 10.1257/jel.20151374.
Raz, Joseph. (1980): The Concept of a Legal System: An Introduction to the Theory of Legal System (2nd ed.). City: Clarendon Press.
Raz, Joseph. (1990): Practical Reason and Norms (2nd ed.). Oxford: Oxford University Press.
Raz, Joseph. (2009a): Between Authority and Interpretation: On the Theory of Law and Practical Reason. Oxford: Oxford University Press.
Raz, Joseph. (2009b): The Authority of Law: Essays on Law and Morality (2nd ed.). Oxford: Oxford University Press.
Rothbard, Murray N. (1998): The Ethics of Liberty. New York: New York University Press.
Schauer, Frederick. (2010): "Was Austin Right after All? On the Role of Sanctions in a Theory of Law". In: Ratio Juris 23 (1): 1–21. doi: 10.1111/j.1467–9337.2009.00441.x.
Schauer. Frederick. (2015): The Force of Law. Cambridge, MA: Harvard University Press.
Schauer, Frederick. (2018): "Response: A Continuing Conversation". In Jurisprudence 9 (2), 385–393. doi: 10.1080/20403313.2017.1333260.
Thaler, Richard H., and Cass R. Sunstein. (2021): Nudge: The Final Edition. New Haven, CT: Yale University Press.
Yaffe, Gideon. (2003): "Indoctrination, Coercion and Freedom of Will". In: Philosophy and Phenomenological Research 67 (2), 335–356.
Woodbury-Smith, Kara. (2020): "The Nature of Law and Potential Coercion". In: Ratio Juris 33(2), 223–240. doi: 10.1111/raju.12288.

Motoki Miura
Faculty of Law, Meiji Gakuin University
motoki.miura@law.meijigakuin.ac.jp

A Short Essay on Applying Interventionist Accounts to Legal Causation Theory*

NOBUAKI YAMAMOTO

Abstract: This paper focuses on legal causation, particularly examining the challenges of factual causation in non-deterministic cases. Traditional methods face difficulties in these scenarios, leading to the proposal of Interventionist Accounts as a framework for addressing legal causation. The paper introduces J. Halpern's Extended Causal Model, an extension of Interventionist Accounts for determining singular causation. However, the Extended Causal Model encounters challenges, and the paper suggests modifications to address imprecision. In conclusion, the paper advocates for the Modified Extended Causal Model as a comprehensive legal causation theory. It addresses challenges in factual causation and provides a unified approach to deterministic and non-deterministic cases.

Keywords: Causation, Responsibility, Counterfactuals, Statistics, Interventionist Accounts, Causal Model

1 Introduction

Legal causation is the basis for assigning legal responsibility, and discussions have developed in several legal fields. Regardless of the theory adopted, it is commonly shared that, in applying the law, it is safe to assume that factual causation – the causal relationship between the event supposed as the cause and the event positioned as the effect – is a crucial factor in determining the existence or non-existence of legal causation in any of the theories.

Then, what are the cases in which the existence or non-existence of factual causation, one element of legal causation, is at issue? The presence or absence of a factual causal relationship may become a point of contention in pollution cases, where the link between exposure to a specific chemical substance and the onset of a disease is in question, or in medical malpractice cases, where the relationship between a particular medical procedure and the patient's subsequent disability is at stake. Litigation involving such cases, like pollution and medical malpractice, often revolves around scientific

* This research was supported by JSPS KAKENHI Grant Number JP21K01112.

findings. They are frequently non-deterministic cases in which the mechanism between the presumed causal event and the consequent event is unknown or uncertain.[1]

To address such non-deterministic cases, the prevailing position in the natural sciences is to comprehend causation in probabilistic terms. Here, we can observe the distinction between legal causation and the natural scientific approach to factual causation.

This paper aims to present a framework for determining factual causation based on a unified foundation with natural scientific causation that can handle non-deterministic cases considering the aforementioned concerns. In doing so, we will focus on the position of Interventionist Accounts, which has gained prominence in recent theories of causation in philosophy.

2 Conventional Arguments

2.1 Counterfactual test

The counterfactual test (conditio sine qua non) has traditionally been used to determine factual causation. In philosophy, David Lewis represents the view that reduces causation to counterfactuals.[2]

However, Lewis's theory of causation is concerned with deterministic cases,[3] and while it is proposed that for non-deterministic cases, it is sufficient to make a counterfactual comparison of the probability of the occurrence of an effect, it is difficult to demonstrate the likelihood of the occurrence of an effect in non-deterministic cases. Furthermore, as a fundamental problem, some critics argue that it is not always clear what kind of laws determine whether a counterfactual conditional statement is true or false.[4] Given that the cases in which factual causation is at issue are non-deterministic cases, it is challenging to determine factual causation in non-deterministic cases using the counterfactual test.

1 Even in the case of "A stabbed B with a knife and B died," there may be cases where the mechanism between the presumed event as the cause and the event as the effect is unknown or uncertain, such as when the wound caused by A is not usually fatal but may have caused death in combination with B's constitution that makes it difficult to stop bleeding.

2 For details of Lewis' theory of causation, see Lewis (1973b). And for details of Lewis's theory of counterfactuals, see Lewis (1973a).

3 Lewis himself also admits that his theory primarily focuses on deterministic cases.

4 Goodman (1983).

2.2 NESS test

The NESS (Necessary Element of a Sufficient Set) test, represented by H. L. A. Hart and Tony Honoré's legal causation theory, has a similarly significant impact on legal causation theory as a counterfactual test.[5] In the NESS test, a cause is "an element in a sufficient set of conditions that is necessary for that sufficient set of conditions to produce an effect." A leading theory in legal interpretation recognizes factual causation when the combination of cause and effect (die Formel der gesetzmäßigen Bedingung) is identified, based on the laws of nature and the laws of probability, and can be summarized as being in the same position as the NESS test.

However, as a prerequisite to determining factual causation, the NESS test requires that the transition of events consistent with the laws be transparent.[6] Thus, as with the counterfactual test, it is challenging to identify factual causation in non-deterministic cases.

2.3 Probability Rising test

The most promising approach to examining legal causation theory that works in non-deterministic cases is the introduction of probability. This is because introducing probabilities allows one to accurately capture phenomena that deterministic rules, such as counterfactuals, cannot. Because of these probabilistic advantages, it is common in the natural sciences to view causation, including non-deterministic cases, in probabilistic terms.[7]

A representative position as a probabilistic theory of causation in philosophy is the probability-rising theory, which states that a cause raises the probability of an effect occurring.[8] For example, if a person catches a cold and develops a fever, the fever may go down the next day if nothing is done, but the probability of the fever going down the next day will increase by taking cold medicine. In this case, taking cold medicine can be the cause of the effect of the fever coming down, and the cause can be deemed to have increased the probability of the effect occurring.

In the probability-rising theory, all of the mechanism of the causation in question doesn't need to be revealed when determining the causation. Therefore, the probabili-

---

5 As representative literature of adopting the NESS test, see Hart/Honoré (1985); Wright (1985); Puppe (2013). For comparison, the legal causation theory of Karl Engisch and the INUS test by John Mackie also share a similar basic idea to the NESS test.

6 For example, Christopher Pulman points out that the "ordinary chain of events" criterion that Hart-Honoré's legal causation theory emphasizes is context-dependent. For details, see Pulman (2014).

7 Pearl (2009), 1–2.

8 As representative literature of probability-rising theory, see Reichenbach (1956); Suppes (1970); Cartwright (1983).

ty-rising theory can be an effective framework for determining causation in non-deterministic cases. However, three problems can be pointed out with the probability-rising theory.

Firstly, the probability-rising theory focuses on statistical linkages and targets general causation. Therefore, to understand legal causation from the standpoint of the probability-rising theory, which targets singular causation established between individual concrete events, the issue is the relationship between general causation and singular causation. The relationship between general causation and singular causation is a difficult question in the theory of causation in philosophy.[9]

Secondly, a counterexample is pointed out, indicating that the probability-rising theory leads to conclusions that differ from our intuitive judgments. Typical counterexamples are the symmetric overdetermination cases. In this scenario, there are overlapping events, each of which alone produces an effect, and each of the two events alone increases the probability of an effect occurring. Therefore, one cannot be said to have increased the probability of the occurrence of the effect by itself, leading to the conclusion that neither of the two events is a cause.[10] However, this conclusion contradicts our intuition that the two events are both causes.

Thirdly, according to the probability-rising theory, the definition of causation includes the concept of a causal effect that "raises the probability of an effect occurring." This creates a problem called pseudo-correlation, in which a statistical linkage that results in a greater probability of an effect cannot deny that an entirely different factor is the cause of the effect.[11] The problem of pseudo-correlation has been recognized as a significant difficulty in the probability-rising theory. Thus, Nancy Cartwright held that X being the cause of Y means that X raises the probability of Y occurring after fixing the causes of Y other than X and factors not included in the causal path from X to Y.[12] However, since background factors are causal concepts, it is difficult to formulate by probability alone what factors should be conditioned as background factors. Thus, Cartwright falls into the cycle of defining causation by causation,[13] and attempting to reduce causation to probability fails.

---

9 For details of the relationship between general causation and singular causation, see Kutach (2014), 2–8.
10 Ibid., 111.
11 Ibid., 105–108; Pearl/Mackenzie (2018), 47.
12 Cartwright (1983), 21–26. For the responses of the theorists of the probability increase theory other than Cartwright, see Kutach (2014), 106–108.
13 Pearl/Mackenzie (2018), 48–49.

3 Interventionist Accounts

3.1 Backgrounds and basic ideas

Considering the problems with the probability-rising theory, it is challenging to construct a legal causation theory that can deal with non-deterministic cases by applying the probability-rising theory. On the other hand, given the advantage of dealing with non-deterministic cases, grasping causation in probabilistic terms is attractive. Looking at recent philosophical theories of causation, Interventionist Accounts that grasp causation in probabilistic terms have become dominant.

Interventionist Accounts can be organized as having been established under two theoretical backgrounds. The first is the philosophical manipulability theory, which attempts to analyze and define the concept of causation in terms of experimentation and manipulability[14]. The other is the scientific manipulability theory, which formulates the methodology scientists have used to elucidate causation[15]. Among scientific manipulability theories, Pearl's theory based on Bayesian networks, which he developed based on Bayesian statistics, has attracted widespread attention. It is often called statistical causal inference because of its characteristic use of statistical methods. It is said that Interventionist Accounts were established in these theoretical backgrounds by the organization of James Woodward.

As inferred from its theoretical background, Interventionist Accounts present a causal theory focusing on "manipulability." In other words, the basic idea of Interventionist Accounts is that the existence of causation between X and Y means that it is possible to manipulate Y indirectly by directly manipulating X.[16] This basic idea of manipulability is nothing more than a counterfactual question.[17] Based on this basic idea, Interventionist Accounts introduce the concept of "intervention," in which X is manipulated from the outside to reflect manipulability in the formulation of causation.

Interventionist Accounts, which attempt to formulate manipulability through the concept of intervention, assume that causation can be discovered through scientific practice and are non-metaphysical positions irrelevant to reducing causation to non-causal elements.[18] In other words, Interventionist Accounts abandon the reductive definition of causation as being analyzed by non-causal concepts. This position of Interventionist Accounts can be understood as an epistemological theory based on the structure of causation.[19]

---

14 As a leading theorist, Georg Henrik von Wright, Peter Menzies, and Huw Price.

15 As a leading theorist, Judea Pearl, Joseph Halpern, Peter Spirtes, Clark Glymour, and Richard Scheines.

16 Woodward (2003), 39–40.

17 Woodward (2009), 236.

18 Kutach (2014), 129.

19 This policy shift in Interventionist Accounts, particularly statistical causal inference, is described by Scheines as an "epistemological turn." See Scheines (2005), 285.

3.2 Methodologies

Interventionist Accounts view causation as a relationship between variables and make causal inferences in line with a causal model modeled by a directed graph[20] consisting of a set of variables and structural equations. In a causal model, structural equations define the values of one variable by the values of other variables and are usually expressed mathematically. However, due to its nature of showing causation in a unidirectional manner from cause to effect, the structural equations are asymmetric, showing only the influence from the right-hand side to the left-hand side. Variables in the causal model are classified into exogenous variables, whose values are not determined by the structural equations, and endogenous variables, whose values are determined by the structural equations.[21]

By constructing a causal model consisting of these elements, we can visualize the structure of the causation in question and prepare for the formulation of manipulability, which is the basic idea of Interventionist Accounts. The causal model constructed is subjective because it reflects the modeler's understanding of causation. However, whether the causal model created is accurate can be confirmed by measuring the variables in the model.

Then, according to Interventionist Accounts, the existence or non-existence of the causation in question is determined by conducting an "intervention" on the constructed causal model and testing whether changing the variable that is presumed to be the cause changes the variable that is positioned as the effect.[22]

Let us now examine what a causal model and causal inference would look like in Interventionist Accounts. For example, let's consider the case of pollution, in which exposure to a chemical substance combined with the constitution of the exposed person causes a disease. Following interventionist methodology, this case can be represented in a causal model, as shown in Figure 1.

In the causal model in Figure 1, exposure to the chemical substance (X) and the constitution of the exposed person (Z) have a causal influence on the onset of disease (Y). Note that X, Y, and Z are all endogenous variables. In this case, the exogenous variables defining X could be, for example, a factory that emits the chemical substance, and the exogenous variables defining Z could be, for example, heredity, but to avoid complications, they are not reflected in the causal model. Thus, constructing a causal model can visually represent the structure of the causation in question. The relationship between X, Y, and Z can be expressed as the structural equation $Y = f(X, Z)$, which mathematically expresses how Y changes in response to the values taken by X and Z.

20 A directed graph consists of a vertex and a directed edge with an orientation represented by an arrow. Interventionist Accounts often use a directed acyclic graph (DAG), which is an acyclic graph without cyclic paths (paths consisting of directed edges from any vertex through another vertex back to the first).

21 For a summary of Interventionist Accounts, see Kutach (2014), 128–133.

22 For a definition of concept of "intervention", see Woodward (2003), 98.

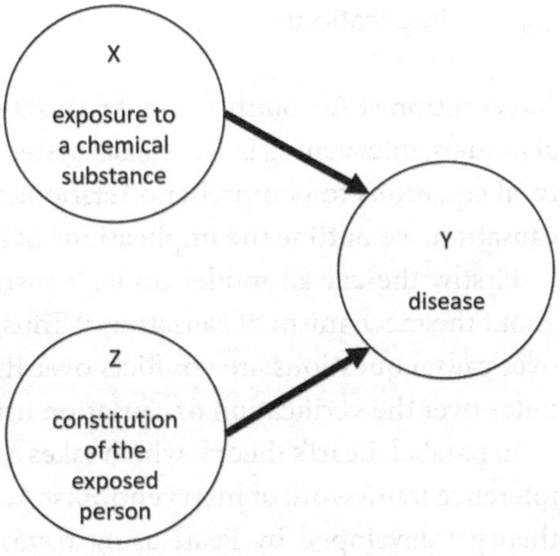

Fig. 1 A causal model of the pollution case

The accuracy of this causal model would then be verified by measuring the endogenous variables X, Y, and Z individually. To determine whether X is the cause of Y in the example in Figure 1, we can examine how Y changes by fixing Z to real-world values while intervening on X. Figure 2 shows the causal model of Figure 1 with interventions.

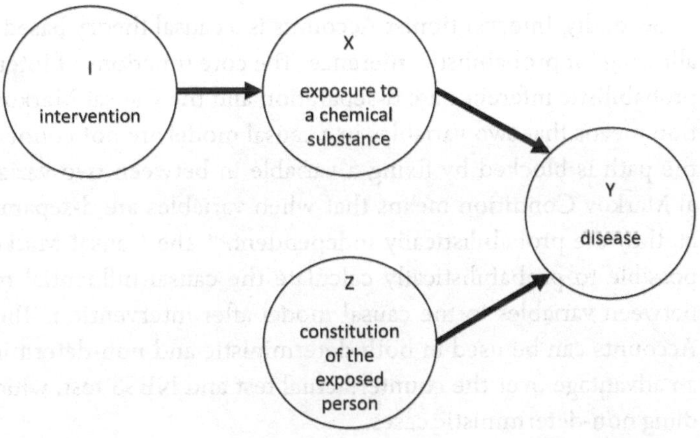

Fig. 2 A causal model of the pollution case with intervention

In the causal model of Figure 2, I is the cause of X, and X depends solely on I. Consequently, I influences Y through X. In this scenario, the value of Z is fixed to its original value and remains constant during the intervention. This setup allows us to assess whether X has a causal influence on Y by examining if the value of Y changes with the intervention I on X. Thus, through the actual scientific practice of intervening on X, we can determine whether X is the cause of Y.

3.3 Implications

Interventionist Accounts facilitate causal inferences through the construction of causal models, intervening in the causal system guided by the model, and employing structural equations to comprehend relationships among variables. When applied to legal causation, we outline the implications of Interventionist Accounts.

Firstly, the causal model under construction reflects the model builder's beliefs about the mechanism of causation.[23] Thus, in Interventionist Accounts, disagreements over causal questions are conflicts over the accuracy of the causal model itself or disputes over the verification of causation using the model.

In parallel, Pearl's theory, which takes a mathematical approach to discuss the causal inference framework of Interventionist Accounts, is grounded in the Bayesian network theory[24] developed by Pearl using Bayesian statistics,[25] in which prior probabilities are updated by pieces of evidence and other factors.[26] In Bayesian statistics, subjectivity diminishes gradually through updating beliefs with evidence, leading to highly objective conclusions.[27] Therefore, in causal inference, faults in the causal model will be exposed during the process of verifying the model using various data.[28] Through data-based verification, the subjectivity of the causal model itself is reduced, and if the causal model turns out to be based on incorrect beliefs about the mechanism of causation, it can be discarded.

Secondly, Interventionist Accounts is a causal theory based on Bayesian networks, allowing for probabilistic inference. The core functions of Interventionist Accounts in probabilistic inference are d-separation and the Causal Markov Condition. D-separation means that two variables in a causal model are not connected in any path or that the path is blocked by fixing a variable in between two variables.[29] Also, the Causal Markov Condition means that when variables are d-separated in the causal model, they are probabilistically independent.[30] The Causal Markov Condition makes it possible to probabilistically calculate the causal influential relationship established between variables in the causal model after intervention. Therefore, Interventionist Accounts can be used in both deterministic and non-deterministic cases, presenting an advantage over the counterfactual test and NESS test, which face difficulties handling non-deterministic cases.

---

23 Pearl/Mackenzie (2018), 89.
24 For details of Bayesian networks, see Pearl (1985).
25 For a summary of Bayesian statistics, see Rowbottom (2015), 61–76.
26 Pearl/Mackenzie (2018), 128–133.
27 Ibid., 90.
28 Ibid., 129–130.
29 Pearl (2009), 16–18.
30 Ibid., 30–32.

Thirdly, various scientific methods are employed to test the existence or non-existence of causation through interventions in causal models. The most representative natural scientific method for verifying causation through intervention is the experimental method, including randomized controlled trials (RCT). However, there are cases in which the artificial intervention required for verification by experimental methods is physically impossible or ethically inappropriate.[31] Therefore, Pearl argues that the existence of causation can also be verified through statistical manipulation of data by introducing the do-calculus method[32] for treating interventions statistically.[33] Do-calculus is an inference rule that uses Causal Markov Conditions to predict intervention effects, enabling causal inference through statistical manipulation of data.[34] Thus, Pearl's causal inference is capable of making causal inferences in cases where experimental methods are impossible or inappropriate.

Fourthly, Interventionist Accounts directly acknowledge that counterfactual reasoning is essential to causal inference, especially in singular causation.[35] However, this is not a position that reduces causation to counterfactuals, as Lewis does.[36] Interventionist Accounts is the position that, given that questions about singular causation are counterfactual, inference based on causal models is necessary to provide answers to questions about singular causation.[37] Thus, like Lewis, it does not require a strict definition of the similarity of possible worlds but seeks to answer causal and counterfactual questions based on the human ability to grasp causation.[38] Interventionist Accounts also holds that the change in the value of variable Y in conjunction with the change in the value of variable X due to an intervention is "invariant" within a certain range and

---

31 For example, it is physically impossible to randomly assign patients to obese and non-obese groups to study the impact of obesity on heart disease, and it is ethically inappropriate to force randomly assigned individuals to smoke for a while to study the impact of smoking on lung cancer. These examples are based on Pearl/Mackenzie (2018), 149–150.

32 Pearl makes a clear distinction between "seeing," which is reasoning by observation, and "doing," which is inference by intervention. Pearl introduces the do-calculus as a calculation method that is different from "seeing," which is inferred by calculation based on Bayesian networks.

33 Ibid., 149–150.

34 For details of causal inference by using do-calculus, see Pearl (2009), 65–106.

35 Pearl/Mackenzie (2018), 260. From this view of Interventionist Accounts, it seems possible to reconstruct Hart and Honoré's recognition of the usefulness of counterfactuals to a certain extent as a test in determining the legal causation.

36 Ibid., 267.

37 This idea of Interventionist Accounts contrasts with Lewis' theory and is similar to that of Horwich, who held that counterfactuals should be explained by causation. See Horwich (1987), 158–161. Horwich himself characterizes causality in terms of lawful combination, causal continuity, and temporal order, taking a position close to that of the regularity theory (Ibid., 129–145).

38 Pearl's theory, based on these ideas, might be evaluated as being grounded in causal realism. It should be noted, however, that Pearl emphasizes the human capacity to grasp causation and the fact that it is consistent in many cases while acknowledging that causal models are subjective. From this statement, we can assume that Pearl is emphasizing the human psychological aspect of grasping causation, and it seems to require careful consideration as to whether or not he is a causal realist.

positions such a general rule as an "invariant general rule." However, a general law of invariance is not a law of exceptionlessness that holds for all values of variables X and Y.[39] Thus, the problem of laws uncertainty faced by Lewis's theory and the NESS test is avoided in Interventionist Accounts, which serves as a framework for determining causation in non-deterministic cases while encompassing counterfactual reasoning.

4 Legal Causation Theory Applying Interventionist Accounts

4.1 Halpern's Extended Causal Model

Interventionist Accounts can be assessed as a practical method for determining causation applicable to both deterministic and non-deterministic cases. Before presenting a legal causation theory using Interventionist Accounts, we will explore the advantages and possibilities of applying them to legal causation theory.

Traditional legal causation theories often construct arguments based on non-causal concepts. However, as highlighted by the limitations of the counterfactual and NESS tests, attempts to reduce legal causation to non-causal concepts encounter significant challenges. The situations where legal causation becomes problematic are often those involving difficulties in determining causation, such as non-deterministic cases. In these instances, the primary question for legal causation theory is not an ontological one but an epistemological one concerning factual causation. Therefore, there is merit in abandoning the strict definition of causation and embracing Interventionist Accounts, an epistemological theory that addresses causal questions.

While there are advantages in applying Interventionist Accounts to legal causation theory, it primarily deals with general causation aligned with the interests of natural scientists. However, Pearl's theory, grounded in Bayesian networks and incorporating counterfactual concepts in causal inference, can be positioned as a theory encompassing the inference of singular causation.

(i) So, how does Interventionist Accounts infer singular causation? Within Interventionist Accounts, the most influential theory of singular causation following Pearl's approach is the Extended Causal Model (ECM) proposed by Halpern, one of Pearl's collaborators. Halpern aims to formulate the Interventionist Accounts method for determining singular causation by introducing the concepts of sufficient cause[40] and normality[41] into the framework. With these concepts incorporated, the ECM is formulated as follows.

39 Woodward (2003), 270–272.
40 Halpern (2019), 24.
41 Ibid., 79–83.

x is considered a cause of y precisely when all the following conditions are met:

AC1: x and y both occur.

AC2:

(i) When all variables, except those on the path from x to y, are fixed to the actual world or relatively unexceptional world values, an intervention to prevent x from occurring results in y not occurring.

(ii) When the subset Z of variables containing x on the path from x to y has the actual value, and the set W of variables with no common part with Z is fixed to actual values, y occurs.

AC3: There is no sub-model that satisfies both AC1 and AC2.[42]

According to the formulation of the ECM, singular causation can only be established between adjacent variables. Singular causation denies the causal chain between individual concrete events, i.e., the transitivity of causation. However, we determine causation based on the assumption that transitivity of causation exists within a certain range, and denying the transitivity of causation may lead to erroneous conclusions. Therefore, Halpern presents the conditions required for causation to be transitive (the transitivity test) as follows:

In the background setting for a particular causation, x1 is the cause of x3 if x1 is the counterfactual causation of x2, x2 is the counterfactual causation of x3, and the following two conditions are satisfied:

(a) For every variable that x2 can take, there exists a corresponding x1 variable.

(b) x2 exists on all causal paths from x1 to x3 in the background setting of the causation.[43]

4.2 Problems and modifications of the Extended Causal Model

The ECM is a theory that incorporates both necessary and sufficient causes in singular causation inference, further developing the NESS test within the Interventionist Accounts methodology. However, understanding the concept of "relatively unexceptional world values" or normality in the ECM and determining it pose theoretical challenges similar to those faced by Hart and Honoré's legal causation theory, which relies on normal transition principles.

In adapting Halpern's ECM for a legal causation theory, clarification is needed for the concept of "relatively unexceptional world values." To modify the concept of normality, it is essential to revisit the nature of factual causation in legal situations.

42 Ibid., 81.
43 Ibid., 41–46.

Legal causation involves a causal relationship where the violation of the law, such as stabbing someone with a knife (A stabbing B), is the cause, and the violation of legal interest (B's death) is the effect, as can be seen from the typical example of "A stabbed B with a knife and B died as a result." In situations questioning the existence of legal causation, the act of breaking the law is viewed as an extraordinary event in factual causation. Therefore, in legal causation theory, "not violating the law," that is, the concept of legality, is a concept that can replace the concept of normality. Based on these considerations, this paper proposes to modify Halpern's ECM to introduce "legal values" in place of "relatively unexceptional world values." In this paper, we will refer to the formulation modified by the concept of legality as the "Modified Extended Causal Model (Modified ECM)," which is as follows:

> x is a cause of y when the following conditions hold:
> LC1: x and y both occur.
> LC2:
> (i) When all variables, except those on the path from x to y, are fixed to the actual world or legal values, an intervention to prevent x from occurring makes y not occur.
> (ii) When the subset Z of variables containing x on the path from x to y has actual values, and the set W of variables with no common part with Z is fixed to actual values, y occurs.
> LC3: There is no sub-model that satisfies LC1 and LC2.

In the Modified ECM, variables not on the examining causal path are fixed as "legal values." The concept of legality is applied to each specific case considering the text of the law. Although the determination of what constitutes a legal event may lack unambiguous clarity, it is deemed clearer than the concept of normality for legal causation theory. Additionally, judgments regarding events in violation of the law are subjective and part of the causal model construction, aligning with the basic approach of Interventionist Accounts.

Like Halpern's ECM, the Modified ECM does not inherently recognize the transitivity of causation. Therefore, the transitivity test is applied as a condition for its establishment when questioning factual causation with transitivity is being questioned that straddles variables that satisfy the conditions of the Modified ECM.

As an example of causal inference using the Modified ECM, let's examine whether x is the cause of y in a scenario where a lethal dose of poison administered by A (x) and a lethal dose of poison administered by B (z) might have led to the death of C (y). Figure 3 illustrates the causal model for this case. Exogenous variables, such as the poison purchase by A and B, are omitted to avoid complications.

An intervention applying the Modified ECM to this case is shown in Figure 4. Here, the intervention (i) on x is made after fixing z to the value of the legal variable, indicating the situation where B does not administer any poison to C. Since x and y satisfy all

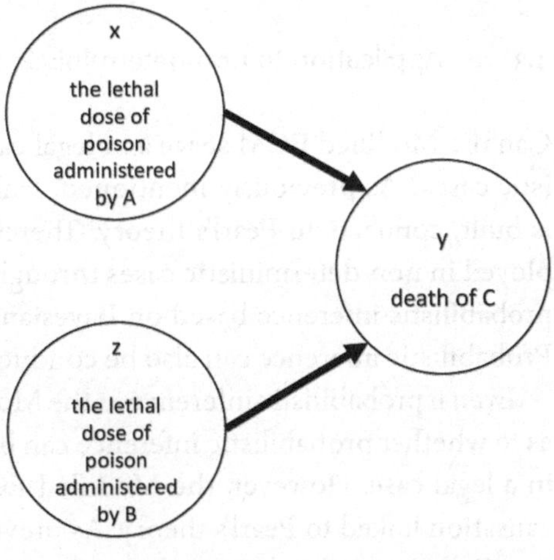

Fig. 3 A causal model of the poisoning case

the Modified ECM conditions, we can infer that x is the cause of y, and the same can be inferred for z and y. Thus, consistent with our intuitive judgment, we can infer that both x and z are causes of y.

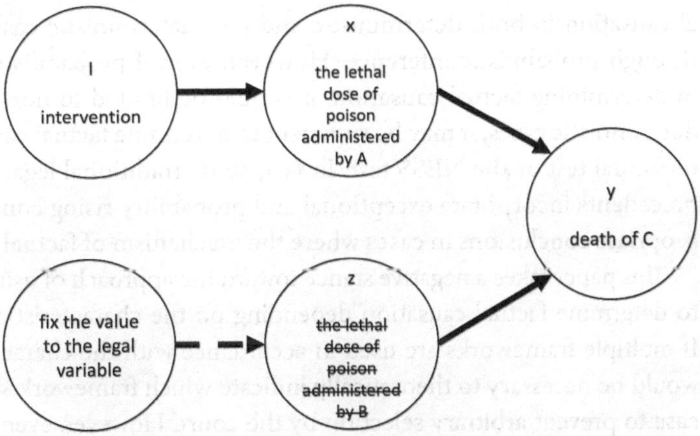

Fig. 4 A causal model of the poisoning case with intervention

4.3 Application to non-deterministic cases

Can the Modified ECM serve as a legal causation theory applicable to non-deterministic cases? As previously mentioned, Halpern's ECM, on which the Modified ECM is built, connects to Pearl's theory. Therefore, similar to Pearl's theory, it can be employed in non-deterministic cases through a framework of causal inference, including probabilistic inference based on Bayesian networks and causal Markov conditions.[44] Probabilistic inference can also be conducted within the Modified ECM.

Even if probabilistic inference in the Modified ECM is possible, a question may arise as to whether probabilistic inference can be utilized to determine the factual causation in a legal case. However, the Modified ECM is a framework for determining factual causation linked to Pearl's theory. As previously demonstrated, Pearl's theory is based on a Bayesian network grounded in Bayesian probability theory, interpreting probability as a measurable degree of belief. The judge's mental process appears to be nothing more than a formation of their own beliefs based on various types of evidence. If it is possible to interpret the judge's formation of beliefs about factual causation as Bayesian probabilistic inference, it would also be plausible to determine factual causation by using probabilistic inference based on the Bayesian network in the Modified ECM.

Thus, the Modified ECM is fundamentally oriented toward determining factual causation in both deterministic and non-deterministic cases in a unified manner through probabilistic inference. However, even if probabilistic reasoning is allowed in determining factual causation, it should be limited to non-deterministic cases. In deterministic cases, it may be sufficient to determine factual causation using the counterfactual test or the NESS test. In fact, some traditional legal causation theories and precedents incorporate exceptional and probability-rising considerations to draw appropriate conclusions in cases where the mechanism of factual causation is unclear.

This paper takes a negative stance toward the approach of using different frameworks to determine factual causation depending on the characteristics of each specific case. If multiple frameworks are used in accordance with the characteristics of each case, it would be necessary to theoretically indicate which framework should be used in which case to prevent arbitrary selection by the court. However, even if a certain typological arrangement is possible, it would be difficult to identify sufficient theoretical criteria for determining which framework to use in specific cases. Certainly, the approach of using multiple frameworks to reach appropriate conclusions regarding the attribution of liability has its appeal. Still, from the perspective of drawing appropriate conclusions regarding the attribution of legal responsibility, it would be desirable to deepen the discussion by limiting legal causation to factual causation and distinguishing it from legal responsibility rather than treating legal causation and legal responsibility as synonymous.

---

44 Ibid., 46–53.

5 Conclusion

In this paper, we reference Interventionist Accounts, a philosophy gaining prominence in recent years, and propose a legal causal theory that can provide a unified judgment for deterministic and non-deterministic cases. This proposal involves a critical examination of Halpern's ECM, a framework for determining singular causation. Interventionist Accounts offers a comprehensive framework for addressing causation questions through the use of causal models and the concept of intervention. Halpern's ECM and the transitivity test play significant roles within Interventionist Accounts as frameworks for singular causation. However, the ECM encounters imprecision issues due to the introduction of the concept of normality. To address this, a Modified ECM is presented, which substitutes the concept of legality for normality.

Based on the preceding discussion, the paper's conclusion is that the Modified ECM, applying Interventionist Accounts, can be established as a legal causation theory capable of unifying deterministic and non-deterministic cases.

6 Bibliography

Cartwright, Nancy (1983): How the Laws of Physics Lie. Oxford: Oxford University Press.

Goodman, Nelson (1983): Fact, Fiction, and Forecast. Fourth Edition. Cambridge, MA: Harvard University Press.

Halpern, Joseph (2019): Actual Causality. Cambridge, MA: MIT Press.

Hart, H. L. A. / Honoré, Tony (1985): Causation in the Law. Second Edition. Oxford: Oxford University Press.

Horwich, Paul (1987): Asymmetries in Time. Problems in the Philosophy of Science. Cambridge, MA: The MIT Press.

Kutach, Douglas (2014): Causation. Cambridge: Polity Press.

Lewis, David (1973a): Counterfactuals. Oxford: Basil Blackwell.

Lewis, David (1973b): "Causation". In: Journal of Philosophy 70 (17), 556–567.

Pearl, Judea (1985): "Bayesian networks. A model of self-activated memory for evidential reasoning". In: Proceedings of the 7th Conference of the Cognitive Science Society, 329–334.

Pearl, Judea (2009): Causality. Models, Reasoning and Inference. Second Edition. Cambridge: Cambridge University Press.

Pearl, Judea / Mackenzie, Dana (2018): The Book of Why. The New Science of Cause and Effect. New York: Basic Books.

Pulman, Christopher (2014): "Voluntary Interventions". In: Pulman, Christopher (ed.) Hart on Responsibility. London: Palgrave Macmillan, 47–70.

Puppe, Ingeborg (2013): "The Concept of Causation in the Law". In: Kahmen, Benedikt and Stepanians, Markus (Eds.) Critical Essays on "Causation and Responsibility". Berlin: De Gruyter, 67–109.

Reichenbach, Hans (1956): The Direction of Time. Berkeley: University of California Press.

Rowbottom, Darrell P. (2015): Probability. Cambridge: Polity Press.

Scheines, Richard (2005): "Causation". In: Horowitz, Maryanne C. (ed.) New Dictionary of the History of Ideas. 1 Vols. Detroit, MI: Charles Scribner Sons, 280–289.
Suppes, Patrick (1970): A Probabilistic Theory of Causality. Amsterdam: North-Holland.
Woodward, James (2003): Making Things Happen. A Theory of Causal Explanation. Oxford: Oxford University Press.
Woodward, James (2009): "Agency and Interventionist Theories". In: Beebee, Helen et al. (eds.) The Oxford Handbook of Causation. Oxford: Oxford University Press, 234–262.
Wright, Richard W. (1985): "Causation in Tort Law". In: California Law Review 73 (6), 1735–1828.

Nobuaki Yamamoto
Faculty of International Social Sciences, Yokohama National University
yamamoto-nobuaki-vx@ynu.ac.jp

Part 4
The Role and Reality of Judges

Way of the Judge*
What is Judicial Virtue?

TOMASZ WIDŁAK

Abstract: This article aims to elaborate on the meaning of judicial virtue by proposing a theoretical model of virtue that accommodates the judicial role in a democratic jurisdiction. First, the article will discern why virtue could be regarded as helpful in considering the judicial role. In the second part, the discussion will move to the issue of the relation between judicial and overall virtue. A concept of the judicial virtue being role-relevant will be proposed. Finally, the discussion will conclude with a proposal of a target-centered model of virtue that accommodates judicial virtue as a role-relevant concept and the demands of the law towards the judicial role.

Keywords: virtue, judicial virtue, virtue ethics, virtue jurisprudence, legal ethics

1 Introduction

Virtue is a critical concept in both Eastern and Western ethical traditions. In the West, thinking about a morally good life in terms of virtues (gr. *aretē*) stems from the ancient Greek philosophy, mainly represented by Plato[1] and Aristotle[2] and later by Roman stoics.[3] In the East, Confucius and his followers – Mencius[4] and Xunzi[5] also used virtue as the central moral category of their ethical teachings.[6] The impact of virtue-oriented moral language was further reinforced over the centuries by great religious systems like Christianity[7], Buddhism[8], and Islam.[9] Unsurprisingly, the notion of virtue had also permeated the secular spheres of medieval and early modern life. The influence

* This article is part of a project financed by the National Science Centre, Poland, project No. 2018/31/B/HS5/03181.

1 See White (2015), 3–15.
2 See Curzer (2018), 104–129.
3 See Becker (2018), 130–152.
4 Shirong (2015), 77–88.
5 Hutton (2015), 113–125.
6 Ivanhoe (2013), 49–69.
7 See Wood (2018), 281–300.
8 See Goodman (2015), 89–97.
9 See Bucar (2018), 206–223.

of virtue-based language is visible in developing unique ethics of the knighthood, the warrior ruling class of Eastern and Western feudal societies. The most notorious examples of such systems were the demanding chivalry ethos[10] in Europe and the *bushidō*, or "the way of the warrior", of the Samurai in Japan.[11] The rise of modernity and the fall of feudalism seemingly brought the downfall of this type of moral language.[12] Its decline was coupled with the rise of rivalling meta-ethical traditions in Western philosophy: deontology and consequentialism. Even though the times of knights, gentle folks and shoguns had long passed, the virtue-centred language survived in ethics, politics, and even law. At least since Elisabeth Anscombe's article titled *Modern Moral Philosophy,* published in 1958,[13] we are witnessing a great revival of virtue ethics in the West. It is also influencing epistemology[14] and spilling over to social sciences, inducing new movements, such as "positive psychology".[15] Recently, virtue theory has gained a foothold in legal theory, where Solum and others first proposed a new perspective called virtue jurisprudence.[16] One of the first and probably most prominent applications of virtue theory to law is the question of the virtues of judges – people bestowed with the power of adjudication. Several questions arise in the face of an attempt to conceive the judicial role in terms of virtues. Is the aretaic approach helpful in better understanding the judicial role in modern democratic society and the responsibility it carries? Is the idea of judicial virtues adequate for conceptualising what it means to be a good judge?

Answering these crucial questions depends on understanding the concept of virtue. As much as the idea of virtue is pervasive and universal in ethics, understanding what the concept of virtue exactly stands for calls for examining the context in which the virtue operates, especially an institutional or professional, role-related one.[17] The point of interest of this article will be to identify what judicial virtue is. It will propose a theoretical model of virtue that accommodates the judicial role in modern democracies. In what follows, this analysis will first argue why virtue could help consider the judicial role. In the second part, the discussion will clarify the meaning of judicial virtue as a role-relevant virtue. Finally, putting the judicial role and the demands of law towards the judiciary in the broader context of virtue, a theoretical model of target-oriented virtue will be proposed.

10 A culturally relevant source of the chivalry code is the Song of Roland; see Gaund/Pratt (2016), 3–133.
11 See Nitobe/Bennett (2019).
12 For the analysis of the decline of virtue ethics, see Frede (2013), 24–148.
13 Anscombe (1958), 1–19.
14 See Trinkaus Zagzebski (1996).
15 See Peterson/Seligman (2004).
16 Solum (2003), 178–213; Farrelly/Solum (2008); Amaya/Michelon (2020).
17 On the importance of professional context in determining what trait counts as virtue or vice, see Oakley/Cooking (2001).

2 Why virtue?

The judicial role is heavily regulated. Both law and various codes of judicial conduct lay down several rules for judges to be followed. Judicial behaviour is also directed by the jurisprudence of disciplinary courts for judges, which consider the consequences of misconduct in performing the judicial role. The rules and guidelines attempt to answer the question: "What is the right thing to do as a judge?". In contrast, the aretaic language prompts answers to an alternative question: "What is the best way of being a judge?" to which the answer could be: it is to be fair, self-controlled, kind, lawful, honourable, prudent, modest, courageous.[18] The difference between these two queries is more than semantic since the former concentrates on the moral and legal assessment of judicial actions, often dealt with in separation. At the same time, the latter aims to capture judicial excellence in who the judges are and who they are becoming in performing their role.

2.1 Virtue language is comprehensive in describing the judicial character

We intuitively grasp that virtue is a quality that makes one an excellent person.[19] Excellence is not limited to moral perfection because virtue can transcend the moral domain. It is a personal quality most often interpreted as a character trait. Moral character traits are usually seen as the most prominent personal qualities because they are defined in terms of moral right and wrong. However, there are also epistemic (or intellectual), aesthetic, prudential, and other traits.[20] Accordingly, when developed, they give rise to intellectual virtues such as wisdom, knowledge, prudence, and other traits that can be virtues like sensitivity to beauty, ability to quickly adapt to changed circumstances, building a high capacity for tolerating stress, amiability, or punctuality. All of these are desirable virtues. However, none of them is "moral" in that it amounts to commanding behaviour that is morally obligatory, prohibited or merely permitted.[21] After all, someone's poor taste in the arts or bad manners may be something we can resent (or even detest), but it would not typically be a moral failure. Arguably, both moral and intellectual virtues are integrated by practical reason, which, among other elements, involves a particular form of moral sensitivity.[22]

---

18 This enumeration is an example of a possible catalogue of judicial virtues reconstructed in a study of legal literature, sources of law, ethical codes and disciplinary judgments in a Central European jurisdiction. The results of this research were discussed and published as a supplementary file to my other work, see Widłak (2025a).
19 Battaly (2015), 5.
20 Miller (2018), 9.
21 Van Hooft (2006), 9.
22 See Russell (2014), 206; cf. ibid., 1385

Virtue may also be considered similar to a specific skill or capacity. While this view is controversial, it is usually agreed that professionals such as judges need to be good craftspeople (or have technical skills) in the first place.[23] One should also possess excellent communication skills to be sensitive and receptive to legally and morally salient aspects of situations. For instance, in some jurisdictions[24], the criteria for judicial selection are the candidate's communicativeness, teamwork, ability to solve disputes between the parties to the judicial proceedings, negotiation skills, decisiveness, and "life experience". Other jurisdictions like Germany generally require "social competencies" without specifying what should be understood under the term. These capacities are often recognised as important, if not crucial, for judges. However, their relation to deontological judicial ethics remains unclear. Using the virtue language offers a framework for a comprehensive understanding of all necessary traits and skills of the judicial personality.[25]

2.2 Virtues motivate and accommodate emotions

This comprehensive view of personal traits and skills that judicial virtue provides helps assess judicial performance or hold judges accountable. While traditional deontic (or rules-based) approaches to assessing judicial performance focus on rule compliance and assessment of outcomes (for instance, the ratio of the judgements given by a particular judge which were annulled or changed in the appellate procedure to those which were upheld), virtue-based accounts open this process up to a more meaningful and profound notion of what it means being a "good judge". To explain this, one needs to underline another important assertion: virtues are not mere habits, nor are they only dispositions to act from excellent reason or judgment (the abilities to understand, discern and judge). Being virtuous has an important affective component – it involves feelings and emotions, which are harmonised with reasons and play an important role in moral response and motivation to act virtuously.[26] In other words, what matters when it comes to virtue is systematically attaining good ends *via* good actions and acting out of good motives.[27] Feeling the right emotions for the right reasons and integrating them into good action makes virtue a holistic, well-rounded ethical pattern, which ensures that it does not boil down to mere intellectual exercise. A just or lawful judge will deal with her cases justly and according to the law because she deeply craves

23 See Solum (2005), 1375 f.
24 Małolepszy/Jakimiec (2020), 115–146.
25 I discuss the judicial selection criteria and the role of aretaic language mentioned in this section more extensively in Widłak (2025a), 201–206, 209–210.
26 See Szutta (2015), 111–133.
27 See Battaly (2015), 59–85.

lawful justice and feels satisfaction or joy if she can actually "do justice" through the prudent application of the law. At the same time, even in cases of the most heinous crimes, she will respond to the defendant without anger, desire for revenge or even aversion. Bringing about justice and peace is her goal, which motivates her instead of becoming famous or praised. A judge who is well-performing in her job without many formal mistakes but is motivated solely by the perspective of being promoted and getting a higher salary may not be acting against any positive rules of judicial conduct. However, she does not necessarily meet the highest moral standards of having an 'impeccable character'[28] and, therefore, is not worthy of promotion to a higher judicial post.[29]

2.3 Virtues offer a dynamic and teleological view of the judicial role

Another advantage of analysing the judicial role from the aretaic perspective lies in the inherently dynamic nature of virtues and the moral and intellectual development framework it offers. The thinking behind most virtue ethics is teleological. For Aristotle, virtues are justified by the essential role they have in attaining happiness, which he calls *eudaimoniā* – the good life, often translated as flourishing or blessedness and prosperity in contrast to any external good like material wealth or pleasure that can adequately be only a means to further goals.[30] *Eudaimoniā* is reached by the perfection of moral character, that is, by practising virtues as the traits of character, which the practical reasoning tells us are essential to living a fulfilling human and individual life.[31] It is important to stress two points: first, *eudaimoniā* is reached by acting out of virtue over a more extended lifetime period[32] and second, it can be perfected infinitely (hence, this form of virtue ethics is a perfectionist approach). In short, happiness as the fulfilment of every life is not a destination to arrive at, but it is earned over the journey by practising and perfecting virtue. Even if one disagrees with an all-encompassing grandiose *telos* of *eudaimoniā*, teleological thinking is rooted in the aretaic normativity. In a weaker version of this assertion presented below, each virtue can be seen as having its unique aim or target.

These assumptions about perfectionism and the dynamic nature of virtuous development have significant consequences in the case of the judicial profession. When the

---

28 See Sec. 61 § 1(2) of Organization of Common Courts, Act of 27 July 2001 (Poland); similar expressions are found in Czech law (*European E-justice portal* (EU), "Types of legal professions: Czechia"), Estonian law (*European E-justice portal* (EU), "Types of legal professions: Estonia") and Latvia (Sec. 51(1) of the Law on Judicial Power (Latvia)).
29 I discuss the role of emotions in virtue also in Widłak (2025b), 637–638.
30 Aristotle et al. (2009), 1097b, 10 f.
31 See Russell (2013), 9.
32 See Aristotle et al. (2009), 1098a, 12.

judicial role is defined in aretaic terms, the judge finds herself on a path of constant moral and intellectual development. Judicial virtues are acquired and perfected; thus, becoming a judge is always a dynamic state of attaining professionalism and ethics, even if taking on the judicial robe is considered a crowning achievement of a legal career in some jurisdictions. Some virtues may be regarded as entry-level necessary dispositions for a judicial candidate; for instance, incorruptibility, courage, temperament and impartiality, diligence and carefulness, learnedness and intelligence are all counted by Solum as "uncontested judicial virtues".[33] Others, like justice and practical wisdom (prudence) or judicial perception[34], can be substantially developed throughout a judicial career. Practical consequences of perceiving one's judicial role through the lens of constant virtue development should encourage value consistency over long periods and integrity in moral deliberation. Consciously pursuing a virtue such as judicial prudence or ethical perception makes a judge aware and self-reflective on how they deal justice in even the most subtle ways, beyond regulation by any deontic rules. A virtuous mindset in judicial professionals enables them to relate to the participants in the court proceedings when an empathetic and mindful judge takes responsibility for understanding the case from the plaintiff's or defendant's perspective. Virtues also benefit their possessor as they enable one to relate to oneself, for instance, by providing a sense of fulfilment and, thus, a powerful motivation based on pursuing internal (rather than external) values of the practice of judging.[35]

2.4 Virtues spread through exemplars

Seeing the judicial role as a path of practising virtues among challenges, sometimes heroically[36], produces another unexpected and powerful effect of the emergence of exemplars.[37] They are real-life or fictional personal role models, carriers of robust personality features, which may be positive (virtuous) or negative (vicious). Exemplars become crucial for virtue development and moral education because they stand for their life stories and professional choices, which invite admiration (or condemnation, in the case of anti-heroes).[38] Exemplars create role models that encourage imitation of their actions but also, on a deeper level, share their affection and moral and legal perception of situations and cases to be dealt with. Judges will easily relate to their judicial heroes, universally or more individually admired personalities. The role and influence

33 See Solum (2005), 1365–1399.
34 See Van Domselaar (2018), 71–87.
35 On how virtues benefit their possessor, see Hursthouse (1999), 163–191.
36 For stories of "judicial heroes", see Graver (2024).
37 See Szutta (2019), 280–290; Amaya (2013), 428–445.
38 See Trinkaus Zagzebski (2017), 30–60.

of judicial exemplars continue through judicial education and training. Perhaps even more importantly, widely known judicial exemplars encourage public trust in the just judicial system on the part of the larger society. This last point cannot be underestimated; as repeatedly argued by many lawyers and recently most prominently by former US Supreme Court Justice Stephen Breyer, the trust generated by the perception of the judiciary is a crucial factor in upholding the rule of law.[39]

3 Virtue and judicial virtue

Against the above background of the examples of possible ethical, methodical, and epistemic advantages that the aretaic interpretation of the judicial role brings, a major conceptual issue about judicial virtue needs to be clarified. What exactly is "judicial virtue" when related to a non-professional or overall virtue? Is judicial virtue such as fairness a specialised, somehow differentiated species of general fairness that may be shared and practised by lawyers and non-lawyers? Or are these two (or more) entirely different virtues? While it is beyond the limits of this chapter to discuss the implications of these questions in detail[40], a position on the relation between the two concepts needs to be taken to further explain the proposed concept of judicial virtue.[41]

It seems unfeasible for judicial virtues to be a set of traits somehow separate or occurring and developing entirely autonomously from the overall virtues possessed (or not possessed at all) by a judge or a judicial candidate *as a* human or a citizen. If that was the case, and "judicial fairness" was an idiosyncratic kind of virtue unpracticed by lay members of the society, the judge in possession of "judicial fairness" would be substantially impaired in the process of sharing in the normative practices of the society. To put it differently – a judge practising a form of the virtue of fairness detached from general understanding (practice) of it within the society could not be perceived as a fair judge. It would not be helpful unless the judiciary is deliberately intended to be isolated in the inscrutable legalistic ivory tower. If judicial virtues are to be meaningful internally to the judiciary and in a broader social and cultural context, they need to relate to overall virtues.

Judges are also strongly expected to maintain moral integrity in and between professional, public, and private life. In this sense, integrity means that at least some (if not most) judicial virtues must be global instead of local virtues.[42] This view also

39 See Breyer (2021); cf. Widłak (2022), 151–166.
40 I deal with some of these questions in detail in Widłak (2025d), 101–157.
41 Cf Oakley/Cooking (2001).
42 "Global trait is a character trait which exhibits both cross-situational consistency in a wide variety of trait-relevant circumstances, as well as stability in repeated instances of the same kind of trait-relevant circumstances" Miller (2014), 418 f.

determines that possessing judicial virtues (like judicial prudence) requires at least some overall virtues. To be a prudent judge (which involves, among other things, being skilled at and knowledgeable about the law), one must be a sensible, mature person in the first place. This connection may even become legally required. Prudence is called for when a legal provision refers to notions like "life experience" to be used by the judge in evaluating evidence.[43] It follows that, first, judicial virtues are not a set of personality traits that are possessed or developed in separation from overall character traits of a judge and, second, they are not reducible to the general virtues either but rather are traits cooperating with or fostering at least some of the general virtues.

4 Judicial virtues as role-centered virtues

What is specific about judicial virtues that distinguishes them from the overall virtues remains to be decided. One promising possibility to endorse is perceiving the moral salience of judicial virtues as based on their role relevance.[44] The judicial role is firmly set in societal relations. However, viewed from the aretaic perspective, its moral importance should not be justified by the utilitarian argument of maximising social utility or the centrality of the judiciary in serving society. Instead, the moral and legal salience of each judge's role derives from their working to advance the welfare of other persons. The role of a judge, as much as that of a medical doctor or a teacher, is a specialised form developed from morally constitutive relationships between individuals.[45] Just as a doctor or a nurse develops from the role of caregiver, the judicial role develops from the morally determinative role of a protector or peacemaker. It is virtuous of a judge to be just or wise in a way that her actions secure, value, or bring to realisation defendants' legal welfare, for instance, in the form of the sense of justice done. In other words, judicial virtue is determined by the judge's role towards defendants, plaintiffs, or other stakeholders who turn to the court for legal protection. They are the traits that make her better (more excellent) in fulfilling the role that the judge plays in the life of these persons, because she is not a judge for herself or the sake of the law, but a judge *for someone* or in someone's case. This assertion explains how the judicial virtue of justice differs from the general or other, less specialised role-related virtue of justice. For instance, the virtue of justice can also be demonstrated by a superior (like a CEO) towards her subordinates (employees) or a father towards his children. However, we tend to have more precise and usually higher expectations towards judicial justice than

43 See, e.g. Sec. 7 of Poland's Code of Criminal Procedure: "The bodies of the proceedings shall shape their conviction based on all the evidence that has been carried out, freely assessed taking into account the principles of sound reasoning and indications of knowledge and life experience."
44 This part refers to the proposal by Garcia (2015), 415–423.
45 Ibid., 419 f.

in the former cases because of the judge's profound role in advancing the legal welfare of those who appeal the presumed instances of unjustness to the court.[46]

One aspect of the role-centred nature of judicial virtues that remains unclear at this point is the role of law in shaping judicial virtue. On the face of it, the role of a medical practitioner could be invoked as a helpful analogy to the role of the judge since both law and medicine are similarly highly professionalised fields. Just as evidence-based medicine creates higher expectations of caring and nursing by medical professionals compared to help and nourishment provided by the Biblical Good Samaritan, the relevant legal knowledge and experience shape the virtues of a judge at the level unattainable to lay people and even some lawyers. This conclusion would, however, reduce the question of the role of the law in determining the nature of judicial virtues to an epistemic problem of whether the judge possesses, and to what degree, a specific set of intellectual virtues like legal knowledge. There is something more to judicial virtue, which is tightly related to the limitations set out by the law-generated institutional context of delivering legal justice by the judge. The law and the resulting judicial position of authority determine a conventional framework, which modifies the relationship between the judge and the stakeholders of the process. It is not merely a simple two-party, reciprocal moral relation of care or benevolence (like between the medical doctor and a patient) because legal and social justice issues are inherent and prevalent within the judicial process. The law may substantially complicate the understanding of the concept of advancing the welfare of the participants of the legal process, given that the judge is also limited by the values (and norms) transcending these individual relations (with a plaintiff or defendant), such as equality before the law, and public interest, or a fair societal distribution of burdens and benefits.[47]

5 Target model of judicial virtue

To give a fuller account of judicial virtues in consideration of the doubts raised in the preceding section, now turn to a proposal of a target-centred model of virtue, which offers a more comprehensive structure of judicial virtues.[48] This working model of target judicial virtue is inspired by some features of Swanton's pluralist framework of virtue ethics[49] and her further work on the concept of target-centeredness of virtue.[50]

46 I develop the idea of role-relevant judicial virtues and draw on some of the same examples in Widłak (2025a), 211–213; Widłak (2025c), 96; Widłak (2025d), 101–119.
47 Cf. Widłak (2025d), 116–119.
48 This section incorporates and expands upon arguments developed in my previous publications, see Widłak (2025a), 212–213; Widłak (2025c), 94–96; Widłak (2025d), 131–137.
49 Swanton (2003).
50 Swanton (2021).

Swanton claims that "a virtue is a good quality of character, specifically a disposition to respond to, or acknowledge, items within its field or fields in an excellent or good enough way".[51] There are two critical notions used for this model: the first is the field, and the second is the target of virtue. A field of virtue is a collection of all items constituting the sphere of concern for the particular virtue.[52] Items can be of various ontological sorts; they may be both internal to the agent (e.g. desires) as well as outside of the agent: physical objects, property, money, other people or situations, and also abstract items like knowledge or beauty.[53] For instance, a life threat made to the judge by a defendant is an item in the field of judicial courage. A bribe or otherwise corruptive proposal is an item in the field of judicial integrity. However, it is essential to highlight that the fields of virtues do not have to be exclusive; there may be items that lie in the fields of more than one virtue; for instance, a defendant's outrageous behaviour in the courtroom may be an item in the fields of both judicial self-control (restraint) and decisiveness. Also, some judicial virtue fields fit in the fields of overall virtues; for instance, the field of judicial knowledge, as a case of scientific knowledge, is arguably a subfield of the Aristotelian virtue of philosophical wisdom.[54] Judicial virtues can be seen as having specific fields, differentiating them from general virtues. The fields or the nature of the items will be, to a large extent, construed legally. The institutional framework of the judicial system necessarily determines which items (challenges) may be appropriately addressed or responded to by the judge. Facts of the case, evidence, behaviour of a defendant in the courtroom, the substantive and procedural law, legal principles, actions by representing lawyers, the legal complexity of the case, public expectation of legal and moral standards of the judicial process, the responsibility for the outcome of the process – these are but small fraction of examples of items predetermined by the legal system to be responded to by judges. The relationship between the law or the institutional framework of the judiciary and the items identified as positioned in the fields of judicial virtue does not need to be direct. The items that can be appropriately addressed by acting from judicial virtues and those that are not will also be determined by the experience of a particular judge, a deep understanding and perception of one's role and its limitations, or through judicial prudence. For instance, an experienced and perceptive judge in a democratic jurisdiction will recognise the value of an egalitarian political community and awaken to the role of a judicial office in fostering civic fraternity.[55] She might thus realise her subtle propensity to reason and act with the feeling of superiority towards other participants of the adjudicative process, even if unconsciously following her position of authority and power or supreme legal

51 Swanton (2003), 19.
52 Ibid., 20 f.
53 Ibid., 20.
54 See Aristotle et al. (2009), 1141a, 108.
55 Amaya (2018), 97–107.

knowledge. It could constitute an item in the field of judicial humility, a virtue oriented on the deep understanding of the value of fundamental equality between people and the judicial role in honouring it.

The items present in the fields of judicial virtues put demands on the virtuous judge to respond to them or acknowledge them in an appropriate (excellent or at least good enough) way.[56] It may be done through different response modes (promoting values, honouring rules, being respectful of status, considering relationships between people, creating, admiring, or handling things appropriately). These responses to the challenges presented by items in the field may hit the aim or goal of virtue or not. Thus, the "features which make traits of character virtues are determined by their targets, aims or point (...)".[57] In other words, traits of character are valued as virtues based on the kind of aims or functions that they realise in the life of a good human being. It may be the flourishing of the individual (the agent of virtue). However, virtues may also target the well-being of others, peace in society, and the preservation of the environment or the legal system. Following this concept, a particular action is right if it hits the target of the relevant virtue. For instance, the aim of lawfulness as a judicial virtue is to uphold the rule of law. A judge acts lawfully when, in response to the government's attempt to surveil a journalist (an item in the field), she invalidates the relevant government action or rejects a request for wiretapping and, by doing so, upholds or strengthens the rule of law through effective judicial control. The target of virtue determines whether the chosen form of response to the world (an item in the field of virtue) is a good or correct one.[58] The response is appropriate if it hits the target of the virtue. Hitting the target of virtue may be regarded, in Aristotelian terms, as hitting "the mean" of each virtue.[59] The mean is a multi-dimensional condition of meeting the requirements of virtue "in the right circumstance, in the right manner, at the right time, to the right extent, for the right reasons, concerning the right people or objects, deploying the right instruments".[60]

This overall target model of virtue accommodates the role-oriented view of judicial virtue presented above in two ways. First, many judicial virtues may be regarded as directly having a target in the form of a particular welfare of others (e. g. kindness, fairness, impartiality). Second, the target of judicial virtue is hit when the virtuous response is proper concerning other participants of the court proceedings, understood as an inherently social process. A judge's response to a bribe by merely denying or ignoring it is not virtuous because it is not a good enough way to react to behaviour that harms the legal welfare of the parties to the case.

56 Swanton (2003), 19.
57 Swanton (2021), 133.
58 Swanton (2021), 7.
59 Aristotle et al. (2009), 1106b, 30 f.
60 Swanton (2021), 137.

6 Conclusion

Judging is like professional writing. Following the rules may be necessary for judging as much as it is for proper writing. One does not, however, become an outstanding writer just by following a code of rules. The same is true for becoming an excellent judge. Aretaic concepts such as virtue are considered thick notions;[61] allow us to normatively grasp a fuller account of a judge's personality and role. It was argued here that virtue language provides for a more comprehensive picture of what it takes to be a good judge by transcending the limits of deontic and consequentialist morality, accommodating emotions or the affective side of action and their role in motivating the judge to act excellently in relations with other human beings, as well as by providing potent patterns of moral and legal education through exemplars. Virtues are excellent qualities of character acted upon from good motives (or fine inner states) and aimed at acknowledging and responding well to the world's challenges. The response takes the form of virtuous action if it hits the target or the aim of each virtue in an excellent or good enough way. Judicial virtues are role-based in that they are defined by the kind of challenges arising in the path of judicial service, including those put there by the law, that can be appropriately recognised and addressed by a virtuous response that hits the specific target. In the case of judicial virtue, the target is directly a form of welfare of the stakeholders of the judicial process (the society, the participants to the proceedings) or at least hitting the target in the sense of attaining Aristotelian mean, involves respecting the welfare of those whom the judge serves in her role of administering justice.

Bibliography

Amaya, Amalia / Michelon, Claudio (Eds.): The Faces of Virtue in Law (2020). Abingdon – New York: Routledge.

Amaya, Amalia (2018): "The virtue of judicial humility". In: Jurisprudence 9(1), 97–107.

Amaya, Amalia (2013): "Exemplarism and Judicial Virtue". In: Law & Literature 25, 428–445.

Anscombe, G. Elisabeth M. (1958): "Modern Moral Philosophy". In: Philosophy 33, 1–19.

Aristotle / Ross, David (Trans.) / Brown, Lesley (Ed.): The Nicomachean Ethics (2009). New York: Oxford University Press.

Battaly, Heather (2015): Virtue. Cambridge – Malden: Polity Press.

Becker, Lawrence C. (2018): "Stoic Virtue". In: Snow, Nancy E. (Ed.): The Oxford Handbook of Virtue. New York: Oxford University Press, 130–152.

Besser-Jones Lorraine / Michael Slote (Eds.) (2015): The Routledge Companion to Virtue Ethics. New York: Routledge.

Breyer, Stephen (2021): The Authority of the Court and the Peril of Politics. Cambridge, MA – London: Harvard University Press.

61 See Williams (1986), 129.

Bucar, Elizabeth M. (2018): "Islamic Virtue Ethics". In: Snow, Nancy E. (Ed.): The Oxford Handbook of Virtue. New York: Oxford University Press, 206–223.

Code of Criminal Procedure, Act of 6 June 1997 (Poland) (Dz. U. 2022, poz. 1375).

Curzer, Howard J. (2018): "Aristotle and Moral Virtue". In: Snow, Nancy E. (Ed.): The Oxford Handbook of Virtue. New York: Oxford University Press, 104–129.

Farrelly, Colin / Solum, Lawrence B. (Eds.): Virtue Jurisprudence (2008). New York: Palgrave Macmillan.

Frede, Dorothea (2013): "The historical decline of virtue ethics". In: Russell, Daniel C. (Ed.), The Cambridge Companion to Virtue Ethics. Cambridge: Cambridge University Press, 124–148.

Garcia, J. L. A. (2015): "Roles and Virtues". In: Besser-Jones, Lorraine / Michael Slote (Eds.): The Routledge Companion to Virtue Ethics. New York: Routledge, 415–423.

Gaund, Simon / Pratt, Karen (Eds., trans.) (2016): "Song of Roland". In: Gaund, Simon / Pratt, Karen (Eds., trans.): The Song of Roland and Other Poems of Charlemagne. New York: Oxford University Press, 3–133.

Goodman, Charles (2015): "Virtue in Buddhist Ethical Traditions". In: Besser-Jones, Lorraine / Michael Slote (Eds.): The Routledge Companion to Virtue Ethics. New York: Routledge, 89–97.

Graver, Hans Peter (2024): Valiant Judges, Iniquitous Law. Thirteen Stories of Heroes of the Law. New York: Routledge.

Hursthouse, Rosalind (1999): On Virtue Ethics. New York: Oxford University Press.

Hutton, Eric L. (2015): "Xunzi and Virtue Ethics". In: Besser-Jones, Lorraine / Michael Slote (Eds.): The Routledge Companion to Virtue Ethics. New York: Routledge, 113–125.

Ivanhoe, Philip J. (2013): "Virtue ethics and the Chinese Confucian Tradition". In: Russell, Daniel C. (Ed.), The Cambridge Companion to Virtue Ethics. Cambridge: Cambridge University Press, 49–69.

Luo, Shirong (2015): "Mencius' Virtue Ethics meets the Moral Foundations Theory: A Comparison". In: Besser-Jones Lorraine / Michael Slote (Eds.): The Routledge Companion to Virtue Ethics. New York: Routledge, 77–88.

Małolepszy Mateusz / Jakimiec Bartłomiej (2020): "Rozdział 9. Kryteria i procedura wyboru sędziów sądów powszechnych w ujęciu prawnoporównawczym". In: Małolepszy Mateusz (Ed.) (2020): Kryteria i procedura wyboru sędziów sądów powszechnych w wybranych państwach europejskich. Warszawa: C. H. Beck, 115–146.

Miller, Christian B. (2018): "Virtue as a Trait". In: Snow, Nancy E. (Ed.): The Oxford Handbook of Virtue. New York: Oxford University Press, 9–34.

Miller, Christian (2014): "The problem of character". In: van Hooft, Stan (Ed.): The Handbook of Virtue Ethics. Durham: Acumen, 418–429.

Nitobe, Inazō / Bennett, Alexander (Ed.) (2019): Bushido. The Samurai Code of Japan. Tokyo – Vermont: Tuttle Publishing.

Oakley, Justin / Cooking Dean (2001): Virtue Ethics and Professional Roles. Cambridge: Cambridge University Press.

Peterson, Christopher / Seligman, Martin E. P. (2004): Character Strengths and Virtues. A Handbook and Classification. New York: Oxford University Press.

Russell, Daniel C. (2014): "Phronesis and the Virtues". In: Polansky, Ronald (Ed.): The Cambridge Companion to Aristotle's Nicomachean Ethics. New York: Cambridge University Press, 203–220.

Russell, Daniel C. (2013): "Virtue ethics, happiness, and the good life". In: Russell, Daniel C. (Ed.), The Cambridge Companion to Virtue Ethics. Cambridge: Cambridge University Press, 7–28.

Snow, Nancy E. (Ed.) (2018): The Oxford Handbook of Virtue. New York: Oxford University Press.
Solum, Lawrence B. (2005): "A Tournament of Virtue". In: Florida State University Law Review 32, 1365–1400.
Solum, Lawrence B. (2003): "Virtue Jurisprudence. Virtue-Centred Theory of Judging". In: Metaphilosophy 34 (1/2), 178–213.
Swanton, Christine (2021): Target Centered Virtue Ethics. New York: Oxford University Press.
Swanton, Christine (2003): Virtue Ethics. A Pluralistic View. New York: Oxford University Press.
Szutta, Natasza (2019): "Exemplarist moral theory – some pros and cons". In: Journal of Moral Education 48, 280–290.
Szutta, Natasza (2015): "Moral Education from the Perspective of Virtue Ethics". In: Diametros. A Journal of Philosophy 46, 111–133.
Trinkaus Zagzebski, Linda (2017): Exemplarist Moral Theory. New York: Oxford University Press.
Trinkaus Zagzebski, Linda (1996): Virtues of the Mind. An Inquire into the Nature of Virtue and the Ethical Foundations of Knowledge. Cambridge: Cambridge University Press.
Van Domselaar, Iris (2018): "The perceptive judge." In: Jurisprudence 9(1), 71–87.
Van Hooft, Stan (2006): Understanding Virtue Ethics. Chesham: Acumen.
White, Nicholas (2015): "Plato and the Ethics of Virtue". In: Besser-Jones, Lorraine / Michael Slote (Eds.) The Routledge Companion to Virtue Ethics. New York: Routledge, 3–15.
Widłak, Tomasz (2022): "Trust and Trustworthiness as Judicial Virtues". In: Krytyka Prawa. Niezależne Studia nad Prawem 14 (4), 151–166.
Widłak, Tomasz (2025a): "Rule of Law and the Criteria for Appointment of Judges:
A Case for Judicial Virtues". In: Hague Journal on the Rule of Law 17, 199–220.
Widłak, Tomasz (2025b): "Judicial resistance and the virtues". In: Oñati Socio-Legal Series 15 (2), 629–647.
Widłak, Tomasz (2025c): "Judicial virtues of independence". In: Widłak, Tomasz (Ed.), Judicial Character in Hard Times. On the Role of Judicial Virtues in Defending the Rule of Law. Cheltenham, UK, Northampton, MA, USA: Edward Elgar Publishing.
Widłak, Tomasz (2025d): Temida z charakterem. Filozoficznoprawny przewodnik po cnotach sędziowskich. Gdańsk – Warszawa: University of Gdańsk Press & Wolters Kluwer Polska.
Williams, Bernard (1986): Ethics and the Limits of Philosophy. Cambridge, MA: Harvard University Press.
Wood, W. Jay (2018): "Christian Theories of Virtue". In: Snow, Nancy E. (Ed.): The Oxford Handbook of Virtue. New York: Oxford University Press, 281–300.

Tomasz Widłak
Faculty of Law and Administration, University of Gdańsk
tomasz.widlak@ug.edu.pl

Challenging the Rule of Law
Stress and Burnout in the Polish Judiciary During the Constitutional Crisis

TERESA CHIRKOWSKA-SMOLAK / MAREK SMOLAK

Abstract: This study investigated the psychological well-being of judges in the midst of Poland's constitutional crisis, emphasizing work-related stress and burnout in a challenging political environment. The judiciary's critical role in upholding democracy and the rule of law places judges at the forefront of political and legal transformations, making them particularly vulnerable to psychological strain.

Utilizing a survey methodology, this study encompasses responses from 475 Polish judges. The Perceived Stress at Work Scale (PSwP) and Oldenburg Burnout Inventory (OLBI) were employed to measure stress and burnout. The findings reveal that Polish judges experience a moderate to high level of perceived stress and burnout, which is significantly more pronounced than that of other social professionals in Poland and legal professionals in other European countries.

These results highlight the unique pressures faced by judges owing to the current political climate. This study underscores the need for systemic interventions in the judiciary, such as mental health support and workload management, to mitigate these challenges. The elevated stress and burnout levels among judges have profound implications for the efficiency of the judiciary and the broader rule of law.

In conclusion, this study provides valuable insights into the mental health challenges confronting legal professionals during political crises. It emphasizes the importance of addressing these issues to maintain the integrity and functionality of judicial systems, particularly in times of political and social upheavals.

Keywords: judges, stress, burnout, constitutional crisis

1 Introduction

At the outset, it is worth noting that in legal considerations we often use the term 'the Polish constitutional crisis'. The term 'the Polish constitutional crisis' has many meanings, so let us clarify what this term means.

According to W. Sadurski, the term means that the legislature and executive of the Polish government to have *de facto* control over judges and their appointments. In 2015 Law and Justice party came to power and significantly altered the composition of the

Polish Constitutional Court, the Supreme Court and the National Council of Judiciary. Law and Justice party used its power to appoint judges to the Polish Constitutional Court in 2015, leading to the Polish Constitutional Court crisis. The government of Poland continued to expand its hold on the judiciary resulting in the 2017 Supreme Court crisis, and the 2019 Polish judicial disciplinary law[1]. The changes in the legislation regarding the Supreme Court, National Council of the Judiciary, and the common courts have left Polish judges highly vulnerable to political pressure and interference.

In the midst of Poland's constitutional crisis, characterized by the ruling party's efforts to restructure the judiciary, an often-overlooked dimension merits attention: the psychological well-being of judges. This crisis, intensifying and intertwined with legal, democratic, and nationalistic elements, spills over into judges' personal and professional lives, necessitating an in-depth analysis of its impact on those responsible for upholding justice[2].

The legal profession, particularly judges and prosecutors, is a guardian of the rule of law, making them especially vulnerable to vicissitudes within the judicial system. Their role in upholding democracy and ensuring impartial justice is paramount; however, in times of political unrest, such as the period marked by the governance of the Law and Justice party (PiS), their position has become increasingly challenging. This period witnessed attempts to influence the judiciary, raising concerns about the erosion of judicial independence and impartiality[3].

The recent shift towards a pro-European coalition government has initiated a change in political focus, aimed at addressing the erosion of the rule of law. However, the lasting impacts of the previous eight years continue to provide a context for understanding the condition of the judiciary during the research period.

The emotional exhaustion and burnout resulting from such a politically charged environment can have significant mental health implications for judges, as illustrated by Rothstein and Eek's research on occupational stress in judicial decision making[4]. The deterioration of the rule of law leads to unpredictable legal outcomes, exacerbating stress and potentially resulting in burnout[5]. This unpredictability and lack of support within the profession can impede judges' professional advancement and decision-making capabilities, ultimately affecting the integrity of the legal field[6].

It is noteworthy that, amidst these challenges, a segment of the judiciary has exhibited resilience and integrity, actively opposing assault on the rule of law. These "brave professionals" demonstrate a commitment to democracy and judicial independence,

---

1 Sadurski (2019), 58; Smolak (2017),27–29.
2 Ibid.
3 Ibid.
4 Rothstein/Eek (2013), 156–164.
5 Pech/Scheppele (2017), 3–47.
6 Guthrie et al. (2001), 777–830.

highlighting the complex interplay between professional obligations and personal well-being in a restrictive legal environment[7].

Bi's study on the occupational burnout among legal professionals in the context of rule-of-law reforms further accentuates this correlation, emphasizing the risks of stress and burnout due to the disparity between professional ideals and practical realities. This aspect is particularly pertinent to Polish judges amidst the constitutional crisis, underscoring the significance of this study in exploring these critical issues[8].

2 The Mental Health of Legal Professionals

Mental health within the legal profession has become a matter of increasing concern, as indicated by a variety of sources, such as national surveys, scholarly publications, professional webinars, and support initiatives. This concern gained prominence in the United States with the establishment of The National Taskforce on Lawyers Well-Being in 2016 and has since extended to encompass the European Union[9]. While the legal profession offers both rewards and intellectual stimulation, it comes with substantial demands and challenging work environments. Lawyers confront the pressure to meet billable hours and client expectations, which can negatively impact their overall well-being. Approximately 30 % of lawyers in the United States report experiencing mental health issues, a trend mirrored globally[10]. This problem affects legal professionals across all areas of practice, with 35 % of those surveyed by the International Bar Association reporting a detrimental impact of their work on mental well-being[11].

According to previous studies, legal professionals are more prone to experiencing depression, anxiety, and stress, and have lower overall mental well-being compared to the general population. This information is outlined in a report by the National Taskforce on Lawyer Well-Being, titled "The Path to Lawyer Well-Being: Practical Recommendations for Positive Change," which was published in August 2017[12]. While limited data are available, it is likely that legal professionals in Poland, particularly judges, face unique challenges that affect their mental well-being. The cultural, political, and policy contexts in Poland significantly impact the interpretation and valuation of mental well-being, which vary globally. Therefore, there is a need for focused research to understand and address the unique challenges faced by Polish legal professionals.

7 Kidder (2005), 132–149; Sekerka/Bagozzi (2007), 132–149; Smolak et al. (2022), 317–320
8 Bi (2017), 581–613
9 Chirkowska-Smolak (2022), 247–260.
10 Kelk et al. (2009), 35–41; National Taskforce on Lawyer Well-Being (2017), [online document, no page numbers].
11 International Bar Association (2020), [online document, no page numbers].
12 National Taskforce on Lawyer Well-Being (2017), [online document, no page numbers].

A solid theoretical foundation is crucial for fully understanding the psychological consequences of stress and burnout in the judiciary. Recent academic research has expanded our understanding of burnout, which is now widely recognized as a multifaceted reaction to prolonged workplace stress characterized by substantial job demands and insufficient resources. The study conducted by Demerouti et al. significantly enriches our understanding of burnout by identifying its primary constituents as exhaustion and disengagement[13]. Exhaustion arises from extended exposure to demanding work conditions that affect emotional, physical, and cognitive states. On the other hand, disengagement represents a psychological detachment from one's work, resulting in a loss of interest and a sense of pointlessness in work tasks. In the judiciary, where judges face high-pressure decision making, substantial workloads, and public scrutiny, these dimensions are particularly relevant. This scenario is not only important for individual well-being but also has far-reaching implications for the judiciary. Burnout can compromise judicial decision making, affect the quality of judgments, and ultimately undermine public trust in the judicial system[14].

Our research integrates the theoretical framework of perceived stress at work proposed by Cohen and Williamson. This approach enables us to comprehend stress as judges' subjective reaction to perceived obstacles or pressures, a particularly relevant aspect in the context of Poland's constitutional crisis[15].

Stress is not solely a product of external circumstances but also results from an individual's interpretation of these circumstances as exceeding their ability to cope. This perspective, put forward by Cohen and Janicki-Deverts, emphasizes the role of the individual in perceiving stressors and determining their capacity to manage them[16]. Perceived stress is a measure of the degree to which individuals evaluate life situations.

In the Polish judiciary, the ongoing constitutional crisis and increasing political interference in judicial affairs exacerbate the stressors experienced by judges, resulting in a climate of uncertainty and instability[17]. This occupational stress significantly impacts judges' performance and decision-making, potentially leading to cognitive biases and diminished reasoning[18]. Prolonged exposure to such stress can have detrimental effects on judges' mental health, including the development of anxiety and depression, which can affect both their personal and professional lives[19].

Our study aims to provide a refined understanding of the psychological well-being of Polish judges, particularly in light of the ongoing constitutional crisis. Our investiga-

---

13 Demerouti et al. (2021), 686–691.
14 Maslach & Leiter (2016), 103–111; Rothstein & Eek (2013), 156–164; Smolak, Sadurski, Chirkowska-Smolak (2020), 247–260.
15 Cohen & Williamson (1988), 31–67.
16 Cohen & Janicki-Deverts (2012), 1320–1334
17 Sadurski (2019), 58–99; Pech & Scheppele (2017), 3–47.
18 Guthrie, Rachlinski, & Wistrich (2001), 777–830.
19 Jouriles & McDonald (2015), 241–249.

tion into the heightened levels of stress and occupational burnout among these judges is not solely academic in nature but rather a crucial examination of the human element within a judiciary facing pressure.

The implications of our research extend beyond the academic realm and offer critical insights into the broader consequences of a stressed Polish legal community. The effects on the quality of justice, public trust in the legal system, and resilience of democracy itself cannot be overstated. Addressing these issues is essential not only for enhancing the judiciary's resilience but also for strengthening the foundations of democracy in Poland.

3 Method

3.1 Purpose of the Study

The primary purpose of this research was to assess and report the levels of perceived stress at work and burnout among Polish judges. Given their pivotal role as defenders of the rule of law, their heightened susceptibility amid political shifts, and the erosion of democracy, this study aims to thoroughly comprehend their current psychological well-being. This study is of paramount importance considering the recent constitutional crisis in Poland, which poses substantial challenges to the mental health of legal professionals. By conducting an extensive analysis of stress and burnout levels within this group, this study aims to provide invaluable insights into the personal sacrifices made by these professionals in maintaining justice and democracy.

3.2 Research Questions

1. What is the level of perceived stress at work and burnout among Polish judges?

This inquiry aimed to quantify and analyze the current state of psychological stress and burnout within professional groups. Specifically, it involves measuring and interpreting the extent of these conditions, thereby providing a snapshot of the mental health status of judges in the context of the recent political and legal changes in Poland.

2. Do lawyers, particularly judges, experience significantly higher stress and burnout than representatives of other social professions in Poland do?

The objective here is to contextualize the findings within a broader societal framework by comparing the levels of stress and burnout experienced by judges with those of other social professional groups with high cognitive demands. This comparative analysis seeks to determine whether the unique challenges faced by legal professionals in their roles contribute to distinctively higher levels of psychological stress and burnout.

3.3 Procedure

The present study is based on an online survey conducted in 2022 as part of a broader endeavor that focuses on the well-being of Polish legal professionals. This survey was carried out among Polish judges using a census sampling method, aimed at encompassing the entire population of potential respondents. The help of court presidents was enlisted to accomplish this.

Prior to the initiation of the survey, participants were required to provide written consent in accordance with ethical standards and were apprised of their right to withdraw from the survey at any juncture, with the assurance that their responses would remain confidential. The research team established a direct communication channel with participants, with the aim of addressing any queries or concerns, fostering a transparent and responsive environment, and reinforcing the ethical integrity of the research.

The sample size required to meet the minimum threshold was determined by using the estimated prevalence of work-related stress and burnout among approximately 10,000 judges in Poland, which was set at 50 %. By employing the standard proportion formula, it was determined that a sample size of 385 judges would be necessary to ensure the statistical validity and representativeness of the results within the designated confidence interval and margin of error.

3.4 Participants

This research project involved a diverse cohort of 475 judges from Poland, encompassing a broad range of demographic and professional characteristics. Among these participants, 289 were female judges, accounting for approximately 60.8 % of the sample, whereas 184 were male judges, representing 38.7 % (Fig. 1). Regarding their professional roles, 302 judges (63.6 %) held non-managerial positions, while 158 (33.3 %) held managerial positions, reflecting a wide spectrum of responsibilities within the judiciary (Fig.2).

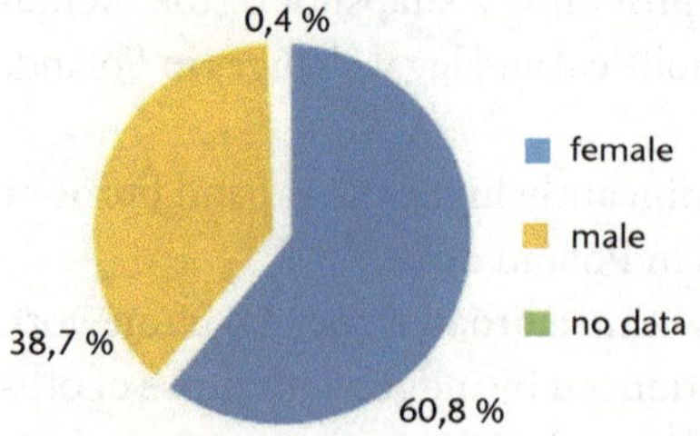

Fig. 1 Gender distribution

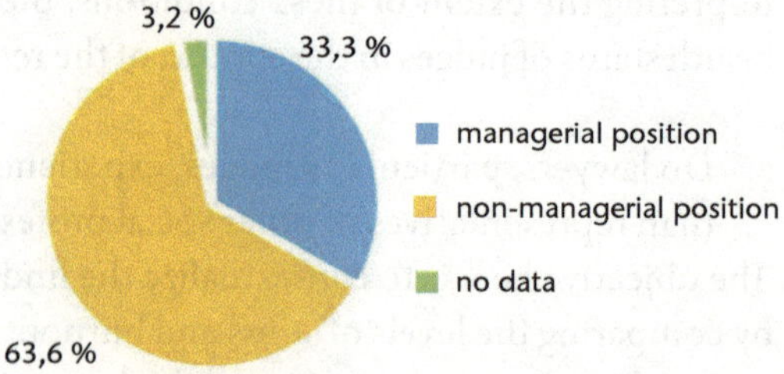

Fig. 2 Professional roles distribution

As for legal specialization, the majority (204 judges, 43 %) came from the civil law field, followed by 136 judges (28.6 %) from the criminal law field, 67 judges (14.1 %) in economic law, 42 judges (8.8 %) in family law, and 22 judges (4.6 %) in labor law, providing a comprehensive representation of various legal domains (Fig.3).

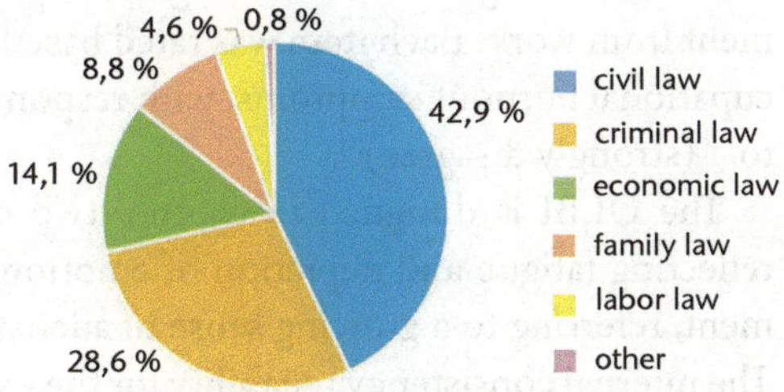

Fig. 3 Legal specialization distribution

The judges also varied in their professional experience, with an average of 19.33 years (SD = 8.33 years) and a range of 1–40 years, highlighting a mix of seasoned and relatively new judges. Similarly, their tenure in their current positions averaged 13.17 years (SD = 7.78 years) and ranged from 1 to 40 years, reflecting different stages of career development. Moreover, the judges reported working an average of 49.64 hours per week (SD = 11.26 hours), indicating the demanding nature of their roles and the need for many judges to work long hours.

3.4.1 Perceived Stress at Work Scale (PSwP)

The Perceived Stress at Work Scale (PSwP) was developed by Chirkowska-Smolak and Grobelny as a tool to measure employees' perceived stress levels in their work environments. This scale comprises ten test items that focus on assessing employees' beliefs about unpredictability, lack of control, and work-related events that may have caused stress in the month preceding the survey. An example item from this scale is: "In the past month, how often have you been angry because of things that happened that were outside of your control at work?" Respondents were asked to indicate the frequency of their specific thoughts and feelings on a scale ranging from 0 (never) to 4 (very often). The items collectively aim to capture the extent of unpredictability, lack of control, and work overload experienced by the employees. The PSwP demonstrated good reliability, with a Cronbach's alpha of 0.85, indicating high internal consistency[20].

20 Chirkowska-Smolak & Grobelny (2016), 131–139.

3.4.2 Oldenburg Burnout Inventory (OLBI)

The OLBI, developed by Demerouti et al. and adapted into Polish by Chirkowska-Smolak, was utilized to measure occupational burnout. This instrument consists of 16 items, with eight items assessing exhaustion and the other eight assessing disengagement from work. Each item was rated based on the degree of agreement regarding occupational burnout symptoms, with response options ranging from 1 (strongly agree) to 4 (strongly disagree)[21].

The OLBI is designed to capture two core dimensions of burnout: exhaustion, reflecting fatigue and depletion of emotional and physical resources, and disengagement, referring to a growing sense of alienation from and cynicism about one's work. The internal consistency reliability for the exhaustion subscale was $\alpha = 0.75$, and for the disengagement subscale, $\alpha = 0.74$, indicating satisfactory reliability[22].

4 Results

4.1 Statistical Description of Burnout and Work-Related Stress Among Judges

This subsection presents the descriptive statistics of the study, focusing on the levels of burnout and work-related stress among Polish judges. The present study aimed to assess burnout on two subscales – exhaustion and disengagement (also referred to as cynicism)–as well as perceived stress at work among Polish judges.

Stress at Work: The level of work-related stress was determined using a scale with a minimum score of 0.20 and a maximum score of 3.90. The average stress level among the judges was 2.03 (SD = 0.72), suggesting a moderate level of perceived stress in the workplace.

Exhaustion: The exhaustion subscale of burnout ranged from a minimum score of 1.25 to a maximum of 4.00, with an average score of 2.85 (SD = 0.53), indicating a relatively high level of exhaustion among judges.

Disengagement (Cynicism): For the disengagement aspect of burnout, the scores varied between 1.25 and 4.00, with an average score of 2.62 (SD = 0.44). This indicates a moderate-to-high level of disengagement among the participants.

Having established the statistical landscape of stress and burnout among Polish judges, we now turn to address our primary research questions: What is the level of perceived stress at work and burnout among Polish judges? Additionally, do lawyers, particularly

21 Demerouti et al. (2003), 12–23; Chirkowska-Smolak (2018), 27–47.

22 Chirkowska-Smolak (2018), 27–47.

judges, experience higher stress and burnout than individuals from other social professions in Poland?

4.2 Perceived stress at work and burnout among Polish judges

This study examined the perceived stress levels of Polish judges in their work environments. In response to our first research question regarding the level of perceived stress at work and burnout among Polish judges, our analysis reveals the following insights. The results of our analysis revealed significant insights, particularly in the comparison of stress levels between judges and the broader working Polish population.

The mean stress score for judges in our study was 2.03 (SD = 0.72), indicating perceived stress levels in professional environments. In contrast to the findings of Chirkowska-Smolak and Grobelny, who reported a mean stress score of 1.57 (SD = 0.69) among a sample of 537 Polish employees, a noticeable difference of approximately 0.46 points was observed. The effect size of this difference, calculated using Cohen's d, is approximately 0.65, indicating a medium to large difference in work-related stress levels between Polish judges and the general working population in Poland[23].

Table 1 presents a summary of the burnout levels among Polish judges based on their exhaustion and cynicism stanine scores, along with relevant descriptive statistics. The findings of the study indicate that the Polish judges in the sample generally experienced high levels of burnout, with an average exhaustion score of 6.79 and a disengagement score of 6.13. Moreover, the median scores of 7 for exhaustion and 6 for disengagement further emphasized this trend. The data revealed a slightly skewed distribution, with a moderate level of cynicism reported by 42.95 % of judges. Notably, approximately 3.37 % of the judges exhibited severe burnout, characterized by the highest stanine score (9) on both the exhaustion and disengagement scales.

Table 1 Burnout (exhaustion and disengagement) among Polish judges.

Metric	Exhaustion Stanines	Disengagement Stanines
Mean	6.79	6.13
Median	7.00	6.00
Standard Deviation	1.69	1.60
Minimum	1.00	1.00
Maximum	9.00	9.00
High Level (Exhaustion)	292 (61.47 %)	
Moderate Level (Exhaustion)	167 (35.16 %)	

23 Chirkowska-Smolak & Grobelny (2016), 131–139.

Table 1 Burnout (exhaustion and disengagement) among Polish judges.

Metric	Exhaustion Stanines	Disengagement Stanines
Low Level (Exhaustion)	16 (3.37%)	
High Level (Disengagement)		204 (42.95%)
Moderate Level (Disengagement)		245 (51.58%)
Low Level (Disengagement)		26 (5.47%)
Severe Burnout	3.37%	3.37%

Source: the authors' own study

These results underscore the need to address Polish judges' mental well-being and the potential stress and challenges inherent in their professional roles.

4.3 Comparative Analysis: Judges vs Other Social Professions in Poland

To further explore our second research question of whether judges experience higher stress and burnout than individuals from other social professions in Poland, we explore how the burnout and stress levels of judges compare to those in other social professions within Poland. An independent sample t-test was conducted to compare the burnout levels of judges and other social professionals in Poland, utilizing mean scores, standard deviations, and sample sizes. The analysis was based on data from the Polish study conducted by Baka and Basińska, which involved social professionals with high cognitive demands, such as teachers, medical personnel, and policemen, with a total sample size of $N = 1804$. For the dimension of exhaustion, the mean score among the social professionals was 2.31 ($SD = 0.55$). The t-test revealed a highly significant difference between the social professionals and the judges, $t(2277) = 19.18$, $p < 0.0001$. This indicates that judges experience significantly higher levels of exhaustion compared to the social professionals. The effect size was large, as indicated by Cohen's d (0.99).

Regarding the dimension of disengagement, the mean score for the social professionals was 2.29 ($SD = 0.55$). The results of the t-test for disengagement were also significant, $t(2277) = 12.096$, $p < 0.0001$, suggesting that judges experience higher levels of disengagement compared to their counterparts in other social professions. The effect size was found to be medium, with Cohen's d at 0.66.

These findings suggest that judges in Poland experience more pronounced levels of exhaustion and disengagement than other social professionals[24].

24 Baka & Basińska (2016), 29–41.

4.4 Comparative Analysis with International Studies

This subsection extends our comparative analysis to an international context, comparing the burnout and stress levels of Polish judges with those of legal professionals in other countries. In our comparative analysis of occupational stress, we examined the perceived stress levels of judges in comparison with two groups of lawyers from the United States, as reported by Krill et al. Lawyers were categorized into two cohorts: those who believed their employer valued professionalism (N = 610) and those who believed their employer valued financial worth (N = 610). Our findings revealed that lawyers who believed their employer prioritized professionalism reported lower stress levels, with a mean of 1.479 (SD = 0.692), while judges in our study exhibited notably higher stress levels, with a mean of 2.03 (SD = 0.72). The results of the t-test were highly significant, with a statistic of -14.56 and a p-value less than 0.0001. The effect size, measured using Cohen's d, was -0.787, indicating a large effect size. This disparity underscores the greater levels of stress experienced by judges than by lawyers who believed their employer valued professionalism[25]. This study included a comparison group of 539 judges and lawyers who assessed their financial worth. The results showed that judges reported higher levels of stress (M = 2.03, SD = 0.72) than did lawyers (M = 1.743, SD = 0.704). The t-test revealed a statistically significant difference with a t-value of -6.41 and a p-value of less than 0.0001. The medium effect size of -0.403 suggests that even when compared to lawyers, judges experience higher levels of stress.

The findings of this study highlight a significant trend in occupational stress experienced by judges in Poland. The results consistently demonstrate that judges report greater levels of perceived stress compared to both groups of lawyers in the United States, with a more pronounced difference observed when compared to lawyers who believe they are valued for their professionalism. These results underscore the unique stressors faced by judges and the intensity of their occupational strain.

Our results contrasted also with those of a Norwegian study by Innstrand et al. that employed a distinct response scale, yet adhered to the same methodological approach. This study included lawyers with various professional backgrounds. Our analysis revealed statistically significant disparities in exhaustion and disengagement levels between both sexes when compared to the Norwegian study, with p-values below 0.05. Cohen's d values indicated substantial effect sizes of 0.886 and 1.038 for exhaustion and 1.180 and 1.185 for disengagement among men and women, respectively. These pronounced distinctions, especially in disengagement, emphasize the gravity of burnout among Polish judges[26].

---

25 Krill et al. (2022), 177.
26 Innstrand et al. (2011), 813–824.

We compared our findings with a German study conducted by Kersten et al., which assessed burnout in high-cognitive-demand professions, including lawyers, but did not specifically target them. Our study's total burnout scores for both genders were higher than those reported in the German study, with the mean total burnout scores for females ($M = 2.781$) and males ($M = 2.661$) being significantly higher. These results suggest a notable difference in the burnout levels between the two studies[27].

In addition, we examined a recent French study by Nickum and Desrumaux, which explored burnout among French lawyers and found a high mean burnout score ($M = 4.07/7$, $SD = 0.95$). When comparing our results with this French study, adjusting for the 7-point scale used by Nickum and Desrumaux, we found that Polish judges experience a higher level of burnout than French lawyers ($t(654) = 5.1875$, $p < 0.0001$, with a Cohen's $d = 0.44$). Although statistically significant, this difference should be interpreted with caution because different measurement tools were used in the two studies[28].

The findings of this study underscore the prevalence of burnout among Polish judges. Moreover, despite employing different methodologies, the variation in burnout levels between Polish judges and French lawyers underscores the pivotal role that cultural, systemic, and environmental factors play in comprehending burnout in the legal profession. This contrast underscores the necessity for a complex and nuanced understanding of burnout, which accounts for the distinct challenges encountered by legal professionals across diverse nations.

In summary, our study reveals a significant prevalence of burnout and stress among Polish judges, characterized by elevated levels of exhaustion and disengagement. The comparative analysis, both nationally and internationally, indicates that these stress levels are notably higher than those in other social professions and in different legal contexts abroad. These findings highlight the unique pressures faced by the judiciary in Poland.

5 Discussion and Conclusion

This study investigated the psychological well-being of Polish judges amidst a profound constitutional crisis, concentrating on heightened levels of work-related stress and burnout. Our findings offer a compelling perspective on the mental health challenges faced by legal professionals, particularly in light of the intensifying crisis and its implications, as emphasized by Sadurski[29].

27 Kersten et al. (2020), 123–137.
28 Nickum & Desrumaux (2023), 349–361.
29 Sadurski (2019), 58–99.

The findings of our study indicate that Polish judges are subjected to higher levels of occupation-related stress when compared to the average employee in Poland. This disparity can be ascribed to the distinct obligations and responsibilities that are inherent to their judicial positions. By drawing a parallel between the stress levels of judges and those of the general working population, we have identified the specific difficulties and pressures that judges in Poland encounter, thereby underscoring the necessity of implementing tailored interventions to alleviate and manage stress within this particular professional cohort.

This research undertakes a nuanced comparative analysis with other social professions in Poland and their European counterparts, situating the singular pressures experienced by judges within a broader societal and international context. Our findings reveal substantial levels of burnout and stress among Polish judges, which we believe are due to the complexities and responsibilities inherent in their judicial roles. These results align closely with those of Bi's study in China, where it was discovered that legal professionals whose contexts firmly adhered to the principles of the rule of law experienced lower levels of burnout, while those confronting a disparity between these principles and their daily practices experienced higher burnout levels[30]. This parallel indicates a pervasive tendency within the legal profession, where the tension between professional principles and practical demands can have a profound impact on occupational stress and burnout. The consistency of these results across various cultural and legal settings highlights the crucial need to align legal practice with rule-of-law ideals to alleviate burnout among legal practitioners.

The alarming magnitude and prevalence of stress and burnout among Polish judges suggest that these legal professionals confront considerably greater levels of stress when compared to individuals engaged in other social professions and the workforce as a whole. Furthermore, this heightened stress, in conjunction with significant exhaustion and detachment, indicates a pervasive problem firmly rooted within their professional roles. This situation resonates with the discourse surrounding the psychological consequences of high-pressure settings[31] and reflects growing concerns about mental health in the legal profession[32].

By carrying out a comparative analysis of burnout among Polish judges, we sought to contrast our results with those of international studies of a similar nature. Despite the limited research into the well-being of legal professionals, this comparative examination provides valuable insights into burnout across diverse cultural and professional contexts. Our comparative analysis indicates that burnout levels among Polish judges are significantly higher than those in similar professional groups in other European countries. This distinction highlights the unique challenges the Polish judiciary faces, which

30 Bi (2017), 581–613.
31 Schaufeli & Buunk (2003), 383–425.
32 Chirkowska-Smolak (2022), 247–260.

are likely exacerbated by the current constitutional crisis and the specific socio-political context of Poland. These findings underscore the pressing need for targeted interventions and further research to better comprehend and address the specific mental health needs of legal professionals, particularly in high-stress environments like the judiciary.

The following factors can contribute to the heightened state of stress and burnout among judges: the complex and high-stakes nature of judicial work coupled with political instability and threats to judicial independence. The intense public scrutiny and the expectation to maintain impartiality in a politically charged atmosphere further exacerbate these challenges. The lack of adequate psychological and institutional support to manage this unique set of challenges leaves judges vulnerable to burnout, a finding consistent with Rothstein and Eek's research on the impact of occupational stress on judicial decision making[33].

The repercussions of burnout among judges extend beyond the realm of individual well-being. The persistent stress and burnout experienced by judges can lead to cognitive impairments, which, in turn, can compromise the quality of judicial decisions. Moreover, it can trigger mental health issues, such as anxiety and depression, and have deleterious effects on both the personal and professional lives of judges. Excessive burnout can result in a disengagement from work, cynicism, and a diminished sense of personal accomplishment, all of which can negatively impact the morale and effectiveness of the judiciary. Given these consequences, it is imperative to implement targeted interventions to manage and mitigate stress and burnout within the judiciary, as suggested by scholarly works on the well-being of lawyers.[34].

Acknowledging the constraints of our study, including its reliance on a convenience sample and self-reported measures, we recognize the need for future research. Longitudinal studies and international comparative analyses would deepen our comprehension of the mental well-being challenges faced by legal professionals, thereby enhancing strategies to bolster the judiciary's resilience in Poland and beyond.

In conclusion, this study demonstrates the critical necessity of addressing the psychological well-being of judges in Poland. In the midst of a constitutional crisis, ensuring the mental health of these crucial legal professionals is essential for maintaining the integrity and efficiency of the judiciary, and by extension, upholding democracy and the rule of law. Our study contributes to the global discourse on burnout in the legal profession, advocating for comprehensive, cross-cultural approaches to these challenges. Prioritizing the mental health of judges is not only a national concern for Poland but a crucial aspect of sustaining democratic institutions and the rule of law on a global scale.

---

33 Rothstein & Eek (2013), 156–164.
34 Chirkowska-Smolak (2022), 247–260.

Bibliography

Baka, Ł., & Basińska, B. (2016). Psychometryczne właściwości polskiej wersji Oldenburskiego Kwestionariusza Wypalenia Zawodowego (OLBI). Medycyna Pracy, 67(1), 29–41.

Bi, X. (2017). Caught between ideal and reality: A study on occupational burnout among inside-system legal professionals under the rule-of-law reform in contemporary China. Chinese Journal of Sociology, 3, 581–613.

Chirkowska-Smolak, T. (2018). Polska adaptacja kwestionariusza do pomiaru wypalenia zawodowego OLBI (The Oldenburg Burnout Inventory). Studia Oeconomica Posnaniensia, 3(6), 27–47.

Chirkowska-Smolak, T. (2022). Stress at work among Polish legal professionals: The role of workload. Ruch Prawniczy, Ekonomiczny i Socjologiczny, 84(1), 247–260. https://doi.org/10.14746/rpeis.2022.84.1.18

Chirkowska-Smolak, T., & Grobelny, J. (2016). Konstrukcja i wstępna analiza psychometryczna Kwestionariusza Postrzeganego Stresu w Pracy (PSwP). Czasopismo Psychologiczne, 1(22), 131–139.

Cohen, S., & Williamson, G. (1988). Perceived stress in a probability sample of the United States. In S. Spacapan & S. Oskamp (Eds.), The social psychology of health (pp. 31–67). New York: Sage Publications.

Cohen, S., & Janicki-Deverts, D. (2012). Who's stressed? Distributions of psychological stress in the United States in probability samples from 1983, 2006, and 2009. Journal of Applied Social Psychology, 42(6), 1320–1334. https://doi.org/10.1111/j.1559-1816.2012.00900.x

Demerouti, E., Bakker, A. B., Vardakou, I., & Kantas, A. (2003): "The convergent validity of two burnout instruments: A multitrait-multimethod analysis". In: European Journal of Psychological Assessment, 19, 12–23.

Demerouti, E., Bakker, A., Peeters, M., & Breevaart, K. (2021): "New directions in burnout research". In: European Journal of Work and Organizational Psychology, 30(5), 686–691. https://doi.org/10.1080/1359432X.2021.1979962

Guthrie, C., Rachlinski, J. J., & Wistrich, A. J. (2001): "Inside the judicial mind". In: Cornell Law Review, 86, 777–830.

Innstrand, S. T., Langballe, E. M., Falkum, E., et al. (2011): "Exploring within- and between-gender differences in burnout: 8 different occupational groups". In: International Archives of Occupational and Environmental Health, 84, 813–824. https://doi.org/10.1007/s00420-011-0667-y

International Bar Association. (2020): "Mental Wellbeing in Legal Profession: Global study report". Retrieved from https://www.ibanet.org/document?id=IBA-report-Mental-Wellbeing-in-the-Legal-Profession-A-Global-Study. accessed 14.12.2023

Jouriles, E. N. & McDonald, R. (2015): "Psychological issues in the judicial system". In: Psychology, Public Policy, and Law, 21(2), 241–249. https://doi.org/10.1037/law0000042

Kelk, N. J., Luscombe, G. M., Medlow, S. D., & Hickie, I. B. (2009): "Courting the Blues: Attitudes Towards Depression in Australia Law Students and Legal Practitioners". Sydney: Brain & Mind Research Institute.

Kersten, M., Fornazin, M., & Muller, E. (2020): "Burnout among professionals with high cognitive demands: A cross-sectional study". In: Journal of Occupational Health Psychology, 25(3), 123–137. https://doi.org/10.1037/ocp0000178

Kidder, R. M. (2005). Moral courage. New York: HarperCollins Publishers.

Krill, P. R., Degeneffe, N., Ochocki, K., & Anker, J. J. (2022): "People, Professionals, and Profit Centers: The Connection between Lawyer Well-Being and Employer Values". In: Behavioral Sciences, 12(6), 177. https://doi.org/10.3390/bs12060177

Maslach, C., & Leiter, M. P. (2016): "Understanding the Burnout Experience: Recent Research and Its Implications for Psychiatry". In: World Psychiatry, 15, 103–111. https://doi.org/10.1002/wps.20311

National Taskforce on Lawyer Well-Being. (2017): "The Path to Lawyer Well-Being: Practical Recommendations for Positive Change". Retrieved from https://lawyerwellbeing.net/wp-content/uploads/2017/11/Lawyer-Wellbeing-Report.pdf; accessed 14.12.2023

Nickum, M., & Desrumaux, P. (2023): "Burnout among lawyers: Effects of workload, latitude, and mediation via engagement and over-engagement". In: Psychiatry, Psychology, and Law, 30(3), 349–361. https://doi.org/10.1080/13218719.2022.2035840

Pech, L., & Scheppele, K. L. (2017): "Illiberalism within: Rule of law backsliding in the EU". In: Cambridge Yearbook of European Legal Studies, 19, 3–47. https://doi.org/10.1017/cel.2017.9

Rothstein, H., & Eek, D. (2013): "The impact of burnout on judicial decision-making". In: Journal of Judicial Administration, 22(3), 156–164.

Sadurski, W. (2019). Poland's constitutional breakdown. Oxford: Oxford University Press.

Schaufeli, W. B., & Buunk, B. P. (2003): "Burnout: An overview of 25 years of research and theorizing". In: M. Schabracq, J. Winnubst, & C. Cooper (Eds.), The Handbook of Work and Health Psychology, 383–425. New York: Wiley.

Sekerka, L. E., & Bagozzi, R. P. (2007): "Moral courage in the workplace: Moving to and from the desire and decision to act". In: Business Ethics: A European Review, 16(2), 132–149.

Smolak, M. (2017), "Employing David Dyzenhaus' Conception of the Culture of Authority and the Culture of Justification for analysing changes proposed be the act on the Supreme Court". In: Ruch Prawniczy, Ekonomiczny i Socjologiczny, 4, 27–29.

Smolak, M., Sadurski, W., & Chirkowska-Smolak, T. (2020): "Rozum publiczny – uzasadnianie sądowe – umysł sędziego". Poznań: Wydawnictwo Naukowe UAM

Teresa Chirkowska-Smolak
Faculty of Psychology and Cognitive Science, Adam Mickiewicz University
chirko@amu.edu.pl

Marek Adam Smolak
Faculty of Law and Administration, Adam Mickiewicz University
smolak@amu.edu.pl

Part 5
Law and Science

Using Science Education for Lawyers to Uphold the Principles of Justice Laid out in Blackstone's Ratio

AMELIA SHOOTER

Abstract: The criminal justice principles laid out by Blackstone's ratio are at risk of being eroded by legal professionals prioritising rational legal decision-making over the evaluation of substantive scientific concerns where the two collide. This is seen in a body of case law from the United States where issues relating to forensic science limitations are raised. The author posits that this is due to legal professionals' greater familiarity with legal reasoning rather than scientific knowledge, arguing that law schools should harness their position to provide contextual scientific education for their students. This will support science-led decision-making and reduce the risk of miscarriages of justice, striving to uphold the principles of Blackstone's ratio.

Keywords: decision-making, education, forensic science, science literacy, lawyers

Introduction

Blackstone's ratio is one of the key principles that invokes fairness in the criminal justice system. The maxim states that "the law holds that it is better that ten guilty persons escape, than that one innocent party suffer."[1] The spirit of this statement is further echoed throughout many notable texts, ranging from the Bible[2] to Zadig.[3] It has also been replicated across common law jurisprudence in multiple jurisdictions[4] – the only difference being the ratio itself, whether expressing two, ten or one hundred guilty persons.

This principle and its deep origins are generally considered to be a driving force behind the presumption of innocence.[5] It has more recently become associated with the innocence movement and pursuit of miscarriages of justice through the work of

1 Blackstone/Hardcastle Browne (1897), 713.
2 Genesis 18: 24–33.
3 Voltaire (1749), 43.
4 *See, e.g.* Secretary of State for the Home Department v. AF (No 3) [2008] EWCA Civ 1148, para 74; Department of Homeland Security v. Thuraissiagiam 591 U.S.
5 Dervan, et al. (2016), 1592.

innocence projects.[6] The innocence movement has – since the 1990s – been using scientific tools at its disposal to 'discover' wrongful convictions.[7] Most notably, DNA evidence has led to high numbers of exonerations,[8] due to its high degree of reliability and validity.[9]

While DNA evidence enjoys a high degree of reliability, other forensic science disciplines lack the same rigorous scientific underpinning, despite their longstanding admissibility.[10] The National Academy of Sciences (hereafter NAS), the United States' premier scientific think-tank,[11] has produced multiple reports evaluating the reliability and validity of common forensic science evidence techniques, finding considerable variability between disciplines.[12] In its 2009 landmark report, *Strengthening Forensic Science in the United States: A Path Forward* (hereafter, *Strengthening*), the headline message from the report declared that "with the exception of nuclear DNA analysis … no forensic method has been rigorously shown to have the capacity to consistently, and with a high degree of certainty, demonstrate a connection between evidence and a specific individual or source."[13]

Despite these concerns, courts' responses have been lacklustre when this evidence has been challenged.[14] In common law jurisdictions, where precedent is binding, concerns about reliability and validity have consistently been set aside in favour of legal process justifications. In a wide-reaching study, Shooter found that judges follow markers of the legal process vision when making decisions relating to forensic science evidence.[15] According to this study, judicial decision-making is driven by following precedent; the institutional competence of trial court decision-makers (i. e. trial judges and juries); finality considerations; and underpinning assumptions about rationality and procedural regularity.[16]

As forensic science is commonplace evidence in trials, it is important that trial court actors – particularly judges, lawyers and jurors – have a strong enough understanding of the probative value of forensic science. It is clear through case law – however – that a knowledge gap exists in legal practitioners' understanding of the limitations of forensic science evidence.[17] Cooper and Shooter have identified that this lack of "science

---

6 South African Innocence Project, About Us, https://innocence.co.za/about.html (accessed 04.01.2024)
7 *See, e.g.* Laurin (2012), 1478.
8 Innocence Project, Cases, https://innocenceproject.org/all-cases/ (accessed 04.01.2024)
9 Crow (1996).
10 *See, e.g.,* Porter (2011), 39 f.; People v. Jennings 252 Ill. 534 (1911).
11 Shooter/Cooper (2019), 443.
12 Edwards/Gatsonis (2009), 87.
13 ibid., 7.
14 Following NAS reports, the FBI initiated a review of both CBLA analysis and microscopic hair analysis. *See,* Beety (2015), 984; FBI National Press Office (2007).
15 Shooter (2020).
16 *Id.*
17 Cooper/Shooter (2022), 3.

literacy" among legal professionals requires further study,[18] as judicial fidelity to legal process values, particularly precedent, is oftentimes at ideological odds with legitimate concerns about reliability and validity of particular forensic science disciplines.[19] Where such conflict exists, there is an increased risk of miscarriages of justice.

This article explores the importance of engaging legal practitioners with scientific concepts and disciplines employed in US legal proceedings, in order to adhere, as much as possible, to the sentiments expressed through Blackstone's Ratio. It does so in four parts. First, it discusses the concept of science literacy, acknowledging the benefits of lawyers' education in scientific principles. Second, it establishes how the current knowledge gap exists amongst lawyers is a natural phenomenon of the education system. Third, it explores case law demonstrating the tendency of legal professionals to overlook substantive scientific issues in favour of legal rationality. Fourth, after reviewing educational programmes for law students, it concludes by recommending that law schools embrace interdisciplinary scientific studies to support aspiring lawyers.

1 About Science Literacy and the Law

Perpetual concerns about lawyers' understanding of forensic science evidence have been raised by the NAS, the leading US scientific scholarly organisation.[20] For example, in *Strengthening,* the NAS stated that legal professionals "lack the scientific expertise necessary to comprehend and evaluate forensic science evidence in an informed manner."[21] Additionally, there is much criticism about the rigour used by judges when making admissibility decisions relating to scientific evidence.[22] Under the *Daubert* admissibility criteria, trial judges are tasked with ensuring that proffered evidence is reliable,[23] using criteria set out in Federal Rule of Evidence 702.[24] Under this standard, judges are required to evaluate the general acceptance of the proffered evidence, alongside the expert's knowledge/experience, scientific underpinning, reliability/peer review and best practice.[25] Despite being tasked with this role, questions remain about the judicial ability to carry out this evaluation,[26] exposing the risk of misattributing the reliability of the evidence, and ultimately, the potential for injustice.

---

18 ibid., 24 f.
19 ibid.
20 National Academy of Sciences, Mission, https://www.nasonline.org/about-nas/mission/ (accessed 04.01.2024).
21 Edwards/Gatsonis (2009), 12 (n12).
22 Moriarty/Saks (2005), 16, 28 f.
23 Daubert v. Merrell Dow Pharmaceuticals Inc. 509 US 579 (1993).
24 Federal Rule of Evidence 702.
25 ibid.
26 *See,* Campbell Moriarty/Saks (2005), (n22).

To support the judicial task, the NAS has, on several occasions, supported and directed the judicial disposal of forensic science, by – for example – instructing judges to take judicial notice of the underpinning scientific principles behind nuclear DNA analysis in 1992.[27] NAS reports have, on other occasions, been critical of the judiciary's ability to understand and apply scientific evidence. Most notably, in *Strengthening*, the report committee noted that legal professionals lack the essential training to comprehend the approaches used in forensic science analysis,[28] recommending an enhanced education provision to increase their science literacy.[29]

This illumination of legal professionals' lack of scientific knowledge has contributed to concerns about the ability of the justice system to stay abreast of scientific changes.[30] However, lawyers and judges are merely among a wider section of the population that has a scientific knowledge gap, and are not the only decision-makers in the justice system. According to the NAS's own 2016 report on science literacy, the need for science literacy in legal settings is an issue "increasingly difficult to ignore,"[31] and science literacy for legal professionals, as a community, differs from other communities, due to the specific use and application of science in the legal system.[32]

The report recognised a wider benefit in general science literacy (i.e. having "knowledge, skills and fluency"[33] in science), as it assists with problem solving.[34] It acknowledged a "democratic" rationale for having a science literate population,[35] as it promotes better decision-making and collective interests.[36] Logically, this includes other public decision-making tasks, including jury decisions. The report suggested that science education for non-scientists would have a wider societal benefit.[37] Specifically, it acknowledged that:

> Research on science literacy at the level of individuals should be complemented by efforts to examine how science literacy emerges in communities of people working together, and how both the nature and effects of science literacy cannot be extricated from the social systems within which they are embedded.[38]

27 McKusick (1992), 23, 133.
28 Edwards/Gatsonis (2009), 27 (n12).
29 ibid., 27 f.
30 Snow/Dibner (2016), 69.
31 ibid.
32 ibid., 110 f.
33 ibid., 17.
34 ibid., 30.
35 ibid., 25.
36 ibid.
37 ibid., 43.
38 ibid.

signifying the importance of both scientific knowledge amongst individuals, and the willingness of societal systems to embrace this knowledge.

The NAS acknowledged the legal community as one such societal system, as individuals regularly use science to assist decision-making "as part of the story."[39] As such, it needs to be "'reconstructed' and understood in proper context before it becomes useful."[40] This accepts that lawyers and judges *need* to be able to analyse or evaluate science before becoming a useful tool in legal proceedings.

Science has long been harnessed by the legal system and used as a decision-making tool. However, when longstanding forensic science evidence is challenged – for example through the findings of *Strengthening* – the "tool" of forensic science evidence does not perform a straightforward task. Under the *Daubert* admissibility test, the trial judge assesses the reliability of evidence based on the legal criteria set out in Federal Rule of Evidence 702, or state equivalent. After being admitted, it is for the trial lawyers to present and/or challenge the forensic science evidence, using the testimony of experts, prepared report(s), NAS reports and other tools to support their legal submissions. As such, it is particularly important that legal professionals can harness the forensic science evidence to advance their legal argument. However, despite the importance of scientific evidence in legal proceedings, there is no formal requirement that legal professionals in the US (and other common law jurisdictions) undertake formal scientific education.

2 Science Literacy in the Curriculum and Legal Practice

Legal instruction is a notably distinct discipline from scientific endeavour, with the educational and professional career path to becoming a lawyer benefiting from a clear structure. In the US, requirements for admission to the bar vary by state, but law schools should – through instruction – prepare students for admission following graduation.[41] Quotas are used to ensure that law graduates are sufficiently prepared for bar examination.[42] Considering this, law schools are focussed towards teaching black-letter law, leaving little room for additional material, which can lead graduates unprepared for the challenges of legal practice.[43] Among law schools, there is a notable absence of integrated scientific (and moreover, other interdisciplinary) education courses – the focus is primarily on legal scholarship.

39 ibid., 77.
40 ibid.
41 American Bar Association (2023), 17.
42 Ibid., 27.
43 Sonsteng et al. (2014), 18.

This may partly be explained by the generally interdisciplinary nature of prior studies, as law is offered exclusively at graduate level in the US. It is therefore logical to assume that there is wide diversity in law students' educational backgrounds. While this is certainly true in theory, law students typically hold undergraduate degrees in political sciences and humanities.[44] This means that those students may not have an adequate foundational understanding of scientific concepts for use as legal tools. Other common law jurisdictions generally suffer from a similar lack of exposure to scientific principles as part of their formal legal education, and in jurisdictions where undergraduate law degrees are commonplace, issues may be exacerbated. For example, in England and Wales, the "qualifying" law degree route through completion of an LLB, *legum baccalaureus,* requires only the completion of seven foundational black-letter legal subjects: criminal law, equity and trust law, land law, EU law, contract law, tort law, and public law, which includes constitutional law, administrative law, and human rights.[45] Neither this degree, nor the following vocational qualification and subsequent period of apprenticeship to the bar (pupillage) require any scientific or interdisciplinary training.[46]

While it is possible for a science graduate (from any discipline) to become a legal practitioner, there is no mandatory requirement for formal scientific qualifications prior to legal study. The lack of formal inclusion into law programmes places a burden on the individual lawyer to inform themselves on how to handle scientific evidence. Due to this absence, the strongest tools at the lawyer's disposal are legal skills, even when dealing with non-legal concepts. These may include: examining the admissibility history of a technique, precedent in treatment, use of advocacy skills to guide the response of decision-makers (including juries), using scientific experts, and making use of reports. This leads to a very legal-centric model of rationalising decisions, which can often be at the expense of substantive scientific issues. While legally sound, this may negatively impact the scientific legitimacy of a decision.

3 Good *Legal* Decision-Making, Bad *Scientific* Decision-Making? Judicial Reasoning in Recent Decisions

Lawyers' use of science in adversarial jurisdictions, for example, in the US, tend to rely on the testimony of expert witnesses. While they are bound to testify to the truth,[47] they remain agents of the party that called them into evidence. Lawyers are then tasked with examining the expert through direct- and cross-examination to elicit and chal-

44 Grey (2023).
45 Bar Standards Board (2019), 4.
46 ibid., Part 3.
47 Federal Rule of Evidence 603.

lenge the expert's testimony. The trial judge makes admissibility decisions, generally applying the *Daubert* admissibility criteria.[48] Additionally, to assist judges,[49] a federal mechanism exists for the appointment of an expert witness, independent of the parties.[50] In practice, despite its utility, this mechanism is seldom used,[51] which can – without a non-partisan scientific voice – contribute towards an exaggeration of the adversarial partisan argument, and a struggle to find the truth, clouded by a so-called "battle of the experts,"[52] evident through a review of appellate case law decisions.

Case law demonstrates that decision-making is also clouded by the routine treatment of scientific concerns as legal issues, despite some lawyers attempting to make use of scientific material. For example, *Strengthening* is routinely used during trials as a cross-examination tool to elicit limitations of proffered evidence.[53] This limited use has not generally extended to appellate courts overturning decisions made on evidence criticised in the report. Where admissibility has been challenged at appeal, appellate decisions routinely default to legal reasoning to dismiss appeals over a substantive engagement with scientific concerns contained in the report.

3.1 Using a Legal Rationale to Dismiss Challenges

Across a data set of 239 appellate decisions where *Strengthening* has been cited, the majority of decisions followed this pattern of scientific avoidance.[54] Several legal mechanisms are used as rational justifications for the transformation and reduction of scientific challenges into legal issues, but reliance on precedent appears most frequently. For example, the court in *Commonwealth v Armstrong* rejected the appellant's challenge that the fingerprint evidence admitted during his trial was unreliable and erroneously admitted.[55] The appellant's challenge focussed on the lack of underpinning evidence around the extent to which the testifying expert could be certain of a match, supported by *Strengthening*.[56] Relying on precedent, the court rejected this challenge, finding that the previous case of *Gambora* had sufficiently explored match certainty and there was no error in the expert's testimony direct-examination.[57]

---

48 Daubert (1993), (n23), although the "general acceptance" standard is retained in some states, *see* Frye v. United States, 293 F. 1013 (D. C. Cir 1923).
49 General Electric Co. v. Joiner 522 U. S. 136 (1997), 150.
50 Federal Rule of Evidence 706.
51 Imwinkelried, (2020), 845; Beety/Oliva (2019), 527 f.
52 *See*, Cruz, (2023).
53 Fishman, (2023), Para 59:14.
54 Cases are on file with the author, 2009–2023.
55 Commonwealth v. Armstrong 211 N. E.3d 622 (Mass. 2023).
56 ibid., 634.
57 ibid.

However, the court did find that the expert had erred during cross-examination, as it made comments that the ACE-V method of fingerprint analysis was error-free.[58] Despite this, the court found that the error was not enough to create a likelihood of a miscarriage of justice,[59] citing precedent again to rationalise the decision to ultimately dismiss the case.[60] By finding that the cross-examination did not amount to prejudicial error, the court implicitly acknowledged two things: first, that the act of cross-examination is a decision-making tool for the jury, deferring to the rationality of the jury's decision; and second, in recognising the error, but not finding it prejudicial, the court emphasised the importance of finality, a principle that upholds legal certainty within the confines of an imperfect legal system.[61] Both of these are hallmarks of legal rationalisation within the legal process vision.[62]

Similarly, in *United States v Hunt,* the court's engagement with relevant scientific literature (including NAS reports) was also grounded in legal reasoning.[63] The appellant challenged the lack of research underpinning firearms evidence, including uncertainties relating to error rates.[64] While the court acknowledged and accepted the NAS reports' findings,[65] it ultimately referred to a 2016 follow-up report to *Strengthening* by the President's Council of Advisors on Science and Technology (PCAST),[66] which stated that its recommendations "did not call for the immediate, wholesale exclusion of firearm toolmark evidence from the courts,"[67] and dismissed the appeal.

This rationalisation sidelined and precluded a review of legitimate scientific limitations, allowing the court to use *legal* directions to dismiss the challenge. Specifically, the court re-affirmed the role of the trial judge as gatekeeper of scientific evidence under *Daubert,*[68] and deferred to the trial court's decision.[69] However, in doing so, it further acknowledged its own legally limited role in reviewing decisions, as well as the difficulties in legal professionals making scientific decisions, saying that in many (other) cases "appellate judges have an obligation to educate themselves and engage in the sometimes difficult work of assessing scientific and technical material,"[70] although the court found little relevance in the instant decision.

---

58 ibid., 635.
59 ibid., 636.
60 ibid.
61 Bator, (1963).
62 *See,* Hart/Sacks (1994), 434.
63 United States v. Hunt, 63 F.4th 1229 (10th Cir 2023).
64 ibid., 1235.
65 ibid., 1236–8.
66 Holdren/Lander (2016).
67 US v. Hunt (2023) 1238 (n63).
68 ibid., 1243.
69 ibid., 1252.
70 ibid.

Additionally, in *Ficklin v Commonwealth*, a review of the trial court's decision to admit firearms evidence was framed exclusively as a legal review of the judicial application of admissibility, using the *Daubert* criteria.[71] In dismissing the appellant's claim, the court reviewed the trial judge's decision through a precedent-based lens, citing cases including *Garrett v Commonwealth, Meskimen v Commonwealth* and *United States v Otero* to find that there was "sufficient agreement"[72] for admission and concluded that the method used to analyse the evidence had sufficient underpinning, ultimately deciding that the trial judge had not abused his discretion in admitting the evidence.[73] This decision, framed as a legal admissibility review, pays considerable deference to the discretion of the trial judge, is grounded in precedent, and avoids scientific engagement.

The scope to review scientific evidence is further narrowed when an appellate court is reviewing an out-of-time postconviction application. This, in practice, restricts judges to review newly discovered evidence, not available at the time of the trial. These further procedural limits can be seen in cases such as *Bodden v Gentry*, where the petitioner submitted a habeas corpus appeal, which included a challenge to tyre-track evidence presented at trial.[74] The petitioner sought to raise the challenge through *Strengthening's* criticism of the underpinning science.[75] The court dismissed the petitioner's claim, finding that the report itself did not provide any evidence that the petitioner herself was innocent,[76] emphasising the importance placed on the legal framework rather than the potential scientific significance of the report's findings. To further emphasise the narrow scope of review, the court referred to the report as "generic" (i. e. not particular to the petitioner's case),[77] further narrowing the scope of such reports for future decisions.

These recent cases, while hand-picked, are representative examples of wider practice. There is evidence to replicate this pattern of decision-making across different scientific disciplines:[78] judicial decisions routinely follow legal procedural reasoning, linked to legal process values when making and rationalising decisions, rather than addressing substantive scientific limitations.[79]

71 Ficklin v. Commonwealth 2022 WL 3640906 (Ky. 2022).
72 ibid., 3.
73 ibid., 4.
74 Bodden v. Gentry 2020 WL 2513672 (D. Nev. 2020).
75 ibid., 8.
76 ibid.
77 ibid.
78 Shooter (2020) (n15).
79 ibid.

3.2 Using Scientific Claims to Support the Legal Rationale

The side-lining of substantive issues, while widespread, is not a blanket practice. There is a considerable number of cases where rationality in legal decision-making and scientific considerations align. For example, in *Carmon v State,* the court found in favour of granting the petitioner a retrial as newly discovered evidence had emerged which undermined the evidence that led to his conviction.[80] The petitioner claimed that *Strengthening* and other scientific reports put into question the firearms testimony heard at trial, as the reports challenged the expert's assertions of certainty.[81] In reviewing the reports' findings, the court acknowledged the issues relating to certainty and subjectivity,[82] but ultimately deferred to the competence of the jury. In granting a retrial, it held that a new jury would be competent to decide the weight of the firearms testimony, taking into account the scientific limitations, while still not engaging fully in substantive scientific discussions.[83]

This is a demonstration of the court using scientific concerns to justify fidelity to legal procedure, but only to the extent that it is needed to support the legal rationale. It emphasises that legal reasoning takes primary importance. This is also seen in *Abruquah v State,* where the ultimate issue was whether the trial court had abused its discretion. The state Supreme Court overturned the petitioner's conviction, following his appeal against the state expert's testimony declaring a firearms match to absolute certainty.[84] The court undertook a detailed and methodical admissibility review of available evidence, under both *Frye* and *Daubert* frameworks.[85] It examined several scientific reports, including *Strengthening,* a further NAS report entitled *Ballistic Imaging*[86] and several additional studies not available at the time of the petitioner's trial.[87] After finding that the general acceptance of the expert's analysis method (required as part of the admissibility test) was "neutral,"[88] it concluded that the trial court had erred in admitting the firearms evidence, and subsequently overturned the conviction, due to the relative importance of the firearms evidence to the case,[89] ultimately finding an abuse of discretion.[90]

---

80 Carmon v. State 2022 WL 17423683 (Conn. Super. Ct. 2022), 16.
81 ibid., 17.
82 ibid., 18.
83 ibid., 26.
84 Abruquah v. State 483 Md. 637 (Md. 2023).
85 ibid.
86 ibid.
87 Additional studies included the 2016 PCAST report, and two further studies examining the rate of false positives, ibid., 669.
88 ibid., 692.
89 ibid., 696–698.
90 ibid.

It appears from these decisions – and others – that scientific progress and rationality without the support of legal reasoning does not reach the benchmark required by courts to consider finding in favour of an appellant, but when there is a legal irregularity, scientific perspectives may be considered. In *Carmon*, the court allowed the appeal through the dual lens of "newly discovered evidence" of scientific progress; and by deferring to the competence of actors within the legal system: a competent juror would be able to weigh the probative value of the evidence.[91] The court did not go so far as to suggest that the newly discovered evidence had the likelihood of undermining the case against the petitioner. Similarly, *Abruquah* was reviewed through the "abuse of discretion" standard,[92] with the court framing the scientific discussion in terms of the trial judge's abuse of discretion when making admissibility decisions.[93]

3.3 Lack of Confidence ... or Competence?

Taking into account decisions where petitioners' scientific challenges have been successful, the success of these challenges is not wholly scientific, but largely made through a dominant legal lens. This dominance of legal rationality over scientific matters is perplexing as progress of thought in scientific communities can still provide a rationale for legal decisions and progress.[94] This begs the question as to why appellate courts have required an additional legal irregularity in order to allow a petitioner's appeal – is this because courts do not have the scientific confidence to make decisions due to legal professionals' knowledge gaps, or that courts do not believe that they have the competence to make decisions based on scientific progress, in light of competing legal procedural elements?

This confidence/competence issue can be explored in several ways, although particularly interest is the interaction between legal and scientific principles from the perspective of the legal professional. An increase in science literacy among lawyers has the ability to progress the law in light of scientific developments and reduce the risk of scientific considerations being overlooked and prevent miscarriages of justice as it can strengthen the rationale for reviewing the interaction between these two disciplines. Cooper's encouragement of the harnessing of the lawyer as the "competent outsider" to science allows lawyers to understand and reconcile potential disparities.[95] Therefore, a logical step towards facilitating this is to provide additional education to equip

91 Carmon v. State (2020) (n80).
92 Abruquah v. State (2023) (n84).
93 *Id.*, at 697.
94 Hart/Sacks (1994), 3 (n62).
95 Cooper (2024)

lawyers and judges with the tools to appreciate scientific evidence on a deeper, interdisciplinary level.

4 Law Schools as a Place for Legal Education, in Society

Legal careers are diverse, making it difficult for law schools to offer comprehensive instruction for students. However, while learning "black letter" subjects is undoubtedly necessary, the current side-lining of scientific concerns by legal professionals highlights the need for a greater focus on the interdisciplinary nature of the law from an early educational standpoint.

Interdisciplinary studies have not wholly been ignored by law schools. Legal educators have recognised the importance of lawyers to apply their work in interdisciplinary fora, with Howell Jackson of Harvard Law School stating that "lawyers … must work in a world in which arguments are framed in quantitative terms and the evaluation and presentation of data are critical to effective advocacy."[96] However, concerns remain that "many law schools may have fallen behind the curve when it comes to preparing students to litigate cases in which expert testimony will be proffered."[97]

Case law demonstrates an initial willingness by lawyers to raise scientific issues, but judicial decision-making generally avoids scientific engagement where it conflicts with legal reasoning. Law schools should be able to equip their students for interdisciplinary law, particularly exploring the junctures where science and law meet, as they do so frequently, and often appear to contrast. Faigman's observation that "justices and judges do somersaults to avoid substantive scientific analysis,"[98] seen in existing case law, has the potential to be – at least somewhat – remedied by adequate interdisciplinary legal education.

There are at least three distinct benefits to law schools incorporating scientific interdisciplinary education prior to professional practice. First, if mandated by professional bodies, all law students will receive comparable scientific education at an early stage in their career. Second, students may also benefit from this approach due to the relative proximity in time between legal studies and prior scientific instruction. Finally, incorporating interdisciplinary studies while at law school is efficient as it allows for legal educators to draw on a range of resources and knowledge from other areas within the institution, which may also be mutually beneficial for other faculties.

There are a variety of options that law schools may wish to consider when integrating interdisciplinary scientific education into their existing frameworks. The limited formal instruction requirements leave space for educators to insert "science in law"

96 Jackson (2003) 321 f.
97 Merlino et al. (2008), 192.
98 Faigman (1999), 26.

or "law in society" content. Making this a mandatory requirement, overseen by professional bodies, would be the most consistent approach, particularly suited to the standard JD programme, although it may be difficult in practice to gain consensus on explicit requirements.

"Science in law" content may be offered effectively in two broad approaches: either through a distinct module or integrated into existing subject areas. Both approaches should be practice-driven and concentrate on the use of science as a tool for effective legal reasoning, rather than exclusively teaching established aspects of science. As philosopher Lon Fuller said in the 1950s, "There is, for example, an almost universal agreement that our primary object is not to impart information. Whatever it is we want the student to get, it is something more durable, more versatile and muscular, than a mere knowledge of rules of law."[99]

The creation of a dedicated "science in law" module may be relatively straightforward in its content as the aim of the module would be generalist. As such, material and/or expertise may be borrowed from other faculties, although content may vary depending on institutional expertise. Practically, students may be asked to use science to support the resolution of legal dilemmas, much like how practical courses currently operate.[100] As its purpose would be to introduce students to scientific principles and generate an appreciation for scientific disciplines, law schools could have considerable flexibility when building such programmes.

Alternatively, scientific education may be introduced into existing modules or co-curricular programmes. If inserted into existing subjects, there are a variety of modules that could be coupled organically with the introduction of scientific principles. While the delivery and availability of these modules vary, potential standard candidate foundational subjects could include contract, criminal, tort law, and evidence. Another method of incorporation may be through the provision of co-curricular (or extra-curricular) activities, which while not mandatory, are also popular among students,[101] particularly as they are generally considered to be authentic experiential learning tools[102] and prepare students for legal employment.[103] Setting students up with science-based co-curricular legal activities may therefore be a fun and engaging experience for participants.

---

99 Fuller (1950), 36.

100 Mullenix (2023).

101 These can be wide-ranging, including participation in activities such as mooting, negotiating, debating, legal advice clinics, innocence projects, journal editing, etc.

102 Nesbitt Cosby (2018), 808.

103 The Inns of Court College of Advocacy, OUP and ICCA National Mooting Competition, https://www.icca.ac.uk/oup-icca-national-mooting-competition/ (accessed 04.01.2024)

Conclusion

The aim of including scientific instruction is not to transform future lawyers into scientists, but empower them with an awareness of scientific principles and generate an openness in using it to assist legal decision-making. This is currently lacking. Lawyers who are equipped with a greater understanding of the principles underpinning science are more likely to make better-informed decisions.[104] For example, an increased awareness of the complexities of forensic science may encourage judges to make more frequent use of the Rule 706 mechanism, something that is reportedly successful when used.[105] Educating lawyers to increase their science literacy also serves to highlight the legitimacy of scientific progress as being a rational independent legal justification, serving the efficiency and quality of the justice system. The principle of using science to uphold and develop the law – moreover – reduces the risk of miscarriages of justice, the principled driving force behind any fair justice system, as set out in Blackstone's Ratio.

Bibliography

Abruquah v State 483 Md. 637 (Md. 2023)
American Bar Association (2023): Standards and Rules of Procedure for Approval of Law Schools. Chicago: American Bar Association.
Bator, Paul M. (1963): "Finality in Criminal Law and Federal Habeas Corpus for State Prisoners". In: Harvard Law Review 76, 441–528.
Bar Standards Board (2019): "Bar Qualification Manual", London: Bar Standards Board.
Beety, Valena E. & Oliva, Jennifer D. (2019): "Evidence on Fire". In: North Carolina Law Rev. 97, 483–528.
Beety, Valena Elizabeth (2015): "Identifying the Culprit in Wrongful Convictions". In: 82 Tennessee Law Review 82, 975–1006.
Bodden v Gentry 2020 WL 2513672 (D. Nev. 2020).
Carmon v State 2022 WL 17423683 (Conn. Super. Ct. 2022).
Cecil, Joe S. & Willging, Thomas E. (1993): Court Appointed Experts: Defining the Role of Experts Appointed under Federal Rule of Evidence 706. Washington DC: Judicial Center.
Commonwealth v Armstrong 211 N. E.3d 622.
Cooper, Sarah (2024): "How do Layers Relate to Science Literacy? A New Methodological Framework". In: American Journal of Trial Advocacy 48, 61–88.
Cooper, Sarah & Shooter, Amelia (2022): "A Case for Conceptualizing Science Literacy for Lawyers". In: Criminal Law Practitioner 13, 3–26.
Crow, James F. (1996): The Evaluation of Forensic DNA Evidence, Washington DC: National Academies Press.

104 Snow/Dibner (2016) 25 (n30).
105 Cecil/Willging (1993), 11 f., 19.

Cruz, Archibald (2023): "The Paradigm Shift in the Proposed Amendment to Federal Rule of Evidence 702". In: Baylor Law Review 75, 265–291.
Daubert v Merrell Dow Pharmaceuticals Inc. 509 US 579 (1993).
Department of Homeland Security v Thuraissiagiam 591 U. S
Dervan, Lucian E., Leo, Richard A., Ryan, Meghan J., Beety, Valena E., Gilchrist, Gregory M., William W., (2016): "Voices on Innocence". In: Florida Law Review 68, 1569–1596.
Edwards, Harry T. & Gatsonis, Constantine (2009): Strengthening Forensic Science in the United States: A Path Forward, Washington DC: National Academies Press.
Faigman, David L. (1999): Legal Alchemy: The Use and Misuse of Science in the Law. New York: W. H. Freeman.
FBI National Press Office (2007): "FBI Laboratory to Increase Outreach in Bullet Lead Cases" https://archives.fbi.gov/archives/news/pressrel/press-releases/fbi-laboratory-to-increase-outreach-in-bullet-lead-cases, accessed 04.01.2024.
Federal Rule of Evidence 603.
Federal Rule of Evidence 702.
Federal Rule of Evidence 706.
Ficklin v Commonwealth 2022 WL 3640906 (Ky. 2022).
Fishman, Clifford (2023): Jones on Evidence, New York: Lawyers Cooperative Publishing.
Frye v United States, 293 F. 1013 (D. C. Cir 1923).
Fuller, Lon L. (1950): "On Teaching Law". In: Stanford Law Review 3, 35–47.
General Electric Co. v Joiner 522 U. S. 136 (1997).
Genesis, Chapter 18.
Grey, Sheryl (2023): "The Top 13 Pre-Law Majors". In: https://www.forbes.com/advisor/education/pre-law-majors/, accessed 04.01.2024.
Hart, Jr, Henry M. & Sacks, Albert M., Ed. William N. Eskridge Jr. & Philip P. Frickey (1994): The Legal Process: Basic Problems in the Making and Application of Law. New York: Foundation Press.
Holdren, John P. & Lander, Eric S. (eds) (2016): Forensic Science in Criminal Courts: Ensuring Scientific Validity of Feature Comparison Methods. Washington DC: Obama White House.
Imwinkelried, Edward J. (2020): "The Admissibility of Scientific Evidence: Exploring the Significance of the Distinction between Foundational Validity and Validity as Applied". In: Syracuse Law Review 70, 817–850.
Innocence Project, "Cases". In: https://innocenceproject.org/all-cases/, accessed 04.01.2024
Jackson, Howell E. (2003): "Analytical Methods for Lawyers". In: Journal of Legal Education 53, 321–327.
Laurin, Jennifer E. (2012): "Still Convicting the Innocent". In: Texas Law Review 90, 1472–1506.
Merlino, Mara, Richardson, James T., Chamberlain, Jared & Springer, Victoria (2008): "Science in the Law School Curriculum: A Snapshot of the Legal Education Landscape". In: Journal of Legal Education 58, 190–213.
Moriarty, Jane Campbell & Saks, Michael J. (2005): "Forensic Science: Grand Goals, Tragic Flaws, and Judicial Gatekeeping". In: Judges' Journal 44, 16–46.
Mullenix, Linda S. (2023): "The Short Unhappy Life of the Negotiation Class". In: University of Michigan Journal of Law Reform 56, 613–698.
National Academy of Sciences, "Mission". In: https://www.nasonline.org/about-nas/mission/, accessed 04.01.2024.

Nesbitt Cosby, Teresa (2018): "To the Head of the Class: Quantifying the Relationship between Participation in Undergraduate Mock Trial Programs and Student Performance in Law School". In: St John's Law Review 92, 797–832.
People v Jennings, 252 Ill. 534 (Illinois, 1911).
Porter, Glenn (2011): "A New Theoretical Framework Regarding the Application and Reliability of Photographic Evidence". In: International Journal of Evidence and Proof 15, 26–61.
Secretary of State for the Home Department v AF (No 3) [2008] EWCA Civ. 1148.
Shooter, Amelia & Cooper, Sarah L. (2019): "A Template for Enhancing the Impact of the National Academy of Sciences' Reporting on Forensic Science". In: British Journal of American Legal Studies 8, 441–464.
Shooter, Amelia (2020): 100 Years of the National Research Council: A Critical Examination of Judicial References to Forensic Science NAS Reports. Birmingham: Unpublished Thesis.
Snow, Catherine E. & Dibner, Kenne A. (2016): Science Literacy: Concepts, Contexts and Consequences. Washington DC: National Academies Press.
Sonsteng, John, Lattner, Leigha, Parks, Emily & Camarotta, David (2014): "The Unfulfilled Promise of Law Schools to Prepare Students for the Practice of Law". In: Sua Sponte 40, 17–62.
South African Innocence Project, "About Us" In: https://innocence.co.za/about.html, accessed 04.01.2024.
The Inns of Court College of Advocacy, "OUP and ICCA National Mooting Competition". In: https://www.icca.ac.uk/oup-icca-national-mooting-competition/, accessed 04.01.2024.
United States v Hunt, 63 F.4th 1229 (10th Cir 2023).
Victor A. McKusick (1992): DNA Technology in Forensic Science. Washington DC: National Academies Press.
Voltaire (1749): Zadig. London: John Brindley.
William Blackstone, ed. William Hardcastle Browne (1897): Commentaries on the Laws of England. New York: L. K. Strouse & Co.

Amelia Shooter
School of Law, University of Nottingham
Amelia.Shooter@Nottingham.ac.uk

Alternative Medicine Meets Legal Theory
Non-Scientific Treatments as a Regulatory Challenge

TOMASZ PIETRZYKOWSKI

Abstract: The paper explores the question of traditional and alternative medicine as a challenge for the public and legal policy-making. A plethora of healing practices rooted in pre-scientific traditions and beliefs remain prevalent in Western as well as Eastern hemispheres. Unsupported by credible empirical evidence and inconsistent with basic scientific knowledge, they offer subjectively perceived improvements, unrelated to the actual efficacy of the treatment. Such pseudo-medical modalities pose a serious regulatory problem that has not yet met the satisfactory, well-considered solutions worldwide. Two extreme regulatory models based on opposite philosophical solutions are examined and found indefensible due to their practical deficiencies and flawed philosophical underpinnings. Therefore, a middle-way based on respect for the patient's genuine autonomy is proposed and outlined.

Keywords: law, medicine, regulation, science, policy, evidence, healthcare.

1 Scientific Medicine

The emergence of scientific medicine occurred as a result of the great discoveries and technological advances of the 17th and 18th centuries. However, the actual institutionalization of medicine as a practice based not on individual observations handed down from generation to generation but rather on systematic research and rigorously verified evidence did not occur until the last century. The process is still far from complete. Thus, everyday medical practice is by no means free of methods and measures whose effectiveness has never been scientifically soundly tested. In many respects, intuitively applied "common sense medicine" still dominates over methods verified by hard evidence. Some studies suggest that the latter may constitute a minority rather than the majority of the therapies actually used[1].

For these reasons, the idea of evidence-based medicine has been intensively developed for several decades[2]. It seeks to develop the strictest possible criteria for ob-

1 Patashnik et al. (2017); Stengenga (2018).
2 Howick (2011); Straus et. al. (2019).

jectively assessing the reliability of evidence of the efficacy and safety of individual treatments. This is because such evidence is generally of different types and quality. The weakest quality of scientific evidence is provided by individual clinical observations and case reports, followed by cohort observational studies, then randomized and properly controlled clinical trials, and, at the highest, by properly conducted meta-analyses of such studies.

Only a critical analysis of the appropriate amount and quality of evidence can allow a given treatment method to be considered positively verified (most probably genuinely effective). The bulk of such evidence must consist of properly designed and controlled randomized clinical trials published in sufficiently credible peer-reviewed journals. Therapies that meet these criteria then become the subject of guidelines established by the relevant expert bodies. Such guidelines serve bringing the daily medical practice as close as possible to the ideal of using treatment methods supported by the best evidence available at the current state of medical knowledge.

Verification of the reliability of the evidence of the effectiveness and safety of individual treatment methods is a continuous process. No scientific findings are definitive and must remain open to revision in view of potential new evidence that may always appear. Nonetheless, the relative level of confidence in particular claims or theories may differ greatly depending on the quality and amount of the relevant evidence. Despite centuries of making medical practice increasingly science-based, it is still encumbered by numerous methods and approaches that have never been properly verified by randomized controlled trials. The consistent application of Evidence-Based Medicine (EBM) principles plays a crucial role in further progress in identifying and eliminating therapies that cannot stand the empirical test of genuine clinical efficacy.

2 So-called Alternative Medicine

Many therapeutic approaches remain outside the boundaries of scientific medicine, especially the part that strives to respect and implement the principles of EBM. In many cases, the belief in their efficacy is based not on the quality of clinical research but on various folk traditions (local or exotic), pre-scientific beliefs, and religious or philosophical systems. Such practices are sometimes collectively called "alternative," "complementary," "traditional," "unconventional," "natural," etc. medicine. Fundamental doubts may be raised by the very nomenclature suggesting that such methods belong to "medicine" and thus lend them a prima facie credibility that they do not, in fact, deserve. Hence, one of the most prominent experts on the subject consistently promotes the use of the term "So-Called Alternative Medicine" (SCAM)[3].

3 Ernst (2018).

This is no less true of increasingly popular terms like "integral," "integrated," or "holistic" medicine. These are meant to imply that they are a kind of equal complement to scientific medicine. Allegedly, only together can they acquire the ability to take a holistic approach to humans and their health. However, this terminology is actually more of a rhetorical and marketing ploy than any characterization of the relationship between scientific and non-scientific approaches to diagnosing and treating diseases. Therefore, a much more appropriate term to encompass the totality of those health practices that do not reckon with reliably verified scientific knowledge is the term "pseudo-medicine."

Not only are pseudo-medical methods and theories plentiful but their catalog remains essentially open. Thus, it is difficult to estimate their popularity; however, most studies indicate that no less than 25–70 % of people living in developed countries use pseudo-medical means or therapies[4]. It can be assumed that in countries with less developed healthcare systems and limited access to scientific medicine, the scale of the impact of such practices is even much higher.

Many of the most popular pseudo-medical methods are based on Far Eastern religious and folk traditions. Among these, Chinese acupuncture is particularly widely used. The practice of acupuncture is based on the theory of "meridians" running through the body to channel life-energy (Qi) flows. This is the strand of pseudo-medicine that perhaps most strenuously aspires to accomplish the status of a scientifically validated therapy.[5] However, the results of the studies show at best the results indicating improvement in patients' subjective feelings (pain, anxiety, discomfort) only[6]. More importantly, they are typically not significantly better than those achieved with sham acupuncture[7]. Moreover, a critical analysis of the quality of these studies, particularly those published in China, indicates that acupuncture is probably nothing more than a kind of "theatrical placebo."[8]

Even less evidence supports the efficacy of other Far Eastern healing practices, such as the Japanese Reiki and Indian Ayurveda. They are generally based on utterly non-scientific theories, explaining the causes of diseases and methods of treating them in a way detached from modern biomedical knowledge. Attempts to demonstrate their clinical efficacy in a way that eliminates the influence of the placebo effect and possible

4 Cf. e. g. Lee et al. (2022), 713–35; Phutrakool/Pongpirul (2022); Eardley et al. (2012); Ernst (2018), 7 f.
5 This aspiration has been fortified by a questionable attitude toward acupuncture of the World Health Organization, which published several reports strongly overrating the effectiveness of that method in a wide range of conditions. See Singh/Ernst (2009), 91–96.
6 E. g. Xu et al. (2018), Kong et al. (2019), Ying et al. (2018).
7 E. g. Deare et al. (2013); Linde et al. (2016); Ju et al. (2017).
8 Colquhoun/Novella (2013), 1360 f.; Rotkiewicz (2023).

other so-called "context effects" invariably reveal that the effectiveness of such therapies is demonstrated only by relatively poorly designed and controlled studies[9].

Even practitioners of the Reiki method avoid claiming that it is a means of affecting the disease. The results are to be achieved due to "getting to the root of the disease to create the best conditions for the body to heal itself"[10]. In so-called Ayurvedic medicine, the basis of the therapeutic effect is the use of herbal products, minerals, and metals (including lead, arsenic, and copper), grounded on pre-scientific notions of health as a balance of the three so-called doshas (Vata, Pitta, and Kapha)[11]. However, the active ingredients in some of the herbs used in it can bring about some therapeutic effects, at least for certain diseases[12]. However, the use of heavy metals also leads to the appearance of cases of poisoning, making Ayurvedic specifics a relatively risky form of pseudo-medicine[13].

Pseudo-medical treatments of Western provenance do not differ essentially from those of Far Eastern traditions. Among the best known is homeopathy, invented in the late 18th century. Interestingly, the idea was born mostly out of justified dissatisfaction with the ineffective and harmful methods prevailing in the medical practices of that time (such as bloodletting). From today's perspective, however, scientific evidence respecting the standards of methodological reliability leaves no doubt that homeopathy is completely ineffective (except for the placebo effect). The resulting improvement in the patient's subjective condition invariably turns out to result mostly from "long, empathetic, compassionate encounters with the homeopath, the placebo effect and other factors that make up the so-called context effect"[14].

Similar features are observed in chiropractic, osteopathy, anthroposophical medicine, Gerson therapy, bioresonance, aromatherapy, uridotherapy, hydrocolonotherapy, detoxification, and many others[15]. There is no substantial evidence that they can actually positively affect health (as opposed to subjective impression of improvement resulting from placebo, natural course of an illness, and other contextual factors). The lack of such evidence, combined with the absence of a convincing and respectful scientific knowledge of the alleged mechanism of action, makes it implausible to regard these treatments as anything else than just another form of pseudo-medicine.

---

9 https://sciencebasedmedicine.org/reiki, accessed 17 August 2025; Lee et al. (2008), 947–954. Ernst/Smith (2019), 61–63.

10 Cf. e.g., https://www.mcgill.ca/oss/article/health-pseudoscience/should-we-take-reiki-seriously, accessed 17 August 2025.

11 Patwardhan (2014); Kumar/Sinh (2020).

12 https://sciencebasedmedicine.org/a-poorly-conceived-study-fails-to-prove-ayurveda-works/, accessed 17 August 2025; Ernst (2019), 263–264.

13 https://www.nccih.nih.gov/health/ayurvedic-medicine-in-depth, accessed 17 August 2025; Ernst, ibid., 263.

14 Ernst, ibid., 112.

15 Ibid.

The diversity and relatively blurred boundaries of pseudo-medical practices do not mean that they are not a phenomenon united by certain key common features. The first is their reliance on theoretical foundations incompatible with scientific knowledge, most often ignoring such knowledge or using it in a fragmentary, if not caricatured, manner. In doing so, they often refer to entities and phenomena (energy and its balance, meridians, chakras, doshas, water memory, etc.), the existence of which cannot be established by any reliable empirical methods and the role of which is a blatant contradiction of the processes and causal relations known to science. Their acceptance is an act of faith, and these concepts themselves often have religious or quasi-religious provenance.

The second defining feature of pseudo-medicine is the lack of sufficiently reliable evidence of its effectiveness. This does not mean that there are no various types of studies, observations, or publications suggesting otherwise. On the contrary, some strands of pseudo-medicine attempt at all costs to create the impression of "scientific evidence" confirming their effect. However, they are characterized by poor quality and how they are conducted, and the verifiability and replicability of their results do not meet methodological standards and rigor. For these reasons, they do not allow for sound consideration of their results as sufficiently reliable confirmations of the hypotheses[16].

The eccentricity of the theories promulgated as explanations for the alleged efficacy of pseudo-medical therapies is therefore matched by the weakness of the evidence intended to confirm the validity of the beliefs on which they are founded. The latter, in turn, usually undermines not only the foundations of medicine, anatomy, or physiology but often also the very foundations of the scientific worldview. Thus, they should be examined in light of the famous methodological principle formulated by Carl Sagan, according to which "extraordinary claims require extraordinary evidence" (ECREE)[17]. In fact, however, the relevant evidence, if it exists at all, is not only very far from being extraordinarily strong but remains at best highly ambiguous and questionable[18].

---

16 In this respect, the evidence of the effectiveness of pseudo-medicine resembles – by no means incidentally only – the attempts carried out for decades to experimentally prove various types of paranormal phenomena: telepathy, telekinesis, precognition, etc. For an example of a thorough, critical analysis of studies that were presented as empirical, "scientific" evidence of their occurrence, see Hansel (1966).

17 For critical discussion of the so-called Sagan Standard see Deming (2016), 1319–1331.

18 This is not to say that a positive impact on subjectively perceived wellbeing and, consequently, quality of life is unimportant. On the contrary, its role in modern medicine is definitely growing. Thus, individual techniques of alternative therapies could be of value even without any effect on improving the objective state of disease progression, if only their positive effect on the patient's perceived level of wellbeing were convincingly proven. In this respect, too, however, the efficacy of the vast majority of pseudo-medicine methods is not significantly superior to the placebo effect. Relatively the most convincing evidence of clinically significant effects on the well-being of patients of certain diseases concerns techniques based on mindfulness and meditation. These, too, should be treated with caution. Mindfulness-based therapies, for

Why do pseudo-medical therapies remain so popular despite their lack of real efficacy? There are many reasons – from inadequate access to medical help and the depersonalized and superficial contact many patients face during medical visits to the attractiveness and simplicity of explanations that substitute for complex pathophysiological and pharmacological mechanisms of disease formation and treatment. Some role may also be played by the charm of exotic mystery as well as the over-cautiousness of many doctors and scientists in evaluating pseudo-medical practices. The most important factor, however, seems to be understandable desperation in the face of the inevitable limitations of real therapeutic possibilities.

All these considerations make pseudo-medicine a significant social and regulatory legal problem. This is because it is an excellent field for consciously or unconsciously exploiting the credulity and ignorance of people struggling with diseases, constituting a group extremely vulnerable to abuse. It also entails numerous risks related to the abandonment or delay of actual treatment, the waste of enormous financial resources often necessary to fully exploit the possibilities of real treatment, and the undesirable negative side effects, as well as the involvement of public institutions in authorizing and lending credibility to activities based on superstition, autosuggestion, or simple quackery.

3 Legal Status of Pseudo-Medical Practices

The immense popularity of pseudo-medical practices and the easy income they bring make the relevant industry an influential player in terms of marketing and lobbying capabilities. Moreover, some governments tend to more or less officially support "their own" medical traditions, treating them as a tool for building their international soft power and balancing foreign cultural influences. Consequently, in many countries, numerous pseudo-medical practices are treated by law as almost equivalent to scientific medicine.

An example of such a policy is the status of acupuncture, whose contemporary importance and popularity have been largely a matter of conscious government policy pursued for several decades. The political role of traditional Chinese medicine in Chinese government policy is evidenced by successive official national programs for its development implemented in the aftermath of strategic decisions made at the 18th CCP Congress in 2012[19]. In 2020, an additional proposal to outlaw speech criticizing Traditional Chinese Medicine (TCM) was considered (although ultimately abandoned).

---

example, have not only been shown to be ineffective in smoking cessation but also in reducing stress and anxiety associated with nicotine withdrawal. One study found a reduction in their levels but eight others did not – see Jackson et. al. (2022).

19 Wang et al. (2021).

Similarly, in Japan, traditional medicinal methods (so-called kampo, although mainly limited to the preparation and use of herbal medicines) have for several decades been treated as legally equivalent to "Western" medicine[20]. Such policy change was implemented after the period of marginalization of kampo in the aftermath of the country's modernization initiated by the Meiji Revolution. In India, traditional Ayurvedic medicine is treated as a parallel, independent treatment system, offered as an exclusive form of therapy by nearly three thousand hospitals and more than 15,000 pharmacies across the country[21]. In Western countries, such practices are not treated as equivalent alternative treatment methods. However, in most cases, they are at least tolerated if not variously legally recognized.

In the legislation of almost all American states, acupuncture has gained the status of a licensed healing practice, and increasingly similar regulations for chiropractic, naturopathy, and reflexology are also appearing. In 1991, by congressional decision, an Office for Alternative Medicine, now called the Center for Complementary and Integrative Health, was established within the structures of the National Institutes of Health. At the level of state legislation, regulations are emerging to protect physicians practicing alternative methods from potential charges for practices contrary to medical knowledge and non-physician practitioners of these methods from potential charges of illegally providing medical services (so-called "safe harbor laws")[22].

In Europe, the solutions to pseudo-medicine are a completely chaotic patchwork. In Germany, the profession of *Heilpraktiker* was legally recognized in the 1930 s, and the then-adopted law remains in force until today. In the vast majority of other European countries, licenses for practitioners of various types of alternative treatments have also been introduced. A special case is Switzerland, where the profession of "alternative and complementary medicine therapist" was legally recognized in 1999, although due to lack of scientific evidence of effectiveness, it was abolished; however, in 2009, by referendum, practitioners of several kinds of complementary medicine were granted the status of a full-fledged part of the health care system financed by public health insurance[23].

Only in a few countries (including Poland and France) do pseudo-medical practices remain an activity performed only on general market principles and not subject to specific regulations by medical law. Diagnosing and treating patients is permitted only by physicians, who are required to use only methods with scientifically proven efficacy[24]. However, the sector of pseudo-medical services provided on a commercial basis

20 Arai/Kawahara (2019), 3–11; Fuyuno (2011), 480.
21 Shi et al. (2021). 51–55.
22 Bellamy (2021).
23 Rist/Schwabl (2009), 76–78.
24 The actual legal situation under the Polish law is, however, far from coherent. For details see Pietrzykowski/Smilowska (2023), 14–27.

remains tolerated, and sometimes doctors themselves join in. Whereas in Poland the medical self-government unequivocally condemns the use of alternative methods (primarily homeopathy) by physicians[25], in France, many pseudo-medical practices are conceived as potentially dangerous due to the links to religious or quasi-religious cults[26].

Interesting solutions have been envisaged in Belgian law. Practitioners of alternative methods are legally obliged to familiarize themselves with the patient's diagnosis by a medical doctor. If the patient has not consulted a relevant physician, the practitioner must first instruct the patient to seek it. If the patient refuses, the practitioner should obtain a written statement from the patient to be kept in the patient's file. The practitioner must also endeavor to ensure that the measures he or she uses do not cause the patient to fail to receive the proper treatment administered by the physician and must inform the patient's physician of his or her own assessment of the patient's condition. These regulations are interesting measures that can reduce the most serious risk of pseudo-medical services, which is the abandonment or delay in undertaking diagnostics and treatment that can realistically improve the patient's health.

Relatively favorable to pseudo-medicine are also the European Union's regulations on drug registration. In 2004, the European Union introduced a simplified procedure for authorizing homeopathic products (provided that the active substance is diluted to such a degree as to guarantee the absence of any effect on the human body). Herbal medicinal products are also subject to a simplified procedure and can be marketed on the condition that they have been in practice for at least 30 years, 15 of them within the European Union. Manufacturers of homeopathic and herbal products, on the other hand, are exempted in this procedure from the obligation to stop clinical studies proving the effectiveness of marketed drugs[27]. In African countries, as in Asia, the legal recognition of traditional treatments as a full-fledged alternative to scientific medicine is almost universal[28].

A general review of the legal situation in major legal systems worldwide suggests that there is a sufficiently thought-over regulatory approach to pseudo-medical practices. The relevant arrangements seem to be a more or less accidental mixture of tolerant recognition, skepticism, and instrumental promotion, based on unclear and incoherent philosophical presumptions. In many cases of legislative proposals and following public debates, the lawmakers seem somewhat intellectually defenseless in

---

25 Resolutions of the Polish Supreme Medical Council opposing the treatment of homeopathy as an acceptable method of treatment have become the subject of antitrust proceedings launched by the Office of Competition and Consumer Protection. Fortunately, the ludicrous allegation of "monopolistic practices" by the medical profession supreme self-regulating body was finally (after 6 years!) abandoned. See the decision of the President of the UOKiK, No. DOK-1/2017 of August 3, 2017.

26 Cloatre et al. (2021), 328–348.

27 Directive 2004/24/EC of 31.04.2004, OJ L 136, 85–90; Directive 2004/27/EC of 31.03.2004, OJ L 136, 34–57.

28 World Health Organization, Global report on traditional and complementary medicine, 2019, 18–19.

facing the phenomenon that combines important and difficult scientific, social, legal, ethical, and psychological considerations. This makes the philosophical analysis and normative argument pertaining to the potential regulatory models fully legitimate, if not urgently needed.

4 Potential Regulatory Models

Regardless of the variety and inconsistency of realistically existing legal solutions, from the point of view of rational legal policy, there are three possible approaches to the regulation of pseudo-medicine referring to different philosophical assumptions. The first allows full freedom of choice for the patient (so-called "health freedom") among all the treatment services offered on the entirely free market, regardless of the scientific or non-scientific paradigm within which they operate ("medical pluralism"). Decisions are made by the patient himself, who may prefer any treatment based on such information as they themselves deem reliable. Anyone offering such services is subject to similar rules of liability for damages, and the standard of professional due diligence, reliability of communication with the patient, and obtaining the patient's informed consent are subject to evaluation by the courts and institutions competent to do so.

However, the well-known weaknesses of the *laissez-faire* model are the anachronistic philosophical and empirical assumptions about the degree of rationality of patients' decisions, particularly the actual ability to acquire and fully understand the information necessary to make a fully informed choice of therapy[29]. Such assumptions do not correspond to reality, even remotely. This is the case in relatively comfortable decision-making conditions and with a sufficient level of medical literacy. It is all the more true when people who are ill, desperate, and helpless make decisions under severe stress. In such circumstances, the rationality of choices is even further distorted by all kinds of self-delusion, motivated reasoning, and subtle misrepresentations provided by practitioners.

Public recognition of pseudo-medical activities can confer credibility, resulting from perceiving state licenses as a seal of official approval. This, in turn, may amplify its capability to exploit many patients' gullibility. Moreover, allocating funds to finance objectively ineffective therapies constitutes an obvious problem in terms of a severe lack of sufficient resources to provide all patients with everything that modern medicine may have to offer. As a result, significant harm may be caused by limiting access to scientifically proven treatments due to the waste of valuable time or indispensable financial resources.

A counter model is to rigorously restrict legally offered treatments to only those with scientifically verified efficacy. Under such a regime, only physicians committed

29 See Pietrzykowski/Smilowska (2021), 1–8.

to using only evidence-based medicine can undertake the diagnosis and treatment of patients. There are no “alternative” medicine methods – medicine is either based on scientific data or it is not medicine and should not be used to make money at the expense of patients seeking help. This model assumes that it is the state’s responsibility to allow only truly competent practitioners to treat patients in ways that are based on the best available scientific evidence. The state is in an incomparably better position than ordinary patients to distinguish genuine from fake therapies; thus, it must organize the health market so that patients are protected from wasting time and money, and the relevant resources are allocated as effectively as possible. This may be called a prohibitionist or statist model.

However, a solution based on a ban on offering patients treatment with scientifically unproven methods has all the disadvantages of prohibition. In practice, it is impossible to effectively enforce a ban when its subject is behavior that enjoys a significant degree of social acceptance. It would require gigantic forces and resources directed at fighting the “black market” of officially banned services. Even if it would reduce their availability, it would most likely increase the overall social and individual harm inflicted by their provision.

The prohibitionist model would also be highly morally questionable, as it would restrict the freedom to voluntarily and knowingly use services that, despite their lack of proven efficacy, may in many cases be harmless for a patient and bring them various subjective benefits (even if mostly in the form of psychological comfort or placebo effects). Therefore, it can be rightfully regarded as excessively paternalistic and constraining individual liberty to the extent beyond a reasonable justification.

5 Genuine Autonomy Model

The disadvantages of both the fully free-market and prohibitionist models prompt the search for an intermediate solution. Although most of the realistically existing ways of regulating pseudo-medicine can be considered some kind of intermediate norm, they generally form haphazard combinations of market and rationing solutions. The optimal intermediate model should be founded on rational and consistent philosophical assumptions. A regulation that meets this condition would be a combination of the right to use any pseudo-medical services offered on a free-market basis while protecting against misinformation, exploitation of ignorance and desperation, and abuse of the authority of medicine and science[30]. It can be described as a patient’s genuine autonomy model.

---

30 Cf. the “robustness principle” advocated as a sound basis of legal measures concerning behaviors resulting from vices in Leitzel (2008).

Measures to protect the patient from misinformation about the nature of the services offered to him should include mandatory warnings about the lack of evidence of the therapeutic efficacy of a particular type of treatment or substance[31]. Placing them on products or in a conspicuous place on the premises where the services in question are provided would by no means be a novelty among consumer protection instruments against various types of products or services. The terms "medicine," "therapy," "treatment," "drug," or "medicinal product" should be reserved by law for the benefit of physicians practicing in accordance with scientific knowledge, and their use to name and advertise pseudo-medical practices and substances should be prohibited.

In addition, the prerequisites for liability for damages for the non-factual presentation of its advantages and alleged effectiveness should be tightened and clarified. Information about such liability and its prerequisites should also be properly displayed and made available to patients. Public funding for pseudo-medical services should be excluded. Mandatory licensing of non-medical entities providing services or producing substances intended to affect the health and well-being of the patient should allow for more effective oversight of the market. The advantages of such solution seem to outweigh the risks of lending such licensed services the impression of official confirmation of their legitimacy.

The application of the above solutions would minimize the risk of abuse of trust and credulity of patients seeking rescue while preserving the right to legally use such services on their own accounts by those aware of the nature of the services offered to them. Providing conditions of voluntariness based on sufficiently accessible and clear information realizes a pattern of real, rather than merely formal, patient autonomy. This provides a more reasonable alternative to prohibition and the strict *laissez-faire* model.

6 Concluding Remarks

The *laissez-faire,* prohibitionist, and genuine autonomy models for regulating pseudo-medical services and substances differ primarily in their underlying empirical and axiological assumptions. The flawed nature of such assumptions affects the real operation of legal rules based on them, potentially distorting the harms and benefits that the regulation can produce. As in the case of almost all other social problems, a model striving to find an Aristotelian "golden mean" between extremes seems to be the most promising and best suited to the extremely complex psychological and sociological conditions of the healthcare system.

Unlike existing regulations, however, a set of such compromise solutions should be founded on a consistent and reliable factual and philosophical basis. What is at stake,

---

31 Cf. Ernst (2009), 343–345.

after all, is the life and health of huge numbers of people, but also, in the long run, the position of science and true expertise in shaping social life.

Bibliography

Arai, Ichiro / Kawahara, Nobuo (2019): "Kampo pharmaceutical products in the Japanese health-care system: Legal status and quality assurance". In: Traditional & Kampo Medicine 6, 3–11.

"Ayurvedic Medicine: In Depth" In: The National Center for Complementary and Integrative Health, https://www.nccih.nih.gov/health/ayurvedic-medicine-in-depth, accessed 17 August 2025.

Bellamy, John (2021), Quack Protection Acts advance in state legislatures, https://sciencebasedmedicine.org/quack-protection-acts-advance-in-state-legislatures/, accessed 17 August 2025.

Chandra, Apoorva (2021): "A Poorly Conceived Study Fails to Prove Ayurveda Works". In: Science-Based Medicine,
https://sciencebasedmedicine.org/a-poorly-conceived-study-fails-to-prove-ayurveda-works/, acccessed 17 August 2025.

Cloatre, Emilie et al. (2021): "Legalities of Healing: Handling Alterities at the Edge of Medicine in France, 1980s–2010s.". In: Osiris 36, 328–348.

Colquhoun, David / Novella Stephen (2013): "Acupuncture is theatrical placebo". In: Anesthesia and Analgesia 116 (6), 1360–3.

Deare, John et al. (2013): "Acupuncture for treating fibromyalgia" In: Cochrane Database of Systematic Reviews 5, Art. No.: CD007070.

Deming, David (2016): "Do extraordinary claims require extraordinary evidence?" In: Philosophia 44 (4), 1319–1331.

Eardley et al. (2012): "CAM use in Europe – The patients' perspective. Part I: A systematic literature review of CAM prevalence in the EU". Cambrella Work Package 4, https://phaidra.univie.ac.at/detail/o:292161, accessed 17 August 2025.

Ernst, Edzard (2018): SCAM. So-Called Alternative Medicine, Exeter: Societas.

Ernst Edzard / Smith, Kevin (2018): More Harm than Good. The Moral Maze of Alternative and Complementary Medicine, Cham: Springer Nature.

Ernst Edzard (2019): Alternative Medicine. A Critical Assessment of 150 Modalities, Cham: Springer Nature.

Fuyuno, Ichiko (2011): "Japan: Will the sun set on Kampo?" Nature 480, s96.

Hansel, Charles E. M. (1966): ESP. A Scientific Evaluation, New York: Charles Schribners Sons.

Howick, Jeremy (2011): The Philosophy of Evidence-Based Medicine, Oxford: Wiley.

Jackson, Sarah et al. (2022): "Mindfulness for smoking cessation". In: Cochrane Database of Systematic Reviews 4, Art. No.: CD013696.

Ju, Yong Zi et al. (2017): "Acupuncture for neuropathic pain in adults". In: Cochrane Database of Systematic Reviews 12, Art. No.: CD012057.

Kong, De Zhao et al. (2019): "Acupuncture for chronic hepatitis B". In: Cochrane Database of Systematic Reviews 8, Art. No.: CD013107.

Lee, Lyn et al. (2022): "Prevalence of use of traditional, complementary and alternative medicine by the general population: A systematic review of national studies published from 2010 to 2019". In: Drug Safety 45, 713–735.

Lee, Myeong So et al. (2008): "Effects of reiki in clinical practice: a systematic review of randomised clinical trials". In: International Journal of Clinical Practice 62, 947–954
Linde, Klaus et al. (2016): "Acupuncture for the prevention of episodic migraine". In: Cochrane Database of Systematic Reviews 6, Art. No.: CD001218.
Novella, Steven (2011): "Reiki". In: Science-Based Medicine, https://sciencebasedmedicine.org/reiki/, accessed 17 August 2025.
Patashnik, Eric M. et al. (2017): Unhealthy Politics: The Battle over Evidence-Based Medicine, Princeton-Oxford: Princeton University Press.
Phutrakool, Phaupong / Pongpirul, Krit (2022): "Acceptance and use of complementary and alternative medicine among medical specialists: a 15-year systematic review and data synthesis" In: Systematic Reviews, 11 (1), 10.
Pietrzykowski, Tomasz / Smilowska, Katarzyna (2023): "Prawo, lekarze i pseudomedycyna". In: Radca. pl 2, 14–27, https://oirp.katowice.pl/add/vrecord/1402630714/1406899157/1402630728_0.pdf, accessed 17 August 2025.
Pietrzykowski, Tomasz / Smilowska, Katarzyna (2021): "The Reality of Informed Consent: empirical studies on patient comprehension" In: Trials 22, 1–8.
Rist, Lukas / Schwabl, Herbert (2009): "Komplementärmedizin im politischen Prozess". In: Forschung Komplementarmedizin 16, 76–78.
Rotkiewicz, Marcin (2023): Akupunktura – placebo doskonałe, https://www.projektpulsar.pl/czlowiek/2205386,1,akupunktura-placebo-doskonale.read, accessed 17 August 2025.
Shi, Yu et al. (2021): "Traditional medicine in India". In: Journal of Traditional Chinese Medical Sciences 8 (Suppl. 1), 51–55.
Singh, Simon / Ernst, Edzard (2009): Trick or Treatment? Alternative Medicine on Trial, London: Corgi.
Stengenga, Jacob (2018): Medical Nihilism, Oxford: Oxford University Press.
Straus, Sharon E. et al. (2019): Evidence-Based Medicine, 5th ed., Edinborough-London: Elsevier.
Wang, Wan-Jing et al. (2021): "Current policies and measures on the development of traditional Chinese medicine in China" In: Pharmacological Research 163, 105187.
World Health Organization (2019): Global report on traditional and complementary medicine, https://www.who.int/publications/i/item/978924151536, accessed 17 August 2025.
Yang, Jie et al. (2018): "Acupuncture for hypertension". In: Cochrane Database of Systematic Reviews 11, Art. No.: CD008821.
Xu, Mangman et al. (2018): "Acupuncture for acute stroke". In: Cochrane Database of Systematic Reviews 3, Art. No: CD003317.

Tomasz Pietrzykowski
Reseach Center for Public Policy and Regulatory Governance, Faculty of Law and Administration, University of Silesia in Katowice.
tomasz.pietrzykowski@us.edu.pl

The paper was prepared in collaboration with Dr. Katarzyna Smilowska from the Silesian Center for Neurology in Katowice, who contributed to its medical aspects, particularly in the proper understanding and application of evidence-based medicine standards.

Part 6
Cosmopolitanism vs. Culture?

International Human Rights Norms in the Culturally Diverse World*

KOSUKE KIYAMA

Abstract: In addressing the challenge posed by cultural diversity to the universality of international human rights norms, this paper critiques a recently proposed strategy anchored in the function of international law. The strategy claims that the international human rights regime benefits all cultural proponents and can be supported despite cultural diversity. This paper argues against this strategy on the grounds that benefit does not entail support and the strategy cannot prepare room for new international mechanisms that protect the rights of members of cultural groups. The paper advocates for an alternative approach that grounds international human rights norms in universally shared interests, offering a more nuanced framework that respects cultural differences.

Keywords: human rights, cultural diversity, the international human rights regime, interests, agency, equality

1 Introduction

1.1 Cultural diversity vs. universality of human rights norms?

On 24 June 1947, the American Anthropological Association (AAA) submitted its famous statement to the United Nations Commission on Human Rights.[1] It is possible to treat the statement as not hostile to human rights but just showing the challenges that the Universal Declaration of Human Rights would face, but the statement has

* This paper was presented at the 2nd IVR Japan International Conference in September 2023, where I received valuable support from Akio Fukuhara and other organizing members; and at the Stirling Political Philosophy Group in October 2023, where I benefited from constructive comments and the support of Fay Niker and others. However, my deepest gratitude goes to Rowan Cruft, who accepted me as a visiting researcher and commented on the early manuscript several times in the Summer of 2023 at Stirling, where academic and administrative staff kept an ideal atmosphere for research. In addition, I am grateful to Christofer Bullsmith for his support in improving the clarity of the paper. Finally, this paper is supported by The Murata Science Foundation M23 Kaijin 003 and JSPS KAKENHI Grant Number JP21K12821.

1 American Anthropological Association (1947).

largely been read as a 'rejection' of the declaration, or 'denial of possibility for engagement'.[2]

Whilst anthropologists, especially in the Boasian clan, have often called their claim "relativism", at the core of the claim is a tolerance for difference.[3] Although mainstream anthropologists' attitudes towards human rights have changed from rejection, through absence, to engagement since 1947[4], at the heart of their stance lies a moral claim, namely: what I call the *cultural diversity respect requirement*.[5]

Cultural diversity respect requirement: There are different cultural systems, and in envisaging human rights, some kind of respect for them is required.

This respect requirement has frequently been invoked to question the universality of international human rights norms. For instance, the Asian Values arguments, at least on the surface, advocate for the equal treatment of certain "Asian Values" in envisaging human rights, often claiming this leads to a change in the ranking of human rights to emphasize economic rights over civil and political rights.[6] Stimulated by this kind of doubt about the universality of human rights, moral, political, and legal philosophers have tried to respond. Some stressed the fact that in the origin of the human rights regime after World War II, such as the drafting process of the Universal Declaration of Human Rights, many people from diverse cultures participated[7], but others argue this does not establish universality because the participants were from a tiny subset of the societies involved and they cannot be seen as representing their cultural moralities as they were just the "elites" of each society.[8]

In the same way that the cultural diversity respect requirement has been used to question the origin of international human rights norms, it has been used to question their content and implementation.[9]

---

2 Eagle (2001), 537, 540.
3 Ibid.
4 Simmons/Feldman (2018), 115.
5 This is different from what Allen Buchanan calls 'ethical pluralism', which 'holds that there is a plurality of valid, that is, rationally defensible moralities, but that none of them is uniquely rational'. Buchanan (2013), 251. The cultural diversity respect requirement is weaker, allowing for the possibility that individuals can critique certain practices within a purportedly different culture. This nuanced perspective aligns with the stance taken by pro-rights anthropologists in the 1990 s. Eagle (2001), 554.
6 For an analysis of this, see Bell (2000), Part II.
7 Gilabert (2018), 92.
8 Miller (2014), 154.
9 As the best treatment of the claim from cultural diversity against human rights, see Nickel (2007), Ch. 11.

1.2 Desiderata to fulfil the cultural diversity respect requirement

However, why is the cultural diversity respect requirement taken seriously? Perhaps there are worries or assumed wrongness in not accommodating cultural diversity in international human rights norms. Assumed wrongness includes:

a) Moral: Parochialism – arbitrary selection or ranking of moral values
First, not respecting cultural diversity and hence betraying the cultural diversity respect requirement is thought to lead to the arbitrary selection or ranking of moral values in human rights.

b) Political: Imposition of arbitrary moral values
Second, it leads to imposing values not shared by others, as was done under the practice of colonialism or imperialism.

c) Practical: Insufficient support for human rights norms from people
Third, failing to meet the cultural diversity respect requirement might lead to hostility towards human rights norms if individuals feel their culture is not respected. This could result in a backlash against human rights endeavours, potentially leading to the failure to achieve human rights.

1.3 Purpose of the paper

The paper aims to explore justificatory strategies for human rights that attempt to accommodate the cultural diversity respect requirement. Specifically, it critically examines a recently proposed approach relying on the function of international law. This strategy argues that the functions and purposes of the international human rights regime benefit all cultural proponents[10] and can be supported without being afflicted by cultural diversity. The paper challenges this strategy by arguing that benefit does not entail support and that it cannot prepare room for new international mechanisms that protect human rights better. Instead, the paper advocates for a strategy grounding international human rights norms in universally shared interests, offering a more robust foundation for universal support. Notably, the paper underscores the moral significance of *equality* and *agency* as the grounding values for international human rights norms to accommodate and respect cultural differences. The subsequent discussion shows how this *dualism* can meet the desiderata shown above.

10 This perspective is not confined to philosophers but is occasionally tacitly endorsed by the AAA, particularly when considering the utilization of human rights law, especially the right to culture, to uphold the norm of respecting cultural diversity. See Eagle (2001), 551.

2 Benefits of the international legal human rights system for culturally diverse groups

2.1 Buchanan's argument

Allen Buchanan, especially in his influential work *The Heart of Human Rights*, proposes a unique way to accommodate the cultural diversity respect requirement. Buchanan positions the international legal human rights system as a foundational element in justifying human rights. Then, he offers several reasons for having the system. Especially relevant here is that Buchanan affirms the importance of the cultural diversity respect requirement and explains the major reason cultural groups have for supporting the system, namely that the system benefits (offers advantages to) cultural groups.[11] These advantages include the safeguarding of cultural groups through individual legal human rights, offering reasonable institutional mechanisms for minority groups to exercise their rights and by giving cultural community members the power to appeal even when states do not recognise them as groups.[12] Alternatively, individual legal human rights contribute to the flourishing of groups by fostering not the interests of the elite in the groups but the rights of each individual.[13]

While Buchanan emphasizes the protective nature of the international legal human rights system for cultural groups, he acknowledges that the system may disadvantage some groups. However, he contends that the overall advantages of the system outweigh the disadvantages, and that there is no viable alternative to the international legal human rights system, considering the substantial transition costs from the current system to an alternative.[14]

This line of argument is intended to avoid moral parochialism or political imposition and gather support for human rights norms, thereby fulfilling the cultural diversity respect requirement. Importantly, it achieves this by focusing on the international legal human rights system rather than appealing to practices specific to any particular culture.[15] Further, the argument appeals to the benefits accrued to cultural groups or

---

11 Buchanan (2013), Ch. 7. Note that Buchanan confines his discussion to cultural groups characterized by 'valid moralities'–moral frameworks that operate effectively in society, relying on internal support rather than coercion and functioning without substantial reliance on irrational beliefs. Ibid., 241 f.

12 Ibid., 264 f.

13 Ibid., 266.

14 Ibid., 272.

15 Charles Beitz, despite differing with Buchanan on several points, considers the international human rights practice as not parochial, viewing it as a theoretical premise. See Beitz (2009), 20 f. However, in my view, determining whether the practice itself is parochial and establishing criteria for such judgment is a highly challenging task. For instance, is the practice deemed non-parochial merely because it involves the contributions of not only Westerners but also Asian or African officials and intellectuals? If so, what percentage of representation from these regions would suffice? Furthermore, does their involvement truly represent the societies they purportedly speak for? The consensus on these questions, grounded in a suitable

their members, assuming that the benefits generate reasons for those cultural groups to support the system without perceiving it as imposed.

2.2 Does benefit entail support? Room for new international mechanisms?

While Buchanan's arguments hold merit, I aim to highlight two key points. First, I contend that his argument for justifying the international legal human rights system based on the benefits it offers to cultural groups is flawed. Second, this argument suppresses the potential for the development of more effective mechanisms for protecting the rights of certain cultural group members.

The first point revolves around the normative relationship between benefit and support. My point is that benefit does not entail support. More specifically, the alleged fact that cultural groups or their individual members benefit from the international legal human rights system does not entail that they should support that system. To illustrate, consider a scenario where a professor provides water to a dehydrated student stuck outside on a hot day but she is fired because of another incident.[16] A student forgets to bring his ID card to enter buildings at the premise and lost a purse for purchasing a can of drink at a vending machine. When he is feeling dehydrated, a professor finds him and invites him to her office, offering several cups of water. In the situation, the student benefits from the professor's actions and uncontroversially should be grateful to her. However, this does not entail that he should support the professor, especially her existence at the university. Imagine the professor is fired after continuously sexually harassing another student, and seeks support to challenge her dismissal. In this situation, the grateful student is surely not morally required to support the professor. From this, what is clear is that benefitting from her (having a reason for gratitude) does not entail he should support her existence at the university. This scenario mirrors Buchanan's argument and shows that the mere benefit cultural groups enjoy from the international legal human rights system is not enough to establish that they should support the system.

Secondly, this point gains special relevance when Buchanan does not allow considering alternatives to the current system and accommodate only reforms of it. He writes: 'Given the significant protections that international legal human rights provide

rationale, seems elusive. In contrast, the interest-based view I advocate in section three offers guidance on assessing whether the current international human rights practice aligns with the cultural diversity respect requirement.

16 From Kiyama (2023a), 89 f. The scenario is similar to the well-known example of a public entertainment announcement used by Robert Nozick. However, the context differs, as Nozick's case is employed to counter the fair play-based argument for obeying the law, where benefitting from the law serves as the foundation for compliance. See Nozick (1974), 93. My argument extends beyond situations where fairness is a crucial consideration. I am indebted to Rowan Cruft for suggesting the consideration of Nozick's case.

for groups and relationships, and given the costs and risks of scrapping the system in favour of some other mode of achieving a comparable level of protection, the best alternative for those whose collectivistic moralities are disadvantaged by some aspects of the existing system may be to lobby for more reform rather than to discard the baby with the bathwater'.[17] Buchanan thereby advocates for reform rather than considering alternative world orders where cultural groups or their members might find more just and effective mechanisms for protecting their important interests. This limitation is grounded in his conception of institutional legitimacy – the Metacoordination View.[18] According to this view, institutions are required to produce benefits compared to their absence[19], but they are not expected 'to be either fully just or optimally efficacious'.[20] Perhaps Buchanan adopts this view thinking that the weak requirement for the legitimacy of institutions, i. e., that they are better than nothing, can acquire wide support.[21]

However, I question the rationale for this view. Even if the current international human rights system benefits cultural groups, we can imagine a system that can prevent the oppression of cultural groups better or includes more just and effective mechanisms for protecting their interests. Indeed, the United Nations' inaction during the Rwandan genocide highlights a significant deficiency in the current system. As a report annexed to a letter from Secretary-General Kofi Annan to the President of the Security Council notes, the genocide was 'a failure by the United Nations system as a whole', especially 'a persistent lack of political will', inter alia around the Security Council.[22] Given such shortcomings in the international legal human rights system, cultural groups facing similar risks may find it impossible to perceive the existing system as sufficiently beneficial. We should explore the possibility of a world order where efforts to prevent tragedies are not hindered by the deficits of the current system and can leverage the potential of individual actors, such as individuals or NGOs while creating new institutional mechanisms for protecting potentially oppressed cultural groups and vulnerable in the groups.

Contrary to this vision, Buchanan advocates for the legitimacy of the current world order, including the Security Council, citing its "ecological" legitimacy, by which he

17 Buchanan (2013), 272.
18 On the importance and examination of the Metacoordination View in Buchanan in general, see Kiyama (2023a).
19 Buchanan (2013), 192; Buchanan (2018), 55, 59.
20 Buchanan (2013), 178.
21 When Buchanan mentions that if institutions are supported by enough number of people through 'unreflective habit', it works well, it seems he would like to associate legitimacy criteria and wide support. See Buchanan (2018), 55. Of course, the paper does not endorse this view because benefit does not entail support, as argued above.
22 S/1999/1257, 3.

means that the Security Council is illegitimate 'in isolation'[23], but the system as a whole can be legitimate. He writes that 'the illegitimacy of even an institution as important as the Security Council need not undermine the legitimacy of other parts of the system'.[24]

I argue that the Metacoordination view of legitimacy, especially when considered ecologically, is highly problematic.[25] It is overly status quo-centred, offering almost no room for supporters of alternative institutions to envision alternative pathways. This view, in effect, hinders the possibility of criticizing and abandoning institutions, placing an undue burden on the vulnerable. Consider this with an analogy to the following scenario. At a university, a teacher exists, and she reiterates academic harassment. A student, suffering from harassment, utters a voice to appeal to the university on the issue. Imagine that the university supports her existence by saying, 'Our educational systems, including teachers, are mostly great and benefit you. Even if the teacher harasses you, our educational system is beneficial and should be supported. So, she should be supported as a part of the university'. This corresponds to the claim of ecological legitimacy. However, I believe that the student need not agree; the most obvious reasons are that the university's statement fails to adequately consider the student's agony, and that he experiences an unreasonable burden stemming from the existence of the teacher and the university's approval of it. If this is so, ecological legitimacy is delusive. Then, it is important that institutions can be criticized, changed, and sometimes replaced without appealing to the guise of "ecological" legitimacy.[26] It means that for some cultural groups, the oppression of them can be better prevented by relying on some possible international mechanisms than the international legal human rights system.

The implications of this analysis are twofold. First, to accommodate the cultural diversity respect requirement, the appeal to benefits cultural groups may enjoy does not work, as benefitting from an institution does not entail that it should be supported. Second, it is important to see how we can criticize, change, and replace existing institutions, embracing the potential for creating new institutions and networks of individual actors. For this, we need some interests or values from which we can guide the endeavour. The interests-based approach that I endorse in the next section can do this job.

---

23 Buchanan (2013), 198

24 Ibid., 203.

25 In this and the next paragraph, I follow Kiyama (2023a), 96–100.

26 The creation of a new institution might have a positive impact on the current unfair institutions. From the concept of introducing a cosmopolitan global parliament as opposed to the association model of states (such as the WTO), Pablo Gilabert explains how the creation of a new institution could foster change of other institutions. See Gilabert (2018), 284.

3 Supremacy of interests-based approaches, inter alia, dualism

In the preceding discussion, I have argued that against Buchanan's conception of human rights, it is important that institutions can be criticised, changed, and replaced to establish a new, desirable order that adequately addresses the cultural diversity respect requirement. To achieve this, we need guiding values to shape the endeavour. This necessitates an approach grounded in values to steer institutional formation.

3.1 Interests-based approaches

For this, we can appeal to interests-based approaches, often referred to in the philosophy of human rights as naturalistic, humanist, or orthodox approaches. This approach posits that human rights fundamentally derive from the interests inherent in human beings, justifying these rights based on those interests. While interpretations of interests may vary among theorists, the basic structure of the argument is as follows.

Most importantly, certain interests are deemed crucial, often linked to interpretations of human dignity. For instance, James Griffin emphasizes interests related to normative agency, while Pablo Gilabert emphasizes broader plural human capacities.[27] Despite differences in depicting how these interests produce rights[28], the basic argument goes like this.[29] *Abstract* rights, conceptualized as claim rights, are derived from the interests inherent in human beings. These abstract rights then manifest as *specific* rights in response to concrete circumstances. James Griffin terms the need to consider social circumstances the requirement of "practicality", implying practical considerations informed by human nature and societies.[30] We can interpret this practicality as accommodating considerations of cultural circumstances in each society relevant to each abstract right. In other words, abstract rights can take different forms according to diverse cultural contexts.[31]

---

27 Griffin (2008); Gilabert (2018).
28 Whilst Griffin espouses a kind of naturalism, Gilabert supports what he calls the dignitarian network, especially influenced by contractualism developed by T. M. Scanlon, to address this issue. Ibid., Ch. 8.
29 Ibid., 33–35.
30 Griffin (2008), 37.
31 See also Gilabert (2018), 45–56.

3.2 Advantages of interests-based approaches in general

Irrespective of the particular interests that interests-based approaches adopt, the approaches offer general advantages in addressing the cultural diversity respect requirement.

Firstly, they enable the framing of human rights to align with social circumstances, including cultural ones, thereby countering accusations of parochialism if abstract rights are not parochial – I will address this worry in the following sub-section. Abstract rights grounded in interests can be formulated as specific rights according to the practicalities of each social context, guiding the formulation and realization of human rights within diverse cultural landscapes.[32]

Secondly, by emphasizing the importance of achieving interests within each social context, interests-based approaches discourage 'self-righteous'[33] interventions by external entities. This strategy typically refrains from justifying the imposition of values, except in cases where vital interests are severely infringed (the Rwandan Genocide would be one such).

Thirdly, the consideration of practicalities ensures that the language of human rights is not perceived as alien within local contexts. Interests-based approaches can contextualize the language, accommodating the significance of the social (including cultural) milieu. This contextualization can garner motivational support for rights, at least to the extent that the context is respected.[34]

In this way, interests-based approaches, in general, alleviate concerns related to moral parochialism, political imposition, and insufficient support for human rights. Critics may contend that these approaches are rooted in the interests of 'isolated individuals', lacking justification for collective moralities that prioritize human relationships.[35] However, interests-based approaches do not necessitate an 'atomistic' view of individuals' interests.[36] The interests and abstract rights need not assume an atomistic form but can be formulated as those requiring references to social circumstances. For instance, consider the interest in or abstract right to *knowledge*[37], the importance of which either derives from other higher-level abstract rights (autonomy or liberty in

32 See also Griffin (2008); Gilabert (2018), 46.

33 I borrow this expression from Gilabert's work. Ibid., 94.

34 In this point, I agree with Daniel Bell in putting the emphasis on local knowledge, but in a more limited way. See Bell (2000), 72.

35 Buchanan (2013), 254, 267; cf. Beitz (2009), 56.

36 Gilabert (2018), 35; Kiyama (2022), 107. In answering this kind of criticism, in his word 'communitarian' critique, Rowan Cruft offers two possibilities to answer. One is the view that I take in the main text, and the other is that the goods that ground human rights depend on the goods of others, and there is interconnectedness between goods (or interests). Cruft (2019), 126 f. I take the former in the paper, but there is no need to deny the latter.

37 I take this example from Kiyama (2022), 65, 107.

Griffin's case) or is shown by itself.[38] At the abstract rights level, the right to knowledge can be articulated generally, allowing for the specification of context-specific rights in diverse social and cultural contexts. For example, in many parts of Japan and the UK, the abstract right to knowledge might be specified as the right to elementary education, aligning with Art. 26 of the Universal Declaration of Human Rights. Conversely, in societies where establishing modern institutions like an elementary school system is impossible or undesirable, such as among the Yanomami people in Brazil, the abstract right might be articulated as a more informal right to parental or collective education.

3.3 Dualism as an interests-based approach

As alluded to in the preceding subsection, however, the viability of this response hinges on whether abstract rights (and the interests from which they are derived) are not 'atomistic' or, more broadly, whether they meet the cultural diversity respect requirement. Many interests-based approaches, such as Griffin's normative agency-based view, have faced criticism for falling short of this requirement – being labelled as parochial, imposing, or incapable of garnering support.[39] However, I argue that a view on interests that ground human rights, which I term dualism[40], can meet the cultural diversity respect requirement.

Dualism modifies the notion of normative agency as elaborated by James Griffin on the one hand, while incorporating interests related to equality as an additional grounding value for human rights on the other hand. To understand why dualism is proposed, it may be instructive to consider Griffin's theory as a comparison. In Griffin's monism, interests that ground human rights are confined to those necessary for normative agency, defined as 'our being able to form a conception of a worthwhile life and then pursue it'.[41] Notably, Griffin emphasizes the value of choice as a component of agency, involving 'deliberating, assessing, choosing, and acting to make what we see as a good life for ourselves'.[42]

However, philosophers such as Rainer Forst and David Miller criticise Griffin, arguing that his framework denies the possibility of a good life that is not chosen. According to them, Griffin excludes the life of a person who finds fulfilment in being a community member without deliberate choices about how they live.[43] So, for Forst, '[e]

38 The latter way is taken by Martha Nussbaum. See Nussbaum (2006).
39 For such criticism against interests-based approaches in general, see Cohen (2008). For criticisms of Griffin and Nussbaum, see Beitz (2009).
40 Kiyama develops the points in this subsection in detail. See Kiyama (2022), Ch. 6.
41 Griffin (2008), 47.
42 Ibid., 33.
43 Miller (2014), 157 f.; Forst (2012), 90.

specially in an intercultural context, Griffin's [agency] seems to be a partial, non-universalizable conception of the good and of a basic human interest in pursuing it'.[44]

To address this criticism, I propose re-settling the element of choice – not at the level of abstract rights but at the level of specific rights. In this proposal, a person is said to live a life of normative agency if they identify the good in their life, irrespective of whether they view it as a chosen life. By broadening the notion of normative agency in this way, we can accommodate the aforementioned criticism. If this is so, at the level of abstract rights, choice is not an integral aspect of human rights. However, choice can be important at the level of specific rights. Consider two hypothetical communities. In a community where the good of all people can be identified and, in fact, are identified – perhaps critics envisage this kind of community – choice cannot be the object of specific rights. However, in a community where it is reasonable to think that for a stably identified life, people need to choose their goods, for example, through the choice of occupation, to have the option of choice to a reasonable degree should be the requirement of the abstract rights accruing from agency.

The second part of this dualism emphasizes interests related to equality as a condition for having a good life or a life of normative agency. Equality, especially political equality, has been criticised as a Western value.[45] However, I contend that by justifying the value of equality not from a cultural trait but from a (perhaps psychological) human interest, we can establish it as a basis for human rights whilst meeting the cultural diversity respect requirement.

To illustrate, Andrea Sangiovanni's argument can be followed, asserting that the *integral sense of self* explains the importance of equality in envisaging human rights.[46] According to Sangiovanni, acts infringing upon equality, such as torture, rape, and genocide, are fundamentally wrong because they undermine an individual's integral sense of self.[47] This sense implies that each person perceives themselves as the creator and

---

44 Ibid., 90. Griffin presents two potentially contradictory responses to the criticism. See Kiyama (2022), 158–162. The first is to uphold the value of choice. He suggests that 'abnegations' of choice can be rational and accommodated by the notion of autonomy (a choice-related aspect of normative agency), as long as they are chosen. Griffin (2008), 153. The second response posits that being a 'self-chooser' is only one facet of normative agency. In this view, a normative agent is not required to live 'an examined life'. Instead, possessing the 'capacity to identify the good' is sufficient to qualify as a normative agent. Ibid., 46; cf. Griffin (2014), 228. The former does not address the criticism because it clings to the value of choice in shaping a good life, even though Griffin tries to defend this by showing that to choose is a prudential value, an 'accomplishment' in human life within his prudential perfectionism (Griffin 2008: p. 151). I doubt that this perfectionism can be justified, but will not explore it further here. The proposal in the main text aligns more with Griffin's latter response.

45 For example, in denying democracy in Singapore, Lee Kuan Yew depicted political equality as unsuitable for Asian culture. See Bell (2000).

46 Even though Sangiovanni shows his argument for equality distinguished from the interests-based approaches (in his words, 'orthodox views' on human rights), I think his view largely shares the same structure as interests-based approaches. See Kiyama 2019.

47 Sangiovanni (2017), 75 f.

enactor of self. When treated as inferior, the integral sense of self is jeopardized, leading to a loss of control over engagement with others and, consequently, self-presentation.[48] If human beings have this 'self-presenting' nature, then having an integral sense of self is an integral and structural element of any flourishing life.[49] This is because 'the most important goods in a human life', such as love, friendship, and raising a family, can have 'values for us' and 'be meaningful to us' only when they are located in our integral lives.[50] Consequently, interests related to equality, specifically those related to the *integral sense of self*, are deemed necessary for the enjoyment of important goods in life.

3.4 Advantages of dualism in meeting the cultural diversity respect requirement

Embracing dualism, i. e. the interests-based view based on freshly-interpreted normative agency and equality, we can meet the cultural diversity respect requirement. First, it does not rely on any particular conception of the good, thus avoiding moral parochialism. Normative agency, in our sense, can be as broad as accommodating diverse cultural groups, whilst the interests related to equality are seen as a necessary element for the agency. Second, dualism refrains from imposing values not shared by others. The argument, grounded in the enjoyment of the interests necessary for any good lives, is dissociated from any colonial or imperial mindset. Third, combined with the general features of interests-based approaches, dualism can accommodate diverse specifications of abstract rights based on agency and equality. As long as specific rights are identified according to social circumstances or practicalities in each context, dualism can acquire support in the culturally diverse world.

4 Conclusion

The paper scrutinized justificatory strategies of human rights that try to accommodate the cultural diversity respect requirement. I contended that the argument based on the benefits provided by the international legal human rights system to cultural groups failed to offer a compelling reason for supporting the system. I continued to argue that instead of appealing to "ecological" legitimacy of instituitons, we need values or interests to guide the creation or change of institutions and endeavours of individual actors. As a strategy that can play this role, the paper espoused interests-based approaches, inter alia, dualism. By showing interests that ground human rights and utilising the considerations of practicalities, the strategy can offer a human rights conception that

48 Ibid., 211.
49 Ibid., 82.
50 Ibid., 82, 241.

is not parochial, avoids imposing values without considering social circumstances, including cultural ones, and can be widely supported.

Bibliography

American Anthropological Association (1947): "Statement on Human Rights". In: *American Anthropologist*, New Series, 49(4), 539–543. Doi: 10.1525/aa.1947.49.4.02a00020

Beitz, Charles (2009): *The Idea of Human Rights*. Oxford: Oxford University Press.

Bell, Daniel (2000): *East Meets West. Human Rights and Democracy in East Asia*. Princeton: Princeton University Press.

Buchanan, Allen (2010): *Human Rights, Legitimacy, & the Use of Force*. Oxford: Oxford University Press.

Buchanan, Allen (2013): *The Heart of Human Rights*. Oxford: Oxford University Press.

Buchanan, Allen (2018): "Institutional Legitimacy". In Sobel, David / Vallentyne, Peter / Wall Steven (Eds.): *Oxford Studies in Political Philosophy*. Oxford: Oxford University Press, 53–78.

Cohen, Jean L. (2008): "Rethinking Human Rights, Democracy, and Sovereignty in the Age of Globalization". In: Political Theory, 36(4), 578–606. Doi: 10.1177/0090591708317901

Cruft, Rowan (2019): *Human Rights, Ownership, and the Individual*. Oxford: Oxford University Press.

Eagle, Karen (2001): "From Skepticism to Embrace. Human Rights and the American Anthropological Association from 1947–1999". *Human Rights Quarterly*, 23(3), 536–559. Doi: 10.1353/hrq.2001.0034

Forst, Rainer (2012): 'The Justification of Human Rights and the Basic Right to Justification. A Reflective Approach" In: Corradetti, Claudio (Ed.): *Philosophical Dimensions of Human Rights. Some Contemporary Views*, New York: Springer, 81–106.

Gilabert, Pablo (2018): *Human Dignity & Human Rights*. Oxford: Oxford University Press.

Griffin, James (2008): *On Human Rights*, Oxford University Press.

Griffin, James (2014): "Replies" In: Crisp, Roger (Ed.): *Griffin on Human Rights*. Oxford: Oxford University Press, 206–232.

Kiyama, Kosuke (2019): "Human Rights Based on Human Dignity. Defence and Elaboration through an Examination of Andrea Sangiovanni's Critique." In: *Journal of Global Studies*, 9, 1–24. Doi: 10.14988/pa.2020.0000000130

Kiyama, Kosuke (2022): *The Philosophy of Human Rights. The Search for Underlying Values in the Modern World*. Tokyo: The University of Tokyo Press. (in Japanese)

Kiyama, Kosuke (2023a): "Human Rights Justified as International Legal Human Rights, not Moral Human Rights? A Critique of Allen Buchanan's Turn on Human Rights". *Journal on Public Affairs*, 19(1), 49–106. (in Japanese). Doi: 10.20776/s18814859-19-1-p49

Kiyama, Kosuke (2023b): "How Should Human Dignity be a Ground for Human Rights? A Preliminary Exploration". *Ratio Publica*, 3(1), 6–20.

Miller, David (2006): *National Responsibility and Global Justice*. Oxford: Oxford University Press.

Miller, David (2014): "Personhood versus Human Needs as Grounds for Human Rights". In: Crisp, Roger (Ed.): *Griffin on Human Rights*. Oxford: Oxford University Press, 152–169.

Nickel, James W. (2007): *Making Sense of Human Rights*. Oxford: Blackwell Publishing.

Nozick, Robert (1974): *Anarchy, State, and Utopia*. Oxford: Blackwell Publishing.

Nussbaum, Martha C. (2006): *Frontiers of Justice. Disability, Nationality, Species Membership.* Cambridge: Harvard University Press.
Simmons, William Paul / Feldman, Lindsey Raisa (2018): "Critical Ethnography and Human Rights Research". In: Smith, Rhona / McConnell, Lee (Eds.): *Research Methods in Human Rights*, Abingdon: Routledge, 114–133.

Kosuke Kiyama
Institute of Humanities and Social Sciences, University of Tsukuba
kosukereal@gmail.com

How Can We Share Cosmopolitan Hope Interculturally?*
Foundation, Permissibility, and Rationality of Cosmopolitan Hope

KENTO MIYATA

Abstract: While cosmopolitanism is significant in a globalized society, globalization reveals the plurality of cultures and it remains unclear how cosmopolitanism can be universally accepted beyond cultural contexts. This paper attempts to discover an intercultural foundation of cosmopolitan hope and defend its permissibility and rationality. Two possible approaches were examined: the overlapping consensus approach (OCA) and the constructivist approach (CA). The CA is more suitable, but it must be supplemented by the unity requirement (UR) to overcome all problems regarding the foundation of cosmopolitan hope. Furthermore, I clarify how UR fosters an expectation for cosmopolitan order and contributes to the constitution of practical identity, which renders cosmopolitan hope permissible and rational.

Keywords: constructivism, cosmopolitanism, hope, overlapping consensus, unity of reason, discourse theory

1 Introduction

Since Diogenes identified himself as *cosmopolitēs*, cosmopolitanism has significantly influenced the intellectual history of human beings. Considering that all human beings must cooperate in solidarity to deal with the many issues of a globalized contemporary society, the cosmopolitanism that justifies and motivates such practical attitudes has become increasingly significant. However, globalization reveals the plurality and heterogeneity of cultures, and it remains unclear how cosmopolitanism can be universally accepted beyond various cultural contexts. Furthermore, numerous factors, such as the global rise of far-right groups, nationalism fostered by populist leaders, wars, and

* This work is based on a manuscript presented at the workshop "Kritische Theorie und kulturelle Differenz", held at Goethe-Universität Frankfurt on May 4–5, 2023. I thank Prof. Dr. Eva Buddeberg and Prof. Dr. Rainer Forst for organizing the workshop, and the participants for their valuable comments. I also acknowledge the financial support of JSPS KAKENHI Grant Numbers JP23K12352 and JP23H00784.

the self-centered pursuit of profits by global economic elites, render a cosmopolitan order more unachievable.

Considering these paradoxical circumstances of a globalized society, this paper attempts to answer two questions. The first is about an intercultural normative foundation of cosmopolitan hope: "How can we share cosmopolitan hope interculturally?" or, more concretely, "In the globalizing world, where can we discover an intercultural normative foundation on which cosmopolitan hope can rely?" The second is about its permissibility and rationality. To rephrase Kant's question, "May we hope for a cosmopolitan order?"

The remainder of this paper is organized as follows: The first section clarifies the meaning of cosmopolitan hope. Then, we approach the question of the intercultural normative foundation of cosmopolitan hope and examine two possible approaches: the Overlapping Consensus Approach (following Charles Taylor) and the Constructivist Approach (following Rainer Forst's critical constructivism). After pointing out some problems with the former, especially from the perspective of the characteristics of Japanese thought (second section), I defend the latter in the third section while maintaining that Forst's critical constructivism must be supplemented in an important respect. In the fourth section, I turn to the second question on the permissibility and rationality of cosmopolitan hope.

2 On the concept of cosmopolitan hope

This paper aims neither to argue for a particular form (or any "conception" in a Rawlsian sense) of cosmopolitan normative order nor to propose some theoretical explanation of hope. However, it is necessary to clarify what *cosmopolitan hope* means in this paper. Therefore, I will define the concepts of *cosmopolitanism* and *hope*, respectively, to the extent necessary for my arguments.

What does cosmopolitanism mean? It refers to the idea that every human should be treated as an equal. However, what *being treated as an equal* means is controversial. First, it can be understood as a statement about institutional order, a demand for the abolition of national boundaries, and the creation of a world state or federation. According to Pogge, this type of cosmopolitanism is called *legal* cosmopolitanism and can be distinguished from *moral* cosmopolitanism, which advocates moral standards or criteria for assessing human agents and their conduct, social institutions, and the state of the world.[1] Although moral cosmopolitanism takes different forms, its various forms share four commitments.[2] (1) Normative Individualism: The ultimate unit of

1 Pogge (2007).
2 Ibid., 316.

moral concern is individual human beings. (2) Impartiality: A cosmopolitan moral criterion considers each included human individual symmetrically. (3) All-inclusiveness: Every human being should be included as the ultimate unit of moral concern. (4) Generality: Persons are the ultimate units of concern not only for their compatriots, fellow religionists, or the like, but also for everyone in general. This paper uses cosmopolitanism to refer only to moral cosmopolitanism, which has these four commitments, though a series of disputes regarding it remains undecided.

Recent literature on hope indicates that the concept of hope is as controversial as that of cosmopolitanism. I cannot dwell on the discussion of hope, but it suffices to define it loosely. The standard definition of hope consists of two elements: belief in the possibility of an uncertain outcome of hope and the desire for that outcome.[3] However, it cannot explain why two people could have equivalent desires and the exact probability estimate assigned to the desired outcome, even though one person hopes and the other despairs (e.g., a cancer patient hopes for recovery and another one despairs while estimating the same probability of recovery). With this problem in mind, Katie Stockdale proposes a third element, namely, "seeing or perceiving in a favorable light the possibility that the desired outcome obtains."[4]

Combining these definitions, I define *cosmopolitan hope* as a mental attitude of seeing or perceiving in a favorable light the possibility that a normative order treating every human being as a moral equal would be obtained. Let us now turn to the first question: How can cosmopolitan hope be shared interculturally? Where can we discover an intercultural normative foundation supporting cosmopolitan hope?

3 The idea of overlapping consensus on cosmopolitan hope?

In a contemporary society characterized by "the fact of pluralism," we are not allowed to appeal to *the* metaphysical or religious grand narrative, which promises the realization of a cosmopolitan normative order in the future, as the intercultural normative foundation of cosmopolitan hope. It is also problematic to appeal only to Western thought by arguing that cosmopolitanism originated from Western thinkers such as Diogenes. To avoid the issue of metaphysics and West-centrism, *the Overlapping Consensus Approach* (hereinafter OCA) can be adopted, in which we expect that hopes expressed in various forms within dominant comprehensive doctrines or intellectual traditions of different cultures will overlap, and then we will discover the intercultural normative foundation of cosmopolitan hope in this overlapping consensus (Charles Taylor adopts this approach to come to an unforced international agreement on hu-

3 Blöser et al. (2020), 2.
4 Stockdale (2021), 16.

man rights[5]). For example, one could expect that hopes expressed in dominant comprehensive doctrines/traditions in the West (e.g., Christianity[6]) and East (e.g., Confucianism[7]) will overlap. While this approach seems appealing in that it respects the perspectives of each culture and tradition, it has three problems.

First, the OCA entails the problem of anti-cosmopolitan cultures. For example, some regions and countries punish homosexual activity, and even impose the death penalty on homosexuals, or oppress ethnic and religious minority groups that demand self-governance and democracy. With these cases considered, it is highly optimistic to believe that a consensus on cosmopolitan hope is achievable.

Second, even if we disregard the problem of anti-cosmopolitan cultures, the assumptions of the OCA are problematic. It assumes that the world can be divided into cultural entities, such as the West and the East, with their own comprehensive doctrines or intellectual traditions. However, such a reification of culture with an emphasis on the differences between cultures is problematic because, as Forst and Tatsuo Inoue point out, it risks falling victim to Orientalism by portraying the East as the "Orient" with an essence that is heterogeneous to the "Occident," effectively labeling it as "the Other" to the West.[8] This perspective could blind "him or her to the internal diversity and dynamic potential [of Asia or the East; K. M.]" and function as "an epistemological device for guaranteeing Western hegemony over Asia"[9] or the East, which is another form of Western centrism.

The third problem is related to the assumptions of the OCA. It assumes that each culture has its own consistent, comprehensive doctrine or intellectual tradition through which cosmopolitan hopes can be expressed. However, this assumption is particularly problematic in Japan because it is doubtful whether any consistent intellectual tradition represents Japanese thought. Here, I refer to an article titled "Thought in Japan,"[10] published in 1957 by Masao Maruyama (1914–1996), a scholar of the history of Japanese political thought.

According to Maruyama, there is no consistent intellectual tradition in Japan, such as Christianity in the West and Confucianism in China. Therefore, he characterizes Japanese thought as "promiscuity," meaning that elements of various thoughts coexist *without any structure that orders them.*

> If we analyze our thoughts and ways of thinking into various elements and track their respective genealogies, we would encounter something Buddhis*tic*, something Confucian-

5 Taylor (1999).
6 Cf. Rorty (1999).
7 Cf. Ivanhoe (2014).
8 Forst (2021), 198f.; Inoue (1999) mentions this point when he criticizes advocates of Asian values, such as Lee Kuan Yew.
9 Inoue (1999), 39.
10 Maruyama (1961), Ch. 1.

> istic, something Shamanistic, something Western – in short, fragments of all thoughts that have left marks on our history. The problem lies in *the disorderly coexistence of these fragments, where logical relationships among them and their respective positions to occupy remain unclear altogether.*[11] [Italics mine]

In the sixth century, Japan absorbed Buddhism from the Korean Peninsula and syncretized it with indigenous worship and Shamanism (*Shinto*). In the seventh century, Japan reformed its political systems and created a bureaucracy and a system of criminal law modeled on China. Confucianism was prevalent among the ruling class at the same time. Buddhism, syncretized with Shinto and Confucianism (and neo-Confucianism), was influential until the nineteenth century. During the Edo period (1603–1867), the Japanese government adopted a national isolation policy (so-called *Sakoku*) from 1639 to 1854. The end of *Sakoku* caused an influx of Western thought into Japan and enabled Japanese people to study abroad, particularly in European countries. Following these countries, in the Meiji period (1868–1912), the Japanese government attempted to modernize Japanese social and political systems to establish a Western-style government. After World War II, Japan was administered by the General Headquarters of the Supreme Commander for the Allied Powers (GHQ) from 1945 to 1952. Its social and political systems were rapidly reformed according to the ideals of liberal democracy under the supervision of the United States.

Maruyama maintains that, through a series of shifts in dominant thoughts, "a tendency arises for various thoughts introduced into Japan in a certain temporal sequence to bring about change only in their spatial arrangement within the inner minds of individuals, so that they, as it were, coexist timelessly; this tendency makes them lose their *historical* structure all the more."[12] Following his thesis, it would be difficult to say that most Japanese share a consistent intellectual tradition or comprehensive doctrine in which cosmopolitan hopes are expressed.

The OCA fails for these reasons. Critics may blame my portrayal of the OCA for its oversimplification. They maintain that the OCA views cultures as more dynamic entities undergoing continuous change during encounters with other cultures, through which reinterpretation of culture occurs.[13] Even if we acknowledge this criticism and modify the OCA to align it with a more dynamic view of culture, doubts remain as to whether it can provide a normative foundation for cosmopolitan hope. First, envisioning an overlap between dynamically changing cultures presents challenges. To visualize the overlap of components, it is necessary to assume that the overlapping components have a more or less robust core and a stable structure. Second, and more importantly, encounters with other cultures may not necessarily lead to reinterpreta-

11 Ibid., 8.
12 Ibid., 11.
13 I thank Jimmy Chia-Shin Hsu for making me aware of the necessity to answer this objection.

tions of their own culture that support a cosmopolitan order. Instead, such interactions may give rise to dominant interpretations that legitimize xenophobic nationalism. Historical examples such as Japan's experience during World War II and the rise of far-right political groups in Europe illustrate this potential consequence. In conclusion, the modified OCA appears to be an unpromising basis for cosmopolitan hope.

However, the OCA is quite right in acknowledging that appealing to *the* grand metaphysical narrative and West-centrism must be avoided in a contemporary society characterized by "the fact of pluralism." Therefore, the question in the Introduction can be reformulated more precisely as follows: "How can we determine the intercultural normative foundation of cosmopolitan hope while avoiding the problems of metaphysics, Western centrism, and anti-cosmopolitan cultures without lapsing into the reification of cultures and presupposing that they share any consistent doctrines/traditions?"

4 (Re-)Construction of cosmopolitan hope

To address this question, Forst's constructivist approach requires further investigation. He contends that human beings are endowed with reason as the capacity to account for their beliefs and actions, which means human beings are "justifying, reason-giving beings."[14] Everyone has a fundamental right to justification as a normative authority that autonomously decides how the normative orders to which they are subject are constructed. According to his critical constructivism, while the norms we must abide by are constructed through dialogical justification among normative authorities, the normative requirement that everyone should be granted the right to justification can be reconstructed from our moral justificatory practice. This is because, by asking recursively about redeeming the categorical validity claim raised in moral justification, we can reconstruct "a *discursive* justification procedure in which the addressees of the norm can assess its reciprocal and general validity, [...] a procedure in which the criteria of reciprocity and generality are decisive."[15] This means that, from the perspective of the person participating in justificatory practice, "moral persons have a fundamental *right to justification*, and a corresponding unconditional *duty to justify* morally relevant actions."[16] Forst argues that his theory of the right to justification is the best starting point for conceptualizing a normative order in a transnational/global context.[17]

Based on his critical constructivism, I present *a Constructivist Approach* (hereinafter CA) to cosmopolitan hope, according to which the normative foundation of cosmopolitan hope lies in the normative requirements that can be reconstructed from our

---

14 Forst (2014b), 13.
15 Ibid., 19 f.
16 Ibid., 21.
17 Cf. ibid., Part 3.

moral justificatory practice. This approach is appealing because it solves some of the problems mentioned in the previous section. First, relying on the reconstruction of our *daily* justificatory practice can provide a normative foundation for cosmopolitan hope without relying on any metaphysical worldview.[18] Second, the problem of Western centrism can also be solved because the justificatory practice (or the experience of demanding justification) is not unique to Western culture but universal. Third, unlike the OCA, the CA does not necessarily assume reified cultural entities with consistent doctrines and traditions. However, dealing with the problem of anti-cosmopolitan cultures is challenging.

Forst presupposes, with Kant, that "the 'community of justification' in moral matters is the community of all human beings as moral persons"[19]. However, this assumption is disputable. For example, some regions and countries punish homosexual activity and enforce death penalties. In those regions and countries, the sexual minority is denied the status of practical authority and excluded from "the space of justification." In other words, the sexual majority assumes that the categorical validity claim of morality can be redeemed if it is justified in the community of the sexual majority (*not* "all human beings"). The normative requirement obtained by the reconstruction of their justificatory practice is also limited; only the sexual majority is granted the right to justification (the same applies to any other anti-cosmopolitan culture, *mutatis mutandis*). Therefore, further arguments are required if Forst is to argue that the validity claim of morality is to be justified in the community of all human beings.

Forst himself seems to believe that the analysis of the categorical validity claim of morality provides support for this argument.

> The validity claim of a moral norm – according to which each person has the duty to do or refrain from doing X – basically indicates that nobody has good reasons to violate this norm. [...] Hence, the categorical validity of the norm requires that in its justification the relevant reasons have been taken up and that each moral person can understand and must accept this foundation.[20]

Furthermore, he argues that this validity claim is based on "the insight into the duty of a justifying and self-determined responsibility toward other similarly self-determined human beings whom one owes certain reasons."[21] According to this explanation, anyone who raises a moral validity claim, through adequate reflection, can realize that they have already gained insight into the duty of justification for all human beings.

---

18 Cf. Forst (2014a), 182.
19 Forst (2014b), 19.
20 Ibid.
21 Ibid., 37.

However, this argument does not sufficiently explain why moral persons involved in moral justification are equated with all human beings. What we can obtain through an analysis of the validity claim is an insight into the duty to recognize anyone who can provide relevant reasons for justification as a moral person. Only when we presuppose a humanistic understanding of morality, according to which all human beings can provide relevant reasons, can we equate moral persons with all human beings. However, this understanding is not shared between cosmopolitans and the above-mentioned sexual majority who impose the death penalty on homosexuals. Thus, a more fundamental question is, "Why must we, as reasonable persons, recognize every human being as a moral person?" If Forst's constructivism fails to provide such an argument, it is exposed to the charge of appealing to the metaphysics of the Kantian noumenon[22] or a contextualist critique that Forst's theory is persuasive only in the Western context where humanism and cosmopolitanism are deeply rooted[23]. Is the CA able to avoid them? In other words, is there any reason to criticize it as unreasonable to deny that all human beings have an equal right to justification without secret recourse to metaphysics or the Western intellectual context?

"Yes" is my answer. We now outline how this is possible. All human beings have the faculty to distinguish between truth and falsity in terms of how the world is and judge what is morally right and wrong with respect to how the world ought to be (or what one must do). The former is called theoretical reason, whereas the latter is called practical reason. Following Jürgen Habermas and Forst, I assume that the use of reason is not monological but dialogical. Both validity claims of truth and moral rightness are redeemed through intersubjective exchanges of arguments and reasons in a free, equal, and sincere speech situation. Therefore, as Habermas argues, we are inevitably committed to counterfactual presuppositions when we raise a validity claim. These presuppositions include "the shared presupposition of a world of independently existing objects, the reciprocal presupposition of rationality or 'accountability,' the unconditionality of context-transcending validity claims such as truth and moral rightness, and the demanding presuppositions of argumentation that force participants to decenter their interpretive perspectives."[24]

Although I agree with his universal pragmatics in general, I am still dissatisfied with it because it does not mention one essential counterfactual requirement to which a reasonable person must inevitably be committed: the unity of the functions of theoretical and practical reason without contradiction (called the *Unity Requirement*, hereinafter UR). Theoretical and practical reasons are related to different themes (i. e., truth and moral rightness). Nevertheless, they are *one and the same reason*, so they must be *unified*. This idea led Kant to state the following:

---

22 Cf. White (2015), 210.
23 Cf. Allen (2016), Ch.4.
24 Habermas (2008), 28.

> I require that the critique of a pure practical reason, if it is to be complete, also be able to present its *unity* with speculative reason in a common principle; because in the end there can be only *one and the same reason*, which must differ merely in its application.[25] [Italics mine]

While his statement that there is one and the same principle common to theoretical reason and practical reason is controversial, it is less controversial that "for the possibility of any use of reason as such, [...] its principles and affirmations must not contradict one another,"[26] which means that the functions of theoretical and practical reason must not be mutually contradictory. Given the unity of reason, if there is a contradiction between my use of theoretical and practical reason, I will contradict *myself* because reason is *my* faculty.

My thesis is that *those who deny that all human beings have an equal right to justification in a practical context will contradict themselves, because they fail to achieve the unity of reason.* We presuppose that the world is the same for everyone and that everyone has an equal say regarding how the world is. When I raise a claim of validity for the truth of a factual proposition, I implicitly or explicitly presuppose that I am obliged to rebut others' counterarguments. In other words, my reason recognizes all human beings as authorities of justification endowed with rationality and accountability in *a theoretical* context. Nevertheless, if I deny that all human beings have the authority of justification in terms of how the world ought to be (what one must do) – that is, if I do not recognize all human beings as having the authority of justification in *a practical* context – my use of reason becomes self-contradictory. Similarly, if the sexual majority deny the minority the right to justification and, at the same time, if they presuppose the sameness of the world for everyone, then they will contradict themselves. *This internal contradiction and failure to meet UR make them unreasonable.*

Based on this thesis, I argue that the intercultural normative foundation of cosmopolitan hope can be discovered in the combination of two presuppositions common to everyday life across cultures. First, a reasonable person lives in a world while explicitly or implicitly presupposing that the world is the same for everyone; thus, all human beings have theoretical authority. The second presupposition is that a reasonable person is subject to UR, so they must resolve contradictions within themselves to remain reasonable. These presuppositions are obtained from the reconstruction of what it means to live as reasonably justifying beings in a world and are common to every cultural lifeworld. In this sense, they belong to universal structures of the lifeworld. By reflexively reconstructing them, any reasonable person living in any culture can construct

25 Kant (2012), 7.
26 Kant (2015), 97.

cosmopolitan hope. This is my answer to the introduction's first question: "How can we share cosmopolitan hope interculturally?"[27]

My approach, the Constructivist Approach supplemented by the Unity Requirement, can resolve all the problems involved in the intercultural normative foundation of cosmopolitan hope. First, it is not metaphysical because it grounds cosmopolitan hope by reconstructing and combining two presuppositions to which reasonable persons living in the lifeworld – that is, the everyday, non-metaphysical world – are counterfactually committed. Second, it is also not West-centric since these counterfactual presuppositions belong to universal structures of the lifeworld, meaning that they are common to all cultures. Third, as argued above, it overcomes the problem of anti-cosmopolitan cultures, which Forst's critical constructivism cannot. Finally, it is not necessary to assume reified cultural entities with consistent doctrines or traditions.

5 May we hope for cosmopolitan order?

Now that the first question has been answered, let us turn to the second question, "May we hope for a cosmopolitan order?" In this section, this issue is approached by considering two aspects. The first aspect is the permissibility of cosmopolitan hope: "Are we permitted to hope for cosmopolitan order?" The second aspect is the rationality of cosmopolitan hope: "Is it rational to commit to hopeful activities (e.g., fantasizing about the hoped-for outcome and relying on it when planning our lives) based on cosmopolitan hope?" In the following section, I answer both questions positively and explain how UR justifies my responses.

5.1 Unity Requirement as an internal hope-maker

As defined in the first section, hope consists of the belief in the possibility of an uncertain object of hope and the desire for that object. This implies that hoping is nonsensical if the object of hope is impossible. We evaluate an agent who commits to hopeful activities based on impossible and thus impermissible hopes as irrational. To demonstrate the rationality of cosmopolitan hope, it is necessary to demonstrate that it is *not impermissible.* What renders hope permissible?

27 Note that this answer does not completely exclude the OCA. When one ponders cosmopolitan hope, one can refer to vocabularies within one's own culture and concretize it based on them. Nevertheless, for reasons I mentioned in the previous section, the OCA alone cannot provide an intercultural normative foundation for cosmopolitan hope.

To address this question, Darrel Moellendorf analyzes the relationship between hope and reasons.[28] He argues that hope resembles belief. Beliefs are sensitive to reasons; therefore, when someone believes in X without sufficient reasons, that belief is regarded as unjustifiable. In the same vein, he maintains that hope is also sensitive to reasons and is permissible if certain necessary conditions of the likelihood of the object of hope are satisfied. In his other article, factors that raise this likelihood and give us reasons to hope are called "hope-makers".[29] To borrow his term, we can ask, "Are there enough hope-makers that give permissibility to cosmopolitan hope?"

It seems to be imperative to provide a negative response. The global rise of far-right groups, nationalism fostered by populist leaders, wars, and self-centered pursuit of profits by global economic elites provide us with little reason to anticipate a cosmopolitan order but rather compels us to despair of its possibility. However, we must distinguish between the two subtypes of hope-makers: *external* and *internal*. The former is beyond our control, such as causality in nature, whereas the latter is within our influence. In other words, the former is conditioned by factors that are external to one's faculty, whereas the latter is within one's power. Building on the arguments developed previously, I maintain that even if we have lost all the external hope-makers, we still have one internal hope-maker stemming from UR: the potential of reason to motivate the agent to act toward a cosmopolitan order.

UR explains not only why anti-cosmopolitanism is unreasonable, but also how our reason autonomously motivates us to act toward a cosmopolitan order. Given UR, if agents do not act toward a cosmopolitan order, they contradict themselves. Just as simultaneously believing two incompatible propositions causes a sense of discomfort originating from inconsistency, violating UR produces a sense of lack of integrity within themselves. Reason autonomously motivates agents to avoid this disintegrity and to act toward a cosmopolitan order.[30] Certainly, this reasonable motivation suffers from the problem of weakness of will. It may be overwhelmed by egocentric inclinations or weakened by external factors. Nevertheless, the potential of reason to motivate agents autonomously is preserved as long as they use reason, and this holds true for all reasonable persons. Therefore, we may expect a cosmopolitan order to be established if external conditions are met. This expectation functions as an internal hope-maker, permitting cosmopolitan hope. Of course, this does not mean that we are *required* to have cosmopolitan hope because, as Moellendorf argues, we must also consider the opportunity cost of having hope – that is, what is lost by it. For example, if "hoping

28 Moellendorf (2020a).
29 Moellendorf (2020b), 252.
30 Regarding how UR motivates our will *practically*, see note 32.

for a particular political campaign victory encourages a strategy that could result in a crushing defeat,"[31] then it is absurd to say, "Nevertheless, hoping is required!"[32]

5.2 Cosmopolitan hope and constitution of identity

This leads us to doubt the rationality of cosmopolitan hope. Holding on to cosmopolitan hope would not benefit the agent. This is particularly true for those under oppression. Therefore, it could be objected that a continuous commitment to cosmopolitan hope is *irrational* when it does not promote an agent's rational ends, even if permitted. For example, according to Adrienne Martin's theory, hope consists of attraction to the hoped-for outcome, assignment of probability to the outcome, and adopting "a stance toward that probability whereby it licenses treating one's attraction to the outcome (and the outcome's attractive features) as a reason for certain ways of thinking, feeling, and/or planning with regard to the hoped-for outcome."[33] Further, she argues that this licensing stance is a practical attitude "governed by a practical norm of rational-ends-promotion."[34] This means that if an agent's hoping does not promote their rational ends (such as maintenance of their life), then their hoping is irrational. Following Martin's theory, some would deny the rationality of cosmopolitan hope.

This objection sounds compelling, but it is one-sided. As Claudia Blöser and Titus Stahl persuasively demonstrate,[35] Martin's theory is myopic in that it evaluates the

31 Moellendorf (2020a), 7.

32 Note that *the absence of a duty to have cosmopolitan hope* does not imply *the absence of a duty to obey the normative requirements concerning the cosmopolitan order*. To obey them is the moral duty of every reasonable person, a duty whose normativity ultimately derives from UR. However, there is some doubt whether UR can be a source of practical normativity that practically binds the will of a reasonable person and imposes a moral duty on them. Like the laws of logic, UR seems to be a requirement of rationality imposing consistency on us and only *theoretically* binding our thinking. The question, then, is whether the unity requirement can generate *practical normativity that binds our will.*
UR is involved with practical normativity because being subject to UR is a necessary condition for living well as the self with personal identity. Let me outline my arguments, though I cannot fully develop them here. To live well in this world, I must have a personal identity and unify myself based on it (patients suffering from dissociative identity disorder fail to do so). The conditions under which I exist as the unified self by personal identity include the requirement that constituent parts of the self must not be contradictory to each other. What follows from this is the requirement that functions of theoretical and practical reason must be unified without contradiction, meaning the subjection to UR. Therefore, violating UR means not only a theoretical failure in thinking (such as supporting mutually contradictory propositions) but also a failure of the constitution of personal identity, which is *a practical failure* in *living as the self with personal identity*. This is why UR can be a source of practical normativity that binds the will of a reasonable person and, as I stated earlier, motivates them to act toward realizing a cosmopolitan order, unless external factors hinder this reasonable motivation. I thank Rainer Forst for recommending that I clarify the relationship between UR and practical normativity.

33 Martin (2014), 62.

34 Ibid., 59.

35 Blöser/Stahl (2017).

rationality of hope only in terms of instrumental rationality. They maintain that there is a criterion other than instrumental rationality in terms of *fundamental hope*, which is a subgroup of hope. According to them, it can be distinguished from *prosaic hope* (e. g., "I hope it will be sunny tomorrow") in that it constitutes the practical identity of a person who commits to hopeful activities.[36] They contend that we have reasons to have fundamental hope because it relates to the constitution of our practical identity.

> In cases of fundamental hope, the central reason to engage in the activities and attitudes characteristic of hope is the fact that the agent sees engaging in these activities as a constitutive part of her identity.[37]

Based on this idea, the criteria for assessing the rationality of hope are not limited to promoting rational ends. The constitution of practical identity through fundamental hope also rationalizes hopeful activities, even if it does not promote an agent's rational ends. For example, "the political activist who hopes for the end of global inequality in full knowledge of its unlikeliness [...] can be justified in believing that she *ought not to lose hope*"[38], "[e]ven if her hoping for political change does not generate any recognizable benefits for her or promote any ends."[39]

Following these arguments, I maintain that even if activities based on cosmopolitan hope do not benefit the agent, they are still rational because of their role in the constitution of practical identities. They constitute identities in two ways. First, the agent sees engaging in these activities as a constitutive part of the identity of *a cosmopolitan*. Second, cosmopolitan hope is related to the constitution of an additional identity: *a reasonable person*. As discussed in the previous section, the normative foundation of cosmopolitan hope is based on the presupposition that we, as reasonable persons, must be subject to UR. Hence, when the agent continues hopeful activities based on cosmopolitan hope, they continue to follow UR and see engaging in these activities as a constitutive part of the identity of a reasonable person. This is not a particular identity, such as that of a mother, philosopher, or activist. Rather, it is an abstract and general identity.

6 Conclusion

Concluding my responses to the two questions, regarding the first question ("How can we share cosmopolitan hope interculturally?"), we can discover the intercultural normative foundation of cosmopolitan hope – it would be better to express *trans*-cul-

36 Ibid., 345.
37 Ibid., 355.
38 Ibid., 356.
39 Ibid., 354.

tural rather than *inter*-cultural, because my approach does not necessarily presuppose any cultural entity, unlike the OCA – within the combination of two presuppositions to which reasonable persons living in the world are counterfactually committed: the sameness of the world for everyone and the unity of theoretical and practical reason. As an internal hope-maker, this normative foundation gives us a reason to hope for a cosmopolitan order, rendering cosmopolitan hope permissible. As argued above, the rationality of cosmopolitan hope is derived from its contribution to the constitution of practical identities. These discussions justify the positive answer to the second question, "May we hope for cosmopolitan order?"

Having delineated the theory of cosmopolitan hope, I will address the Rortyan question deliberately omitted so far: "Isn't it nonsense to seek *the foundation* for cosmopolitan hope?"[40] This is meaningful because explicating the foundation of cosmopolitan hope provides reasons for hope and makes it more robust. In general, hope is fragile because it lacks certain beliefs. With this in mind, clarifying the foundation, permissibility, and rationality of cosmopolitan hope is necessary to prevent hope from collapsing, and to motivate us to act toward a cosmopolitan order. This necessity is becoming more urgent for people such as the Japanese, who share no consistent intellectual tradition in which cosmopolitan hope can be rooted.

Bibliography

Allen, Amy (2016): The End of Progress. Decolonizing the Normative Foundations of Critical Theory. New York: Columbia University Press.

Blöser, Claudia / Stahl, Titus (2017): "Fundamental Hope and Practical Identity". In: Philosophical Papers 46(3), 345–371.

Blöser, Claudia et al. (2020): "Hope in political philosophy". In: Philosophy Compass 15(5), 1–9.

Forst, Rainer (2014a): "Justifying Justification: Reply to My Critics". In: Ibid.: Justice, Democracy and the Right to Justification. London, New York: Bloomsbury, 169–216.

Forst, Rainer (2014b): The Right to Justification. Elements of a Constructivist Theory of Justice. trans. Flynn, Jeffrey. New York: Columbia University Press.

Forst, Rainer (2021): Die Noumenale Republik. Kritischer Konstruktivismus nach Kant. Berlin: Suhrkamp.

Habermas, Jürgen (2008): "Communicative Action and the Detranscendentalized 'Use of Reason'". In: Ibid.: Between Naturalism and Religion. Philosophical Essays. trans. Cronin, Ciaran. Massachusetts, Cambridge: Polity Press, 24–76.

Inoue, Tatsuo (1999): "Liberal Democracy and Asian Orientalism". In: Bauer, Joanne R. / Bell, Daniel A. (Eds.) The East Asian Challenge for Human Rights. Cambridge: Cambridge University Press, 27–59.

Ivanhoe, Philip J. (2014): "Confucian Cosmopolitanism." In: Journal of Religious Ethics 42(1), 22–44.

40 Rorty (1989).

Kant, Immanuel (2012): Groundwork of the Metaphysics of Morals. revised ed. trans. Gregor, Mary et al. (Eds.) with introduction by Korsgaard, Christine M. New York: Cambridge University Press.
Kant, Immanuel (2015): Critique of Practical Reason. revised ed. trans. Gregor, Mary with a revised introduction by Reath, Andrews. Cambridge: Cambridge University Press.
Martin, Adrienne M. (2014): How We Hope: A Moral Psychology. Princeton, Oxford: Princeton University Press.
Maruyama, Masao (1961): Nihon no shisō. Tokyo: Iwanami Shoten.
Moellendorf, Darrel (2020a): "Hope and Reasons." In: Normative Orders Working Paper published by Forschungsverbund "Normative Ordnungen" der Goethe-Universität Frankfurt am Main, 1–18.
Moellendorf, Darrel (2020b): "Hope for Material Progress in the Age of the Anthropocene". In: Blöser, Claudia / Stahl, Titus (Eds.) The Moral Psychology of Hope. London, New York: Rowman & Littlefield International, 249–264.
Pogge, Thomas (2007): "Cosmopolitanism". In: Goodin, Robert E. et al. (Eds.) A Companion to Contemporary Political Philosophy, 2nd ed. Massachusetts, Oxford, Victoria: Blackwell Publishing, Vol.1, 312–331.
Rorty, Richard (1989): Contingency, Irony, and Solidarity. Cambridge: Cambridge University Press.
Rorty, Richard (1999): "Failed Prophecies, Glorious Hopes". In: Ibid.: Philosophy and Social Hope. London: Penguin Books, 201–209.
Stockdale, Katie (2021): Hope Under Oppression. New York: Oxford University Press.
Taylor, Charles (1999): "Conditions of an Unforced Consensus on Human Rights". In: Bauer, Joanne R / Bell, Daniel A (Eds.) The East Asian Challenge for Human Rights. Cambridge: Cambridge University Press, 124–144.
White, Stephen K. (2015): "Does Critical Theory Need Strong Foundations?" In: Philosophy and Social Criticism 41(3), 207–211.

Kento Miyata
Faculty of Commerce, Otaru University of Commerce
kmiyata@res.otaru-uc.ac.jp

Freedom of Movement for All?
Toward a More Individualist Relational Equality

YUICHIRO MORI

Abstract: In his article, Daniel Sharp developed a relational egalitarian argument against immigration restrictions. In his view, while affluent states' immigration restrictions against disadvantaged immigrants are morally objectionable because they are an exercise of unequal power, similar restrictions against those from affluent states are not. In this paper, I challenge Sharp's restrictive treatment of who can make a complaint against immigration restrictions based on relational equality. First, I outline and critically examine Sharp's argument and argue that his relational egalitarian argument should also condemn immigration restrictions against immigrants from affluent states. Second, I reply to three objections to my argument: objections based on democracy, structural injustice, and the danger of territorial domination.

Keywords: immigration, equality, relational equality, relational egalitarianism, unequal power, individualism, democracy, structural injustice

1 Introduction

For a decade, the well-known "distributive vs. relational" debate on egalitarian theories of justice has been said to determine one's view on the extent to which a state may have discretion over immigration restrictions.[1] In a coauthored book, Christopher Wellman famously argued that those defending open borders from egalitarian perspectives are committed to luck egalitarianism, the most representative version of distributive egalitarianism, according to which it is bad or unjust if and only if some are worse off than others in terms of their holdings or well-being due to uncontrollable causes.[2] If we switch from luck egalitarianism to relational egalitarianism, the egalitarian case for open borders would be much weaker because, unlike the relationship between citizens of the same sociopolitical community, that between immigrants and citizens is thin and, therefore, the disparities between them do not give rise to oppression. By

---

1 Among those considered to be in the distributive camp (above all, so called "luck egalitarians") are Cohen (1989), Temkin (1993), Knight (2009), and Segall (2014). Among those considered to be in the relational camp are Anderson (1999), Scheffler (2003), Kolodny (2014), and Schemmel (2021).

2 Wellman (2011), 60–64.

so arguing, he indirectly provided an argument for states' unlimited discretion over immigration restrictions.[3]

Against this intellectual background, Daniel Sharp developed his relational egalitarian argument against immigration restrictions.[4] In his view, affluent states' immigration restrictions against disadvantaged immigrants are morally objectionable because they exercise unequal power over these disadvantaged immigrants. He also contended that when those excluded are immigrants from affluent states (typically, the United States and Western European countries), there is no morally objectionable relational inequality since there is no instance of unequal power over these immigrants.

In this paper, I challenge Sharp's restrictive treatment of who can make a complaint against immigration restrictions based on relational equality. In Section 2, I outline Sharp's relational egalitarian argument. In Section 3, I critically examine his relational egalitarian argument and argue that it should also condemn immigration restrictions against immigrants from affluent states. In Section 4, I reply to some anticipated objections to my argument. In Section 5, I conclude with a few practical implications for my more individualist position.

2 Sharp's Relational Egalitarian Argument

Sharp's relational egalitarian argument against immigration restrictions is as follows:[5]

> R1: From the viewpoint of relational equality, one party's exercise of unequal power over the other is morally objectionable.[6]
>
> R2: Citizens in affluent states, when engaging in immigration restrictions (e.g., closing borders) against disadvantaged immigrants, exercise unequal power over them.[7]
>
> R3: Therefore, from the viewpoint of relational equality, immigration restrictions by citizens in affluent states against disadvantaged immigrants are morally objectionable.

In claiming R2, Sharp characterizes immigration restrictions as a state intentionally foreclosing the goods and opportunities present in its territory from immigrants.[8] He claims that for it to be an exercise of unequal power over immigrants, which is morally

---

3 His *direct* argument for states' discretion is based on freedom of association (ibid., 13–56).

4 Sharp (2022).

5 In addition to R1 and R2, Sharp's argument is based on the claim that "the [relational] egalitarian objection to being subject to another's greater power is applicable whenever one is subject to another person's greater power in the relevant manner" (ibid., 650, 658–660). Throughout this article, I set aside this premise since the disagreement between Sharp and myself does not concern this.

6 ibid., 650 f.

7 ibid., 660–666.

8 ibid., 661.

objectionable from the standpoint of relational equality, it needs to be a form of *significant* power over the immigrants, and the power inherent in the state's immigration restrictions against immigrants needs to be *unequal*.[9]

When affluent states engage in immigration restrictions against disadvantaged immigrants, Sharp claims that the two conditions described above are satisfied.[10] First, these restrictions are a form of significant power over these immigrants because the goods and opportunities from which immigrants are excluded (e.g., access to labor markets and improved economic prospects, territorially located public goods such as security, social welfare benefits, and associative ties) are objectively important to their lives,[11] and these disadvantaged immigrants cannot access them otherwise.

Second, the power inherent in affluent states' immigration restrictions against disadvantaged immigrants is unequal to that inherent in poor (or middle-income) states' immigration restrictions against immigrants from affluent states. According to Sharp, for two tokens of power to be equal, they need to have equal significance, and the significance of a given token of exclusionary power depends on what one is excluded from and whether the exclusion is decisive. When the United States excludes Hondurans and Honduras excludes Americans, for instance, the goods and opportunities denied to Hondurans are distinct from those denied to Americans because access to the territories of wealthy states comes with access to opportunities not similarly present in worse-off states. Unlike Americans, Hondurans cannot access the kinds of important goods and opportunities (they are excluded from) in their own countries when the two countries engage in mutual exclusion. Thus, Sharp concludes that the power involved when the United States excludes Hondurans and that involved when Honduras excludes Americans is not equal in significance.

In contrast, Sharp argues that when immigration restrictions are exercised against immigrants from affluent states, they do not constitute *unequal* power over them. When the United States excludes Canadians and Canada excludes Americans, for instance, the value of the goods and options denied to Canadians is roughly equivalent to those denied to Americans. Also, both Canadians and Americans can access the kinds of goods and options (they are excluded from) in their own countries, respectively. In this case, the two tokens of power are equal in significance. For another instance, even when Honduras unilaterally excludes Americans, this does not constitute unequal power over them in the relevant sense because the exclusionary power

---

9 In addition to the two conditions, Sharp contends that a state's immigration restrictions need to create power inequalities between *persons* because relational egalitarians are ultimately concerned about inequalities between persons (e.g., citizens in a receiving state and immigrants) rather than those between immigrants and the state itself (ibid., 665). I set aside this further condition throughout this article since the disagreement between Sharp and myself does not concern this.

10 ibid., 661–663.

11 By the goods and opportunities being "objectively" important, Sharp means that people have a weighty interest (rather than a merely subjective preference) in them (ibid., 655).

of Honduras would be much weaker than that of the United States if the latter were to exercise it over the former, based on differences in the goods and options withheld and in people's ability to access them otherwise.[12] Therefore, Sharp concludes that there is no morally objectionable relational inequality when those excluded are immigrants from affluent states.

3 Critical Examination

As explained in the previous section, Sharp contends that when immigration restrictions are exercised against immigrants from affluent states, they do not constitute an unequal power over these immigrants. This conclusion seems plausible when we treat immigrants from affluent states as *collective* agents who stand vis-à-vis citizens of a receiving state (as Sharp does in his argument). The overall goods and opportunities denied to Canadians as a *group* when the United States excludes them are arguably roughly equal in significance to those denied to Americans as a group when Canada excludes them. The overall goods and opportunities denied to Americans as a group when Honduras excludes them are certainly much less important than those denied to Hondurans as a group when the United States excludes them.

However, when we view each immigrant from an affluent state as an individual who stands vis-à-vis the receiving state represented by its citizens, we can see the situation differently. When a state, whether affluent or not, closes its border to an immigrant who seeks entry, thereby foreclosing the goods and opportunities present in its territory from him or her, the goods and opportunities withheld from *this individual* are much greater in significance than those withheld from citizens of the excluding state if the former does so. This seems true regardless of whether the excluded immigrant is from a poor or affluent state and unless he or she possesses such great economic or political power as to significantly affect the political decisions of the excluding state by his or her own choice (e.g., a billionaire who can threaten political decision-makers of the excluding state by indicating the possibility of withdrawal of his or her investment from its domestic economy). This means that in usual cases, states (and ultimately their citizens) do exercise unequal power over immigrants, whether they come from poor or affluent states. Since relational egalitarians are ultimately concerned with an equal relationship between individuals rather than groups,[13] there is no necessary

12 Although Sharp does not state explicitly, he seems to endorse this conclusion, considering his contention that "the significance of the power exercised by well-off states against worse-off individuals is much greater than the significance of the power exercised by worse-off states against well-off individuals owing to differences in the goods and options withheld and in people's ability to access them otherwise" (ibid., 666).

13 "[Egalitarian political movements] assert the equal moral worth of *persons*" (Anderson (1999), 312). As pointed out in Footnote 9, Sharp concedes that relational egalitarians are ultimately concerned about inequalities between persons.

reason why we need to see a relevant power relation only (or primarily) from a group perspective.

When we view each immigrant from affluent states as an individual, we can see the differences in situations between them concerning how important the goods and opportunities are to their lives and whether the state's exclusion is decisive. As mentioned in the previous section, Sharp argues that goods, such as access to labor markets and improved economic prospects, security, social welfare benefits, and associative ties, are objectively important to the lives of disadvantaged immigrants from poor or middle-income states. This is also true for the worse-off in affluent states. Also, even among affluent states, there are variations in the availability of the above-mentioned goods and opportunities, depending on the effectiveness of antidiscrimination laws in labor markets, the effectiveness of protection from violent crimes, the generosity of social welfare, and so on, which contribute to the decisiveness of states' exclusion from these goods. Female immigrants from Japan might have an objectively important interest in access to more gender-equal labor markets (and, therefore, improved economic prospects) in the United States. Immigrants from the United States who appear to lack physical strength (and therefore become an easy target of violent crimes) might have an objectively important interest in moving to Japan where the crime rate is much lower. Poor immigrants from the United States might have an objectively important interest in the much more generous social welfare benefits of Sweden, and so forth.

Above all, when it comes to associative ties, not only the worse-off but also the better-off in affluent states have an objectively important interest in them. This is especially true in the case of love: if I, a middle-class citizen in one of the affluent states, fall in love with someone living in another country, and she is not able to move out of her state for some reasons (e.g., she is paralyzed and needs to be in bed all day), I would have a sufficiently important interest in moving to that state and have a romantic relationship with her (so long as she consents to do so). Because love is an existential commitment to a *particular* person, it would be highly misplaced to reply to me that I could seek another girlfriend in my own country.

For these reasons, I think that to be consistent and loyal to the ultimate concern of relational egalitarians, Sharp's relational egalitarian argument should condemn not only immigration restrictions against disadvantaged immigrants from poor (or middle-income) states but also those against immigrants from affluent states. To this point, one might stress that those living in affluent states, however disadvantaged they might be, are still generally in a better position than the disadvantaged in poor states; for instance, poor Americans in the United States are far better off than poor people in Burundi. If so, one might continue: the former have less urgent interests in the goods and opportunities denied to them when states engage in immigration restrictions than the latter.

Although I do not dispute this, I have to point out that the difference in seriousness in economic situations also exists between those from poor and middle-income states.

Sharp contends that while relatively disadvantaged or middle-class immigrants from middle-income states do not face severe poverty, they nonetheless have an objectively important interest in their standard of living that goes beyond the threshold of minimal decency.[14] If the differences in economic situations between those from poor and middle-income states do not disqualify the latter from making a complaint based on the relational egalitarian argument, it is unclear why they should be different in the case of the poor from affluent states. Considering that there are also some affluent individuals in poor states (e.g., elites and family members of a political leader), it is arbitrary to draw a border between those qualified and unqualified for relational egalitarian complaints based solely on where these immigrants come from.

4 Objections and Replies to Them

4.1 Objection from Democracy and National Responsibility

Against my argument in the previous section that a state's exclusion from the goods and opportunities present in its territory can be decisive even for (poor) immigrants from affluent states, it might be objected that since these immigrants have the right to vote on the political decision-making of their own wealthy, democratic states, they can make their states provide the goods and opportunities in which they have objectively important interest (e.g., security and social welfare benefits). They can do so by exercising their political rights and changing their states' current policies (e.g., introducing more effective control against violent crimes and a more generous social welfare system). Therefore, the objection is that if their states maintain their current policies, their citizens, whether poor or affluent, are collectively responsible for the consequences of their states' policies and thus are not entitled to make a complaint against immigration restrictions of foreign states by saying that their exclusion is decisive.

While it is true that citizens in affluent states, unlike those in poor (or middle-income) states, have a political right to influence their states' decision-making, it is a separate question whether they can effectively change their states' policies in their favor without undue cost.[15] Considering that the rich have greater de-facto power over the political decision-making of states even under a democratic leadership, and the poor often have limited bargaining power vis-à-vis their rich compatriots, especially in this age of globalization, it does not seem to me an easy task for worse-off individuals in affluent states to collectively exercise their political rights to counter the resistance from

14 Sharp (2022), 661.

15 "[T]he significance of a given token of exclusionary power depends on whether the exclusion is decisive: whether the excluded party can easily and without undue cost access the relevant kinds of goods in some other way" (ibid., 662).

the rich and to provide their own states with the goods and opportunities in which they have objectively important interest.

Admittedly, the decisiveness of foreign states' exclusion of the poor from affluent states will be significantly weakened if their own states fulfill the condition in which all of them can access the goods and opportunities present in their territory in which they have objectively important interests. However, since there are still some (or many) affluent states that have yet to achieve this ideal condition and it is not only the poor but also the rich who are responsible for the *status quo* of these states, it would be unfair to ask these poor individuals to incur all the cost of not winning the political battle against their rich compatriots and, therefore, being unable to access the relevant goods and opportunities in the territory of their own states, just because they happen to be in a fellow-citizen relationship with these rich individuals. After all, the goods of associative ties, in which everyone (whether poor or affluent) has objectively important interests and a commitment to particular individuals, is relevant. As was discussed in the case of love, the objection from democracy above seems out of place since the decisiveness of exclusion in such cases lies not in the incapacity of the home states but in the irreplaceable nature of the goods themselves.

4.2 Objection from the Relevance of Structural Injustice

Against my argument in the previous section that relational egalitarians should condemn not only the affluent states' exercise of unequal power over immigrants from the poor (or middle-income) states but also the exercise of unequal power over those from the affluent states, it might be objected that they need not do so because only the former is an instance of structural injustice. Since immigration restrictions by affluent states against immigrants from poor (or middle-income) states have historically been employed as a way of colonization,[16] the objection goes that the meaning and significance of each of these restrictions ought not to be evaluated in isolation but to be seen as a whole with relation to this context of structural injustice; they are all parts of the unjust global structure in which citizens of affluent states, whether consciously or unconsciously, systematically exploit those in poor (or middle-income) states. The immigration restrictions against those from affluent states, on the other hand, do not involve any structural injustice of the relevant kind, so relational egalitarians, the objection might conclude, need not worry about them, no matter how significant their impact on individual immigrants may be.

There are two major reasons that egalitarians have focused on structural injustices. First, as John Rawls claimed when justifying his choice of what he called "the basic

16 Cole (2011), 223 f.

structure of society" as the primary focus of justice, its effects are "so profound."[17] Second, the unjust structure is in a recursive cycle with individual acts of injustice in the sense that the former makes it easy for the latter to occur, and the frequent occurrence of the latter helps the maintenance and entrenchment of the former in turn. This means that merely prohibiting individual acts of injustice is of little help, and to combat the whole injustice effectively, we need to eradicate unjust structure, the real cause of injustices, by paying due attention to it from theories of justice and equality.[18]

Although I have no quarrel with this objection regarding the importance of paying attention to structure when theorizing equality, I do not think that egalitarians, whether distributive or relational, have to be concerned only about structural injustices. To clarify this, let me introduce two distinct types of structuralism on justice: *inclusive* and *exclusive*.[19] The inclusivist claims that justice ought to be concerned *not only* with individual acts *but also* with structures, whereas the exclusivist claims that justice ought to be concerned *only* with the latter. All we can safely argue from the two reasons above is the inclusivist position (after all, what the profoundness of effects and recursive characteristics mentioned above show is the seriousness of unjust structure and not the triviality of merely individual acts of injustice), and the objection above would commit a *non sequitur* if it were to infer the exclusivist position from the inclusivist one. Since the idea of relational equality itself can be applied to purely personal as well as social or political relationships,[20] and an individual act of immigration restrictions can exert a significantly profound effect on the lives of individuals, regardless of its being an instance of structural injustice, it is unclear why relational egalitarians should (or could) concern only those arising from the structure.[21]

---

17 Rawls (1999), 6 f.

18 For the most notable theory of justice having focused on unjust structure, see Young (1990).

19 I owe this distinction to a similar argument by Tatsuo Inoue, who distinguished "inclusive/exclusive institutionalism" on distributive justice. See Inoue (2012), 89 f.

20 Scheffler (2015), 24–31.

21 By saying this, I do not deny the possibility that the consideration of structural injustice provides an *additional* argument (from the perspective of relational equality) against immigration restrictions, which is to be applied only to those restrictions exercised by affluent states against immigrants from the poor (or middle-income) states. As famously pointed out by Thomas Pogge, citizens in affluent states are said to have inflicted harm on those in poor (or middle-income) states through the practices backed by international institutions that are structural in nature exemplified by those backed by the World Trade Organization and International Monetary Fund that have impeded the economic development of these developing states (Pogge (2008)). These practices of institutional harm can be seen as exercising unequal power, so relational egalitarians would have reasons to concern about them *in addition to* individual acts of immigration restrictions in general. As remedies to these institutional harms, the first thing to do is to reform the harm-imposing international institutions themselves, but since it would take many years to completely reform them, it is argued that citizens in affluent states also have the responsibility to mitigate harms by other measures, such as the redistribution of economic goods to and receiving immigrants from the poor (or middle-income) states (Inoue (2012), 250–267). As this responsibility to mitigate harm is based on the fact that the citizens of affluent states themselves have perpetuated or benefitted from these harm-imposing practices, it can be given priority over other duties and, therefore, affluent states may prioritize receiving immigrants

4.3 Objection from the Danger of Territorial Domination

Against my argument in the previous section that we should see the power relation involved in immigration restrictions from an individual perspective and that relational egalitarians should also condemn those restrictions against immigrants from affluent states, it might be objected that this will lead to the powerful states' colonization of the weaker ones. By sending their people and facilitating their settlements to new destinations, the objection is that powerful states can territorially dominate weaker ones. To counteract this domination, the objection might conclude that citizens in weaker states need to retain wider discretion over immigration restrictions against those coming from these powerful states.

Two replies can be made against this objection. First, whether the flow of immigrants from one state to another leads to the former's domination over the latter depends not only on how affluent the sending state is but also on how different the comparative size (in terms of territory and population) of the two states is. For instance, if Nigeria were to accept all Luxembourgers who wish to immigrate there, there seems to be little chance of Luxemburg dominating Nigeria, considering that the former is much smaller than the latter in size. By contrast, if Russia, considered to be a middle-income state, encourages its people to immigrate to Finland, there does seem to be a danger of territorial domination, although Finns are, on average, more affluent than Russians.

Second, the danger of domination also depends on the number of immigrants. If the flow of these immigrants is traceable to active endorsement on the part of their governments (e.g., if Russia's government actively takes part in sending its people and facilitating their settlement in Crimea, a part of Ukraine), these immigrants and their government can rightly be seen as collective agents, even under my individualist construal of a relational egalitarian argument. In such exceptional cases, the citizens of destination states, whether poor or affluent, are entitled to engage in immigration restrictions, which are comparable to acts of self-defense against invading troops. At the same time, for citizens to appeal to this self-defense argument for immigration restrictions, the danger of domination needs to be concrete rather than abstract. Therefore, it would not justify *unlimited* discretion over immigration restrictions against those coming from affluent or powerful states.

---

from these harmed states when their capacity to accept immigrants is limited. At the same time, since states' immigration restrictions are the exercise of unequal power over immigrants, whether they come from poor or affluent states, it would be objectionable from the standpoint of relational equality for the affluent states to deny entry to immigrants from other affluent states when they have the capacity to receive them as well.

5 Conclusion

In this paper, I critically examined Sharp's own treatment of his relational egalitarian argument and argued for a more individualist position as to who is eligible for a relational egalitarian complaint against immigration restrictions.

Before closing, I wish to refer to two practical implications of my argument in this paper. First, since states' immigration restrictions constitute the exercise of unequal power over immigrants regardless of where they come from if what I argued in this paper is correct, it is morally objectionable from a relational egalitarian ground for a state to deny entry to even immigrants from affluent states as long as it can accept them, and there is no compelling reason not to do so.

Second, when the number of immigrants who wish to seek entry into a state exceeds the capacity of this state to accept them, it is morally permissible for the state to prioritize those among them who have more urgent interests, which is consistent with relational equality. The state may prioritize those having familial ties with its own citizens over those who do not. It may prioritize those who are worse off over those better off in terms of their socioeconomic situations. However, since disadvantaged individuals do exist in affluent states as do privileged individuals in poor ones, it would not be morally permissible for a state to discriminate against them only based on where they come from.[22]

Bibliography

Anderson, Elizabeth (1999): "What Is the Point of Equality?" In: *Ethics* 109 (2), 287–337. https://doi.org/10.1086/233897.

Cohen, Gerald (1989): "On the Currency of Egalitarian Justice." In: *Ethics* 99 (4), 906–944. https://doi.org/10.1086/293126.

Cole, Phillip (2011): "Open Borders. An Ethical Defense." In: Wellman, Christopher / Cole, Phillip: *Debating the Ethics of Immigration. Is There a Right to Exclude?* Oxford: Oxford University Press, 172–313.

Eidelson, Benjamin (2015): *Discrimination and Disrespect*. Oxford: Oxford University Press.

Inoue, Tatsuo (2012): *On Global Justice* [*Sekai Seigi Ron*]. Tokyo: Chikuma Shobo.

---

22 Except for the cases where the affluent states aim at fulfilling their responsibility to mitigate institutional harms (see Footnote 21). Even setting aside these cases, there remains a question of whether a state is permitted to consider (as one factor among others) whether an immigrant comes from a poor or affluent state, especially when the information of his/her individual economic situation is hard to obtain. In such cases, it might be permissible for the state to use the wealthiness of his/her state as a proxy for his/her economic situation as an individual. However, even in such cases, I think that the state should try to take into consideration his/her specific situation as well when making decision if he/she is to provide the relevant information reasonably available to the decision maker. For more on the treatment as an individual, see Eidelson (2015), 127–170.

Knight, Carl (2009): *Luck Egalitarianism. Equality, Responsibility, and Justice*. Edinburgh: Edinburgh University Press.
Kolodny, Niko (2014): "Rule Over None II." In: *Philosophy and Public Affairs* 42 (4), 287–336. https://doi.org/10.1111/papa.12037.
Pogge, Thomas (2008): *World Poverty and Human Rights. Cosmopolitan Responsibilities and Reforms* (2nd Edition). Cambridge and Malden, MA: Polity.
Rawls, John (1999): *A Theory of Justice* (Revised Edition). Cambridge, MA: Harvard University Press.
Scheffler, Samuel (2015): "The Practice of Equality." In: Fourie, Carina / Schuppert, Fabian / Wallimann-Helmer, Ivo (Eds.): *Social Equality. On What It Means to be Equals?* Oxford: Oxford University Press, 20–44.
Scheffler, Samuel (2003): "What Is Egalitarianism?" In: *Philosophy and Public Affairs* 31 (1), 5–39. https://doi.org/10.1111/j.1088-4963.2003.00005.x.
Schemmel, Christian (2021): *Justice and Egalitarian Relations*. Oxford: Oxford University Press.
Segall, Shlomi (2014): *Equality of Opportunity*. Oxford: Oxford University Press.
Sharp, Daniel (2022): "Relational Equality and Immigration." In: *Ethics* 132 (3), 644–679. https://doi.org/10.1086/718076.
Temkin, Larry (1993): *Inequality*. New York: Oxford University Press.
Wellman, Christopher (2011): "Freedom of Association and the Right to Exclude." In: Wellman, Christopher / Cole, Phillip: *Debating the Ethics of Immigration. Is There a Right to Exclude?* Oxford: Oxford University Press, 13–155.
Young, Iris Marion (1990): *Justice and the Politics of Difference*. Princeton: Princeton University Press.

Yuichiro Mori
Graduate School of Law, Hokkaido University
ymori@juris.hokudai.ac.jp

This research was funded by Grants-in-Aid for Scientific Research (B) 18H00790 from Japan Society for the Promotion of Science (JSPS) and the 2023 Murata Science Foundation Grants.

Part 7
Law and Sexuality

Reconsideration of Autonomy-based Principle*
On Raz's Liberal Perfectionism

MING-YUAN CHIN

Abstract: Positioned as a cornerstone of freedom and human dignity, personal autonomy shields individuals from undue state intrusion, emerging as a fundamental human right that ensures freedom of decision-making. However, challenges arise when autonomy clashes with state-defined ideals of the "good," as seen in perfectionism theory. This article argues that the government's responsibility is to avoid interference and actively promote positive freedom, fostering diverse paths to autonomy. Drawing on J. S. Mill's "harm principle" and Joseph Raz's concept of "autonomy-based freedom," the article explores the evolution of personal autonomy, advocates for value pluralism, and examines the tension between Raz's perfectionism and Mill's harm principle. Additionally, it critiques Raz's dismissal of the "right to autonomy," offering counterarguments and shedding light on the interplay between autonomy and constitutional theory. Finally, it addresses the constitutional void stemming from unforeseen issues like the legalization of same-sex marriage, navigating the intersection of fundamental human rights and personal autonomy.

Keywords: Personal Autonomy, Perfectionism, Harm Principle, Value Pluralism, Autonomy Rights

1 Introduction

Personal autonomy holds a crucial position, especially in the constitutional field. Respect for personal autonomy, equal to honoring "human dignity," is considered the foundation of freedom. It not only eliminates the power of the state to unjustly interfere with the individual's sphere but also constitutes a fundamental human right ensuring the individual's freedom of decision-making and activity. This principle expresses the tenets of individualism and reflects the core ideals of all rights protected by the Constitution and is considered key to resolving issues in various areas of society.

* This article, presented at the "The 2nd IVR Japan International Conference (IVRJ 2023)" on September 17, 2023 at Chiba University, has undergone significant revisions. I would like to thank Prof. Jimmy Chia-Shin Hsu, Prof. Hirohide Takikawa, and other esteemed participants for their valuable insights.

However, the autonomy that individuals can exercise under the constraints of assuming a position of "good" sought by the state's authority, as in the case of "perfectionism theory", contradicts the autonomy-based principle that individuals seek to achieve. It results in decisions regarding the "good" being unilaterally imposed on individuals with limited choices.

On the other hand, issues such as the legalization of same-sex marriage present a constitutional gap regarding fundamental human rights that were not anticipated during the Constitution's framing. Marriage is highly connected to the realization of individual dignity and autonomy. In this context, it can be argued that same-sex marriage is achievable through the consideration of the autonomy-based principle. Utilizing the autonomy-based principle as a universal moral theory and considering the examination of the pursuit of happiness in Article 13 of the Constitution of Japan, the theories of legal philosophy and constitution are likely to converge in practical terms. While realizing the core autonomy rights of individuals, the boundaries of rights between individuals are limited by the principle of harm. Furthermore, by respecting and protecting the core autonomy of individuals, the government must not only prevent the loss of autonomy but also provide various options for individuals to achieve autonomy and avoid excessive intervention in the individual's sphere. In other words, the government not only has the duty to uphold the negative freedom of the harm principle, i. e., the duty of non-interference, but also has the duty to go beyond that and actively realize and protect positive freedom.

This article compares and develops arguments based on John Stuart Mill's "harm principle," emphasizing Joseph Raz's "autonomy-based principle" from *The Morality of Freedom*. It delves into the development of personal autonomy, advocates for embracing societal value pluralism, and explores the incompatibility between Raz's perfectionism and Mill's harm principle. Additionally, it discusses Raz's rejection of the "right to autonomy" and presents counterarguments, aiming to explore the intersection of autonomy theory and constitutional theory.

2 The Concept of Autonomy

When explaining the concept of autonomy, it is essential to take note of its multifaceted nature. Gerald Dworkin highlights the diverse usage of the term "autonomy." According to Dworkin, autonomy is sometimes associated with freedom (for instance, in Berlin's terms, negative and positive freedom), occasionally with self-governance or sovereignty, and at times used to symbolize personal will, dignity, integrity, uniqueness, independence, responsibility, self-awareness, and self-identification. What remains consistent across these usages is that autonomy is a characteristic of a person, a quality deemed valuable[1]. This article primarily relies on Joseph Raz's theory to explain the concept of autonomy.

The modern concept of autonomy is primarily developed based on Kant's moral theory. According to Kant, autonomy is the highest principle of reason and morality. It involves acting according to universal moral laws while not constrained by natural desires such as sensual inclinations. Raz notes that his personal autonomy differs from Kant's moral autonomy and should not be confused with the concept of moral autonomy, which is only indirectly related[2]. Kantian autonomy demands adherence to categorical imperatives and self-governance. Conversely, Raz's conception of personal autonomy centers primarily on choosing a "good life" for oneself.

Raz points out that specific concepts of personal well-being in Western societies are ideals of personal autonomy. This autonomy is significantly determined by our actions and involves the capacity to set lifetime goals and choose interpersonal relationships, making it a critical component of happiness. The underpinning philosophy for personal autonomy suggests that people should create their own lives, emphasizing notions of self-creation and self-choice. In essence, autonomous individuals possess the ability to control their own "good life" through a series of decisions made throughout their lives, as Raz states: "The autonomous person is a (part) author of his own life[3]."

However, to increase this ideal of personal autonomy, a society must inherently contain a multitude of distinct forms characterized by diverse and often incompatible value systems. Achieving the ideal of personal autonomy necessitates a range of choices. The existence of various value systems, such as notions of the "good," is crucial for actualizing an autonomous life. Consequently, a standpoint of 'value pluralism' must be assumed before delving into discussions about autonomy.

2.1 Value Pluralism

Value pluralism contrasts with the traditionally supported monism in Western societies. According to Berlin, monism derives from longstanding faith and aims to ultimately resolve all contradictions within that faith. Monism, as the single criterion resolving multiple contradictions, compels individuals to pursue the most significant "monistic" value[4]. On the other hand, value pluralism acknowledges the existence of incommensurable values that are diverse and might conflict with each other[5].

---

1 Dworkin, Gerald (1988): The Theory and Practice of Autonomy. New York: Cambridge University Press, 5 f.; Hattori, Takahiro (2000): "Jiritsugainen to Patānarizumu (The Concept of "Autonomy" and Paternalism)". In: Okayama Law Journal 49 (3&4), 356.
2 Raz, Joseph (1988): The Morality of Freedom. New York: Oxford University Press, 370.
3 ibid., 369.
4 Hama, Shin-ichirō (2008): Bārin no Jiyūron (Berlin's Theory of Freedom). Tokyo: Keisō Shobō, 45 f.
5 ibid., 47 f.

Raz's standpoint appears influenced by Isaiah Berlin[6]. According to Raz, value pluralism establishes the value of tolerance by recognizing all forms of human life, even those that are incompatible, through tolerance[7]. This value of tolerance derives from Kant's concept of personal respect, valuing others' lives and treating their humanity as an end in itself[8]. In essence, a "plural" society that embraces personal uniqueness without denying it and practices tolerance toward diverse personalities is a moral virtue that Raz finds desirable. To uphold personal autonomy in all forms of life, it's necessary to restrain conflicting attitudes in human behavior and values through a perspective rooted in tolerance. A society based on the values of tolerance, or value pluralism, allows individuals to create and secure diverse autonomous lives.

However, among the chosen values, intolerance often emerges, especially toward other moral virtues or pursuits. Intolerance arises when one does not tolerate individuals possessing moral virtues they lack, potentially leading to persecution or harassment. Raz interprets the "use of coercion" by political theorists as a potential manifestation of intolerance[9]. Tolerance, as a unique moral virtue, involves not generating aversion or hostility toward others' ways of living. Maintaining an attitude of tolerance and suppressing tendencies toward aversion or hostility toward others' ways of living has inherent moral value (or virtue).

To respect personal autonomy, it is necessary to tolerate bad or immoral actions within certain bounds. Tolerance restrains tendencies toward intolerance in accepting and pursuing morally acceptable preferences of others. Clashes of values between people generate intolerant emotions. To resolve such conflicts, a stance of tolerating others is essential. Raz terms this competitive pluralism, which offers a relationship with tolerance and a posture of respecting autonomy. Therefore, the principle of toleration is derived in which tolerance and intolerance can coexist[10].

In a society based on value pluralism, various incompatible forms of life are morally permissible[11]. This is due to how different lifestyles possess unique virtues, allowing individuals to obtain their excellence through pursuing them. For example, there is no distinct right or wrong when comparing the lifestyles of an extroverted, socially inclined person and an introverted, reserved individual, as they likely possess different character traits and aspire to different ideals. Regardless of the pursued form of

---

6 Hama, Shin-ichirō (2006): "Aizaia Bārin no Kachi Tagenron: Gendai Seigiron Niokeru Sono Kanōsei (Isaiah Berlin's Value-Pluralism)". In: The Doshisha law review 51 (4), 3.

7 Raz (1988), 401 (n2).

8 Raz, Joseph (2001): Value, Respect, and Attachment. New York: Cambridge University Press, 130–138.

9 Raz (1988), 403 (n2).

10 ibid., 406 f.

11 ibid., 397. In this context, Raz differentiates between value pluralism and moral pluralism. He argues that while value pluralism reflects the coexistence of multiple, often conflicting values, moral pluralism encompasses a broad range of moral perspectives, including diverse conceptions of what constitutes a meaningful or morally fulfilling life.

life, pursuing a form that entails alternative and incompatible modes yields its virtues. Thus, value pluralism affirms the diverse forms of life individuals pursue and promotes respect for each within a society that seeks to maximize them.

However, pursuing a specific lifestyle also implies relinquishing other virtues. As mentioned previously, since all values are incompatible with one another, selecting one value implies not pursuing others. Simultaneously possessing all values is impossible. For instance, a Christian cannot worship a Buddha statue, and a Buddhist cannot worship according to Christian scriptures.

Various types of goods have distinct forms, and different values must be held to achieve autonomy. However, the diversity of these goods showcases the impossibility of simultaneously possessing all virtues and the incommensurability of values. Autonomy, understood as the capacity to select and engage with a multitude of values based on the assumptions of value pluralism, inherently possesses value[12].

The demand for a sufficient range of choices for autonomy is discussed in section 2.2. This range goes beyond mere quantity, requiring a spectrum of diverse virtues that are mutually incompatible. Without the presence of value pluralism representing incompatible virtues, we would be unable to create diverse forms of autonomous lives. Hence, autonomy obliges value pluralism.

2.2 Autonomy-Based Principle

Raz advocates value pluralism and derives the "principle of tolerance," which promotes respecting each other's autonomy by recognizing incomparable and valuable styles of life. Tolerance is one facet of respecting autonomy. Given the above, it is possible to derive an "autonomy-based principle" as a concrete instantiation of value pluralism and the principle of tolerance.

According to Raz, personal autonomy emphasizes the state where people possess certain capacities. To enable individuals to lead autonomous lives, they must fulfill three obligations, or "conditions of autonomy," as the basis for autonomy. The three conditions of autonomy are shown as (1) independence from coercion and manipulation, (2) appropriate mental abilities, and (3) an adequate range of options[13].

(1) The obligation of independence requires refraining from the use of coercion or manipulation to treat people as objects, thereby respecting their independence. The use of coercion and manipulation to undermine a person's will is considered an infringement upon their autonomy. J. S. Mill's harm principle demands non-interference

12 Raz (2001), 157 f. (n8).
13 Raz (1988), 372, 407 f. (n2).

with actions as long as they do not cause harm to others. In the absence of harm, this obligation essentially requires non-interference in human actions.

(2) Developing appropriate mental abilities is necessary for leading an autonomous life. These abilities encompass mental, cognitive, and inferential capacities, as well as emotional, health-related, and physical capabilities. This concept is often discussed as paternalism. For instance, Mill's harm principle is limited only to mature individuals, excluding those who are immature[14]. Thus, autonomy is thought to be possessed by those with the ability to make judgments and utilize internal capacities.

(3) The creation of an adequate range of options for people is required. The criteria for appropriate options should take into account an individual's temporal and spatial context. For example, a balance must be ensured between long-term, significant choices and short-term, less impactful ones (e. g., university admissions or job opportunities) while addressing both the diversity and quantity of options. To pursue autonomy and autonomous lives, individuals need a diverse range of options to engage in self-exploration and self-realization activities. These activities not only involve choosing which abilities to enhance but also which abilities not to develop.

Hama argues that Isaiah Berlin's distinction between 'negative freedom' and 'positive freedom' is useful in understanding the autonomy-based principle[15]. Negative freedom, or freedom from coercion, corresponds to the demand of (1) independence from coercion and manipulation. As Raz pointed out, securing and facilitating autonomy through the obligations of (2) appropriate mental abilities and (3) an adequate range of options equates to positive freedom[16]. According to the autonomy-based principle, if negative freedom is not secured, achieving positive freedom becomes impossible.

2.3 Harm Principle and Autonomy

Raz believes that the autonomy-based principle can be integrated with Mill's harm principle[17]. The harm principle asserts that the only legitimate reason for forcibly interfering with an individual is to prevent harm to others. However, the use of coercion based on the autonomy-based duty is not justified unless harm exists. Therefore, Raz defines harm as not only violating someone's autonomy but also adversely affecting that person's future and possibilities. In other words, actions that infringe upon someone's autonomy violate the autonomy-based duty.

14 Mill, John Stuart (2001): On Liberty. Ontario: Batoche Books, 14.
15 Hama, Shin-ichirō (1995): "Josefu Razu Niokeru Riberarizumu no Tetsugakuteki Kisozuke (On Joseph Raz's Philosophy of Liberalism)". In: The Doshisha law review 47 (2), 139–140.
16 Raz (1988), 408 f. (n2).
17 ibid., 413.

Raz's reinterpretation of the harm principle is broader than Mill's, seeing it as a tool to promote well-being rather than an obstacle to pursuing moral goods. The autonomy principle, central to a good life, obligates individuals to fulfill the conditions of autonomy. Raz aligns the harm principle with perfectionism, asserting the government's duty not only to provide options for citizens' excellence but also to eliminate bad choices and encourage good ones. He provides examples such as the provision of educational systems and national health insurance through taxation, subsidies for public transportation[18]. This perspective supports autonomy and demands perfectionist policies for its realization. However, Raz's endorsement of paternalism through perfectionism raises a potential contradiction with liberalism, as it may undermine the value of tolerance espoused by value pluralism, reflecting what Raz describes as a "manifestation of intolerance[19]."

3 Perfectionism

This section explores Raz's liberal perfectionism in relation to the autonomy-based principle, presenting critiques of his theory and addressing concerns and reflections on its implications.

3.1 Raz's Liberal Perfectionism

Raz supports "liberal perfectionism" in his political morality, viewing political freedom to be rooted in personal autonomy and integral to a good life. While endorsing the autonomy principle as a form of perfectionism, he asserts that the government's duty to promote personal autonomy is limited to what is valuable for individual well-being, or the "good." The core of this position lies in fostering personal autonomy and pursuing meaningful goals and relationships, with the government facilitating this by encouraging virtuous choices and eliminating immoral ones.

According to Raz, applying perfectionism prevents the decline of personal autonomy, safeguarding individuals from pursuing futile lives or goals. Notably, he rejects the use of force, advocating instead for subsidies, encouragement, and promotion through advertising to achieve perfectionist ideals. However, tension arises as Raz emphasizes respecting diverse values while promoting specific worthwhile goals, potentially conflicting with 'value pluralism,' which could lead to a return to the singular value of "monism."

---

18 ibid., 415.
19 ibid., 403.

3.1.1 Raz's Concept of "Good"

To evaluate which values are worth achieving, understanding Raz's concept of the "good," particularly "intrinsic goods," is crucial[20]. Raz distinguishes between "instrumental goods" and "intrinsic goods" based on their dependence on outcomes. Instrumental goods derive their value from achieving specific results, while intrinsic goods are inherently valuable, independent of any outcomes. Raz emphasizes the pursuit of intrinsic goods for autonomous individuals, such as "constituent valuable goods" and ultimately "ultimate valuable goods." However, Raz does not provide a clear answer regarding the content of these "ultimate valuable goods" or the task of identifying objectively ultimate values.

Raz defines the "public good" as a benefit not dominated by specific individuals but potentially jointly controlled by beneficiaries within a society[21]. He classifies goods into "temporary public goods" and "natural public goods." For example, a city's water supply is a "temporary public good" because water distribution can be controlled. "Natural public goods," also known as "collective goods," can foster a tolerant society. However, pursuing ultimate valuable collective goods raises questions about their alignment with "value pluralism." In society, collective goods based on specific choices exist, such as recognizing same-sex marriage, which is considered a collective good[22]. These choices provide opportunities for autonomous lives, making the collective good inherently valuable and thus an intrinsic good.

3.1.2 Perfectionism as "Valuable Personal Autonomy"

Raz argues that the government's role is to safeguard valuable personal autonomy, emphasizing the inherent goodness of autonomy and its societal impact. While the state has the authority to limit choices, it should encourage choices deemed valuable[23]. However, concerns arise about potential paternalism and the state's ability to accurately evaluate which choices are valuable. Raz faces challenges in providing a clear method for identifying what is valuable, and ambiguities persist in defining valuable choices. Jeremy Waldron highlights the dependence of autonomy's value on the objects individuals choose, suggesting that failure can promote potential growth[24]. Nevertheless,

20 ibid., 200.
21 ibid., 198 f.
22 ibid., 206.
23 ibid., 207.
24 Waldron, Jeremy (1989): "Autonomy and Perfectionism in Raz's Morality of Freedom". In: S Cal L Rev 62 (3&4), 1128.

the state's role in evaluating these values raises concerns about citizens' opportunities for self-determination and their ability to correct mistaken judgments.

3.2 Harm Principle and Paternalism

Raz incorporates Mill's harm principle into his own concept of "valuable autonomy," which is grounded in perfectionism. As introduced in the previous section, Raz acknowledges that this concept is vulnerable to critiques of paternalism. The idea that the state could influence individual interests carries the risk of paternalism. To some extent, Raz appears to embrace paternalistic thinking by encouraging the state to limit citizens' choices while promoting and rewarding "good" choices and eliminating harmful options. However, this approach may potentially contradict Mill's harm principle. Therefore, a deeper understanding of Mill's harm principle is necessary. In this section, Mill's stance on paternalism will be examined through quotes from *On Liberty* to determine whether Raz's interpretation aligns with it.

3.2.1 Reaffirmation of Mill's Harm Principle

In *On Liberty*, Mill advocates for individual freedom while presenting the harm principle, which justifies constraints on personal liberty. The harm principle asserts that the government should not interfere with an individual's actions unless those actions cause harm to others. In other words, the only legitimate reason for interference is to prevent harm to others. Any other interference, as it significantly diminishes individual happiness and autonomy, is rejected by Mill.

However, Mill does not entirely reject paternalism[25]. He applies the harm principle selectively to mature individuals capable of "spontaneous progress[26]." He limits its application to those who are immature, underage, dependent, or in need of assistance, justifying protection for the development of basic judgment skills and resistance to external harm. Gerald Dworkin distinguishes between strong and weak paternalism[27]: strong paternalism uniformly interferes without considering individual choice, while weak paternalism intervenes based on assumptions of benefit due to insufficient information or impaired judgment. Mill's examples, such as protecting an unaware per-

25 I would like to refer to an introduction of Chin. See Chin, Ming-yuan / Adachi, Hidehiko (2023): "The Harm Principle and Same-Sex Marriage". In: Kanazawa law review 66 (1), 86 f.
26 Mill (2001), 14 (n14).
27 Dworkin, Gerald (2020): "Paternalism". In: Stanford Encyclopedia of Philosophy. https://plato.stanford.edu/entries/paternalism/, accessed 08.16.2025.

son from crossing a dangerous bridge[28], illustrate permissible intervention when the loss of autonomy is severe and irrecoverable. He also opposes contracts of enslavement that compromise autonomy[29], emphasizing the value of individual self-determination. If the impairment of personal autonomy is predicted to be so severe that it is irrecoverable, intervention may be justified.

3.2.2 Harm Principle as Weak Paternalism

In essence, Mill's concern lies in the arbitrary use of "for your own good" as a justification for imposing strong paternalism against an individual's will. However, Mill does not reject the application of "weak paternalism" in cases involving immature individuals or to prevent irreparable loss of autonomy.

Naomi Nakamura, while acknowledging that many scholars traditionally interpret Mill as an anti-paternalist, argues that the form of paternalism Mill opposes is strong paternalism, which contradicts an individual's will[30]. Therefore, Mill's application of the harm principle is restricted to mature individuals, allowing for the acceptance of "weak paternalism" in other cases.

Under this premise, mature individuals with full judgment capacity have the right to determine their own lifestyle and should not be interfered with, as long as they do not engage in actions that harm autonomy. In other words, regardless of how others perceive their choices, individuals have the right to decide their lifestyle and learn through trial and error. Such individuals must be afforded the utmost respect to make their own decisions, ensuring that their autonomy and self-determination are upheld.

In contrast, imposing specific valuable goals on others in a coercive manner constitutes strong paternalism. Actions such as withholding relevant information or eliminating choices can restrict individuals' ability to shape their own lives. According to Mill, this is harmful not only to individuals but also to society, as it deprives people of the opportunity to contribute to society through their experiences, trial, and error.

3.2.3 Perfectionism as Strong Paternalism

Raz's liberal perfectionism can be considered a form of "strong paternalism" because it supports state intervention based on an individual's "valuable goals." Raz assumes that the state presupposes what constitutes a good life for individuals and universally

---

28 Mill (2001), 88 (n14).
29 ibid., 94.
30 Nakamura, Naomi (2007): Patānarizumu no Kenkyū (Research on Paternalism). Tokyo: Seibundō, 232f.

interferes with choices deemed valueless without questioning the reasons behind each choice. If a choice is considered valuable, it is only because the object of that choice is deemed "good." According to Raz's perfectionist principle, if an individual's choices are directed towards valueless or vulgar goals, the state preemptively restricts those choices, constrains personal autonomy, and engages in coercive interference. As a result, the state enforces strong paternalism, leading to the "tyranny of the majority" that Mill warns against. The promotion of strong paternalism restricts the development of individual personalities, hinders their formation, and molds individuals to fit the state's model, contradicting liberal principles. Therefore, this interpretation is unacceptable.

To resolve this contradiction in perfectionism, it should be reinterpreted through Mill's harm principle and the autonomy-based principle. Under the harm principle, paternalism applies only to those lacking basic judgment capacity. This is aligned with the autonomy condition of possessing appropriate internal capacities in the autonomy-based principle. In other words, individuals with judgment capacity, who can utilize their internal capacities, have the freedom to be free from interference and can choose freely among various options, whether valuable or valueless.

3.2.4 Critical Reception of Raz's Liberal Perfectionism

Gerald Dworkin diverges from Raz by defining paternalism as interference with a person's liberty based on considerations of their welfare, happiness, or interests[31]. Strong paternalism, however, raises concerns about infringing on autonomy and limiting freedom and self-determination. Dworkin questions the legitimacy of Raz's strong paternalism, particularly when safety concerns lead to miscalculations of individual interests.

Hidetoshi Tamaki argues that when a government, in pursuit of moral values, implements non-coercive perfectionist policies, it becomes difficult to justify such actions under an autonomy-based principle[32]. He contends that perfectionism is incompatible with autonomy, the latter being a higher priority. Even non-coercive moral policies may involve coercive measures, such as taxation, which could infringe upon autonomy.

Similarly, Tatsuo Inoue expresses concern about Raz's liberal perfectionism[33]. Inoue describes value pluralism as "a liberal bulwark" against a society that imposes a uniform conception of the ideal life through governing powers. However, Inoue criticizes Raz, arguing that whether liberal perfectionism functions as a liberal bulwark

31 Dworkin, Gerald (1972): "Paternalism". In: The Monist 56 (0), 65–68.

32 Tamaki, Hidetoshi (2004): "Riberarizumu no Saikōchiku (Reconstructing liberalism)". In: Hirai, Ryosuke (Ed.): Seigi: Gendaishakai no Kōkyōtetsugaku wo Motomete (Justice: In search of a public philosophy for modern society). Kyoto: Saganoshoin, 178.

33 Inoue, Tatsuo (2021): Zōhoshinsōban Tashahe no Jiyū: Kōkyōsei no Tetsugaku Toshite no Riberarizumu (New edition Freedom to Others: Liberalism as a Philosophy of Public Nature). Tokyo: Keisō Shobō, 21 f.

depends on Raz's list of "valuable choices for living a good life," which remains unclear. This uncertainty might lead to imposing a singular view of the good on people, eliminating "tolerance for the bad" and undermining the acceptance of a "diversity of good."

Francesco Biondo proposes the concept of "autonomy as freedom," drawing on A. K. Sen's theory, and takes a position against Raz's perfectionism[34]. According to Biondo, Sen defines freedom as the right of individuals to make decisions about their lives, regardless of others' intentions. While utilitarianism seeks to maximize collective utility and happiness, liberalism prioritizes individual rights, particularly in the context of how individuals choose to live. This aligns with Mill's harm principle, allowing individuals the freedom to live their lives, even if it contradicts the "good," and acknowledging the "right to do wrong."

In essence, value lies in the act of choosing itself, even if the choice contradicts societal conceptions of the good. Autonomy rests in the individual's right to choose, and individuals must take responsibility for those choices. Growth occurs through the interplay of errors and conflicts between individual and collective happiness, rooted in the uncompromising nature of value pluralism.

The critique of Raz's argument centers on its failure to acknowledge the "right to do wrong" or the "freedom to make mistakes" within liberal perfectionism. The argument asserts that Raz's emphasis on valuable choices overlooks the intrinsic value of the act of choosing itself. According to this perspective, autonomy is grounded in the individual's ability to choose freely, regardless of the perceived value of the choice. Critics argue that Raz's monistic interpretation, aligned with perfectionism, contradicts the "value of choice" in individual happiness by disregarding the diverse perspectives people hold on happiness.

A proposed revision calls for a reevaluation of perfectionism, advocating that even if an individual's lifestyle is deemed incorrect, the act of choosing should be respected. The "freedom to make mistakes" must be upheld. The suggestion is to reconstruct Raz's ideas by aligning them with Mill's harm principle and the autonomy-based principle. This approach emphasizes the need for the state to respect personal autonomy and individual responsibility while acknowledging that policy decisions may inherently carry a perfectionist character.

4 Right to Autonomy?: About Article 13 of the Japanese Constitution

By introducing the concept of autonomy, Raz argues that the failure to improve conditions for autonomy constitutes harm and imposes a duty on the government to enhance it. The duty to improve autonomy is a moral obligation for all individuals in

34 Biondo, Francesco (2005): "Two Types of Liberal Perfectionism". In: Ratio Juris 18 (4), 523.

society, including sovereigns, to respect the autonomy of others. This respect includes the values of value pluralism and tolerance, as Raz emphasizes, and is essential for individuals to exercise their rights as subjects in the modern constitutional order.

However, Raz rejects the notion of an autonomy-based right, contending that the existence of the statement "X has a right" depends on whether X's interests justify the imposition of obligations on others[35]. According to Raz, the right to autonomy can only be justified if the interests of the right-holder warrant imposing a societal obligation to create a social environment conducive to autonomous living. Conversely, if an individual's interests are insufficient to justify such an obligation, particularly if it places a heavy burden on others, Raz argues that no right to autonomy exists[36].

Although societal systems and individual actions may limit opportunities for autonomous living, Raz's argument does not imply the nullification of all rights. Still, his criteria may support only specific rights, excluding many widely accepted ones. Nicole Hassoun argues that Raz's autonomy-based explanation requires constraints, as it may not align with numerous recognized rights, particularly those related to bodily safety and health[37]. Therefore, opposing Raz's claim that autonomy-based rights do not exist may be a more appropriate stance. Nonetheless, it is evident that limits must be established between individual rights to prevent harm and protect the autonomy of both the "self" and "others."

Considering the historical development of civil society and constitutional law in modern nation-states, there is a need to emphasize individuals as "creators of their own lives" from an individualistic perspective. However, when incorporating "self-determination" into a constitutional system, one cannot ignore the necessary social conditions, systems, and other premises required to realize autonomy. While many rights have been claimed as individual freedoms, these rights often serve to achieve common interests, and realizing individual freedom remains a challenge. Within the framework of natural law, the boundaries between individual and common interests can become ambiguous, making it unclear how common interests contribute to achieving individual rights. Thus, when incorporating individual self-determination into the list of human rights, it is essential to consider the boundaries between individuals, apply the harm principle, and avoid undermining the autonomy of both the "self" and "others."

In the Japanese Constitution, specific articles, such as those guaranteeing "freedom of religion" and "freedom of speech," typify and safeguard human rights. To exercise autonomy rights effectively, a fundamental framework consistent with moral theories is required. Beyond enumerating individual rights, the constitution can also generate

35 Raz (1988), 166 (n2).
36 ibid., 247.
37 Hassoun, Nicole (2014): "Raz on the Right to Autonomy". In: European Journal of Philosophy 22 (1), 104 f.

new human rights, such as "individual autonomy rights," distinct from core autonomy rights, as recognized by Article 13 of the Japanese Constitution[38].

Establishing such rights through the autonomy-based principle is possible, and is essential to consider how this right can interact with other legal rules to be reasonably realized. However, the academic literature on Article 13 of the Japanese Constitution is extensive and beyond the scope of this discussion[39]. Additionally, in balancing constraints on other rights to achieve common social interests, the autonomy-based principle can enable the realization of "positive freedom" to pursue individual well-being and autonomy.

The government has a responsibility to create an environment that respects autonomy based on value pluralism and tolerance. Recognizing diverse personalities is crucial, and the government should establish systems that allow individuals the freedom to explore various options and engage in trial and error, ultimately achieving autonomy. This perspective advocates for the creation and enhancement of legal frameworks that accommodate diverse value systems, particularly noting the absence of legal provisions for same-sex marriage in Japan. Providing options within the marriage institution could address the legal inequalities faced by same-sex couples under Japan's current legal framework.

5 Conclusion

This article explores the relationship between value pluralism, tolerance, and autonomy through Joseph Raz's autonomy-based principle. In a society with diverse and incomparable values, individuals can lead autonomous lives by respecting and tolerating one another. When citizens are unable to achieve autonomy due to their circumstances, the government should work to improve the situation. Autonomy is defined as the ability to make choices about one's life, including setting personal goals and making decisions aligned with inherent values. Values are not classified hierarchically, and while mainstream values may guide overarching societal goals, government policies

38 Japanese constitutional law scholar Professor Koji Sato highlights "personal autonomy" as a new approach to addressing issues caused by an active and welfare state. He considers the examination of autonomy-related problems essential and explores them in relation to the Article 13 of the Japanese Constitution "right to pursue happiness." See Sato, Koji (2002): Nihonkoku Kempō to "Hōnoshihai" (The Constitution of Japan and the "rule of law"). Tokyo: Yūhikaku, 135–137.

39 The theories surrounding Article 13 of the Japanese Constitution include the "General Interest Theory (Ippantekijiyū Setsu)" and the "Personality Interest Theory (Jinkakuteki-rieki Setsu)." The General Interest Theory interprets Article 13 as granting "freedom of action in all areas of life," while the Personality Interest Theory views it as a "collection of rights with interests essential to an individual's personal existence." See Ashibe, Nobuyoshi and Takahashi, Kazuyuki (2019): Kempō (The Constitution of Japan) (7th). Tokyo: Iwanami Shoten, 121.

should practice perfectionism within limits. Non-mainstream values, such as individual beliefs, should not be constrained unless they cause harm to others. Tolerance for diverse values is essential to respecting personal autonomy, preventing the homogenization of values, and preserving individual freedom.

The ability to choose one's life purpose implies mutual respect for others as autonomous agents, creating a moral obligation to respect autonomy. This obligation, grounded in the harm principle, prohibits coercion unless harm is caused, with harm defined as a violation of autonomy conditions: independence, mental abilities, and access to a wide range of options.

In contrast to Raz's liberal perfectionism, the author advocates for the "freedom to make mistakes" and respects individuals as the authors of their own lives through diverse choices. Realizing personal autonomy requires promoting conditions that accommodate varied values. When the government unjustly restricts autonomy, it constitutes harm and justifies resistance from citizens. Recognizing individual diversity, the government should establish legal systems that embrace diverse values, correct discriminatory practices, and support the legalization of same-sex marriage.

Ming-Yuan Chin
Graduate School of Law, Keio University
kawaichichin@keio.jp

(This research was funded by The Keio University Doctorate Student Grant-in-Aid Program from Ushioda Memorial Fund.)

A Rawlsian Critic on Stability Problem of Public Reason*

Same-Sex Marriage Debates in Taiwan as an Example

KUAN-TING CHEN

Abstract: This paper aims to offer a Rawlsian critique of the concept of public reason by (re)contextualizing it within Rawls' theory of stability. The analysis highlights a potential issue: the concept of public reason, as it's currently understood, might not guarantee stability inherently. This investigation is carried out through both theoretical reflection and a case study, emphasizing the possible instability of the public reason framework. By exploring into the motivations and reasons involved, the underlying problem becomes clearer. Rawls' idea of public reason seems to exclude religious and comprehensive ideals, which could push citizens to provide external or weaker internal reasons. This becomes noticeable in the same-sex marriage debates in Taiwan, which serves as an example. In the early 2010 s, the concept of public reason gained popularity and seemed to have a positive impact on the progress of same-sex marriage. However, the conservative backlash in a 2018 public vote undoubtedly gives us a reason to reflect on the effectiveness of the public reason. This paper analyzes the relationship between public reason and different conservative actors' motivations to clarify why public reason, which excludes comprehensive doctrine, eventually fails to generate motivations and ensure stability.

Keywords: Public reason, Stability, Internal Reason, Legalizing Same-Sex Marriage, Religion

1 Introduction

In every democratic country, there must be many controversial social issues under debates, such as adultery, death penalty or same-sex marriage. Sometimes, these issues

* I would like to thank invaluable comments from Chao-Ju Chen, Hung-Ju Chen, Po-Chung Chow, Jimmy Chia-Shin Hsu, Seow Hon Tan, Lin Tsui, and all participants at The 9th Asian Constitutional Law Forum (Taiwan 2022), The 2022 Annual Meeting of the Chinese Association of Political Science (Taiwan 2022) and The 2nd IVR Japan International Conference (Japan 2023).

may result in radical discussions with differing viewpoints, which eventually lead to a more serious conflict between each side. Consequently, it is crucial to determine an appropriate approach for public discussion.

To response these crucial problem, public reason, the principle that participants in public debates should present non-comprehensive doctrines, was introduced by John Rawls. While spreading widely, this notion has also encountered criticism from various perspectives, such as Communitarianism, Socialism or Feminism. Although these critiques provide invaluable insights, they often approach their arguments from an external viewpoint not firmly rooted in Rawls' original idea, which make proponents of Rawls generally cautious about adopting these critical perspectives.

Unlike those perspectives above, this paper, therefore, aims to offer a 'Rawlsian' critique. To establish my critique, a brief outline of Rawls' evolving perspective will be provided. Subsequently, a 'Rawlsian' critique will be introduced, distinguishing between 'internal reasons' driven by motivation and 'external reasons' lacking such motivation. The challenge with the notion of public reason, as I perceive it, lies in its potential to lack compelling force, especially for individuals who adhere to comprehensive doctrine such as religious doctrines. This deficiency ultimately gives rise to concerns regarding its compatibility with Rawls' initial emphasis on the stability. After a theoretical discussion, I use a case study in Taiwan to illuminate the problem in the real world. In Taiwanese same-sex marriage debate, the doctrine of public reason with liberal wings idea initially seemed workable and hopeful in the 2010 s, especially the declaration of the Interpretation No. 748 also gave such a signal of the hope. However, the big win of the conservative wings in the referendum of 2018 was a backlash, which also provides us an opportunity to reflect the idea of public reason. My reflection here will focus on the relation between public reason and different actors' motivations in this backlash event. In my analysis, this backlash event can be explained by two factors: the exclusive function of the public reason and the polarization after exclusion. Both factors can trigger negative emotions for people not to accept the public consensus and then leads to the instability.

2 The Stability Problem and the Idea of Public Reason

2.1 The Idea of the Stability in TJ

Before directly criticizing public reason, we should realize the role of public reason in Rawls' theory. For Rawls, the idea of public reason is associated to the idea of stability. Therefore, we should begin with the idea of stability in Rawls' most famous book, *A Theory of Justice* (hereafter *TJ*).

Rawls puts much emphasis on the problem of the stability, 1/3 part of *TJ* is about stability and present through his congruence argument. But it does not catch people's eyes: most legal and political thinkers ignore this part in *TJ*[1]. In *TJ*, stability is very crucial. Rawls says:

> … the scheme of social cooperation must be stable: it must be more or less regularly complied with and its basic rules willingly acted upon; and when infractions occur, stabilizing forces should exist that prevent further violations and tend to restore the arrangement.[2] One conception of justice is more stable than another if the sense of justice that it tends to generate is stronger and more likely to override disruptive inclinations and if the institutions it allows foster weaker impulses and temptations to act unjustly … it is evident that stability is a desirable feature of moral conceptions. Other things equal, the persons in the original position will adopt the more stable scheme of principles.[3]

For Rawls, his theory must be a realistic utopia, which implies that his political theory must be practicable, he not only concerns the question of the way how to choose the principles of justices but also concerns how these p*rinciples work in the real world. To ensure this, there are two main arguments in his TJ: the argument of the* ***sense of justice*** *and the argument of the* ***good of justice.***

In the argument of the sense of justice, Rawls tries to ensure that people have a special ability to follow principles of justice. Such a special ability is what he calls "the sense of justice". To support this claim, Rawls mentions the role of "motives" first time:

> The stability of a conception depends upon ***a balance of motives:*** the sense of justice that it cultivates and the aims that it encourages must normally win out against propensities toward injustice. To estimate the stability of a conception of justice (and the well-ordered society that it defines), one must examine the ***relative strength of these opposing tendencies.***[4]

Remember Rawls' point here: stability relies on the fact that it must ***fit people's motivation.*** Thus, Rawls must figure out how can this kind of motivation be possible, which means that people can and will follow just principles. This project concludes the main idea of the argument of the *sense of justice* and the argument of the *good of justice.* In this argument, Rawls borrows some key concepts from Lawrence Kohlberg, one of the most famous developmental Psychologists of Rawls' time, to develop his own "moral development theory[5]. Rawls agrees that some people may act unreasonable

---

1 Samuel Freeman, one of the most famous Rawls' students, says: "Rawls has said (in conversation) that he thinks the congruence argument was one of the most original contributions he made in A Theory of Justice and that he is puzzled why it did not attract more comment." *See* Freeman (2003), 308 (n2).
2 Rawls (1999), 5.
3 Idid., 398.
4 Idid., 398 (emphasis added by me).
5 Idid., 407–419. According to Rawls, this development can be divided into three stages: the morality of authority, the morality of the association, and the morality of principles. In first stage, people only follow

and immorally, but it does not mean that all people would not be motivated to follow his principles of justice. People have the sense of justice as a special motivation to do just, and they fail to do that is because their ability is not mature. When people in the well-ordered society develop their sense of justice well, they finally could have such an ability to act morally and just. And in the latter part, Rawls tries to justify that to do justice is fitting people's own good. Even people, however, have the sense of justice, they may not follow the principles of justice. Perhaps these principles conflict with their own goods or goals. Thus, Rawls tries to point out that these principles are the best way to fulfil their autonomy, a fully Kantian concept. Therefore, people would not have opposing motives to act against principles of justice[6]. Through these arguments, Rawls makes an account of the stability in *TJ*.

2.2 The Stability and the Role of Public Reason[7]

In the 1980 s, critics such as Communitarianism argued that Rawls presupposed an "odd" conception of the person, a Kantian person in *TJ*; however, we should not take for granted that all people should become such a "Kantian person"[8]. To avoid such a theoretical weakness, Rawls, therefore, decided to revised his original account in *TJ*.

In his *Political Liberalism* (hereafter *PL*), Rawls presents his idea as *pollical*, not *metaphysical*[9]. Due to the *reasonable Pluralism*, what Rawls means is the fact that *a plurality of conflicting reasonable comprehensive doctrines, religious, philosophical, and moral, is the normal result of its culture of free institutions*[10], Rawls, therefore, quits his Kantian project in TJ and tries to develop another way to ensure his principle possible and stable. For Rawls, the stability of his theory must not depend on some *comprehensive doctrine* because the particular *comprehensive doctrine* may conflict with another. Thus,

---

the commands form the authority (E. g. their parents) to act morally. They have no ability to reasoning how to be moral. In second, stage, people are possible to act morally because they can think form some figures in the society. Due to the association, people may feel guilt or shame, and it means that their sense of justice is much more mature than the former stage. In the final stage, people not only intend to act morally, but also start reasoning how to act morally: they have the ability of reasoning to figure out what principle they should follow, and this is the most mature stages in Rawls' *TJ*.

6 Idid., 450.

7 As Eduardo M. Peñalver mentions, there are two ways to understand Rawls' public reason: one is about the legitimacy, the other is about the stability. Most criticism focused on the legitimacy problem that whether Rawls account is just or justified in a theoretical way. On the contrary, the story about the stability, an interpretation which is more sensitive to the practical aspect, is less discussed. *See* Peñalver (2007), 515. My analysis below is also about the issue of the stability rather than legitimacy.

8 A general portrait, *see* Sandel (2005), 212–215.

9 Rawls (2005), 10.

10 Idid., 441.

Rawls would search for a *political* idea to support his principles, and that is the "public reason".

As mentioned above, the role of the public reason in *PL* is to support principles of justice without comprehensive doctrine. Therefore, there are some restricts to the content of the public reason which Rawls states:

> we are not to appeal to comprehensive religious and philosophical doctrines – to what we as individuals or members of associations see as the whole truth-nor to elaborate economic theories of general equilibrium, say, if these are in dispute.[11]

It seems that public reason is the secular reason because of the separation between religious doctrines and public reasons. However, according to Rawls, religious reason is a kind of comprehensive doctrine, but it doesn't mean that public reason is just secular reason. The restrictions of public reason are stricter than the idea of "secular". For Rawls, some secular reasons, even which liberal-wing prefers may still be the comprehensive: the account in his *TJ* is such a case that he afterward emphasizes the features of "political" in his new book, Political Liberalism. The "political" character of the public reason could be summarized in the following three points:[12]

> First, their principles apply to basic political and social institutions (the basic structure of society);
> Second, they can be presented independently from comprehensive doctrines of any kind (although they may, of course, be supported by a reasonable overlapping consensus of such doctrines); and
> Finally, they can be worked out from fundamental ideas seen as implicit in the public political culture of a constitutional regime, such as the conceptions of citizens as free and equal persons, and of society as a fair system of cooperation.

After sketching Rawls' account in *PL*, we should continue to the issue of stability, which may be the most important in *PL*. To understand the main idea in *PL*, we should compare another concept, *modus vivendi,* the treaty in the background of the tolerance of religion in the 16th and 17th centuries. The content of such a treaty is that people should not impulse their own faith or belief to others, because this may lead to conflicts and wars: it is not advantageous for either side to violate it. However, if one side is strong enough, it would be prudential for them to violate this treaty.[13]In Rawls' interpretation, the consensus on *modus vivendi* is not stable because it is on the outcome of political bargaining and the foundation of this consensus is very contingent. Thus, Rawls

11 Idid., 224.
12 Idid., 453.
13 Idid., 146f.

provides another alternative consensus: *overlapping consensus. Overlapping consensus* is different from the *modus vivendi* because the former is dependent on the reasonable foundation. For Rawls, this reasonable foundation just lies in public reason.

According to Rawls, if reasonable pluralism is the reality of our society, the consensus must not rely on some *comprehensive doctrine*. On the contrary, it should depend on another way to gain its reasonableness. And through the idea we just mentioned above: *the conceptions of citizens as free and equal persons and of society as a fair system of cooperation*, Rawls believes that the public reason, the reason which Rawls separates from the *comprehensive doctrine*, could gain this reasonableness.

3 The Obstacles of Public Reason: A Theoretical Framework

In section 2, we have overviewed the whole picture of stability in Rawls' former account (*TJ*) and his later account (*PL*). This shift, for Rawls, is to avoid a Kantian conception of the person. Thus, the idea of public reason is provided to re-ensure stability in his theory. In section 3, I will reflect Rawls project in his *PL*. I think that Rawls has offered enough key hints for us: the stability relies on the fact that it ***fits people's motivation***[14].

3.1 Rawls and Internal Reason

However, before delving into this critique, it is necessary to introduce a brief discussion about the issue between reasons and motives. This preliminary analysis will serve to illuminate the barriers that may impede the concept of public reason.

To illustrate this connection, let's begin with a practical example: choosing breakfast items at a convenience store. This scenario often requires people to make reasonable decisions among an array of choices. In such moments, people may offer reasons for their selections, such as "Drink milk for its high calcium content" or "Tea is beneficial for health." The validity of these statements rests not on personal preferences but rather resembles objective facts, independent of individual motivations or desires. Even if someone like Daniel, who lacks a preference for tea, randomly picks up a bottle of tea, his choice remains rational due to the cited health benefits.

Conversely, an alternative approach to decision-making emerges. We might sometimes assert, "I desire something sweet, so I'll select this cake for breakfast," or "As a sincere Buddhist, I should refrain from the hotdog." These statements derive from our genuine inclinations, aligning their validity with our individual perspectives. Consider

14 Rawls (1999), 398.

Amy, a sincere Buddhist, who consciously opts for a vegetable salad over a hotdog; her choice is rooted in a personally motivating factor.

The distinction between these two types of reasons lies not in their content but in their structure. While the same reason could classify as the former for person A, it might be categorized as the latter for person B. For example, the incentive to protect the environment may drive environmentally conscious citizens to favor recycled products. This motivation propels their actions. However, this same reason might not wield the same compelling force for the broader populace, who may acknowledge the reason of using recycled goods without feeling a personal imperative. This distinction, as articulated by Bernard Williams, highlights the divergence between the "external reason" that appeals to the masses and the "internal reason[15]" that resonates with environmentalists.

The theoretical disagreements between Internalism and Externalism about reason are complicated[16], so it is not the place here to discuss such a meta-ethical question about whether external reason exists. In fact, Rawls himself says little in this meta-ethical issue. The key point is that to satisfy the criteria which Rawls presents in *TJ*, the reason we provide must be a kind of internal reason: the agents must be capable of being motivated by such a reason. As mentioned above, Rawls presents in *TJ* that stability should regard ***people's motivation***. In *TJ*, the reason Rawls provides not only to describe how a principle is permittable to be promoted but also to involve ***actual or possible motivation***. This claim implies that the reason which Rawls provides must be an internal reason rather than an external one[17].

3.2 Fragility of Public Reason

Understanding the concept of stability as articulated by Rawls in TJ is crucial. It embodies two fundamental aspects: (1) The stability of a reason hinges on the extent of its support from our motivation, whether actual or potential. A reason lacking motivating power would fail to establish stability. (2) Additionally, this motivation should not be overshadowed by competing motivations.

For Rawls, public reason is a way to create and justify a special consensus for our society. This consensus is the foundation of a well-ordered society. It means that people in this society must share the similar viewpoint. If not, it would be impossible for

15 Williams (1981), 101–13.

16 A clear elucidation of this issue, *see* Seitiya (2012).

17 Prof. Jeremy Waldron also concludes that Rawls comes closest to internalism through another way. But he also mentions that Rawls' account in this dimension is normative rather than philosophical. *See* Waldron (2007), 111 f.

people to gather in a well-ordered form. The legal or political institutions should be justified and accepted in the same way to all(most) people in this society.

Besides, people not only have to justify and accept the legal and political institutions in the same way, but they must also accept this public reason with vivid and strong motivation. It could not, as Rawls points out in *PL*, be just a *modus vivendi*. On the contrary, they must accept this reason *sincerely*. It implies that people should *internalize* public reason.

As mentioned above, to maintain stability, public reason, on the one hand, should be their internal reason. In addition, they should have a *strong* motivation to accept or internalize public reason sincerely. If such a motive is not strong enough, the public reason could not have a requirement power in their motivation set to overwhelm other motivations. These are conditions that should be satisfied to maintain stability. But in Rawls' *PL* account, the idea of public reason could not fulfil these conditions.

For Rawls, we should not appeal to comprehensive religious and philosophical doctrines. However, these comprehensive religious and philosophical doctrines usually have appealed to those who believe in them: these doctrines provide a whole picture about what they should do and who they are, or we can say: a character of themselves. These doctrines are part of their personal identity and they would be strong internal reasons for those people. And if we ask those people not to seek comprehensive doctrines in the public sphere, it means that they should abandon, as Habermas points out, what they sincerely treasure most: their whole life picture and their identity[18].

According to Rawls, we should ask them to abandon their strong internal reason. But for those who believe in comprehensive doctrines, this requirement may stimulate negative motives against the idea of public reason because it shocks their identity. That is the first potential obstacle.

In fact, Rawls has noticed this problem. In his "*The Idea of Public Reason Revisited*", Rawls provides a "wider view of public reason" and says that we don't need to abandon all sorts of religious or comprehensive doctrines. Those doctrines may be introduced into a public political discussion if they can provide a reason not solely in their comprehensive points but also provide some public ideas[19]. If those people who wholly believe in religious or comprehensive doctrines can provide some religious or comprehensive opinions which fit the public reason, their opinions, in Rawls' "wider view of public reason", are acceptable and reasonable. It means that those people need to *transfer* their religious or comprehensive opinions into a public form[20]: they should present their original doctrines in a new public way. However, there may be some possible obstacles in this "transformation".

18 *See* Habermas (1995), 126.
19 *See* Rawls (2005), 462.
20 *See* Waldron (2012), 863.

For those people who believe in religious or comprehensive doctrines, reasons for political or legal institutions they prefer are their "internal reasons", and those internal reasons are just religious or comprehensive doctrines. For them, their "transformation" is to provide a reason which they do not wholly believe (or maybe they do not believe at all). There are two potential problems here. First, their transformation may fall: their religious or comprehensive doctrines may not be present in a public form smoothly. Thus, their public justification falls. In this situation, those people may feel upset (or angry), and it may stimulate some negative emotions and motivations against the other side (those who use public reasons well). Second, even though they can transfer their doctrines in a "public form", in their viewpoint, what they present now is less compelling to them[21]. What they provide in public, just as Dworkin points out[22], is not the thing they *sincerely* believe: those reasons are not their "true" internal reasons are in their minds. "Belief", as a motive-related concept, plays a unique role in our thought: to believe something implies a disposition or motivation to act on this belief.[23] Although we could provide a reason to keep them from presenting their religious belief in public, this disposition or motivation is still in their minds. And it's not allowed to ask people to abandon their belief in the liberal society. For them, what they really believe is not the things they present in public, and then there may be no reliable power of motivation in their motivation set to support it. If the consensus is overlapping in this way, it is still fragile.

4 Case Study: Same-sex Marriage Debates in Taiwan

4.1 Background

On May 17, 2019, the Legislative Yuan of Taiwan passed the *Act for the Implementation of Judicial Yuan Interpretation No. 748*. Under this law, same-sex couples are granted legal rights to inheritance and medical decision-making. Additionally, same-sex couples are required to adhere to the obligations of the monogamous system. As a result, Taiwan made history by becoming the first Asian country to legalize same-sex marriage.[24]

However, the journey was not without obstacles. Like other countries, the same-sex marriage in Taiwan has been very controversial for a long time. Many people and NGOs engage in this discussion, leading to vigorous debates that reverberate across

---

21 Peñalver (2007), 535.
22 Dworkin (2006), 65.
23 Carter (2014), 1213 f.
24 Nonetheless, during that period, the legal status of same-sex couples (referred to as Article 2 Relationship) remained distinct from heterosexual marriage. For instance, until 2023, same-sex couples were not granted the right to jointly adopt filiation, indicating a disparity in legal privileges. A critical introduction about this issue, *see* Chen (2019).

Taiwanese society. Particularly for those not directly involved in the discourse on same-sex marriage, the public discussions on social media platforms often represent one of the primary channels through which they access information about this matter. Indeed, these debates wield a considerable influence over people's decision-making processes, irrespective of their stance – whether positive or negative – on the issue.

Among these participants, one group stands out prominently: the Family Guardian Coalition (FGC, 台灣宗教團體愛護家庭大聯盟), a prominent right-wing non-governmental organization rooted in the Christian faith[25]. Owing to their religious background, FGC does not accept Same-sex marriage at all[26]. Throughout these debates, the FGC often presents reasons and perspectives on marriage that are unconventional and divergent from those of others. Notably, they contend that same-sex marriage is "Inhumane, immoral, and harmful to health[27]." Many individuals find these assertions incredulous and subject them to ridicule. Those opposing the FGC often find their stance to be unreasonable. Critics have taken aim at the FGC, asserting that all participants in public discussions should adhere to the principle of providing a "public reason," a well-known concept attributed to Rawls. For example, Kris Chu (朱家安), a prominent public writer on the Internet, is particularly vocal in criticizing the FGC. He frequently asserts that the FGC's eccentricity stems from their reluctance to present a public reason devoid of religious beliefs[28]. Kris Chu's claim implies that public discourse necessitates the provision of arguments grounded in the public domain. Such a claim was popular on social media and the Internet, garnering widespread acceptance. Consequently, the camp aligned with liberal viewpoints appeared to have gained the upper hand in the debate, at least within the realm of online discourse.

On May 24, 2017, the Justices of Constitutional Court issued Interpretation No. 748, declaring part of Taiwan's Civil Code, which in essence prohibits same-sex marriage, unconstitutional. This news cheered the liberal-wings up. It seems that liberal-wings' "*public reason model*" really works[29].

However, the more radical conflict quickly came. After Interpretation No. 748, FGC and their partners (E.g. 下一代幸福聯盟, Coalition for the Happiness of our Next Generation) promoted new voting proposals against same-sex marriage and claimed that "*Let Marriage and Family Matters be decided by the people* (婚姻家庭,人民決定)".

---

25 More detailed about this NGO's background and impact, *see* Ho (2020) 147–150.
26 Surely, the context for Taiwanese against same-sex marriage may be more complicated: traditional Chinese culture from a Confucianism may also play a role in this issue. However, in Rawls' theoretical framework, even such a Confucianism can also be a comprehensive doctrine. Besides, an empirical study using Taiwan's dataset also shows the connection between the religious belief and the unfriendly attitude to the same-sex marriage, *see* Tang/Chang (2021).
27 *See* the report from You (2016).
28 *See* generally Chu (2016).
29 For example, Prof. Chueh-An Yen, a leading liberal legal scholar in National Taiwan University, was optimistic and said that the "public reason" was frequently used in these debates. *See* Yen (2017), 93.

And the result of the referendum in 2018 really shock: almost 75 percent of voters voted "yes" on FGC's proposals[30]. Dur to this unfriendly signal from the society of Taiwan, many LGBT people felt great pain and therefore killed themselves after the referendum of 2018[31]. It seems that public reason, a well-known Rawlsian concept, did not ensure the stability, which Rawls concern most. On the contrary, it finally led to trouble: the failure in the referendum in 2018 seemed as an example, and the conflict between the two sides gets much more radical after those public debates. Additionally, according to a survey from TEDS (Taiwan's Election and Democratization Study), even the *Act for Implementation of J. Y. Interpretation No. 748* was finally passed by the Legislative Yuan in 2019, there were still 38 % of people who do not support at all and 15.2 % people who do not support this Act[32]. It looks like public reason model did not ensure citizens agreed or solved the problem – the conflict still exists.

4.2 Some Potential Doubts

To some readers, the preceding paragraphs might lead to confusion, prompting them to question whether the discussion pertains to family law's specific issue – legalizing same-sex marriage – rather than delving into the broader concepts of justice principles. Addressing this object of inquiry, a crucial query emerges: Does Rawls indeed intend to extend his "public reason" to this context? Additionally, sceptics may wonder why NGOs and citizens, not being governmental entities, should be bound by the constraints of public reasons. The significance of these questions lies in their potential to shape our analysis. If both questions receive negative answers, the discourse on public reason might be irrelevant and inappropriate for this case.

Rawls' response to these inquiries is affirmative. Within Rawls' framework, the realm of public reasons primarily encompasses what he terms "basic political and social institutions," and the family is unequivocally regarded as one of these fundamental institutions.[33] Legal structures governing the family are closely intertwined with numerous fundamental rights. Furthermore, contemplating the permissible forms of family within the legal framework necessitates envisioning oneself *as a legislator.* It means that these people indeed talking about what is most reasonable way for the statutes[34] (of marriage); therefore, people in these debates, indeed as Rawls emphasis, is arguing *as a collective body, and is exercising the final political and coercive power over*

30 An overview of the movement of FGC and their partner, *see* Kuan (2021).
31 More detail information about the LGBT's suicidal rate after the referendum, *see* Lin et al (2019).
32 *See* TEDS. (2019).
33 Rawls (2005), 466–474.
34 Idid., 444 f.

on another in enacting laws[35]. Consequently, a valid and compelling rationale exists for examining the intricate interplay between public reason and the ongoing dialogue surrounding the legalization of same-sex marriage".

4.3 Analysis

To display my analysis, I will first address the reasons put forth by the conservative wings. These reasons, as outlined in an article published on their official website, can be summarized as follows:[36]:

A. The impossibility of fertility within same-sex marriage unions stands as a defining contrast between same-sex relationships and traditional marriage.
B. Concerns are raised about the potential adverse impact of same-sex marriage on family continuity and demographic growth within Taiwan.
C. The contention is made that same-sex marriage does not align with the best interests of children.
D. Same-sex marriage is not a universally recognized human right.

My attempt here is not to answer whether these reasons are correct. Even though these reasons may not be correct, they, at the first glance, are provided in a "public form": These reasons seem not to appeal for any comprehensive doctrines, especially in a religious sense[37]. However, as we just analysis in section 3, these reasons are fragility and unpowerful in their motivation set.

First, under the constraint of public reason, people need to "transform" their voice into a public form, and some people may fail and therefore be ignored. This transformation is not an easy job, requiring an array of knowledge or cultural resources; as a result, many folk country people who embrace Confucianism or traditional Chinese culture will not be (re)presented in these public debates and then will be ignored easily. In fact, some citizens from rurality once complained that they were not regarded as partners to communicating during discussion[38]. For these people, since their voices are not (re)presented directly in these discussions, they do not have a consensus in this political issue with other side; for them, their moral motivation are still constituted by their own comprehensive doctrine about marriage; and they, therefore, will not have a strong moral motivation to overwhelm their personal or private interests. Besides, those people may feel upset while feeling ignored, and it may cause negative

35 Idid., 214.
36 Coalition for the Happiness of our Next Generation (2014).
37 *See* Lai (2017).
38 *See* the report from Yen (2016).

motivations against the other side (those who use public reasons to support same-sex marriage). As we mention above, those who be excluded from the public domain may be upset. Even we could exclude their opinions form the public domain, their anger and other negative motivation remain in their own private sphere. Their belief is one of the constitutive parts of their thought and it's hard for them to abandon. Those excluded "loser" would gather as groups and start to discuss their viewpoints together. The members in these groups believe that what they wholly believe is good and those things in the public domain is bad, they also exchange their viewpoints frequently and regularly. Unfortunately, due to be excluded from the public domain, they are not welcome to engage into the public discussion and then they have less opportunities to gain some "opposite opinions" to challenge their own partial opinions. Thus, the effects of information and reputation cascades in these like-mind groups, according to Cass Sunstein' studies[39], would leads to the polarization and lead to more negative motivation. We could say that the practice of the public reason may generate the polarization and would be self-defeated to the idea of stability[40] (the whole picture about these people's motivation structure, please see *Table 1, row2*).

However, even though those people can transform their voices into a public form and then engage in these debates, there are still some obstacles in their motivation structure. Roughly speaking, their reasons are not totally transformed in a public sense, and therefore, will be attacked by those liberal wings easily.

In fact, the core argument for conservative wings lies in the value of family, or in an accurate sense, the value of children. In *Reason A*, they argue that the crucial element of marriage is *fertility*, which implies that one of the core values of the family is to birth children, and *Reason B*, therefore, can also be derived from it. Besides, for the conservative wing, the value of family not only lies in the possibility of the birth of children but also lies on how children in these families can live well, which constitutes the essence of their *Reason C*. To sum up, these reasons imply a comprehensive doctrine, a conception of good about *what a good family is*.

Since these reasons, indeed, imply on a comprehensive doctrine, we can provide two kinds of interpretation. To take the *Reason C*, for example, *Reason C* argues that same-sex marriage will product a "unhappy result" to those children raised by same-sex marriage couples. Thus, to against such a claim, liberal wings usually provided an array of happy examples or researches result from the studies of social work. On one hand, if conservative wings sincerely care about "best interest of children" as they claim, they should take these "counter examples" seriously, or even should revise their claims. However, they usually ignored these counter-examples, which means that the

39 *See* Sunstein (2002). To link the connection between the exclusion and the problem, *see* Peñalver (2007), 538.

40 To put the problem of the stability and the polarization in a theoretical discussion, *see* Peñalver (2007), 540. A more general and theoratical discussion about this issue, *see* Talisse (2009).

"best interest of children", in a way, is only an external reason and therefore cannot generate a real motivational power in their mind (see *Table 1, row3, Interpretation I*). But on the other hand, as these conservative wings have their own "conception of good" when they are understanding "children's best interest", we, in an accurate sense, can say that these reasons they provided are not public reason; therefore, since these reasons are not public reason, they cannot eventually guarantee the stability that Rawls really cares about (see *Table 1, row4, Interpretation II*).

Based on the analysis above, we can observe that emphasizing on public reason does not necessarily ensure stability. The reason for this lack of assurance lies in the fact that public reason is insufficient to ensure strong and consistent motivations among people. This is particularly evident because public reason must exclude comprehensive doctrines, potentially leading actors to endorse these laws or policies based on external reasons. And the case of legalizing same-sex marriage in Taiwan, specifically the backlash during the 2018 referendum, vividly illustrates the failure of Rawls' account of public reason.

Table 1 People's Motivation Structures

Agent	Moral Motivation (sense of Justice)	Non-Moral Motivation	Result
Citizens from Rurality Transforming unsuccessfully and therefore be ignored	Still constituted by their own comprehensive doctrine, no power	The Consensus against their own belief. More negative Motives due to exclusion.	Their Moral motives has no real power to overcome Non-Moral Motives.
Progressive Conservative Participants Transforming unsuccessfully and usually be objected by Liberal wings	**Interpretation (I):** provide public reason in an external sense	The Consensus against their own belief	Their Moral motives has no real power to overcome Non-Moral Motives.
	Interpretation (II): do not provide public reason	No real conflict. Due the exclusion, their view will be polarized.	No real conflict, no consensus

5 Conclusion

This paper aims to reflect the idea of public reason from a "Rawlsian" perspective. To do this, I've used Rawls' idea of stability and expanded it to consider a more pessimistic view of public reason. While Rawls' original notion of finding a balance between motives is appealing, an interesting conflict arises when we compare this with his concept of public reason. It seems that in his eagerness to distance himself from his Kantian interpretation, Rawls might give up his foundational concept in *TJ* too soon. However, a careful analysis shows that the idea of public reason doesn't always ensure stability. This claim is supported not just through theory but also through a relevant case study from Taiwan that highlights the inherent instability within the framework of public reason. By examining the motivations and reasons involved, we get a clearer grasp of the heart of the issue. At the core of Rawls' public reason is the exclusion of strong religious and ideological beliefs. Ironically, this exclusion could encourage people to offer external reasons or even weaker internal reasons. An illustrative example of this can be seen in Taiwan's discussion about same-sex marriage, where the boundaries of public reason were tested. On the flip side, even when individuals try to adjust their comprehensive beliefs to fit the public sphere, their reasons still mainly come from their personal understanding of what's good. These challenges, whether they're apparent or potential, pose crucial obstacles to Rawls' vision.

In this paper, I illustrate Rawls' concept public reason while also exploring potential obstacles through his idea of stability. Rawls' original emphasis on achieving balance in motivations is full of wisdom. To follow this perspective, it's crucial to be more attuned to people's thoughts and feelings. A nuanced understanding of human behavior and decision-making is essential to grasping how actions influence others. Thus, how to craft an impassioned reason that can resonate in our society is not avoided. Although this effort certainly presents a significant challenge, it's crucial for realizing Rawls' well-order society.

Bibliography

Carter, Stephen L. (2014): "The Challenge of Belief. In: Bonston University Law Review 94, 1213–1223.

Chen, Chao-Ju (2019): "A Same-sex Marriage that is Not the Same: Taiwan's Legal Recognition of Same-sex Unions and Affirmation of Marriage Normativity". In: Australian Journal of Asian Law 20 (1), 59–68.

Chu, Kris (2016): Will God Say No? A Philosophical View on Same Sex Marriage. Taipei: Comma Press. (In Chinese).

Coalition for the Happiness of our Next Generation (2014): "Preserving the value of family; "Against Same-sex marriage". In: Coalition for the Happiness of our Next Generation. https://web.archive.org/web/20210806093437/https://taiwanfamily.com/related-posts/artice02, accessed 19.11.2023. (in Chinese)

Dworkin, Ronald (2006): Is Democracy Possible Here?: Principles for a New Political Debate. New Jersey: Princeton University Press.

Freeman, Samuel (2003): "Congruence and the Good of Justice. In Samuel Freeman (Ed.), The Cambridge Companion To Rawls. Cambridge: Cambridge University Press, 277–315.

Habermas, Jürgen (1995): "Reconciliation Through the Public Use of Reason: Remarks on John Rawls's Political Liberalism". In: The Journal of Philosophy 92, 109–131.

Ho, Ming-sho (2020): "The Religion-Based Conservative Countermovement in Taiwan: Origin, Tactics and Impacts". In David Chiavacci, Simona Grano & Julia Obinger (Eds.), Civil Society and the State in Democratic East Asia: Between Entanglement and Contention in Post High Growth. Netherlands: Amsterdam University Press, 277–315.

Kuan, Hsiaowei (2021): "Taiwan's 'Civil Code v Special Law' Debate in the Same-Sex Marriage Controversy: A Populist Threat to the Rule of Law?". In Brian Christopher Jones (Ed.), Democracy and Rule of Law in China's Shadow, Oxford: Hart Publishing, 105–128.
Lai, Ten-Herng (2017): "Saving the Traditional Chinese, Family Guardian Coalition, the Dress code Conservatism and the Hypocrisy". In: Watchout Philosophy Group (Ed.), Reading Philosophy in The Modern World, Taipei: Athena Press, 149–156. (In Chinese).
Lin, I. Hsuan, Ko, Nai-Ying, Huang, Yu-Te, Chen, Mu-Hong, Lu, Wei-Hsin, & Yen, Cheng-Fang (2019): "Effect of Same-Sex Marriage Referendums on the Suicidal Ideation Rate among Nonheterosexual People in Taiwan". In: International Journal of Environmental Research and Public Health 16(18), 3456.
Peñalver, Eduardo M. (2007): "Is Public Reason Counterproductive?" In: West Virginia Law Review 110(1), 515–544.
Rawls, John. (1999): A Theory of Justice (Revised Edition ed., 1971). Cambridge, Massachusetts: Harvard University Press.
Rawls, John. (2005): Political Liberalism (Expended Edition ed., 1996). New York: Columbia University Press.
Sandel, Michael J. (2005): Public Philosophy: Essays on Morality in Politics. Cambridge, Massachusetts: Harvard University Press.
Seitiya, Kieren. (2012): "Introduction: Internal Reasons". In: Kieran Setiya & Hille Paakkunainen (Eds.), Internal Reasons: Contemporary Readings. Cambridge, Massachusetts: MIT Press, 1–34.
Talisse, Robert B. (2009): "Dilemmas of public reason: pluralism, polarization, and instability". In: Thorn Brooks & Fabian Freyenhagen (Eds.), The Legacy of John Rawls. New York: Continuum, 107–124.
Tang, Cheng-Yi, & Chang, Jen-Ho. (2021): "Moderating Role of Religion Between Implicit and Explicit Attitudes on Opinions Same-Sex Marriage: A Study from Taiwan Implicit Association Test Database". In: Bulletin of Educational Psychology 53(1), 151–172. (In Chinese).
TEDS. (2019): "TEDS2019 Telephone and Mobile Phone Interview Survey of the Presidential Satisfaction – The Twenty-Eighth Wave". In: Taiwan's Election and Democratization Study, http://teds.nccu.edu.tw/teds_plan/list.php?g_isn=133&g_tid=0&g_cid=5, accessed. (in Chinese)
Waldron, Jeremy (2007): "Public Reason and Justification in the Courtroom.: In: Journal of Law, Philosophy and Culture 1(1), 107–134.
Waldron, Jeremy. (2012): "Two-Way Translation: The Ethics of Engaging with Religious Contributions in Public Deliberation". In: Mercer Law Review 63, 845–868.
Williams, Bernard. (1981): Moral Luck. Cambridge: Cambridge University Press.
Yen, Chueh-An (2017): "An analysis from Institutionalism and Anti-Discrimination. In: Taiwan Law Journal, 328, 96. (in Chinese)
Yen, Zen-Kai. (2016): "'Pro Same-sex Marriage movement and FGC only debated in Taipei Urban' Yang Chang-zhen: The elders in the countryside were not regarded as partners for communicating". In: The Storm Media, 18.12.2016. https://www.storm.mg/article/202691, accessed 19.11.2023. (in Chinese)

You, Yi-Jhen (2016): "FGC: same-sex marriage is Inhumane, immoral, and harmful to health". In: New Talk news, 24.10.2016.https://newtalk.tw/news/view/2016-10-24/78454, accessed 19.11.2023. (in Chinese)

Kuan-Ting Chen
Cornell Law School (USA)/ College of Law, National Chengchi University (Taiwan)
Kc2283@cornell.edu

Decriminalising Male Homosexual Acts, Protecting Opposite-Sex Marriage

An Analysis of Singapore's Shift in the Stance towards Homosexuality

SEOW HON TAN

Abstract: Singapore's previous criminal regulation of male homosexual conduct has been the subject of much scrutiny, both within the country and internationally. Previously, acts of 'gross indecency' between male persons, whether in private or in public, had been criminalised under Singapore's Penal Code in a provision inherited from colonial times. The law was retained in 2007 even though the government said in parliament that the law would not be 'proactively enforced'. The law was finally repealed in 2023 alongside the introduction of a constitutional provision to safeguard the laws and policies related to opposite-sex marriage. This article examines the shift in Singapore's stance and approach towards the regulation of homosexual conduct and explains the societal forces and legal thinking underlying the shift.

Keywords: homosexuality, same-sex marriage, traditional marriage, LGBTQ+, 377A

1 Introduction

Singapore's regulation of male homosexual conduct has been the subject of much scrutiny, both within the country and internationally. Previously, acts of 'gross indecency' between male persons, whether in private or in public, had been criminalised under section 377A of Singapore's Penal Code [Section 377A].[1] Section 377A was inherited from the time when Singapore was a British colony. It was retained amidst much controversy after an extensive criminal law review in 2007. In retaining the provision, the government said in parliament that it would not be 'proactively enforced'.[2] Activist groups continued to campaign for repeal of the provision after parliament's decision in 2007. Lawsuits to challenge the constitutionality of Section 377A were mounted unsuccessfully in the Singapore courts. The Attorney-General then publicly represent-

1 Penal Code 1871.

2 Parliamentary Debates Singapore (23 October 2007), col 2401.

ed in 2018 that private same-sex acts between consenting male persons would not be prosecuted.[3] The law remained the subject of much controversy. Section 377A was finally repealed in 2023 after extensive dialogues[4] between the government and interested parties, which included LGBTQ+ groups, community and religious leaders, and youths. Alongside the repeal, there was a constitutional amendment to protect the laws and policies supporting the institution of opposite-sex marriage.[5]

This article examines Singapore's approach to the regulation of male homosexual conduct in the last two decades, analysing the reasons for the shift from continued criminalisation of male homosexual acts to the decision to protect opposite-sex marriage in the Constitution of the Republic of Singapore [Singapore's Constitution].[6] Part 2 examines the legislative move to retain Section 377A in 2007. Part 3 considers some of the social and legal moves to challenge Section 377A after the 2007 parliamentary decision. Parts 4 and 5 examine the reasons underlying the government's decision to decriminalise male homosexual acts alongside a constitutional amendment to protect opposite-sex marriage and the intended effects of such moves. The conclusion in Part 6 summarises more broadly Singapore's counter-cultural approach in contrast to worldwide trends in relation to LGBTQ+ rights.

2 Section 377A and the 2007 Parliamentary Review

Prior to its repeal, Section 377A of the Penal Code made it an offence for male persons to commit acts of gross indecency with other male persons. The proscription made no distinction between public and private acts. The Penal Code, which contained much of Singapore's criminal law, was retained after Singapore ceased to be a British colony and became an independent nation in 1965. A previous version of it was based on the Indian Penal Code, which was first drafted by the Indian Law Commission over which a British politician, Lord Macaulay, presided. Section 377A became part of Singapore law in 1938, when Singapore was a British colony. Section 377A was based on a British provision that was made law in 1885.[7]

Before the extensive 2007 criminal law review, the former Section 377 of the Penal Code criminalised sexual acts 'against the order of nature' with any man, woman, or animal. The government revealed in 2004 in parliament that there had not been prosecution for consensual oral sex in private between a male and a female for many years,

---

3 Attorney-General's Chambers (2018).
4 Tham, Yuen-C (2022).
5 Constitution of the Republic of Singapore (Amendment No. 3) Act 2022.
6 Constitution of the Republic of Singapore (2020 Rev Ed).
7 Criminal Law Amendment Act 1885.

'except in cases involving minors or those who are physically or mentally vulnerable'.[8] The former Section 377 was repealed in 2007 and replaced with a provision covering sexual acts with corpses, while bestiality was covered under a new Section 377B.

Section 377A was not a source of controversy for many decades although the statistics released for a ten-year period showed that as many as 185 persons had been convicted between 1997 and 2006. A controversy over LGBTQ+ issues which implicated the Singapore government briefly ensued in Singapore around 2003 when the then-Prime Minister Goh Chok Tong revealed, in an interview with Time Magazine, that the government had employed homosexuals in sensitive government positions.[9] At that time, while the majority in Singapore was said to be largely morally conservative on issues of sexuality, LGBTQ+ themes had been featured in theatre productions. In 2007, a teacher in a prestigious boys' school in Singapore admitted on his blog that he was gay.[10] The fact that this 'coming out' made the news perhaps indicated the overall conservative stance of many in the nation.

A debate in the public square ensued before the parliamentary debate in 2007. The government sought feedback via an online portal on the proposed criminal law reforms. The majority who gave feedback called for the retention of the law in what the then-Prime Minister Lee Hsien Loong [Lee] thought was a very organized campaign.[11] Online petitions were started by those seeking retention as well as those seeking repeal, culminating in an online petition for repeal being presented in parliament by a nominated member of parliament [MP] arguing that the provision was an 'unconstitutional derogation from the constitutional guarantee of equality and equal protection of the law as set out in Article 12(1) of the Constitution'.[12]

Section 377A was retained in 2007 by parliament. The debate over its retention took centre stage even though there were many other provisions of the Penal Code being updated and added. The debate was perhaps one of the most polarized in the history of Singapore's parliament, though its retention was a foregone conclusion as the ruling party in parliament was moving its retention and did not lift the party whip for its MPs to vote at will. The then-Senior Minister for Law Ho Peng Kee as well as Lee stated the government's position in their speeches, while 15 other MPs commented on Section 377A, with 11 supporting its retention.[13] Lee decided that as society was not ready for its repeal, a compromise would be achieved through retaining Section 377A with the understanding that there would be no 'pro-active enforcement' of the law. This was

8 Parliamentary Debates Singapore (6 January 2004).
9 Price, David C (2003).
10 Jacob, Paul (2007).
11 Parliamentary Debates Singapore (23 October 2007) (Prime Minister Lee Hsien Loong). For an analysis of the 2007 parliamentary debates, see Tan, Seow Hon (2009).
12 Parliamentary Debates Singapore (22 October 2007) (Mr Siew Kum Hong).
13 Parliamentary Debates Singapore (23 October 2007).

thought to give homosexuals space for personal fulfilment while signalling society's endorsement of heteronormativity.

The arguments made in parliament for repeal included the following. First, it was argued there was no proper ground for criminalization of consensual adult same-sex acts which did not cause any tangible harm.[14] Second, the law was thought to be discriminatory towards male homosexuals, who would be regarded as criminals.[15] Third, it was argued that the perceived immorality of same-sex acts stemmed from religious beliefs that were not publicly accessible reasons and therefore could not be the foundation of law in a secular pluralist democracy.[16] Fourth, the retention of such a law was a hindrance to Singapore becoming an open and inclusive society that was attractive from a more cosmopolitan point of view.[17]

The main argument for retaining the law was straightforwardly based on heteronormativity. The law was seen as a moral signpost as well as a legal safeguard.[18] If male same-sex acts were criminalised, there would be a bar in principle from moving in the manner that other jurisdictions in the world had – of approving same-sex marriages and recognising other LGBTQ+ rights such as adoption of children, according of legal benefits related to housing and tax, and so on. While heteronormativity might have carried a negative connotation in some jurisdictions, it was thought that the majority in Singapore viewed 'a heterosexual stable family' as a 'social norm' which was desirable to teach in schools and which parents sought to foster in their children.[19]

3 Aftermath of 2007 Parliamentary Debates

3.1 Activism and Legal Challenges

After 2007, social activism on LGBTQ+ issues accelerated. Amongst other things, a non-profit movement Pink Dot Sg[20] organised yearly events and another group called Ready4Repeal[21] held its first townhall in 2018 to urge the public to take their stories related to such issues to their MPs.

Two sets of legal challenges were also mounted in the courts.

14 Parliamentary Debates Singapore (22 October 2007) (Mr Siew Kum Hong).
15 Ibid.
16 Parliamentary Debates Singapore (22 October 2007) (Mr Hri Kumar).
17 Parliamentary Debates Singapore (22 October 2007) (Mr Siew Kum Hong).
18 Parliamentary Debates Singapore (22 October 2007) (Mr Christopher de Souza).
19 Parliamentary Debates Singapore (23 October 2007) (Prime Minister Lee Hsien Loong).
20 http://pinkdot.sg, accessed 28.12.23.
21 http://ready4repeal.com, Access Date 28.12.23.

The first set of challenges[22] involved Tan Eng Hong, who was arrested for engaging in oral sex in a cubicle in a public toilet of a shopping complex and was initially charged under Section 377A, and Lim Meng Suang and his partner Kenneth Chee Mun-Leon who had been in a 'romantic and sexual relationship'[23] with each other since 1997. Tan Eng Hong's charge was later substituted with another charge under Section 294(a) of the Penal Code, concerning the commission of an obscene act in a public place, but he pursued the case to challenge the constitutionality of Section 377A. Lim Meng Suang and Kenneth Chee said they experienced discrimination which was reinforced by Section 377A, the effect of which was in their view to label them as criminals regardless of whether it was enforced. With Section 377A, it was 'always at the back of their minds that if authorities wanted to, they could arrest them and charge them'[24] under Section 377A. The challenge of constitutionality was raised under Articles 9 and 12 of the Singapore Constitution. Article 9 concerned the right to life and personal liberty. The Court of Appeal dismissed the idea of a constitutional right to privacy or personal autonomy under the notion of 'personal liberty', essentially rejecting the approach of the United States Supreme Court towards the due process clauses of the United States Constitution.[25] Article 12 concerned the right to equality and freedom from discrimination. In deciding Section 377A was not discriminatory, the Court of Appeal applied Singapore's reasonable classification test, determining that the classification was based on intelligible differentia (singling out males committing acts of gross indecency with other males) which bore a rational relation to the objective of the law, which was to enforce societal morality. The Court of Appeal also held that the courts were not to be 'mini-legislatures'[26] and could not inquire into the legitimacy of the objectives the legislature had chosen to pursue. That said, on occasion, the differentia could be so illogical as to be unintelligible, such as for example if the law banned women from driving, in which case the law would be unconstitutional for violating Article 12.[27]

The second set of challenges resulted in the Court of Appeal's decision in *Tan Seng Kee v Attorney-General*.[28] The Court of Appeal dismissed the case on the ground of the lack of locus standi on the parts of the plaintiffs, as they could not be prosecuted. The challenges were raised in relation to Articles 9, 12, and 14 of the Singapore Constitution. The Court of Appeal came to the decision that none of these were violated. In relation to Article 9(1), the Court of Appeal reiterated its previous decision not to 'trespass onto Parliament's territory'[29] by assessing whether a law was 'fair, just and

22 *Lim Meng Suang v Attorney-General* (2014). For an analysis, see Tan, Seow Hon (2016).
23 Ibid., para 15.
24 *Lim Meng Suang v Attorney-General* (2013), para 7.
25 *Lim Meng Suang v Attorney-General* (2014), paras 44–45.
26 Ibid., 70 and 77.
27 Ibid., para 114.
28 *Tan Seng Kee v Attorney-General* (2022).
29 Ibid., para 264.

reasonable' before it could be regarded as constitutional. In relation to Article 14(1)(a) which protected freedom of speech and expression, the Court of Appeal dismissed the argument that 'acts of gross indecency' were regarded as expression protected under Article 14, which in its context was taken primarily to protect 'speech' rather than 'expression' of intimacy between persons.[30] Moreover, Section 377A could not be said to have a chilling effect on gay rights advocacy.[31] But the critical difference from the earlier set of cases was that the Court of Appeal suggested there were in fact two different approaches to the 'reasonable classification test' which was used to decide if a law violated Article 12's equality provision, and declined to decide which of the two approaches it would adopt, leaving it for 'further reflection on a suitable occasion in the future'.[32] The different approaches would not be discussed in this article, but the refusal of the court to decide proved to be a motivating factor which led the government after the case to surmise that there was a significant legal risk that the Court of Appeal might find Section 377A to be unconstitutional vis-à-vis Article 12.[33]

3.2 Effectiveness of Section 377A as a Safeguard Against Advancement in LGBTQ+ Rights

The objective of retaining Section 377A as a moral signpost was raised in the 2007 debates, even though such an objective might have been highly dubitable in countries which regard a failure to accord LGBTQ+ rights as morally repugnant and discriminatory behaviour. The effectiveness of law serving as a form of moral signalling may arguably vary from culture to culture. In a more conformist culture, or in a society which defers to or respects governmental authority, the influence of law on morality may be more pronounced. Even in less conformist or deferential cultures, the influence of law cannot be denied: such influence is the very reason for activists to campaign for the removal of criminal laws even if they are not enforced, because of the stigmatisation involved when an act is criminalised.

Moral signalling aside, the existence of Section 377A, rendering homosexual acts between male persons illegal, entailed various consequences on principle. For example, it was thought that, on principle, same-sex marriage and civil unions could not be legalised, adoption could not be available to homosexual couples, schools set up in Singapore and regulated by Singapore law would continue to teach from a perspective of heteronormativity, and higher age ratings could be stipulated for media content depicting homosexuality. However, the expectation that Section 377A would serve as a

30 Ibid., paras 277–285.
31 Ibid., paras 295–299.
32 Ibid., para 329.
33 Shanmugam, K (2022), para 128.

safeguard on principle to stop other legal developments in relation to LGBTQ+ rights was not always met. In 2018, the Singapore High Court granted an adoption order to a male individual who sought to adopt his own biological son conceived through an overseas surrogacy arrangement. He intended to coparent with his homosexual partner. This was despite the court recognizing that there was a public policy, revealed in the retention of Section 377A in 2007, as well as section 12(1) of the Women's Charter, opposed to same-sex family units, whether these units consisted of one or two homosexual parents. The court noted that an adoption order would have an appreciable effect on traditional parenting norms in Singapore, which Lee was eager to preserve in 2007. The policy against same-sex family units would be violated by the order. However, the policy did not arise from the relevant statute relating to adoption of children. The central policy in the relevant statute pertaining to adoption, the child's welfare, prevailed.[34] The court thus narrowly interpreted the most pertinent legal policies implicated by a statute, by giving a much greater weight to the legal policy directly found in the statute within which the provision was situated, instead of reading the several statutes as closely associated. But, surely, adoption is not an isolated act. A family unit necessarily forms after adoption, parenting follows, values are imparted to the child, and so on.[35] With the court's narrow interpretation of pertinent legal policies that it had to give effect to, Section 377A failed to do the work that some expected of the provision. This was another factor that might have led to the government's change in tactic as far as its objective of preventing further changes in LGBTQ+ rights was concerned, in view of the perceived moral conservatism in the nation, in the 2023 amendments.

4 Lead-Up to the 2023 Amendments

In 2018, the Attorney-General declared publicly that he would not prosecute consenting adult male persons who had committed private homosexual acts, in the exercise of prosecutorial discretion, as it was not in the public interest to prosecute such acts. This move was significant because the legal effect of Lee's statement in Parliament in 2007 that Section 377A would not be pro-actively enforced had, until then, been dubitable in view of the separation of powers of the different branches of government. The Attorney-General's prosecutorial discretion could not be fettered by Lee's statement in Parliament. But even after the Attorney-General's declaration, a question remained, though, as to the binding effect in law of the declaration, and whether the Attorney-General could change his mind. This question was resolved by the Court of Appeal in *Tan Seng Kee v Attorney-General* when it held that the Attorney-Gener-

34 *UKM v. Attorney-General* (2018).
35 For a critique of this decision, see Tan, Seow Hon (2019).

al's articulation of prosecutorial policy concerning a general class of persons – namely, homosexual men[36] – to give effect to the public policy reflected in the Lee's speech in 2007 created a substantive legitimate expectation on the part of individuals of the class concerning sexual activity between two consenting adult men engaging in the acts in private.[37] Section 377A was said to be unenforceable in its entirety so that the political package envisaged by the Prime Minister would be given effect to and homosexual men would not face the legal uncertainty and consequent sense of harassment.[38] Reasonable notice should be given in clear and unambiguous terms if the Attorney-General wished to resile from his representation.[39] The fact that Section 377A remained on the law books remained a sore point, however, as opponents noted that gays were stigmatised as criminals for private sexual behaviour which was important to them as expressions of intimacy.

Although the Court of Appeal determined that male homosexuals had no locus standi to challenge the constitutionality of Section 377A as there was no real or credible threat of prosecution,[40] the government remained concerned that other routes existed for the judicial finding that Section 377A was unconstitutional.[41] While the government did not give this particular example, this might occur if some other law or policy that differentiated between male homosexuals and others was challenged. For example, if the definition of marriage under the Interpretation Act or section 12 of the Women's Charter were challenged for violating Article 12 of the Singapore Constitution, a substantive argument might be made in defence of the definition of marriage – that same-sex marriage could not be legally permissible as it necessarily involved acts criminalised under Section 377A. If so, the legal validity of Section 377A would become an issue that the courts had to examine. In any case, the government determined that there was a significant legal risk of the courts finding that Section 377A was unconstitutional. In *Tan Seng Kee v Attorney-General*, even though it did not have to do so as it had dismissed the challenge based on a lack of locus standi, the Court of Appeal considered the substantive constitutional challenges based on Articles 9, 12, and 14, suggesting that there was no violation of Articles 9 and 14 but being less definite about constitutionality according to Article 12. The Minister for Law, K Shanmugam, explained that the Court of Appeal noted that Section 377A might fail the reasonable classification test used in relation to Article 12 if it was understood according to the *Syed Suhail*[42] approach.[43] He also noted that the Court had, since *Tan Seng Kee v*

36 *Tan Seng Kee v Attorney-General* (2022), para 132.
37 Ibid., para 137.
38 Ibid., para 152.
39 Ibid., para 138.
40 Ibid., para 153.
41 Shanmugam, K (2022), paras 206–211.
42 *Syed Suhail bin Syed Zin v Attorney-General* (2021).
43 Shanmugam, K (2022), paras 191–193.

Attorney-General, applied the *Syed Suhail* test and approach in two other cases. There was therefore a risk that the courts would find Section 377A to be unconstitutional in relation to Article 12.[44]

It should be noted that the government did not take the view that Section 377A was unconstitutional. If it had done so, the view that Article 12 was violated would mean that the government regarded opposite-sex and homosexual acts as on par in a pertinent moral sense, such that the criminal regulation of homosexual, but not opposite-sex, acts constituted unconstitutional discrimination. Such a view can have knock-on effects in principle on the distinction that the government now seeks to draw between same-sex and opposite-sex relations in many laws and policies as well, as the distinction can be similarly discriminatory. Rather, Section 377A was repealed to avert the possibility of the courts taking a different view from the government as to the constitutionality of Section 377A. If Section 377A had been struck down in the courts, the decision 'could lead to a whole series of consequences which would be very damaging to our Singaporean society' in the government's view.[45] A judicial decision was 'binary, zero sum'. It would be made without considering 'the consequential effects of that decision on the definition of marriage'. Challenges of laws relating to marriage as well as laws and policies related to housing, education, and media content that differentiated between opposite-sex and same-sex relations were likely to follow upon Section 377A being struck down by the courts. Rather than face such a possibility, parliament amended the Singapore Constitution to protect opposite-sex marriage. The constitutional move to protect opposite-sex marriage and supporting laws and policies are not incoherent in principle because they stem from parliament's view that differentiation of the two types of relations does not constitute discrimination under Article 12.

The then-anticipated repeal and constitutional amendment were subject to numerous extensive community consultations, after which they were announced at the National Day Rally speech[46] of Lee in 2022, before they came into effect in 2023.

5 Legal and Jurisprudential Significance of the 2023 Constitutional Amendment

The Women's Charter was enacted in 1961 to provide for monogamous marriages, their solemnisation and registration, regulation of rights and duties of married persons, and so on.[47] 'Monogamous marriage' is defined in section 2(1) of the Interpretation Act[48]

44 Ibid., paras 195–196.
45 Shanmugam, K (2022), para 262.
46 Lee, Hsien Loong (2022).
47 Women's Charter 1961, Preamble.
48 Interpretation Act 1965.

as a marriage which is recognised, by the law of the place where it is contracted, as the voluntary union between one man and one woman to the exclusion of all others during the continuance of the marriage. Section 12(1) of the Women's Charter also specifies that marriages between persons who at the date of the marriage are not respectively male and female are void.

The new Article 156, introduced in 2023 alongside the repeal of Section 377A, is titled 'Institution of Marriage' and it states:

(1) The Legislature may, by law, define, regulate, protect, safeguard, support, foster and promote the institution of marriage.

(2) Subject to any written law, the Government and any public authority may, in the exercise of their executive authority, protect, safeguard, support, foster and promote the institution of marriage.

(3) Nothing in Part 4 invalidates a law enacted before, on or after the date of commencement of the Constitution of the Republic of Singapore (Amendment No. 3) Act 2022 by reason that the law –
   (a) defines marriage as a union between a man and a woman; or
   (b) is based on such a definition of marriage.

(4) Nothing in Part 4 invalidates an exercise of executive authority before, on or after the date of commencement of the Constitution of the Republic of Singapore (Amendment No. 3) Act 2022 by reason that the exercise is based on a definition of marriage as a union between a man and a woman.

Article 156(1) of the Singapore Constitution emphasizes what is already within legislative powers to 'define, regulate, protect, safeguard, support, foster and promote the institution of marriage'. Article 156(2) emphasizes the existence of executive powers to protect, safeguard, support, foster and promote the same, subject to any written law. The first two sub-sections are neutral as far as the definition of marriage is concerned: the legislature and the executive would have the same powers to support the institution of marriage even if the definition of marriage in section 12(1) of the Women's Charter or section 2(1) of the Interpretation Act are changed in future. As Articles 4 and 162 of the Singapore Constitution express that laws must comply with the Singapore Constitution, which is the supreme law in Singapore, the law passed by the legislature must comply with the Singapore Constitution. The next two sub-sections are not neutral: Article 156(3) aims to protect laws that define or are based on opposite-sex marriage only from being invalidated for seeming to be inconsistent with Part 4 of the Singapore Constitution, which constitutionally guarantees a list of fundamental liberties, while Article 156(4) suggests the same where the exercise of executive powers is based on such a definition.

The definition of marriage itself, on the other hand, is not constitutionally entrenched. Constitutionally entrenching the definition of marriage itself would have made it harder to amend the definition which is currently contained in ordinary legislation, that is, the Interpretation Act and the Woman's Charter. Ordinary legislation may be amended by a simple majority vote. In contrast, if the definition of marriage had been constitutionally entrenched, according to Article 5(2) of the Singapore Constitution, a special two-thirds majority of parliamentary votes (excluding nominated MPs) is required for constitutional amendment of most of the provisions of the Singapore Constitution. However, Articles 156(3) and 156(4) go further than merely 'hard-coding' the definition of marriage, even though some opponents of the repeal of Section 377A in Singapore had hoped for entrenchment of the definition of marriage.[49] Merely hard-coding the definition would not have safeguarded the laws and policies that serve to 'protect, safeguard, support, foster and promote' the institution of opposite-sex marriage from court challenges based on alleged violation of the rights and liberties listed in Part 4. If Section 377A had been repeatedly challenged, the same would have realistically happened to the laws and policies that 'define, regulate, protect, safeguard, support, foster and promote' opposite-sex marriage. The next frontiers for advancing LGBTQ+ rights would be to invalidate the laws and policies which differentiated between opposite-sex and same-sex relationships. If the laws and policies were challenged, there was a risk that the courts take a different opinion from parliament and the executive on whether the rights and liberties listed in Part 4 of the Singapore Constitution were violated. Thus, if the government was concerned about the courts taking a different view from the government on the constitutionality of Section 377A, it would be concerned about the possible next frontiers for legal challenges.

Article 156 represents the government's unequivocal endorsement of heteronormativity as well as a pre-emptive strike against judicial activism. The broadest range of laws and policies that are likely to be needed to support the institution of marriage are anticipated by the extensive range of verbs used – 'protect, safeguard, support, foster and promote' – in the first two sub-sections. The third and fourth sub-sections state that laws and policies related to marriage *as the union of one man and one woman*, but *not any other definition of marriage* (should that change in future) are not unconstitutional in light of Part 4 of the Singapore Constitution. This in substance conveys that same-sex and opposite-sex relations are not on par, with only the laws and policies based on the latter definition expressed to be not violating Part 4 of the Constitution. Substantively, a special status is accorded to the institution of opposite-sex marriage, arguably rendering it as having special importance alongside fundamental liberties. Parliament also signalled that what was happening elsewhere – the 'perils of court-led change', 'with drastic social repercussions that polarise society'[50] – was unwelcome. Parliament therefore chose to express that laws and policies made in favour of oppo-

49 Elangovan, Navene (2022).
50 Parliamentary Debates Singapore (28 November 2022) (Mr Masagos Zulkifli).

site-sex marriage did not violate Part 4 of the Constitution in its best attempt to shield such laws and policies from judicial challenges and pre-empt judicial activism.

At the very least, the fact of including Article 156 alongside repeal puts paid to the argument that Section 377A was repealed because the government was no longer morally disapproving of homosexual conduct, or that it was of the view there should be no governmental interference in private consensual sexual behaviour. The endorsement of heteronormativity meant that same-sex and opposite-sex relationships do not deserve the same support and protection of laws and policies relating to housing, education, media content, and so on. Thus, Justice Scalia's view in the United States Supreme Court case of *Lawrence v Texas*[51] – that moral disapproval of homosexual conduct was necessary for 'preserving the traditional institution of marriage' and that marriage laws would be left on shaky grounds if public morality was neutral between homosexual and heterosexual acts, which proved prescient in *United States v Windsor*[52] and *Obergefell v Hodges*[53] – was addressed by Singapore's constitutional amendment.

6 Conclusion: An Unusual Move in Favour of Heteronormativity

In contrast to the United States Congress, for example, which not too long ago passed the Respect for Marriage Act[54] which aims to ensure that all states and the federal government recognise same-sex marriages that are validly entered into in any state, the Singapore government moved in favour of protecting opposite-sex marriage. Article 156 represents a counter-cultural move by the Singapore government in view of worldwide trends towards same-sex marriage when anti-sodomy laws were repealed or judicially struck down in those jurisdictions. Constitutionally entrenching the definition of marriage as a union between male and female might have been a bonus to supporters of opposite-sex marriage. But constitutional entrenchment is inadequate if the laws and policies that support marriage as a specific kind of institution are challenged and struck down by the courts. Marriage does not occur in a social vacuum. In Singapore, it is often the culmination of dating, and not pre-arranged. Dating in turn occurs within a moral, social, and cultural milieu which suggests to parties who a potential mate or spouse is. To meaningfully protect the institution of opposite-sex marriage, laws and policies to secure the moral, social, and cultural milieu are necessary. Therefore, to give legal form to its affirmation of the importance of the traditional family unit as a building block of society, Singapore's government focused on protecting the laws and

51 *Lawrence v Texas* (2003).
52 *United States v Windsor* (2013).
53 *Obergefell v Hodges* (2013).
54 Respect for Marriage Act (2022).

policies that support the moral ecology within which opposite-sex marriage occurs by unequivocally affirming heteronormativity through Article 156(3) and (4).

Bibliography

Attorney-General's Chambers (2018): "Government has not removed or restricted prosecutorial discretion for Section 377A, public prosecutor retains full prosecutorial discretion". In: Attorney-General's Chambers Newsroom, 2.10.18 https://www.agc.gov.sg/newsroom/government-has-not-removed-or-restricted-prosecutorial-discretion-for-section-377a-public-prosecutor-retains-full-prosecutorial-discretion/, accessed 28.12.23.

Constitution of the Republic of Singapore (2020 Rev Ed).

Constitution of the Republic of Singapore (Amendment No. 3) Act 2022.

Criminal Law Amendment Act 1885, 48 & 49 Vict. c. 69.

Elangovan, Navene (2022): "S377A repeal: Proposed constitutional amendment to protect marriage definition without 'hard-coding' it, says Edwin Tong". In: Today Online, 22.08.22 https://www.todayonline.com/singapore/ndr-2022-377a-constitution-marriage-edwin-tong-1974591, accessed 28.12.23.

Interpretation Act 1965 (2020 Rev Ed), Singapore.

Jacob, Paul (2007): "A teacher's disclosure and the issue is out in the open". In: The Straits Times, 67, 15.09.07.

Lawrence v Texas (2003) 539 US 558.

Lee, Hsien Loong, "National Day Rally Speech". In: Prime Minister's Office Newsroom, 21.08.22 https://www.pmo.gov.sg/Newsroom/National-Day-Rally-2022-English, accessed 28.12.23.

Lim Meng Suang v Attorney-General [2013] SGHC 73.

Lim Meng Suang v Attorney-General [2014] SGCA 53.

Obergefell v Hodges (2013) 576 US 644.

Parliamentary Debates Singapore: Official Report, Vol. 77 (6 January 2004).

Parliamentary Debates Singapore: Official Report, Vol. 83 (October 2007).

Parliamentary Debates Singapore: Official Report, Vol. 95 (28 November 2022).

Penal Code 1871 (2020 Rev Ed), Singapore.

Price, David C (2003): "Singapore: It's in to be out". In: Time, 10.08.03 https://content.time.com/time/subscriber/article/0,33009,474512,00.html, accessed 28.12.23.

Respect for Marriage Act (2022), United States.

Shanmugam, K (2022): "Second Reading of Penal Code (Amendment) Bill – Speech by Mr K Shanmugam, Minister for Home Affairs and Minister for Law". In: Media Room, 28.11.22 https://www.mha.gov.sg/mediaroom/parliamentary/second-reading-of-penal-code-amendment-bill/, accessed 28.12.23.

Syed Suhail bin Syed Zin v Attorney-General [2021] 1 SLR 809.

Tan Seng Kee v Attorney-General [2022] SGCA 16.

Tan, Seow Hon (2009): "Pragmatism, Morals Legislation and the Criminalization of Homosexual Acts in Singapore". In Journal of Comparative Law 3(2), 285–304.

Tan, Seow Hon (2016): "Between Judicial Oligarchy and Parliamentary Supremacy". In: Singapore Journal of Legal Studies 2016, 307–335.

Tan, Seow Hon (2019): "Surrogacy, Child's Welfare, and Public Policy in Adoption Applications: *UKM v Attorney-General*". In: Singapore Journal of Legal Studies 2019, 263–273.